31 Days Before Your CCNA Exam

Second Edition

Allan Johnson

Cisco Press ▪ 800 East 96th Street ▪ Indianapolis, Indiana 46240 USA

31 Days Before Your CCNA Exam
A Day-by-Day Review Guide for the
CCNA 640-802 Exam
Second Edition

Allan Johnson

Copyright® 2009 Cisco Systems, Inc.

Published by:
Cisco Press
800 East 96th Street
Indianapolis, IN 46240 USA

Printed in the United States of America

Second Printing June 2009

Library of Congress Cataloging-in-Publication Data

Johnson, Allan, 1962-

 31 days before your CCNA exam : a day-by-day review guide for the CCNA

640-802 exam / Allan Johnson. -- 2nd ed.

     p. cm.

 Originally published: Indianapolis, IN : Cisco Press, c2007 under

title: 31 days before your CCNA exam / Scott Bennett.

 ISBN 978-1-58713-197-4 (pbk.)

1. Electronic data processing personnel--Certification. 2. Computer networks--Examinations--Study guides. I. Bennett, Scott, CCNA 31 days

before your CCNA exam. II. Title. III. Title: Thirty one days before your CCNA exam.

TK5105.5.B443 2008

004.6--dc22

2008044139ISBN-13: 978-1-58713-197-4
ISBN-10: 1-58713-197-8

Associate Publisher
Dave Dusthimer

Cisco Press Program Manager
Jeff Brady

Executive Editor
Mary Beth Ray

Managing Editor
Patrick Kanouse

Senior Development Editor
Christopher Cleveland

Project Editor
Mandie Frank

Copy Editor
Barbara Hacha

Technical Editors
Rick Graziani,
Kenneth Stewart

Editorial Assistant
Vanessa Evans

Book & Cover Designer
Louisa Adair

Composition
TnT Design, Inc.

Indexer
Lisa Stumpf

Proofreader
Paula Lowell

CISCO

Warning and Disclaimer

This book is designed to provide information about exam topics for the Cisco Certified Network Associate (CCNA) Exam 640-802. Every effort has been made to make this book as complete and as accurate as possible, but no warranty or fitness is implied.

The information is provided on an "as is" basis. The authors, Cisco Press, and Cisco Systems, Inc. shall have neither liability nor responsibility to any person or entity with respect to any loss or damages arising from the information contained in this book or from the use of the discs or programs that may accompany it.

The opinions expressed in this book belong to the author and are not necessarily those of Cisco Systems, Inc.

Trademark Acknowledgments

All terms mentioned in this book that are known to be trademarks or service marks have been appropriately capitalized. Cisco Press or Cisco Systems, Inc., cannot attest to the accuracy of this information. Use of a term in this book should not be regarded as affecting the validity of any trademark or service mark.

Corporate and Government Sales

The publisher offers excellent discounts on this book when ordered in quantity for bulk purchases or special sales, which may include electronic versions and/or custom covers and content particular to your business, training goals, marketing focus, and branding interests. For more information, please contact:

U.S. Corporate and Government Sales
1-800-382-3419   corpsales@pearsontechgroup.com

For sales outside the United States please contact:
International Sales   international@pearsoned.com

Feedback Information

At Cisco Press, our goal is to create in-depth technical books of the highest quality and value. Each book is crafted with care and precision, undergoing rigorous development that involves the unique expertise of members from the professional technical community.

Readers' feedback is a natural continuation of this process. If you have any comments regarding how we could improve the quality of this book, or otherwise alter it to better suit your needs, you can contact us through email at feedback@ciscopress.com. Please make sure to include the book title and ISBN in your message.

We greatly appreciate your assistance.

Americas Headquarters	Asia Pacific Headquarters	Europe Headquarters
Cisco Systems, Inc.	Cisco Systems (USA) Pte. Ltd.	Cisco Systems International BV
San Jose, CA	Singapore	Amsterdam, The Netherlands

Cisco has more than 200 offices worldwide. Addresses, phone numbers, and fax numbers are listed on the Cisco Website at **www.cisco.com/go/offices.**

CCDE, CCENT, Cisco Eos, Cisco Lumin, Cisco Nexus, Cisco StadiumVision, the Cisco logo, DCE, and Welcome to the Human Network are trademarks; Changing the Way We Work, Live, Play, and Learn is a service mark; and Access Registrar, Aironet, AsyncOS, Bringing the Meeting To You, Catalyst, CCDA, CCDP, CCIE, CCIP, CCNA, CCNP, CCSP, CCVP, Cisco, the Cisco Certified Internetwork Expert logo, Cisco IOS, Cisco Press, Cisco Systems, Cisco Systems Capital, the Cisco Systems logo, Cisco Unity, Collaboration Without Limitation, EtherFast, EtherSwitch, Event Center, Fast Step, Follow Me Browsing, FormShare, GigaDrive, HomeLink, Internet Quotient, IOS, iPhone, iQ Expertise, the iQ logo, iQ Net Readiness Scorecard, iQuick Study, IronPort, the IronPort logo, LightStream, Linksys, MediaTone, MeetingPlace, MGX, Networkers, Networking Academy, Network Registrar, PCNow, PIX, PowerPanels, ProConnect, ScriptShare, SenderBase, SMARTnet, Spectrum Expert, StackWise, The Fastest Way to Increase Your Internet Quotient, TransPath, WebEx, and the WebEx logo are registered trademarks of Cisco Systems, Inc. and/or its affiliates in the United States and certain other countries.

All other trademarks mentioned in this document or Website are the property of their respective owners. The use of the word partner does not imply a partnership relationship between Cisco and any other company. (0805R)

About the Author

Allan Johnson entered the academic world in 1999 after ten years as a business owner/operator to dedicate his efforts to his passion for teaching. He holds both an MBA and an M.Ed in Occupational Training and Development. He taught CCNA courses at the high school level for seven years and has taught both CCNA and CCNP courses at Del Mar College in Corpus Christi, Texas. In 2003, Allan began to commit much of his time and energy to the CCNA Instructional Support Team providing services to Networking Academy instructors worldwide and creating training materials. He now works full time for the Academy in Learning Systems Development.

About the Technical Reviewers

Rick Graziani teaches computer science and computer networking courses at Cabrillo College in Aptos, California. Rick has worked and taught in the computer networking and information technology field for almost 30 years. Prior to teaching, Rick worked in IT for various companies, including Santa Cruz Operation, Tandem Computers, and Lockheed Missiles and Space Corporation. He holds an M.A. in computer science and systems theory from California State University Monterey Bay. Rick also does consulting work for Cisco Systems and other companies. When Rick is not working, he is most likely surfing. Rick is an avid surfer who enjoys longboarding at his favorite Santa Cruz surf breaks.

Kenneth Stewart teaches computer science and computer networking courses at Flour Bluff High School and Delmar College in Corpus Christi, Texas. Kenneth has worked in the field for more than 18 years and taught for the past 11 years. Prior to teaching, Kenneth was a Nuclear, Biological, and Chemical Warfare Specialist in the 82nd Airborne Division at Ft. Bragg, North Carolina. He holds two degrees in computer science and is earning another in occupational career and technology development from Texas A&M Corpus Christi.

Dedication

For my wife, Becky. Without the sacrifices you made during the project, this work would not have come to fruition. Thank you providing me the comfort and resting place only you can give.

Acknowledgments

As the author of the widely successful first edition of this book, Scott Bennett entrusted me to carry on the mission. Thanks Scott, for allowing me to take over this project.

When I began to think of whom I would like to have as Technical Editors for this work, Rick Graziani and Kenneth Stewart immediately came to mind. Both are outstanding instructors and authors in the Cisco Network Academy community. Thankfully, when Mary Beth Ray contacted them, they were willing and able to do the arduous review work necessary to make sure you get a book that is both technically accurate and unambiguous.

Rick is a long-time technology instructor with a world-renowned reputation among both students and teachers of the CCNA and CCNP curricula. When I began to teach CCNA courses in 2000, it wasn't long before I discovered Rick's outstanding resources online. These are available to anyone who sends him an email requesting the password; just Google his name to find his website. Rick and I coauthored the *Routing Protocols and Concepts: CCNA Exploration Companion Guide*, so I know how he works. I knew he would do an outstanding job editing this material before you see it.

Kenneth Stewart often pulls double duty teaching CCNA courses part time at Del Mar College while maintaining a full load teaching various technology classes at Flour Bluff High School here in my hometown of Corpus Christi. In his spare time, he also likes to write books. His students compete on a national level, including networking, web authoring, and robotics. Ken's excitement in the classroom is contagious, and his commitment to the integrity of the teaching materials he uses is unsurpassed. As the excellent coauthor of *Designing and Supporting Computer Networks: CCNA Discovery Learning Guide*, I knew Ken would serve you, the reader, admirably.

Thank you, Rick and Ken, for not only serving as technical editors to this effort, but for being my friends.

This book is a concise summary of the work of Cisco Press CCNA authors. Wendell Odom's *CCNA Official Exam Certification Library*, Third Edition and Steve McQuerry's *Authorized Self-Study Guide CCNA Preparation Library*, Seventh Edition were two of my main sources. The different approaches these two authors—both CCIEs—take toward the CCNA material gives the reader the breadth and the depth needed to master the CCNA exam topics.

The Cisco Network Academy authors for the Exploration series of Companion Guides take the reader deeper, past the CCNA exam topics, with the ultimate goal of not only preparing the student for CCNA certification, but for more advanced college-level technology courses and degrees, as well. Thank you to Mark Dye, Rick Graziani, Wayne Lewis, Rick McDonald, Antoon W. Rufi, and Bob Vachon for their excellent treatment of the material; it is reflected throughout this book.

Mary Beth Ray, executive editor, amazes me with her ability to juggle multiple projects at once, steering each from beginning to end. I can always count on her to make the tough decisions. Thank you, Mary Beth, for bringing this project to me.

This is my fourth project with Christopher Cleveland as development editor. His dedication to perfection pays dividends in countless, unseen ways. Thank you again, Chris, for providing me with much needed guidance and support. This book could not be a reality without your persistence.

Contents at a Glance

Introduction   xxv

Part I: Networking Basics   1

Day 31: Network Devices, Components, and Diagrams   3

Day 30: Network Models and Applications   13

Day 29: Network Data Flow from End-to-End   21

Part II: Switching Concepts and Configuration   31

Day 28: Connecting Switches and Ethernet Technology   33

Day 27: Network Segmentation and Switching Concepts   43

Day 26: Basic Switch Configuration and Port Security   53

Day 25: Verifying and Troubleshooting Basic Switch Configurations   61

Day 24: Switching Technologies and VLAN Concepts   71

Day 23: VLAN and Trunking Configuration and Troubleshooting   87

Day 22: VTP and InterVLAN Routing Configuration and Troubleshooting   97

Part III: Addressing the Network   107

Day 21: IPv4 Address Subnetting   109

Day 20: Host Addressing, DHCP, and DNS   123

Day 19: Basic IPv6 Concepts   137

Part IV: Routing Concepts and Configuration   145

Day 18: Basic Routing Concepts   147

Day 17: Connecting and Booting Routers   161

Day 16: Basic Router Configuration and Verification   167

Day 15: Managing Cisco IOS and Configuration Files   179

Day 14: Static, Default, and RIP Routing   191

Day 13: EIGRP Routing   211

Day 12: OSPF Routing   227

Day 11: Troubleshooting Routing   245

Part V: Wireless Concepts and Configuration   251

Day 10: Wireless Standards, Components, and Security   253

Day 9: Configuring and Troubleshooting Wireless Networks   261

Part VI: Basic Security Concepts and Configuration   265

Day 8: Mitigating Security Threats and Best Practices   267

Part VII: ACL and NAT Concepts and Configuration   277

Day 7: ACL Concepts and Configurations   279

Day 6: Verifying and Troubleshooting ACL Implementations   289

Day 5: NAT Concepts, Configuration, and Troubleshooting   297

Part VIII: WAN Concepts and Configuration   307

Day 4: WAN and VPN Technologies   309

Day 3: PPP Configuration and Troubleshooting   329

Day 2: Frame Relay Configuration and Troubleshooting   337

Day 1: CCNA Skills Review and Practice   353

Part IX: Exam Day and Post-Exam Information   375

Exam Day   377

Post-Exam Information   379

Index   381

Contents

Introduction   xxv

Part I: Networking Basics   1

Day 31: Network Devices, Components, and Diagrams   3

CCNA 640-802 Exam Topics   3

Key Points   3

Devices   3

Switches   3

Routers   5

Media   5

LANs and WANs   7

Networking Icons   7

Physical and Logical Topologies   8

The Hierarchical Network Model   9

The Enterprise Architecture   10

Network Documentation   11

Study Resources   12

Day 30: Network Models and Applications   13

CCNA 640-802 Exam Topics   13

Key Points   13

The OSI and TCP/IP Models   13

OSI Layers   14

TCP/IP Layers and Protocols   15

Protocol Data Units and Encapsulation   16

Growth of Network-Based Applications   17

Quality of Service   17

Increased Network Usage   17

The Impact of Voice and Video on the Network   18

Study Resources   19

Day 29: Network Data Flow from End-to-End   21

CCNA 640-802 Exam Topics   21

Key Points   21

The TCP/IP Application Layer   21

The TCP/IP Transport Layer   21

TCP Header   22

Port Numbers   23

Error Recovery   24

Flow Control   25

Connection Establishment and Termination   25

UDP   26

The TCP/IP Internet Layer   26

The TCP/IP Network Access Layer   27

Data Encapsulation Summary   28

Using Layers to Troubleshoot   29

Study Resources   29

Part II: Switching Concepts and Configuration   31

Day 28: Connecting Switches and Ethernet Technology   33

CCNA 640-802 Exam Topics   33

Key Topics   33

Ethernet Overview   33

Legacy Ethernet Technologies   34

CSMA/CD   35

Legacy Ethernet Summary   35

Current Ethernet Technologies   36

UTP Cabling   36

Benefits of Using Switches   37

Ethernet Addressing   38

Ethernet Framing   39

The Role of the Physical Layer   40

Study Resources   41

Day 27: Network Segmentation and Switching Concepts   43

CCNA 640-802 Exam Topics   43

Key Topics   43

Evolution to Switching   43

Switching Logic   44

Collision and Broadcast Domains   45

Frame Forwarding   45

　　Switch Forwarding Methods   45

　　Symmetric and Asymmetric Switching   46

　　Memory Buffering   46

　　Layer 2 and Layer 3 Switching   46

Accessing and Navigating Cisco IOS   46

　　Connecting to Cisco Devices   46

　　CLI EXEC Sessions   47

　　Using the Help Facility   48

　　CLI Navigation and Editing Shortcuts   48

　　Command History   49

　　IOS Examination Commands   50

　　Subconfiguration Modes   50

Storing and Erasing Configuration Files   51

Study Resources   52

Day 26: Basic Switch Configuration and Port Security   53

CCNA 640-802 Exam Topics   53

Key Topics   53

Basic Switch Configuration Commands   53

Configuring SSH Access   55

Configuring Port Security   56

Shutting Down and Securing Unused Interfaces   58

Study Resources   59

Day 25: Verifying and Troubleshooting Basic Switch Configurations   61

CCNA 640-802 Exam Topics   61

Key Points   61

Troubleshooting Methodology   61

Verifying Network Connectivity   62

Interface Status and the Switch Configuration   65

　　Interface Status Codes   65

Duplex and Speed Mismatches   66

Common Layer 1 Problems On "Up" Interfaces   67

CDP as a Troubleshooting Tool   68

Study Resources   70

Day 24: Switching Technologies and VLAN Concepts   71

CCNA 640-802 Exam Topics   71

Key Points   71

VLAN Concepts   71

Traffic Types   72

Types of VLANs   72

Voice VLAN Example   73

Trunking VLANs   74

Dynamic Trunking Protocol   75

VTP Concepts   76

VTP Modes   77

VTP Operation   77

VTP Pruning   78

STP Concepts and Operation   78

RSTP Concepts and Operation   80

Configuring and Verifying STP   82

PVST+, PVRST, and MIST   82

Configuring and Verifying the BID   82

PortFast   84

Configuring RSTP   84

Troubleshooting STP   84

Study Resources   85

Day 23: VLAN and Trunking Configuration and Troubleshooting   87

CCNA 640-802 Exam Topics   87

Key Points   87

Sample Topology   87

VLAN Configuration and Verification Commands   88

Configuring and Verifying Trunking   91

Troubleshooting VLAN and Trunking Problems   93

Study Resources   95

Day 22: VTP and InterVLAN Routing Configuration and Troubleshooting   97

CCNA 640-802 Exam Topics   97

Key Points   97

VTP Configuration and Verification   97

VTP Troubleshooting   102

Inter-VLAN Routing Configuration and Verification   103

Troubleshooting Inter-VLAN Routing   105

Study Resources   106

Part III: Addressing the Network   107

Day 21: IPv4 Address Subnetting   109

CCNA 640-802 Exam Topics   109

Key Topics   109

IPv4 Addressing   109

Header Format   109

Classes of Addresses   110

Purpose of the Subnet Mask   111

Subnetting in Four Steps   112

Determine How Many Bits to Borrow   113

Determine the New Subnet Mask   114

Determine the Subnet Multiplier   114

List the Subnets, Host Ranges, and Broadcast Addresses   114

Subnetting Example 1   114

Subnetting Example 2   115

Subnetting Example 3   115

VLSM   116

Summarizing Subnet Addresses   118

Private and Public IP Addressing   119

Study Resources   120

Day 20: Host Addressing, DHCP, and DNS   123

CCNA 640-802 Exam Topics   123

Key Topics   123

Addressing Devices   123

ARP   124

DNS   126

DHCP   127

Configuring on a Cisco Router as a DHCP Server   128

Network Layer Testing Tools   132

    Ping   132

Study Resources   134

Day 19: Basic IPv6 Concepts   137

CCNA 640-802 Exam Topics   137

Key Topics   137

Overview of IPv6   137

IPv6 Address Structure   139

    Conventions for Writing IPv6 Addresses   139

    Conventions for Writing IPv6 Prefixes   139

    IPv6 Global Unicast Address   140

    Reserved, Private, and Loopback Addresses   141

    The IPv6 Interface ID and EUI-64 Format   141

    IPv6 Address Management   142

Transitioning to IPv6   142

Study Resources   144

Part IV: Routing Concepts and Configuration   145

Day 18: Basic Routing Concepts   147

Key Topics   147

Packet Forwarding   147

    Path Determination and Switching Function Example   148

Routing Methods   149

Classifying Dynamic Routing Protocols   150

    IGP and EGP   150

    Distance Vector Routing Protocols   150

    Link-State Routing Protocols   151

    Classful Routing Protocols   151

    Classless Routing Protocols   152

Dynamic Routing Metrics   152

Administrative Distance   153

IGP Comparison Summary   154

Routing Loop Prevention   155

Link-State Routing Protocol Features   156

    Building the LSDB   156

    Calculating the Dijkstra Algorithm   157

    Convergence with Link-State Protocols   158

Study Resources   158

Day 17: Connecting and Booting Routers   161

CCNA 640-802 Exam Topics   161

Key Topics   161

Router Internal Components   161

IOS   162

Router Bootup Process   162

Router Ports and Interfaces   164

Router Connections   164

Study Resources   166

Day 16: Basic Router Configuration and Verification   167

CCNA 640-802 Exam Topics   167

Key Topic   167

Basic Router Configuration   167

Verifying Network Connectivity   175

Study Resources   177

Day 15: Managing Cisco IOS and Configuration Files   179

CCNA 640-802 Exam Topics   179

Key Topics   179

The Cisco IOS File System   179

    IFS Commands   179

    URL Prefixes for Specifying File Locations   181

    Commands for Managing Configuration Files   182

    Cisco IOS File Naming Conventions   182

Manage IOS Images   183

    Backing Up an IOS image   184

    Restoring an IOS Image   185

    Recovering an IOS Image Using a TFTP Server   186

    Recovering an IOS Image Using Xmodem   187

Recovering a Lost Password   188

Study Resources   189

Day 14: Static, Default, and RIP Routing   191

CCNA 640-802 Exam Topics   191

Key Topics   191

Static Route Configuration   191

    Static Routes Using the "Next Hop" Parameter   193

    Static Routes Using the Exit Interface Parameter   193

    Default Static Routes   194

RIP Concepts   197

    RIPv1 Message Format   197

    RIPv1 Operation   198

    RIPv1 Configuration   198

    RIPv1 Verification and Troubleshooting   199

    Passive Interfaces   203

    Automatic Summarization   204

    Default Routing and RIPv1   206

    RIPv2 Configuration   207

    Disabling Autosummarization   208

    RIPv2 Verification and Troubleshooting   208

Study Resources   209

Day 13: EIGRP Routing   211

CCNA 640-802 Exam Topics   211

Key Topics   211

EIGRP Operation   211

EIGRP Message Format   212

RTP and EIGRP Packet Types   212

DUAL   214

Administrative Distance   214

EIGRP Configuration   214

The network Command   215

Automatic Summarization   216

Manual Summarization   217

EIGRP Default Route   219

Modifying the EIGRP Metric   219

Modifying Hello Intervals and Hold Times   220

EIGRP Verification and Troubleshooting   221

Study Resources   226

Day 12: OSPF Routing   227

CCNA 640-802 Exam Topics   227

Key Topics   227

OSPF Operation   227

OSPF Message Format   227

OSPF Packet Types   228

Neighbor Establishment   228

Link-State Advertisements   229

OSPF Network Types   230

DR/BDR Election   230

OSPF Algorithm   231

Link-State Routing Process   232

OSPF Configuration   233

The router ospf Command   234

The network Command   234

Router ID   235

Modifying the OSPF Metric   236

Controlling the DR/BDR Election   237

Redistributing a Default Route   238

Modifying Hello Intervals and Hold Times   238

Verifying and Troubleshooting OSPF   239

Study Resources   243

Day 11: Troubleshooting Routing   245

CCNA 640-802 Exam Topics   245

Key Topics   245

The Basic Commands   245

VLSM Troubleshooting   246

Discontiguous Networks   246

Troubleshooting RIP   247

Troubleshooting EIGRP and OSPF Interface Issues   248

Troubleshooting Neighbor Adjacency Issues   249

Study Resources   250

Part V: Wireless Concepts and Configuration   251

Day 10: Wireless Standards, Components, and Security   253

CCNA 640-802 Exam Topics   253

Key Topics   253

Wireless Standards   253

Wireless Modes of Operation   254

Wireless Frequencies   254

Wireless Encoding and Channels   255

Wireless Coverage Area   256

CSMA/CA   256

Wireless Security Risks   257

Wireless Security Standards   258

Study Resources   259

Day 9: Configuring and Troubleshooting Wireless Networks   261

CCNA 640-802 Exam Topics   261

Key Topics   261

Implementing a WLAN   261

    Wireless LAN Implementation Checklist   262

    Wireless Troubleshooting   264

Study Resources   264

Part VI: Basic Security Concepts and Configuration   265
Day 8: Mitigating Security Threats and Best Practices   267

CCNA 640-802 Exam Topics   267

Key Topics   267

The Importance of Security   267

    Attacker Terminology   267

    Thinking Like an Attacker   268

    Balancing Security and Availability   269

    Developing a Security Policy   269

Common Security Threats   270

    Vulnerabilities   270

    Threats to Physical Infrastructure   271

    Threats to Networks   271

    Types of Network Attacks   271

General Mitigation Techniques   273

    Host and Server Security   273

    Intrusion Detection and Prevention   273

    Security Appliances and Applications   273

Maintaining Security   275

Study Resources   276

Part VII: ACL and NAT Concepts and Configuration   277
Day 7: ACL Concepts and Configurations   279

CCNA 640-802 Exam Topics   279

Key Topics   279

ACL Concepts   279

    Defining an ACL   279

    Processing Interface ACLs   279

Types of ACLs   280

ACL Identification   281

ACL Design Guidelines   281

Configuring Standard Numbered ACLs   282

Standard Numbered ACL: Permit Specific Network   282

Standard Numbered ACL: Deny a Specific Host   283

Standard Numbered ACL: Deny a Specific Subnet   283

Standard Numbered ACL: Deny Telnet Access to the Router   284

Configuring Extended Numbered ACLs   284

Extended Numbered ACL: Deny FTP from Subnets   285

Extended Numbered ACL: Deny Only Telnet from Subnet   285

Configuring Named ACLs   286

Standard Named ACL Steps and Syntax   286

Standard Named ACL: Deny a Single Host from a Given Subnet   286

Extended Named ACL Steps and Syntax   287

Extended Named ACL: Deny a Telnet from a Subnet   287

Adding Comments to Named or Numbered ACLs   287

Complex ACLs   288

Study Resources   288

Day 6: Verifying and Troubleshooting ACL Implementations   289

CCNA 640-802 Exam Topics   289

Key Topics   289

Verifying ACLs   289

Troubleshooting ACLs   291

Problem 1: Host Has No Connectivity   291

Problem 2: Denied Protocols   292

Problem 3: Telnet is Allowed #1   293

Problem 4: Telnet Is Allowed #2   294

Problem 5: Telnet Is Allowed #3   294

Study Resources   295

Day 5: NAT Concepts, Configuration, and Troubleshooting   297

CCNA 640-802 Exam Topics   297

Key Topics   297

NAT Concepts   297

  A NAT Example   298

  Dynamic and Static NAT   299

  NAT Overload   299

  NAT Benefits   300

  NAT Limitations   300

Configuring Static NAT   301

Configuring Dynamic NAT   301

Configuring NAT Overload   303

Verifying NAT   303

Troubleshooting NAT   304

Study Resources   306

Part VIII: WAN Concepts and Configuration   307

Day 4: WAN and VPN Technologies   309

CCNA 640-802 Exam Topics   309

Key Topics   309

WAN Technology Concepts   309

  WAN Components and Devices   309

  WAN Physical Layer Standards   311

  WAN Data Link Protocols   312

  WAN Switching   312

WAN Connection Options   313

  Dedicated Connection Options   314

  Circuit-Switched Connection Options   314

  Packet-Switched Connection Options   315

  Internet Connection Options   317

  Choosing a WAN Link Option   319

VPN Technology   320

  VPN Benefits   320

  Types of VPN Access   320

  VPN Components   322

  Establishing Secure VPN Connections   322

Study Resources   326

Day 3: PPP Configuration and Troubleshooting   329

CCNA 640-802 Exam Topics   329

Key Topics   329

HDLC   329

HDLC Encapsulation   329

Configuring HDLC   330

Verifying HDLC   331

PPP Concepts   331

The PPP Frame Format   331

PPP Link Control Protocol (LCP)   332

PPP Configuration and Verification   334

Basic PPP   334

Study Resources   336

Day 2: Frame Relay Configuration and Troubleshooting   337

CCNA 640-802 Exam Topics   337

Key Topics   337

Frame Relay Concepts   337

Frame Relay Components   338

Frame Relay Topologies   339

NBMA Limitations and Solutions   340

Inverse ARP and LMI Concepts   341

Inverse ARP and LMI Operation   342

Configuring and Verifying Frame Relay   343

Full Mesh with One Subnet   344

Partial Mesh with One Subnet per PVC   347

Frame Relay Verification   348

Troubleshooting WAN Implementations   349

Troubleshooting Layer 1 Problems   350

Troubleshooting Layer 2 Problems   350

Troubleshooting Layer 3 Problems   351

Study Resources   352

Day 1: CCNA Skills Review and Practice   353

   Key Topics   353

   CCNA Skills Practice   353

         Introduction   353

         Topology Diagram   353

         Addressing Table   354

         VLAN Configuration and Port Mappings   355

         ISP Configuration   355

         Task 1: Configure Frame Relay in a Hub-and-Spoke Topology   356

         Task 2: Configure PPP with CHAP   356

         Task 3: Configure Static and Dynamic NAT on HQ   356

         Task 4: Configure Default Routing   357

         Task 5: Configure Inter-VLAN Routing   357

         Task 6: Configure and Optimize EIGRP Routing   357

         Task 7: Configure VTP, Trunking, the VLAN Interface, and VLANs   357

         Task 8: Assign VLANs and Configure Port Security   358

         Task 9: Configure STP   358

         Task 10: Configure DHCP   359

         Task 11: Configure a Firewall ACL   359

   CCNA Skills Practice (Answers)   360

         Task 1: Configure Frame Relay in a Hub-and-Spoke Topology   360

         Task 2: Configure PPP with CHAP   362

         Task 3: Configure Static and Dynamic NAT on HQ   362

         Task 4: Configure Default Routing   364

         Task 5: Configure Inter-VLAN Routing   364

         Task 6: Configure and Optimize EIGRP Routing   365

         Task 7: Configure VTP, Trunking, the VLAN Interface, and VLANs   367

         Task 8: Assign VLANs and Configure Port Security   369

         Task 9: Configure STP   370

         Task 10: Configure DHCP   371

         Task 11: Configure a Firewall ACL   372

   CCNA Skills Challenge   374

Part IX: Exam Day and Post-Exam Information   375

Exam Day   377

What You Need for the Exam   377

What You Should Receive After Completion   377

Summary   378

Post-Exam Information   379

Receiving Your Certificate   379

Determining Career Options   379

Examining Certification Options   380

If You Failed the Exam   380

Summary   380

Index   381

Icons Used in This Book

Router

Wireless
Router

Wireless
Access Point

Hub

Hub
(alternate)

Multilayer Switch

Switch

ATM Switch
Relay Switch

WAN Switch

PBX Switch

Cisco ASA

Router with
Firewall

PIX Firewall

Firewall

VPN
Concentrator

DSLAM

CSU/DSU

Access Server

Voice-Enabled
Access Server

Modem

IP Phone

Phone

Server

IP/TV Broadcast
Server

Network
Management
Server

Network
Management
Server

Web
Server

Laptop

PC

Network Cloud

——————— Ethernet Connection

Serial Line
Connection

 Wireless Connection

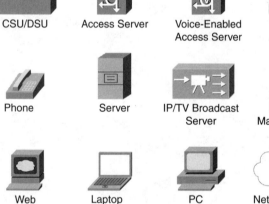

Command Syntax Conventions

The conventions used to present command syntax in this book are the same conventions used in
the IOS Command Reference. The Command Reference describes these conventions as follows:

- **Boldface** indicates commands and keywords that are entered literally as shown. In actual configuration examples and output (not general command syntax), boldface indicates commands
  that are manually input by the user (such as a **show** command).

- *Italic* indicates arguments for which you supply actual values.

- Vertical bars (|) separate alternative, mutually exclusive elements.

- Square brackets ([ ]) indicate an optional element.

- Braces ({ }) indicate a required choice.

- Braces within brackets ([{ }]) indicate a required choice within an optional element.

Introduction

You are almost there! If you're reading this Introduction, you've probably already spent a considerable amount of time and energy pursuing your CCNA certification. Regardless of how you got to this point in your travels through your CCNA studies, *31 Days Before Your CCNA Exam* most likely represents the last leg of your journey on your way to the destination: to become a Cisco Certified Network Associate. However if you are like me, you might be reading this book at the *beginning* of your studies. If such is the case, this book provides you with an excellent overview of the material you must now spend a great deal of time studying and practicing. I must warn you, though; unless you are extremely well versed in networking technologies and have considerable experience configuring and troubleshooting Cisco routers and switches, this book will *not* serve you well as the sole resource for CCNA exam preparation. Therefore, let me spend some time discussing my recommendations for study resources.

Study Resources

Cisco Press offers an abundance of CCNA-related books to serve as your primary source for learning how to install, configure, operate, and troubleshoot medium-size routed and switched networks. See the inside cover of this book for a quick list of my recommendations.

Foundational Resources

First on the list must be Wendell Odom's *CCNA Official Exam Certification Library*, Third Edition (ISBN: 1587201836). If you do not buy any other books, buy this set of two. Wendell's method of teaching, combined with his technical expertise and down-to-earth style, is unsurpassed in our industry. As you read through his books, you sense that he is sitting right there next to you walking you through the material. The practice exams and study materials on the CD in the back of the book are worth the price of the book. There is no better resource on the market for a CCNA candidate.

Next on the list must be Steve McQuerry's *Authorized Self-Study Guide CCNA Preparation Library*, Seventh Edition (ISBN: 1587054647). These two books are indispensable to those students who take the two Cisco recommended training classes for CCNA preparation: Interconnecting Cisco Network Devices 1 (ICND1) and Interconnecting Cisco Network Devices 2 (ICND2). These courses, available through Cisco Training Partners in a variety of formats, are usually of a very short duration (1 to 6 weeks) and are geared toward the industry professional already working in the field of networking. Steve's books serve the reader well as a concise, but thorough, treatment of the CCNA exam topics. His method and approach often differ from and complement Wendell's approach. I recommend that you also refer to these books.

If you are a Cisco Networking Academy student, you are blessed with access to the online version of the CCNA curriculum and the wildly popular Packet Tracer network simulator. Although there are two versions of the CCNA curriculum—Discovery and Exploration—I chose to use the four CCNA Exploration courses in my daily review of the exam topics. The Exploration curriculum provides a comprehensive overview of networking, from fundamentals to advanced applications and services. The Exploration courses emphasize theoretical concepts and practical application, while providing opportunities for students to gain the skills and hands-on experience needed to design, install, operate, and maintain networks in small-to-medium businesses, as well as enterprise and service provider environments. In an Academy class, not only do you have access to Packet Tracer, but you have access to extensive, guided labs and real equipment on which to practice your CCNA skills. To learn more about CCNA Exploration and to find an Academy near you, visit http://www.cisco.com/web/learning/netacad/course_catalog/CCNAexploration.html.

However, if you are not an Academy student but would like to benefit from the extensive authoring done for these courses, you can buy any or all of the CCNA Exploration Companion Guides (CG) and Lab Study Guides (LSG) of the Academy's popular online curriculum. Although you will not have access to the Packet Tracer network simulator software, you will have access to the tireless work of an outstanding team of Cisco Academy Instructors dedicated to providing students with comprehensive and engaging CCNA preparation course material. The titles and ISBNs for the CCNA Exploration CGs and LSGs are as follows:

- Network Fundamentals (CG ISBN: 1587132087; LSG ISBN: 1587132036)

- Routing Protocols and Concepts (CG ISBN: 1587132060; LSG ISBN: 1587132044)

- LAN Switching and Wireless (CG ISBN: 1587132079; LSG ISBN: 1587132028)

- Accessing the WAN (CG ISBN: 1587132052; LSG ISBN: 158713201X)

You can find these books at www.ciscopress.com by clicking the **CISCO NETWORKING ACADEMY** link.

Supplemental Resources

In addition to the book you hold in your hands, I recommend two more supplemental resources to augment your final 31 days of review and preparation.

First, Eric Rivard and Jim Doherty are coauthors of *CCNA Flash Cards and Exam Practice Pack, Third Edition* (ISBN: 1587201909). The text portion of the book includes more than 700 flash cards that quickly review exam topics in bite-sized pieces. Also included are nearly 200 pages of quick-reference sheets designed for late-stage exam preparation. And the included CD features a test engine with more than 500 CCNA practice exam questions.

Second, Wendell Odom has put together an excellent collection of more than four hours of personal, visual instruction in one package, titled *CCNA Video Mentor, Second Edition* (ISBN: 1587201917). It contains a DVD with 20 videos and a lab manual. Wendell walks you through common Cisco router and switch configuration topics designed to develop and enhance your hands-on skills.

The Cisco Learning Network

Finally, if you have not done so already, you should now register with the Cisco Learning Network at http://cisco.hosted.jivesoftware.com/. Sponsored by Cisco, the Cisco Learning Network is a free social-learning network where IT professionals can engage in the common pursuit of enhancing and advancing their IT careers. Here you will find many resources to help you prepare for your CCNA exam, as well as a community of like-minded people ready to answer your questions, help you with your struggles, and share in your triumphs.

So which resources should you buy? That question is largely up to how deep your pockets are or how much you like books. If you're like me, you must have it all! I admit it. My bookcase is a testament to my Cisco "geekness." But if you are on a budget, choose one of the foundational study resources and one of the supplemental resources, such as Wendell Odom's certification library and Rivard/Doherty's flash cards. Whatever you choose, you will be in good hands. Any or all of these authors will serve you well.

Goals and Methods

The main goal of this book is to provide you with a clear and succinct review of the CCNA objectives. Each day's exam topics are grouped into a common conceptual framework that uses the following format:

- A title for the day that concisely states the overall topic

- A list of one or more CCNA 640-802 exam topics to be reviewed

- A Key Topics section to introduce the review material and quickly orient you to the day's focus

- An extensive review section consisting of short paragraphs, lists, tables, examples, and graphics

- A Study Resources section to provide a quick reference for locating more in-depth treatment of the day's topics

The book counts down starting with Day 31 and continues through exam day to provide post-test information. You will also find a calendar and checklist that you can tear out and use during your exam preparation inside the book.

Use the calendar to enter each actual date beside the countdown day and the exact day, time, and location of your CCNA exam. The calendar provides a visual for the time that you can dedicate to each CCNA exam topic.

The checklist highlights important tasks and deadlines leading up to your exam. Use it to help you map out your studies.

Who Should Read This Book?

The audience for this book is anyone finishing preparation for taking the CCNA 640-802 exam. A secondary audience is anyone needing a refresher review of CCNA exam topics—possibly before attempting to recertify or sit for another certification to which the CCNA is a prerequisite.

Getting to Know the CCNA 640-802 Exam

For the current certifications, announced in June 2007, Cisco created the ICND1 (640-822) and ICND2 (640-816) exams, along with the CCNA (640-802) exam. To become CCNA certified, you can pass both the ICND1 and ICND2 exams, or just the CCNA exam. The CCNA exam covers all the topics on the ICND1 and ICND2 exams, giving you two options for gaining your CCNA certification. The two-exam path gives people with less experience a chance to study for a smaller set of topics at one time. The one-exam option provides a more cost-effective certification path for those who want to prepare for all the topics at once. This book focuses exclusively on the one-exam path using the entire list of exam topics for the CCNA 640-802 exam.

Currently for the CCNA exam, you are allowed 90 minutes to answer 50–60 questions. Use the following steps to access a tutorial at home that demonstrates the exam environment before you go to take the exam:

Step 1   Visit http://www.vue.com/cisco.

Step 2   Look for a link to the certification tutorial. Currently, it can be found on the right side of the web page under the heading Related Links.

Step 3   Click the Certification tutorial link.

When you get to the testing center and check in, the proctor verifies your identity, gives you some general instructions, and then takes you into a quiet room containing a PC. When you're at the PC, you have a few things to do before the timer starts on your exam. For instance, you can take the tutorial to get accustomed to the PC and the testing engine. Every time I sit for an exam, I go through the tutorial, even though I know how the test engine works. It helps me settle my nerves and get focused. Anyone who has user-level skills in getting around a PC should have no problems with the testing environment.

When you start the exam, you are asked a series of questions. Each question is presented one at a time and must be answered before moving on to the next question. The exam engine does not let you go back and change your answer. The exam questions can be in one of the following formats:

- Multiple choice
- Fill-in-the-blank
- Drag-and-drop
- Testlet
- Simlet
- Simulation

The multiple-choice format requires that you point and click a circle or check box next to the correct answer or answers. Cisco traditionally tells you how many answers you need to choose, and the testing software prevents you from choosing too many or too few.

Fill-in-the-blank questions typically require you only to type numbers. However if words are requested, the case does not matter unless the answer is a command that is case sensitive (such as passwords and device names when configuring authentication).

Drag-and-drop questions require you to click and hold, move a button or icon to another area, and release the mouse button to place the object somewhere else—typically in a list. For some questions, to get the question correct, you might need to put a list of five things in the proper order.

Testlets contain one general scenario and several multiple-choice questions about the scenario. These are ideal if you are confident in your knowledge of the scenario's content because you can leverage your strength over multiple questions.

A simlet is similar to a testlet in that you are given a scenario with several multiple-choice questions. However, a simlet uses a network simulator to allow you access to a simulation of the command line of Cisco IOS Software. You can then use **show** commands to examine a network's current behavior and answer the question.

A simulation also uses a network simulator, but you are given a task to accomplish, such as implementing a network solution or troubleshooting an existing network implementation. You do this by configuring one or more routers and switches. The exam then grades the question based on the configuration you changed or added. A newer form of the simulation question is the GUI-based simulation, where a graphical interface like that found on a Linksys router or the Cisco Security Device Manager is simulated.

What Topics Are Covered on the CCNA Exam

The topics of the CCNA 640-802 exam focus on the following eight key categories:

- Describe how a network works.

- Configure, verify and troubleshoot a switch with VLANs and interswitch communications.

- Implement an IP addressing scheme and IP Services to meet network requirements in a medium-size enterprise branch office network.

- Configure, verify, and troubleshoot basic router operation and routing on Cisco devices.

- Explain and select the appropriate administrative tasks required for a WLAN.

- Identify security threats to a network and describe general methods to mitigate those threats.

- Implement, verify, and troubleshoot NAT and ACLs in a medium-size enterprise branch office network.

- Implement and verify WAN links.

Although Cisco outlines general exam topics, it is possible that not all topics will appear on the CCNA exam and that topics that are not specifically listed might appear on the exam. The exam topics provided by Cisco and included in this book are a general framework for exam preparation. Be sure to check the Cisco website for the latest exam topics.

Cisco Networking Academy Student Discount Voucher

If you are a Cisco Networking Academy student, you have the opportunity to earn a discount voucher to use when registering and paying for your exam with Pearson VUE. To receive the discount voucher, you must complete all four courses of the CCNA Exploration curriculum and receive a score of 75 percent or higher on your first attempt of the final exam for the final CCNA Exploration course, *Accessing the WAN*. The amount of the discount varies by region and testing center, but typically it has been as much as 50% off the full exam price. Log in to the Academy Connection and click Help at the top of the page to research more information on receiving a discount voucher.

Registering for the CCNA 640-802 Exam

If you are starting your *31 Days to Your CCNA* today, register for the exam right now. In my testing experience, there is no better motivator than a scheduled test date staring me in the face. I'm willing to bet it's the same for you. Don't worry about unforeseen circumstances. You can cancel your exam registration for a full refund up to 24 hours before taking the exam. So if you're ready, you should gather the following information in Table I-1 and register right now!

Table I-1   Personal Information for CCNA 640-802 Exam Registration

Item	Notes
Legal Name	
Social Security or Passport Number	
Cisco Certification ID or Test ID[1]	
Cisco Academy Username[2]	
Cisco Academy ID Number[2]	
Company Name	
Valid Email Address	
Voucher Number[2]	
Method of Payment	

[1]Applies to exam candidates if you have previously taken a Cisco certification exam (such as the ICND1 exam)

[2]Applies to Cisco Networking Academy students only

To register for an exam, contact Pearson VUE via one of the following methods:

- **Online**: http://www.vue.com/cisco.

- **By phone**: In the United States and Canada call 1-800-829-6387, option 1, then option 4. Check the website for information regarding other countries.

The process and available test times will vary based on the local testing center you choose.

Remember, there is no better motivation for study than an actual test date. *Sign up today.*

Part I

Networking Basics

Day 31:   Network Devices, Components, and Diagrams

Day 30:   Network Models and Applications

Day 29:   Network Data Flow from End-to-End

Network Devices, Components, and Diagrams

CCNA 640-802 Exam Topics

- Describe the purpose and functions of various network devices.
- Select the components required to meet a network specification.
- Describe the components required for network and Internet communications.
- Interpret network diagrams.
- Differentiate between LAN/WAN operation and features.

Key Points

At its most fundamental level, a network can be divided into four elements:

- The rules
- The messages
- The media
- The devices

For today's exam topics, we will focus on the devices used in today's networks, the media used to interconnect those devices, and the different types of network topologies.

Devices

Hubs and switches are used to connect end devices to a single LAN. The following describes when to use a hub and when to use a switch:

- Hubs are typically chosen as an intermediary device within a very small LAN where bandwidth usage is not an issue or cost limitations exist. In today's networks, hubs are being replaced by switches.
- Switches are preferred over hubs as a local-area network (LAN) intermediary device because a switch can segment collision domains and provide enhanced security.

Switches

When choosing a switch, the main factors to consider are the following:

- **Cost**: Determined by the number and type of ports, network management capabilities, embedded security technologies, and optional advanced switching technologies.

- **Interface characteristics**: Sufficient number of ports for now as well as future expansion; uplink speeds; mixture of UTP and fiber; modularity.

- **Hierarchical network layer**: Switches at the access layer have different requirements than switches at the distribution or core layers.

Access Layer Switches

Access layer switches facilitate the connection of end devices to the network. Features of access layer switches include the following:

- Port security

- VLANs

- Fast Ethernet/Gigabit Ethernet

- Power over Ethernet (PoE)

- Link aggregation

- Quality of service (QoS)

Cisco access layer switches include the Catalyst Express 500, Catalyst 2960, Catalyst 3560, and Catalyst 3750 Catalyst product lines.

Distribution Layer Switches

Distribution layer switches receive the data from the access layer switches and forward the data to the core layer switches. Features of distribution layer switches include the following:

- Layer 3 support

- High forwarding rate

- Gigabit Ethernet/10 Gigabit Ethernet

- Redundant components

- Security policies/access control lists

- Link aggregation

- Quality of service (QoS)

Cisco distribution layer switches include the Catalyst 4500, Catalyst 4900, and Catalyst 6500 product lines.

Core Layer Switches

Core layer switches make up the backbone and are responsible for handling the majority of data on a switched LAN. Features of core layer switches include the following:

- Layer 3 support

- Very high forwarding rate

- Gigabit Ethernet/10 Gigabit Ethernet

- Redundant components

- Link aggregation

- Quality of service (QoS)

The Catalyst 6500 product line is ideal for dedicated core switches in very large network environments.

Note   You are not required to know the Cisco Catalyst product line for the CCNA exam. Exam questions are platform neutral. Examples given here are for your information only.

Routers

Routers are the primary devices used to interconnect networks—LANs, WANs, and WLANs. When you choose a router, the main factors to consider are the following:

- **Expandability**: Provides flexibility to add new modules as needs change.

- **Media**: Determines the type of interfaces the router needs to support the various network connections.

- **Operating system features**: Determines the version of IOS loaded on the router. Different IOS versions support different feature sets. Features to consider include security, QoS, VoIP, routing complexity, and other services.

Media

Messages are encoded and then placed on the media. Encoding is the process of converting data into patterns of electrical, light, or electromagnetic energy so that it can be carried on the media.

Table 31-1 summarizes the three most common networking media in use today.

Table 31-1   Networking Media

Media	Example	Encoding
Copper	Twisted-pair cable usually used as LAN media	Electrical voltages
Fiber optics	Glass or plastic fibers in a vinyl coating usually used for long runs in a LAN and as a trunk	Electromagnetic waves
Wireless	Connects local users through the air	Electromagnetic waves

Each media type has its advantages and disadvantages. When you choose the media, consider each of the following:

- **Cable length**: Does the cable need to span across a room or from building to building?

- **Cost**: Does the budget allow for using a more expensive media type?

- **Bandwidth**: Does the technology used with the media provide adequate bandwidth?

- **Ease of installation**: Does the implementation team have the ability to install the cable, or is a vendor required?

- **Susceptible to EMI/RFI**: Is the local environment going to interfere with the signal?

Table 31-2 summarizes media standards for LAN cabling.

Table 31-2   Media Standard, Cable Length, and Bandwidth

Ethernet Type	Bandwidth	Cable Type	Maximum Distance
10BASE-T	10 Mbps	Cat3/Cat5 UTP	100 m
100BASE-TX	100 Mbps	Cat5 UTP	100 m
100BASE-TX	200 Mbps	Cat5 UTP	100 m
100BASE-FX	100 Mbps	Multimode fiber	400 m
100BASE-FX	200 Mbps	Multimode fiber	2 km
1000BASE-T	1 Gbps	Cat5e UTP	100 m
1000BASE-TX	1 Gbps	Cat6 UTP	100 m
1000BASE-SX	1 Gbps	Multimode fiber	550 m
1000BASE-LX	1 Gbps	Single-mode fiber	2 km
10GBASE-T	10 Gbps	Cat6a/Cat7 UTP	100 m
10GBASE-SX4	10 Gbps	Multimode fiber	550 m
10GBASE-LX4	10 Gbps	Single-mode fiber	2 km

End devices are those pieces of equipment that are either the original source or the final destination of a message. Intermediary devices connect end devices to the network to assist in getting a message from the source end device to the destination end device.

Connecting devices in a LAN is usually done with unshielded twisted-pair (UTP) cabling. Although many newer devices have an automatic crossover feature that allows you to connect either a straight-through or crossover cable, most devices currently require you to use one or the other.

Use straight-through cables for the following connections:

- Switch to router Ethernet port
- Computer to switch
- Computer to hub

Use crossover cable for the following connections:

- Switch to switch
- Switch to hub
- Hub to hub
- Router to router (Ethernet ports)
- Computer to computer
- Computer to router Ethernet port

LANs and WANs

A local-area network (LAN) is a network of computers and other components located relatively close together in a limited area. LANs can vary widely in size from one computer in a home office to hundreds of computers in a corporate office; however, in general, a LAN spans a limited geographical area. The fundamental components of a LAN include the following:

- Computers

- Interconnections (NICs and the media)

- Networking devices (hubs, switches, and routers)

- Protocols (Ethernet, IP, ARP, DHCP, DNS, and so on)

A wide-area network (WAN) generally connects LANs that are geographically separated. A collection of LANs connected by one or more WANs is called an *internetwork*—thus we have the Internet. The term *intranet* is often used to refer to a privately owned connection of LANs and WANs.

Depending on the type of service, connecting to the WAN is normally done in one of four ways:

- RJ-11 connection to a dialup or DSL modem

- Cable coaxial connection to a cable modem

- 60-pin serial connection to a CSU/DSU

- RJ-45 T1 Controller connection to a CSU/DSU

With the growing number of teleworkers, enterprises have an increasing need for secure, reliable, and cost-effective ways to connect people working in small offices or home offices (SOHOs) or other remote locations to resources on corporate sites. Remote connection technologies to support teleworkers include the following:

- Traditional private WAN technologies, including Frame Relay, ATM, and leased lines

- IPsec virtual private networks (VPNs)

- Remote secure VPN access through a broadband connection over the public Internet

Components needed for teleworker connectivity include the following:

- **Home office components**: Computer, broadband access (cable or DSL), and a VPN router or VPN client software installed on the computer.

- **Corporate components**: VPN-capable routers, VPN concentrators, multifunction security appliances, authentication, and central management devices for resilient aggregation and termination of the VPN connections.

Networking Icons

Before you can interpret networking diagrams or topologies, you first must understand the symbols or icons used to represent different networking devices and media. The icons shown in Figure 31-1 are the most common networking symbols for CCNA studies.

Figure 31-1   Networking Icons

Desktop
Computer

Laptop

Firewall

IP Phone

LAN Switch

Router

Server

Hub
(alternate)

Wireless
Router

Wireless
Access Point

LAN
Media

WAN
Media

Wireless
Media

Physical and Logical Topologies

Network diagrams are more often referred to as *topologies*. A topology graphically displays the interconnection methods used between devices.

Physical topologies refer to the physical layout of devices and how they are cabled. There are seven basic physical topologies, as shown in Figure 31-2.

Figure 31-2   Physical Topologies

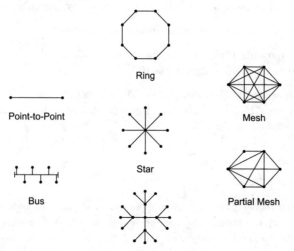

Logical topologies refer to the way a signal travels from one point on the network to another and are largely determined by the access method—deterministic or nondeterministic. Ethernet is a non-deterministic access method. Logically, Ethernet operates as a bus topology. However, Ethernet networks are almost always physically designed as a star or extended star.

Other access methods use a deterministic access method. Token Ring and Fiber Distributed Data Interface (FDDI) both logically operate as ring, passing data from one station to the next. Although these networks can be designed as a physical ring, like Ethernet, they are often designed as a star or extended star. But logically, they operate like a ring.

The Hierarchical Network Model

Hierarchical network design involves dividing the network into discrete layers. Each layer provides specific functions that define its role within the overall network. By separating the various functions that exist on a network, the network design becomes modular, which facilitates scalability and performance. The hierarchical design model is broken up into three layers as follows:

- **Access layer**: Provides local and remote user access

- **Distribution layer**: Controls the flow of data between the access and core layers

- **Core layer**: High-speed redundant backbone

Figure 31-3 shows an example of the hierarchical model.

Figure 31-3   The Hierarchical Model

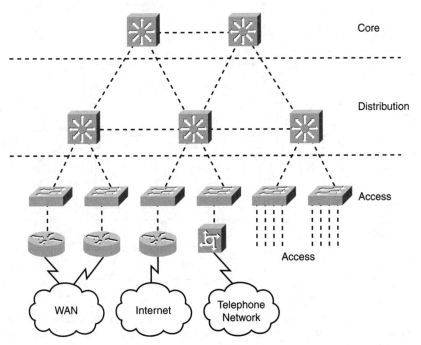

The Enterprise Architecture

The Cisco Enterprise Architecture is designed to provide network planners with a roadmap for network growth as the business moves through different stages. By following the suggested roadmap, IT managers can plan for future network upgrades that will integrate seamlessly into the existing network and support the ever-growing need for services. The Cisco Enterprise Architecture consists of the following modules:

- **Enterprise Campus Architecture**: Refers to a group of buildings that contain many LANs.

- **Enterprise Edge Architecture**: Offers connectivity to voice, video, and data to and from service providers.

- **Enterprise Branch Architecture**: Extends the applications and services within the campus to multiple remote locations.

- **Enterprise Data Center Architecture**: Manages and maintains the enterprise's data systems (such as its server farms).

- **Enterprise Teleworker Architecture**: Connects employee home offices and "road warriors" to the network resources of the enterprise.

Figure 31-4 shows a graphical representation of the Cisco Enterprise Architecture and how each module interconnects.

Figure 31-4   Modules of the Enterprise Architecture

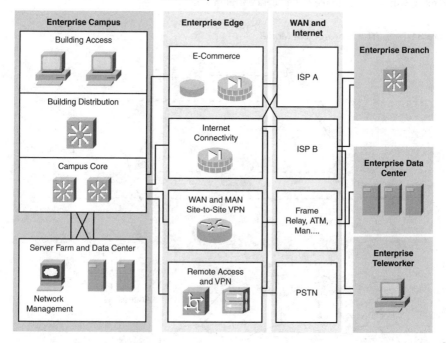

Figure 31-5 shows a network diagram depicting most of the modules of the Enterprise Architecture in a sample implementation of the Enterprise Architecture—the Enterprise Data Center is excluded. Notice how the three layers of the hierarchical model (access, distribution, and core) are integrated into the Enterprise Architecture.

Figure 31-5   An Example of the Enterprise Architecture

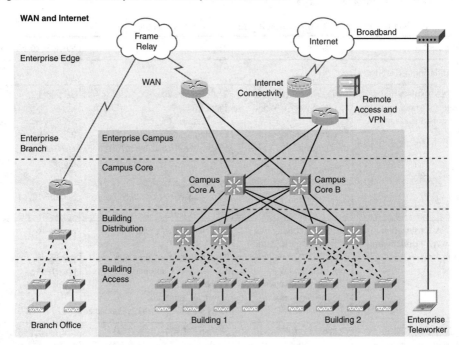

Network Documentation

Documentation for your network should include, at a minimum, the following major categories:

- **Router and switch documentation**: Includes device type, IOS image, hostname, location, addresses, and other important information.

- **End-system documentation**: Includes device names, OS, addressing details, network impact (such as bandwidth usage).

- **Network topology diagram**: Includes all devices and shows the connections as well as the interface designations and addressing scheme.

More often than not, a network's documentation is less than complete. To complete the documentation, you might have to gather information directly from the devices. Commands that are useful to this process include the following:

- **ping**: Tests direct connectivity between two devices

- **telnet**: Tests remote access as well as Layer 7 functionality

- **show ip interface brief**: Verifies interface statuses

- **show ip route**: Verifies routing operations

- **show cdp neighbor detail**: Gathers useful information about directly connected Cisco devices

Study Resources

For today's exam topics, refer to the following resources for more study.

Resource	Chapter	Topic	Where to Find It
Foundational Resources			
CCNA Exploration Online Curriculum: Network Fundamentals	Chapter 1, "Living in a Network-Centric World" Chapter 2, "Communicating over the Network"	The Network as a Platform The Platform for Communications LANs, WANs, and Internetworks	Section 3.2 Sections 2.1.3–2.1.6 Section 2.2
	Chapter 10, "Planning and Cabling Networks"	LANs: Making the Physical Connection LAN and WAN: Getting Connected	Section 10.1 Section 10.2.1
CCNA Exploration Network Fundamentals Companion Guide	Chapter 1, "Living in a Network-Centric World" Chapter 2, "Communicating over the Network" Chapter 10, "Planning and Cabling Networks"	The Network as a Platform The Platform for Communications LANs, WANs, and Internetworks LANs: Making the Physical Connection LAN and WAN: Getting Connected	pp. 10–16 pp. 37–40 pp. 41–44 pp. 368–373 pp. 374–388
CCNA Exploration Online Curriculum: LAN Switching and Wireless	Chapter 1, "LAN Design"	Switched LAN Architecture Matching Switches to Specific LAN Functions	Section 1.1 Section 1.2
CCNA Exploration LAN Switching and Wireless Companion Guide	Chapter 1, "LAN Design"	Switched LAN Architecture Matching Switches to Specific LAN Functions	pp. 2–15 pp. 15–39
CCNA Exploration Online Curriculum: Accessing the WAN	Chapter 1, "Introduction to WANs" Chapter 6, "Teleworker Services" Chapter 8, "Network Troubleshooting"	Providing Integrated Services to the Enterprise Business Requirements for Teleworker Services Establishing the Network Performance Baseline	Section 1.1 Section 6.1 Section 8.1
CCNA Exploration Accessing the WAN Companion Guide	Chapter 1, "Introduction to WANs" Chapter 6, "Teleworker Services" Chapter 8, "Network Troubleshooting"	Providing Integrated Services to the Enterprise Business Requirements for Teleworker Services Establishing the Network Performance Baseline	pp. 3–17 pp. 379–384 pp. 526–541
ICND1 Official Exam Certification Guide	Chapter 1, "Introduction to Computer Networking Concepts"	All topics within the chapter	pp. 5–15
ICND1 Authorized Self-Study Guide	Chapter 1, "Building a Simple Network"	Exploring the Functions of Networking	pp. 3–21
Supplemental Resources			
CCNA Flash Cards and Exam Practice Pack	ICND1, Section 1	Building a Simple Network	pp. 4–36

Network Models and Applications

CCNA 640-802 Exam Topics

- Describe common networked applications, including web applications.
- Describe the purpose and basic operation of the protocols in the OSI and TCP models.
- Describe the impact of applications (Voice over IP and Video over IP) on a network.

Key Points

As a new student to networking, one of the very first topics you probably learned was the layers of the OSI and TCP/IP models. Now that you have completed your studies and are reviewing for the CCNA exam, you more than likely can see the benefit of using these models. Each helps our understanding of networks in its own way. Today we review the OSI and TCP/IP models, as well as the applications and protocols that are commonly used in networks.

The OSI and TCP/IP Models

To understand how communication occurs across the network, we use layered models as a framework for representing and explaining networking concepts and technologies. Network models provide a variety of benefits:

- Reduce complexity
- Standardize interfaces
- Assist understanding
- Promote rapid product development
- Support interoperability
- Facilitate modular engineering

Initially, networks were built on proprietary standards and hardware. Layered models, such as the TCP/IP and OSI models, support interoperability between competing vendor product lines.

The OSI model development began in the 1970s with the goal to provide a standards-based suite of protocols that would allow communication between all computer systems. Although the U.S. government required the use of OSI products in the 1980s and 1990s, the Defense Advanced Research Projects Agency (DARPA) under the Department of Defense—and with the help of researchers at various universities—had designed the competing TCP/IP model. For various reasons, including the popularity of TCP/IP, by 1983 the ARPANET had chosen TCP/IP as its principle protocol suit. By 1994, all U.S. government agencies were required to switch over from OSI protocols to TCP/IP.

Today, we use the OSI model principally as a tool for explaining networking concepts. However, the protocols of the TCP/IP suite are the rules by which networks now operate. Because both models are important, you should be well versed in each model's layers as well as how the models map to each other. Figure 30-1 summarizes the two models.

Figure 30-1   The OSI and TCP/IP Models

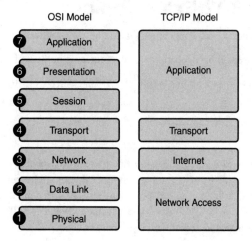

It can be confusing using two models. However, this simple rule might help. When discussing layers of a model, we are usually referring to the OSI model. When discussing protocols, we are usually referring to the TCP/IP model. So let's quickly review the OSI layers and the TCP/IP protocols.

OSI Layers

Table 30-1 summarizes the layers of the OSI model and provides a brief functional description.

Table 30-1   The OSI Model Layers and Functions

Layer	Functional Description
Application (7)	Refers to interfaces between network and application software. Also includes authentication services.
Presentation (6)	Defines the format and organization of data. Includes encryption.
Session (5)	Establishes and maintains end-to-end bidirectional flows between endpoints. Includes managing transaction flows.
Transport (4)	Provides a variety of services between two host computers, including connection establishment and termination, flow control, error recovery, and segmentation of large data blocks into smaller parts for transmission.
Network (3)	Refers to logical addressing, routing, and path determination.
Data link (2)	Formats data into frames appropriate for transmission onto some physical medium. Defines rules for when the medium can be used. Defines means by which to recognize transmission errors.
Physical (1)	Defines the electrical, optical, cabling, connectors, and procedural details required for transmitting bits, represented as some form of energy passing over a physical medium.

The following mnemonic phrase where the first letter represents the layer ("A" stands for "Application") can be helpful to memorize the name and order of the layers from top to bottom.

All People Seem To Need Data Processing

TCP/IP Layers and Protocols

The TCP/IP model defines four categories of functions that must occur for communications to be successful. Most protocol models describe a vendor-specific protocol stack. However, because the TCP/IP model is an open standard, one company does not control the definition of the model.

Table 30-2 summarizes the TCP/IP layers, their functions, and the most common protocols.

Table 30-2   The TCP/IP Layer Functions

TCP/IP Layer	Function	Example Protocols
Application	Represents data to the user and controls dialog.	DNS, Telnet, SMTP, POP3, IMAP, DHCP, HTTP, FTP, SNMP
Transport	Supports communication between diverse devices across diverse networks.	TCP, UDP
Internet	Determines the best path through the network.	IP, ARP, ICMP
Network access	Controls the hardware devices and media that make up the network.	Ethernet, Frame Relay

In coming days, we will review these protocols in more detail. For now, a brief description of the main TCP/IP protocols follows:

- **Domain Name System (DNS):** Provides the IP address of a website or domain name so a host can connect to it.

- **Telnet:** Allows administrators to log in to a host from a remote location.

- **Simple Mail Transfer Protocol (SMTP), Post Office Protocol (POP3), and Internet Message Access Protocol (IMAP):** Used to send email messages between clients and servers.

- **Dynamic Host Configuration Protocol (DHCP):** Assigns IP addressing to requesting clients.

- **Hypertext Transfer Protocol (HTTP):** Used to transfer information between web clients and web servers.

- **File Transfer Protocol (FTP):** Allows the download and upload of files between an FTP client and FTP server.

- **Simple Network Management Protocol (SNMP):** Used by network management systems to monitor devices attached to the network.

- **Transmission Control Protocol (TCP):** Allows virtual connections between hosts on the network to provide reliable delivery of data.

- **User Datagram Protocol (UDP):** Allows faster, unreliable delivery of data that is either lightweight or time-sensitive.

- **Internet Protocol (IP):** Provides a unique global address to computers for communicating over the network.

- **Address Resolution Protocol (ARP):** Finds a host's hardware address when only the IP address is known.

- **Internet Control Message Protocol (ICMP):** Used to send error and control messages including reachability to another host and availability of services.

- **Ethernet:** The most popular LAN standard for framing and preparing data for transmission onto the media.

- **Frame Relay:** Also a framing standard; one of the most cost-effective WAN technologies used to connect LANs.

Protocol Data Units and Encapsulation

As application data is passed down the protocol stack on its way to be transmitted across the network media, various protocols add information to it at each level. This is commonly known as the encapsulation process. The data structure at any given layer is called a protocol data unit (PDU). Table 30-3 lists the PDUs at each layer of the OSI model.

Table 30-3   PDUs at Each Layer of the OSI Model

OSI Layer	PDU
Application	Data
Presentation	Data
Session	Data
Transport	Segment
Network	Packet
Data link	Frame
Physical	Bits

The communication process from any source to any destination can be summarized with the following steps:

1. Creation of data at the application layer of the originating source end device

2. Segmentation and encapsulation of data as it passes down the protocol stack in the source end device

3. Generation of the data onto the media at the network access layer of the stack

4. Transportation of the data through the internetwork, which consists of media and any intermediary devices

5. Reception of the data at the network access layer of the destination end device

6. Decapsulation and reassembly of the data as it passes up the stack in the destination device

7. Passing this data to the destination application at the application layer of the destination end device

Growth of Network-Based Applications

Besides all the common applications we discuss in networking studies, programmers and entrepreneurs are continuously developing applications to take advantage of network resources and the Internet. Today, people create, store, and access information as well as communicate with others on the network using a variety of applications. In addition to the traditional email and web browser applications, people are increasingly using newer forms of communication including instant messaging, blogs, podcasting, peer-to-peer file sharing, wikis, and collaborative tools that allow viewing and working on documents simultaneously. The online gaming industry has grown exponentially over the past several years. All these applications and online experiences place great demands on the network infrastructure and resources. One way of handling the sheer volume of data is to rank packets based on the quality of service that the source application needs—especially considering the increased use of the network in general and the recent rise of voice and video applications that have a very low tolerance for delay and jitter.

Quality of Service

The priority and guaranteed level of service to the flow of data through the network is increasingly important as new applications place greater demands on the processing power and bandwidth of the networks we use. When we place a call over an IP phone, we want at least as good a service as we receive on a traditional land line. Therefore, networks need to use quality of service (QoS) mechanisms to ensure that limited network resources are prioritized based on traffic content. Without QoS implementation, an email message or web page request crossing a switch or a router will have the same priority as voice or video traffic.

Each type of application can be analyzed in terms of its QoS requirements on the network, so if the network meets those requirements, the application will work well.

Increased Network Usage

Applications have tended to increase the need for more bandwidth while demanding lower delay. Here are some of the types of data applications that have entered the marketplace and their impact on the network:

- **Graphics-capable terminals and printers:** Increased the required bytes for the same interaction as the old text-based terminals and printers.

- **File transfers:** Introduced much larger volumes of data, but with no significant response time requirements.

- **File servers:** Allow users to store files on a server—which might require a large volume of data transfer, but with a much smaller end-user response time requirement.

- **The maturation of database technology:** Making vast amounts of data available to casual users, vastly increasing the number of users wanting access to data.

- **The migration of common applications to web browsers:** Encourages more users to access data.

- **The growth of email:** The general acceptance of email as both a personal and business communications service has greatly increased the amount of email traffic.

- **The rapid commercialization of the Internet:** Enabling companies to offer data directly to their customers via the data network rather than via phone calls.

The Impact of Voice and Video on the Network

Currently, voice and video are in the midst of a migration to traditional IP data networks. Before the late 1990s, voice and video used separate networking facilities. Most companies today are either migrating or plan to migrate to IP phones, which pass voice data over the data network inside IP packets using application protocols generally referred to as voice over IP (VoIP).

Figure 30-2 show a few details of how VoIP works from a home high-speed Internet connection, with a generic voice adapter (VA) converting the analog signal from a normal telephone to an IP packet.

Figure 30-2   Converting from Sound to Packets with a VA

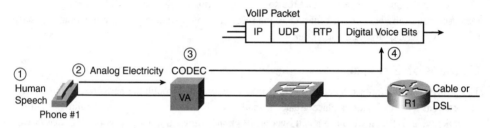

VoIP does not place a demand on the network for additional capacity. A voice call typically consumes less than 30 kbps of bandwidth. However, VoIP is sensitive to delay, jitter, and packet loss:

- **Low delay:** VoIP requires a very low delay between the sending phone and the receiving phone—typically less than 200 milliseconds (.2 seconds). This is a much lower delay than what is required by typical data applications.

- **Low jitter:** Jitter is the variation in delay. VoIP requires very low jitter as well, whereas data applications can tolerate much higher jitter. For example, the jitter for consecutive VoIP packets should not exceed 30 milliseconds (.03 seconds) or the quality degrades.

- **Loss:** If a VoIP packet is lost in transit because of errors or because a router doesn't have room to store the packet while waiting to send it, the lost VoIP packet is not retransmitted across the network. Lost packets can sound like a break in the sound of the VoIP call.

Video over IP has the same performance issues as voice. However, video requires a lot more bandwidth—anywhere from 300 kbps to 10 Mbps, depending on the quality demanded.

To support the QoS requirements of voice, video, and other quality or time-sensitive applications, routers and switches can be configured with a variety of QoS tools. These configurations are beyond the scope of the CCNA exam topics.

Study Resources

For today's exam topics, refer to the following resources for more study.

Resource	Chapter	Topic	Where to Find It
Foundational Resources			
CCNA Exploration Online Curriculum: Network Fundamentals	Chapter 1, "Living in a Network-Centric World"	Examples of Today's Popular Communication Tools	Section 1.1.2
		Networks Supporting the Way We Play	Section 1.1.5
		Providing Quality of Service	Section 1.4.4
	Chapter 2, "Communicating over the Network"	Using Layered Models	Sections 2.4.3–2.4.8
	Chapter 3, "Application Layer Functionality and Protocols"	Applications: The Interface Between the Networks	Section 3.1
CCNA Exploration Network Fundamentals Companion Guide	Chapter 1, "Living in a Network-Centric World"	Examples of Today's Popular Communication Tools	pp. 4–5
		Networks Supporting the Way We Play	p. 8
		Providing Quality of Service	pp. 21–23
	Chapter 2, "Communicating over the Network"	Using Layered Models	pp. 41–44
	Chapter 3, "Application Layer Functionality and Protocols"	Applications: The Interface Between the Networks	pp. 65–71
ICND1 Official Exam Certification Guide	Chapter 2, "The TCP/IP and OSI Models"	All topics within the chapter	pp. 17–39
	Chapter 6, "Fundamentals of TCP/IP Transport, Applications, and Security"	TCP/IP Applications	pp. 146–153
ICND1 Authorized Self-Study Guide	Chapter 1, "Building a Simple Network"	Understanding the Host-to-Host Communication Model	pp. 31–43
Supplemental Resources			
CCNA Flash Cards and Exam Practice Pack	ICND1, Section 1	Building a Simple Network	pp. 4–36

Network Data Flow from End-to-End

CCNA 640-802 Exam Topics

- Use the OSI and TCP/IP models and their associated protocols to explain how data flows in a network.

- Determine the path between two hosts across a network.

- Identify and correct common network problems at Layers 1, 2, 3 and 7 using a layered model approach.

Key Points

The exam topics for this day cover a wide range of content. Much of today's review is a quick summary of the TCP/IP layers and their operations as data is sent from source to destination. Many of the key points will be fleshed out more fully in coming days. However, this is the only day we will discuss the operation of the transport layer. So we will spend quite a bit of time on the Transmission Control Protocol (TCP) and the User Datagram Protocol (UDP). We will also review basic troubleshooting methodologies.

The TCP/IP Application Layer

The application layer of the TCP/IP model provides an interface between software, like a web browser, and the network itself. The process of requesting and receiving a web page works like this:

1. HTTP request sent including an instruction to "get" a file—which is often a website's home page.

2. HTTP response sent from the web server with a code in the header—usually either 200 (request succeeded and information is returned in response) or 404 (page not found).

The HTTP request and the HTTP response are encapsulated in headers. The content of headers allows the application layers on each end device to communicate. Regardless of the application layer protocol (HTTP, FTP, DNS, and so on), all use the same general process for communicating between application layers on the end devices.

The TCP/IP Transport Layer

The transport layer, through TCP, provides a mechanism to guarantee delivery of data across the network. TCP supports error recovery to the application layer through the use of basic acknowledgment logic. Adding to the process for requesting a web page, TCP operation works like this:

1. Web client sends an HTTP request for a specific web server down to the transport layer.

2. TCP encapsulates the HTTP request with a TCP header.

3. Lower layers process and send the request to the web server.

4. Web server receives HTTP requests and sends a TCP acknowledgement back to the requesting web client.

5. Web server sends the HTTP response down to the transport layer.

6. TCP encapsulates the HTTP data with a TCP header.

7. Lower layers process and send the response to the requesting web client.

8. Requesting web client sends acknowledgement back to the web server.

If data is lost at any point during this process, it is TCP's job to recover the data. HTTP at the application layer does not get involved in error recovery.

In addition to TCP, the transport layer provides UDP—a connectionless, unreliable protocol for sending data that does not require nor need error recovery. Table 29-1 lists the main features supported by the transport protocols. The first item is supported by TCP and UDP. The remaining items are supported only by TCP.

Table 29-1   TCP/IP Transport Layer Features

Function	Description
Multiplexing using ports	Function that allows receiving hosts to choose the correct application for which the data is destined, based on the destination port number.
Error recovery (reliability)	Process of numbering and acknowledging data with Sequence and Acknowledgment header fields.
Flow control using windowing	Process that uses a sliding window size that is dynamically agreed upon by the two end devices at various points during the virtual connection. The window size, represented in bytes, is the maximum amount of data the source will send before receiving an acknowledgement from the destination.
Connection establishment and termination	Process used to initialize port numbers, Sequence and Acknowledgment fields.
Ordered data transfer and data segmentation	Continuous stream of bytes from an upper-layer process that is "segmented" for transmission and delivered to upper-layer processes at the receiving device, with the bytes in the same order.

TCP Header

TCP provides error recovery, but to do so, it consumes more bandwidth and uses more processing cycles than UDP. TCP and UDP relies on IP for end-to-end delivery. TCP is concerned with providing services to the applications of the sending and receiving computers. To provide all these services, TCP uses a variety of fields in its header. Figure 29-1 shows the fields of the TCP header.

Figure 29-1   TCP Header Fields

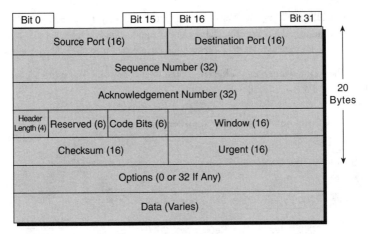

Port Numbers

The first two fields of the TCP header—source and destination ports—are also part of the UDP header shown later in Figure 29-6. Port numbers provide TCP (and UDP) a way to multiplex multiple applications on the same computer. Web browsers now support multiple tabs or pages. Each time you open a new tab and request another web page, TCP assigns a different source port number and sometimes multiple port numbers. For example, you might have five web pages open. TCP will almost always assign destination port 80 for all five sessions. However, the source port for each will be different. This is how TCP (and UDP) multiplexes the conversation so that the web browser knows in which tab to display the data.

Source ports are usually dynamically assigned by TCP and UDP from the range starting 1024. Port numbers below 1024 are reserved for well-known applications. Table 29-2 lists several popular applications and their well-known port numbers.

Table 29-2   Popular Applications and Their Well-Known Port Numbers

Port Number	Protocol	Application
20	TCP	FTP data
21	TCP	FTP control
22	TCP	SSH
23	TCP	Telnet
25	TCP	SMTP
53	UDP, TCP	DNS
67, 68	UDP	DHCP
69	UDP	TFTP
80	TCP	HTTP (WWW)
110	TCP	POP3
161	UDP	SNMP
443	TCP	SSL
16,384–32,767	UDP	RTP-based Voice (VoIP) and Video

Error Recovery

Also known as reliability, TCP provides error recovery during data transfer sessions between two end devices who have established a connection. The sequence and acknowledgment fields in the TCP header are used to track every byte of data transfer and ensure that missing bytes are retransmitted.

In Figure 29-2, the Acknowledgment field sent by the web client (4000) implies the next byte to be received; this is called *forward acknowledgment*.

Figure 29-2   TCP Acknowledgment Without Errors

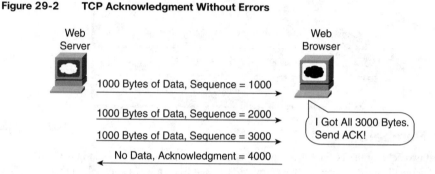

Figure 29-3 depicts the same scenario, except that now we have some errors. The second TCP segment was lost in transmission. Therefore, the web client replies with an ACK field set to 2000. The web server will now resend data starting at segment 2000. In this way, lost data is recovered.

Figure 29-3   TCP Acknowledgment With Errors

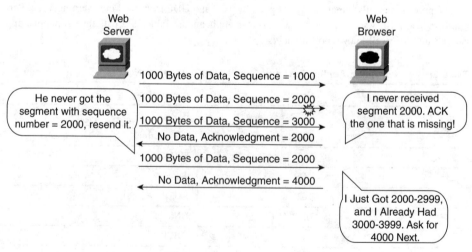

Although not shown, the web server also sets a retransmission timer, awaiting acknowledgment, just in case the acknowledgment is lost or all transmitted segments are lost. If that timer expires, the web server sends all segments again.

Flow Control

Flow control is handled by TCP through a process called *windowing*. The two end devices negotiate the window size when initially establishing the connection; then they dynamically renegotiate window size during the life of the connection, increasing its size until it reaches the maximum window size of 65,535 bytes or until errors occur. Window size is specified in the window field of the TCP header. After sending the amount of data specified in the window size, the source must receive an acknowledgment before sending the next window size of data.

Connection Establishment and Termination

Connection establishment is the process of initializing sequence and acknowledgment fields and agreeing on port numbers and window size. The three-way connection establishment phase shown in Figure 29-4 must occur before data transfer can proceed.

Figure 29-4   TCP Connection Establishment

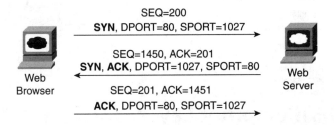

In the figure, DPORT and SPORT are the destination and source ports. SEQ is the sequence number. In bold are SYN and ACK, which each represent a 1-bit flag in the TCP header used to signal connection establishment. TCP initializes the Sequence Number and Acknowledgment Number fields to any number that fits into the 4-byte fields.

After data transfer is complete, a four-way termination sequence occurs that uses an additional flag, called the FIN bit, as shown in Figure 29-5.

Figure 29-5   TCP Connection Termination

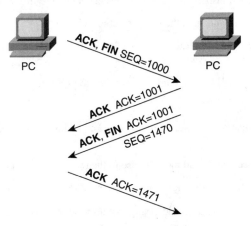

UDP

TCP establishes and terminates connections between endpoints, whereas UDP does not. Therefore, UDP is called a *connectionless protocol*. It provides no reliability, no windowing, no reordering of the data, and no segmentation of large chunks of data into the right size for transmission. However, UDP does provide data transfer and multiplexing using port numbers, and it does so with fewer bytes of overhead and less processing than TCP. Applications that use UDP are ones that can trade the possibility of some data loss for less delay, such as VoIP. Figure 29-6 compares the two headers.

Figure 29-6   TCP and UDP Headers

2	2	4	4	4 bits	6 bits	6 bits	2	2	2	3	1
Source Port	Dest. Port	Sequence Number	Ack. Number	Offset	Reserved	Flags	Window Size	Checksum	Urgent	Options	PAD

TCP Header

2	2	2	2
Source Port	Dest. Port	Length	Checksum

UDP Header

* Unless Specified, Lengths Shown
Are the Numbers of Bytes

The TCP/IP Internet Layer

The Internet layer of the TCP/IP model and its Internet Protocol (IP) defines addresses so that each host computer can have a different IP address. In addition, the Internet layer defines the process of routing so that routers can determine the best path to send packets to the destination. Continuing with the web page example, IP addresses the data as it passes from the transport layer to the Internet layer:

1. Web client sends an HTTP request.

2. TCP encapsulates the HTTP request.

3. IP encapsulates the transport segment into a packet, adding source and destination addresses.

4. Lower layers process and send the request to the web server.

5. Web server receives HTTP requests and sends a TCP acknowledgement back to the requesting web client.

6. Web server sends the HTTP response down to the transport layer.

7. TCP encapsulates the HTTP data.

8. IP encapsulates the transport segment into a packet, adding source and destination addresses.

9. Lower layers process and send the response to the requesting web client.

10. Requesting web client sends acknowledgement back to the web server.

The operation of IP not only includes addressing, but also the process of routing the data from source to destination. IP will be further discussed and reviewed in the upcoming days.

The TCP/IP Network Access Layer

IP depends on the network access layer to deliver IP packets across a physical network. Therefore, the network access layer defines the protocols and hardware required to deliver data across some physical network by specifying exactly how to physically connect a networked device to the physical media over which data can be transmitted.

The network access layer includes a large number of protocols to deal with the different types of media that data can cross on its way from source device to destination device. For example, data might need to travel first on an Ethernet link, then cross a Point-to-Point (PPP) link, then a Frame Relay link, then an Asynchronous Transfer Mode (ATM) link, and then finally an Ethernet link to the destination. At each transition from one media type to another, the network access layer provides the protocols, cabling standards, headers, and trailers to send data across the physical network.

Many times, a local link address is needed to transfer data from one hop to the next. For example, in an Ethernet LAN, Media Access Control (MAC) addresses are used between the sending device and its local gateway router. At the gateway router—depending on the needs of the outbound interface—the Ethernet header might be replaced with a Frame Relay header that will include data-link connection identifier (DLCI) addresses. In Frame Relay, DLCI addresses serve the same purpose as MAC addresses in Ethernet—to get the data across the link from one hop to the next so that the data can continue its journey to the destination. Some protocols, such as Point-to-Point Protocol (PPP), do not need a link address because only one other device is on the link that can receive the data.

With the network access layer, we can now finalize our web page example. The following greatly simplifies and summarizes the process of requesting and sending a web page:

1. Web client sends an HTTP request.

2. TCP encapsulates the HTTP request.

3. IP encapsulates the transport segment into a packet, adding source and destination addresses.

4. Network access layer encapsulates packet in a frame, addressing it for the local link.

5. Network access layer sends the frame out as bits on the media.

6. Intermediary devices process the bits at the network access and Internet layers, and then forward the data toward the destination.

7. Web server receives the bits on the physical interface and sends up through the network access and Internet layers.

8. Web server sends a TCP acknowledgement back to the requesting web client.

9. Web server sends the HTTP response down to the transport layer.

10. TCP encapsulates the HTTP data.

11. IP encapsulates the transport segment into a packet, adding source and destination addresses.

12. Network access layer encapsulates packet in a frame, addressing it for the local link.

13. Network access layer sends the frame out as bits on the media.

14. Lower layers process and send the response to the requesting web client.

15. Response travels back to the source over multiple data links.

16. Requesting web client receives response on the physical interface and sends the data up through the network access and Internet layers.

17. Requesting web client sends a TCP acknowledgement back to the web server.

18. Web page is displayed in requesting device's browser.

Data Encapsulation Summary

Each layer of the TCP/IP model adds its own header information. As the data travels down through the layers, it is encapsulated with a new header. At the network access layer, a trailer is also added. This encapsulation process can be described in five steps:

Step 1   Create and encapsulate the application data with any required application layer headers. For example, the HTTP OK message can be returned in an HTTP header, followed by part of the contents of a web page.

Step 2   Encapsulate the data supplied by the application layer inside a transport layer header. For end-user applications, a TCP or UDP header is typically used.

Step 3   Encapsulate the data supplied by the transport layer inside an Internet layer (IP) header. IP is the only protocol available in the TCP/IP network model.

Step 4   Encapsulate the data supplied by the Internet layer inside a network access layer header and trailer. This is the only layer that uses both a header and a trailer.

Step 5   Transmit the bits. The physical layer encodes a signal onto the medium to transmit the frame.

The numbers in Figure 29-7 correspond to the five steps in the list, graphically showing the same encapsulation process.

Figure 29-7   Five Steps of Data Encapsulation

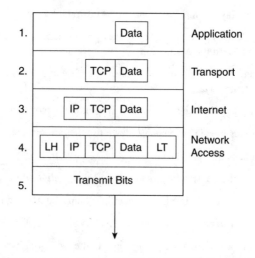

Note   The letters LH and LT stand for link header and link trailer, respectively, and refer to the data link layer header and trailer.

Using Layers to Troubleshoot

You should already have extensive experience troubleshooting network problems—whether in an actual work environment, in a lab environment, or a combination of both. By now, you have developed your own troubleshooting methodology. Maybe you like to check the physical layer first. Is the cabling correct? Are all interface status lights green? Maybe you like to ping everything to gather information about where connectivity is lacking. Then you use the results of your connectivity tests to isolate problems and drill down deeper. Maybe you just intuitively search for solutions, using your past experience to guide.

Regardless of your method, a systematic troubleshooting methodology can help you troubleshoot problems more efficiently and with better success. There are three main methods for troubleshooting networks using the layers of the OSI model:

- **Bottom up:** Start with the physical components and move up through the layers until the problem is isolated. Use this approach when the problem is suspected to be a physical one. Most networking problems reside at the lower levels, so implementing the bottom-up approach often results in effective results.

- **Top down:** Start with the end-user application and move down through the layers until the problem is isolated. Use this approach for simpler problems or when you think the problem is with a piece of software.

- **Divide and conquer:** Start by collecting user experience, documenting the symptoms, and then, using that information, make an informed guess at which OSI layer to start your investigation. After you verify that a layer is functioning properly, assume that the layers below it are functioning, and work up the OSI layers. If an OSI layer is not functioning properly, work your way down the OSI layer model.

To effectively troubleshoot network problems, take the time to select the most effective network troubleshooting method. Today we are just reviewing the general methods used to troubleshoot network problems. In the coming days, we discuss troubleshooting in more detail as we explore implementation-specific situations in switching and routing technologies.

Study Resources

For today's exam topics, refer to the following resources for more study.

Resource	Chapter	Topic	Where to Find It
Foundational Resources			
CCNA Exploration Online Curriculum: Network Fundamentals	Chapter 2, "Communicating over the Network"	The Platform for Communications	Section 2.1
		LANs, WANs, and Internetworks	Section 2.2
		Network Addressing	Section 2.5
	Chapter 3, "Application Layer Functionality and Protocols"	Making Provisions for Applications and Services	Section 3.2
		Application Layer Protocols and Services Examples	Section 3.3

Resource	Chapter	Topic	Where to Find It
	Chapter 4, "OSI Transport Layer"	All topics within the chapter	Chapter 4
	Chapter 5, "OSI Network Layer"	IPv4	Section 5.1
		Networks—Dividing Hosts into Groups	Section 5.2
		Routing—How Our Data Packets are Handled	Section 5.3
	Chapter 7, "Data Link Layer"	All topics within the chapter	Chapter 7
CCNA Exploration Network Fundamentals Companion Guide	Chapter 2, "Communicating over the Network"	The Platform for Communications	pp. 34–40
		Using Layered Models	pp. 47–54
		Network Addressing	pp. 55–57
	Chapter 3, "Application Layer Functionality and Protocols"	Making Provisions for Applications and Services	pp. 71–76
		Application Layer Protocols and Services Examples	pp. 76–92
	Chapter 4, "OSI Transport Layer"	All topics within the chapter	pp. 99–127
	Chapter 5, "OSI Network Layer"	IPv4	pp. 136–144
		Networks: Dividing Hosts into Groups	pp. 144–153
		Routing: How Our Data Packets are Handled	pp. 153–163
	Chapter 7, "Data Link Layer"	All topics within the chapter	pp. 243–273
ICND1 Official Exam Certification Guide	Chapter 2, "The TCP/IP and OSI Networking Models"	All topics within the chapter	pp. 17–39
	Chapter 6, "Fundamentals of TCP/IP Transport, Applications, and Security"	TCP/IP Layer 4 Protocols: TCP and UDP	pp. 133–146
ICND2 Official Exam Certification Guide	Chapter 3, "Troubleshooting LAN Switching"	Generalized Troubleshooting Methodologies	pp. 110–116
ICND1 Authorized Self-Study Guide	Chapter 1, "Building a Simple Network"	Understanding the Host-to-Host Communications Model	pp. 31–43
		Understanding the TCP/IP Internet Layer	pp. 43–62
		Understanding the TCP/IP Transport Layer	pp. 63–84
Supplemental Resources			
CCNA Flash Cards and Exam Practice Pack	ICND1, Section 1	Building a Simple Network	pp. 4–36
	ICND1, Section 2	Understanding TCP/IP	pp. 38–68

Part II

Switching Concepts and Configuration

Day 28:   Connecting Switches and Ethernet Technology

Day 27:   Network Segmentation and Switching Concepts

Day 26:   Basic Switch Configuration and Port Security

Day 25:   Verifying and Troubleshooting Basic Switch
                Configurations

Day 24:   Switching Technologies and VLAN Concepts

Day 23:   VLAN and Trunking Configuration and
                Troubleshooting

Day 22:   VTP and InterVLAN Routing Configuration and
                Troubleshooting

Connecting Switches and Ethernet Technology

CCNA 640-802 Exam Topics

- Explain the technology and media access control method for Ethernet networks.

- Select the appropriate media, cables, ports, and connectors to connect switches to other network devices and hosts.

Key Topics

Ethernet has continued to evolve from the 10BASE2 flavor capable of speeds up to 185 Mbps to the newest 10GigE (10 Gigabit Ethernet) capable of speeds up to 10 Gbps. Since 1985, IEEE has continued to upgrade the 802.3 standards to provide faster speeds without changing the underlying frame structure. This feature, among others, has made Ethernet the choice for LAN implementations worldwide. Today we review Ethernet technologies and operation at both the data link and physical layer.

Ethernet Overview

802.3 is the IEEE standard for Ethernet, and both terms are commonly used interchangeably. The terms Ethernet and 802.3 both refer to a family of standards that together define the physical and data link layers of the definitive LAN technology. Figure 28-1 shows a comparison of Ethernet standards to the OSI model.

Figure 28-1   Ethernet Standards and the OSI Model

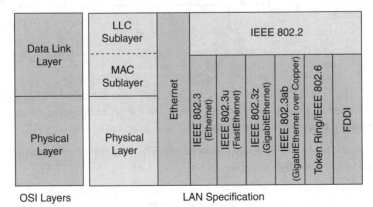

Ethernet separates the functions of the data link layer into two distinct sublayers:

- **Logical Link Control (LLC) sublayer:** Defined in the 802.2 standard.

- **Media Access Control (MAC) sublayer:** Defined in the 802.3 standard.

The LLC sublayer handles communication between the network layer and the MAC sublayer. In general, LLC provides a way to identify the protocol that is passed from the data link layer to the network layer. In this way, the fields of the MAC sublayer are not populated with protocol type information, as was the case in earlier Ethernet implementations.

The MAC sublayer has two primary responsibilities:

- **Data Encapsulation:** Includes frame assembly before transmission, frame parsing upon reception of a frame, data link layer MAC addressing, and error detection.

- **Media Access Control:** Because Ethernet is a shared media and all devices can transmit at any time, media access is controlled by a method called Carrier Sense Multiple Access with Collision Detection (CSMA/CD).

At the physical layer, Ethernet specifies and implements encoding and decoding schemes that enable frame bits to be carried as signals across both unshielded twisted-pair (UTP) copper cables and optical fiber cables. In early implementations, Ethernet used coaxial cabling.

Legacy Ethernet Technologies

Ethernet is best understood by first considering the two early Ethernet specifications—10BASE5 and 10BASE2. With these two specifications, the network engineer installs a series of coaxial cables connecting each device on the Ethernet network, as shown in Figure 28-2.

Figure 28-2   Ethernet Physical and Logical Bus Topology

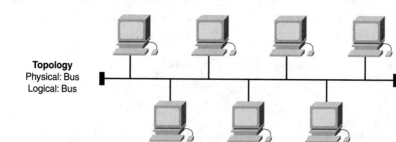

Topology
Physical: Bus
Logical: Bus

The series of cables creates an electrical circuit, called a bus, which is shared among all devices on the Ethernet. When a computer wants to send some bits to another computer on the bus, it sends an electrical signal, and the electricity propagates to all devices on the Ethernet.

With the change of media to UTP and the introduction of the first hubs, Ethernet physical topologies migrated to a star as shown in Figure 28-3.

Regardless of the change in the physical topology from a bus to a star, hubs logically operate similar to a traditional bus topology and require the use of CSMA/CD.

Figure 28-3   Ethernet Physical Star and Logical Bus Topology

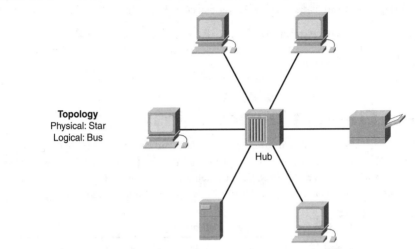

Topology
Physical: Star
Logical: Bus

Hub

CSMA/CD

Because Ethernet is a shared media where every device has the right to send at any time, it also defines a specification for how to ensure that only one device sends traffic at a time. The CSMA/CD algorithm defines how the Ethernet logical bus is accessed.

CSMA/CD logic helps prevent collisions and also defines how to act when a collision does occur. The CSMA/CD algorithm works like this:

1. A device with a frame to send listens until the Ethernet is not busy.

2. When the Ethernet is not busy, the sender(s) begin(s) sending the frame.

3. The sender(s) listen(s) to make sure that no collision occurred.

4. If a collision occurs, the devices that had been sending a frame each send a jamming signal to ensure that all stations recognize the collision.

5. After the jamming is complete, each sender randomizes a timer and waits that long before trying to resend the collided frame.

6. When each random timer expires, the process starts again from the beginning.

When CSMA/CD is in effect, it also means that a device's network interface card (NIC) is operating in half-duplex mode—either sending or receiving frames. CSMA/CD is disabled when a NIC autodetects that it can operate in—or is manually configured to operate in—full duplex mode. In full duplex mode, a NIC can send and receive simultaneously.

Legacy Ethernet Summary

Today, you might occasionally use LAN hubs, but you will more likely use switches instead of hubs. However, keep in mind the following key points about the history of Ethernet:

- The original Ethernet LANs created an electrical bus to which all devices connected.

- 10BASE2 and 10BASE5 repeaters extended the length of LANs by cleaning up the electrical signal and repeating it—a Layer 1 function—but without interpreting the meaning of the electrical signal.

- Hubs are repeaters that provide a centralized connection point for UTP cabling—but they still create a single electrical bus, shared by the various devices, just like 10BASE5 and 10BASE2.

- Because collisions could occur in any of these cases, Ethernet defines the CSMA/CD algorithm, which tells devices how to both avoid collisions and take action when collisions do occur.

Current Ethernet Technologies

Refer back to Figure 28-1 and notice the different 802.3 standards. Each new physical layer standard from the IEEE requires many differences at the physical layer. However, each of these physical layer standards uses the same 802.3 header, and each uses the upper LLC sublayer as well. Table 28-1 lists today's most commonly used IEEE Ethernet physical layer standards.

Table 28-1   Today's Most Common Types of Ethernet

Common Name	Speed	Alternative Name	Name of IEEE Standard	Cable Type, Maximum Length
Ethernet	10 Mbps	10BASE-T	IEEE 802.3	Copper, 100 m
Fast Ethernet	100 Mbps	100BASE-TX	IEEE 802.3u	Copper, 100 m
Gigabit Ethernet .	1000 Mbps	1000BASE-LX, 1000BASE-SX	IEEE 802.3z	Fiber, 550 m (SX) 5 km (LX)
Gigabit Ethernet	1000 Mbps	1000BASE-T	IEEE 802.3ab	Copper, 100 m
10GigE (Gigabit Ethernet)	10 Gbps	10GBASE-SR, 10GBASE-LR	IEEE 802.3ae	Fiber, up to 300 m (SR), up to 25 km (LR)
10GigE (Gigabit Ethernet)	10 Gbps	10GBASE-T	IEEE 802.3an	Copper, 100 m

UTP Cabling

The three most common Ethernet standards used today—10BASE-T (Ethernet), 100BASE-TX (Fast Ethernet, or FE), and 1000BASE-T (Gigabit Ethernet, or GE)—use UTP cabling. Some key differences exist, particularly with the number of wire pairs needed in each case and in the type (category) of cabling.

The UTP cabling used by popular Ethernet standards include either two or four pairs of wires. The cable ends typically use an RJ-45 connector. The RJ-45 connector has eight specific physical locations into which the eight wires in the cable can be inserted, called pin positions or, simply, pins.

The Telecommunications Industry Association (TIA) and the Electronics Industry Alliance (EIA) define standards for UTP cabling, color coding for wires, and standard pinouts on the cables. Figure 28-4 shows two TIA/EIA pinout standards, with the color coding and pair numbers listed.

Figure 28-4   TIA/EIA Standard Ethernet Cabling Pinouts

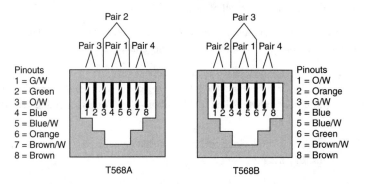

For the exam, you should be well prepared to choose which type of cable (straight-through or crossover) is needed in each part of the network. In short, devices on opposite ends of a cable that use the same pair of pins to transmit need a crossover cable. Devices that use an opposite pair of pins to transmit need a straight-through cable. Table 28-2 lists typical devices and the pin pairs they use, assuming that they use 10BASE-T and 100BASE-TX.

Table 28-2   10BASE-T and 100BASE-TX Pin Pairs Used

Devices That Transmit on 1,2 and Receive on 3,6	Devices That Transmit on 3,6 and Receive on 1,2
PC NICs	Hubs
Routers	Switches
Wireless Access Point (Ethernet interface)	N/A
Networked printers (printers that connect directly to the LAN)	N/A

1000BASE-T requires four wire pairs because Gigabit Ethernet transmits and receives on each of the four wire pairs simultaneously.

However, Gigabit Ethernet does have a concept of straight-through and crossover cables, with a minor difference in the crossover cables. The pinouts for a straight-through cable are the same— pin 1 to pin 1, pin 2 to pin 2, and so on. The crossover cable crosses the same two-wire pair as the crossover cable for the other types of Ethernet—the pair at pins 1,2 and 3,6—as well as crossing the two other pairs (the pair at pins 4,5 with the pair at pins 7,8).

Benefits of Using Switches

A collision domain is a set of devices whose frames could collide. All devices on a 10BASE2, 10BASE5, or any network using a hub risk collisions between the frames that they send, so all devices on one of these types of Ethernet networks are in the same collision domain and use CSMA/CD to detect and resolve collisions.

LAN switches significantly reduce, or even eliminate, the number of collisions on a LAN. Unlike hubs, switches do not create a single shared bus. Instead, switches do the following:

- Switches interpret the bits in the received frame so that they can typically send the frame out the one required port, rather than all other ports.

- If a switch needs to forward multiple frames out the same port, the switch buffers the frames in memory, sending one at a time, thereby avoiding collisions.

In addition, switches with only one device cabled to each port of the switch allow the use of full-duplex operation. Full-duplex means that the NIC can send and receive concurrently, effectively doubling the bandwidth of a 100 Mbps link to 200 Mbps—100 Mbps for sending and 100 Mbps for receiving.

These seemingly simple switch features provide significant performance improvements as compared with using hubs. In particular:

- If only one device is cabled to each port of a switch, no collisions can occur.

- Devices connected to one switch port do not share their bandwidth with devices connected to another switch port. Each has its own separate bandwidth, meaning that a switch with 100 Mbps ports has 100 Mbps of bandwidth per port.

Ethernet Addressing

The IEEE defines the format and assignment of LAN addresses. To ensure a unique MAC address, the first half of the address identifies the manufacturer of the card. This code is called the organizationally unique identifier (OUI). Each manufacturer assigns a MAC address with its own OUI as the first half of the address. The second half of the address is assigned by the manufacturer and is never used on another card or network interface with the same OUI. Figure 28-5 shows the structure of a unicast Ethernet address.

Figure 28-5   Structure of Unicast Ethernet Address

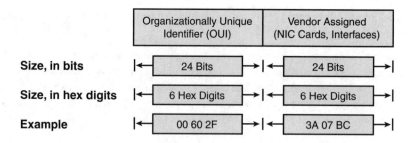

Ethernet also has group addresses, which identify more than one NIC or network interface. The IEEE defines two general categories of group addresses for Ethernet:

- **Broadcast addresses:** The broadcast address implies that all devices on the LAN should process the frame and has a value of FFFF.FFFF.FFFF.

- **Multicast addresses:** Multicast addresses are used to allow a subset of devices on a LAN to communicate. When IP multicasts over an Ethernet, the multicast MAC addresses used by IP follow this format: 0100.5exx.xxxx, where any value can be used in the last half of the address.

Ethernet Framing

The physical layer helps you get a string of bits from one device to another. The framing of the bits allows the receiving device to interpret the bits. The term *framing* refers to the definition of the fields assumed to be in the data that is received. Framing defines the meaning of the bits transmitted and received over a network.

The framing used for Ethernet has changed a couple of times over the years. Each iteration of Ethernet is shown in Figure 28-6, with the current version shown at the bottom.

Figure 28-6   Ethernet Frame Formats

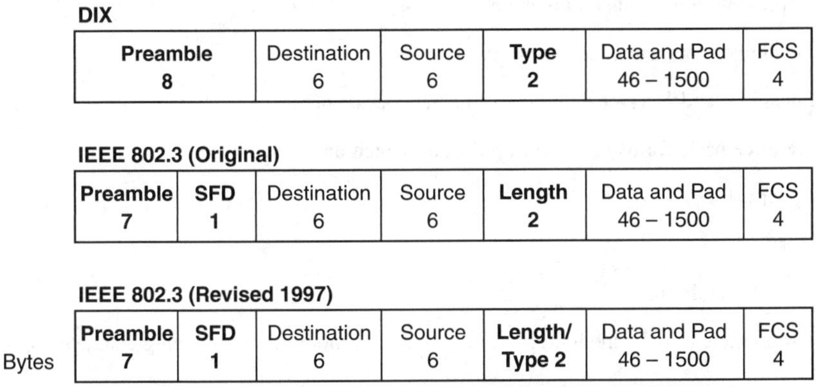

DIX

Preamble	Destination	Source	Type	Data and Pad	FCS
8	6	6	2	46 – 1500	4

IEEE 802.3 (Original)

Preamble	SFD	Destination	Source	Length	Data and Pad	FCS
7	1	6	6	2	46 – 1500	4

IEEE 802.3 (Revised 1997)

Bytes

Preamble	SFD	Destination	Source	Length/ Type 2	Data and Pad	FCS
7	1	6	6		46 – 1500	4

The fields in the last version shown in Figure 28-6 are explained further in Table 28-3.

Table 28-3   IEEE 802.3 Ethernet Field Descriptions

Field	Field Length in Bytes	Description
Preamble	7	Synchronization
Start Frame Delimiter (SFD)	1	Signifies that the next byte begins the Destination MAC field
Destination MAC address	6	Identifies the intended recipient of this frame
Source MAC address	6	Identifies the sender of this frame
Length	2	Defines the length of the data field of the frame (either length or type is present, but not both)
Type	2	Defines the type of protocol listed inside the frame (either length or type is present, but not both)
Data and Pad	46–1500	Holds data from a higher layer, typically a Layer 3 PDU (generic), and often an IP packet
Frame Check Sequence (FCS)	4	Provides a method for the receiving NIC to determine whether the frame experienced transmission errors

The Role of the Physical Layer

We have already discussed the most popular cabling used in LANs—UTP. But to fully understand the operation of the network, you should know some additional basic concepts of the physical layer.

The OSI physical layer accepts a complete frame from the data link layer and encodes it as a series of signals that are transmitted onto the local media.

The delivery of frames across the local media requires the following physical layer elements:

- The physical media and associated connectors
- A representation of bits on the media
- Encoding of data and control information
- Transmitter and receiver circuitry on the network devices

There are three basic forms of network media on which data is represented:

- Copper cable
- Fiber
- Wireless (IEEE 802.11)

Bits are represented on the medium by changing one or more of the following characteristics of a signal:

- Amplitude
- Frequency
- Phase

The nature of the actual signals representing the bits on the media will depend on the signaling method in use. Some methods may use one attribute of a signal to represent a single 0 and use another attribute of a signal to represent a single 1. The actual signaling method and its detailed operation are not important to your CCNA exam preparation.

Study Resources

For today's exam topics, refer to the following resources for more study.

Resource	Chapter	Topic	Where to Find It
Foundational Resources			
CCNA Exploration Online Curriculum: Network Fundamentals	Chapter 8, "OSI Physical Layer"	All topics within the chapter	Chapter 8
	Chapter 9, "Ethernet"	Overview of Ethernet	Section 9.1
		Ethernet—Communication through the LAN	Section 9.2
		The Ethernet Frame	Section 9.3
		Ethernet Media Access Control	Section 9.4
		Ethernet Physical Layer	Section 9.5
		Address Resolution Protocol (ARP)	Section 9.7
	Chapter 10, "Planning and Cabling Networks"	Making LAN Connections	Section 10.2.2
CCNA Exploration Online Curriculum: LAN Switching and Wireless	Chapter 2, "Basic Switch Concepts and Configuration"	Key Elements of Ethernet/ 802.3 Networks	Section 2.2.1
CCNA Exploration Network Fundamentals Companion Guide	Chapter 8, "OSI Physical Layer"	All topics within the chapter	pp. 279–306
	Chapter 9, "Ethernet"	Overview of Ethernet	pp. 315–320
		Ethernet: Communication through the LAN	pp. 320–324
		The Ethernet Frame	pp. 324–334
		Ethernet MAC	pp. 334–342
		Ethernet Physical Layer	pp. 342–347
		Address Resolution Protocol (ARP)	pp. 355–361
	Chapter 10, "Planning and Cabling Networks"	Making LAN Connections	pp. 380–384
CCNA Exploration LAN Switching and Wireless Companion Guide	Chapter 2, "Basic Switch Concepts and Configuration"	Key Elements of Ethernet/ 802.3 Networks	pp. 46–52
ICND1 Official Exam Certification Guide	Chapter 3, "Fundamentals of LANs"	All topics within the chapter	pp. 45–69
ICND1 Authorized Self-Study Guide	Chapter 1, "Building a Simple Network"	Understanding Ethernet	pp. 104–115
		Connecting to an Ethernet LAN	pp. 115–124
	Chapter 2, "Ethernet LANs"	Understanding the Challenges of Shared LANs	pp. 139–144
Supplemental Resources			
CCNA Flash Cards and Exam Practice Pack	ICND1, Section 3	Understanding Ethernet	pp. 70–84

Network Segmentation and Switching Concepts

CCNA 640-802 Exam Topics

- Explain network segmentation and basic traffic management concepts.
- Explain basic switching concepts and the operation of Cisco switches.

Key Topics

Today we review the concepts behind switching, including the history of the development of switching, how switching actually works, as well as the variety of switch features. We also review how to access Cisco devices, the basic IOS commands to navigate the command-line interface (CLI) and the details of how configuration files are managed.

Evolution to Switching

Today's LANs almost exclusively use switches to interconnect end devices; however, this was not always the case. Initially, devices were connected to a physical bus—a long run of coaxial backbone cabling. With the introduction of 10BASE-T and UTP cabling, the hub gained popularity as a cheaper, easier way to connect devices. But even 10BASE-T with hubs had the following limitations:

- A frame being sent from one device may collide with a frame sent by another device attached to that LAN segment. Devices were in the same collision domain sharing the bandwidth.
- Broadcasts sent by one device were heard by, and processed by, all other devices on the LAN. Devices were in the same broadcast domain. Similar to hubs, switches forward broadcast frames out all ports except for the incoming port. Switch ports can be configured on various VLANs, which will segment them into broadcast domains.

Ethernet bridges were soon developed to solve some of the inherent problems in a shared LAN. A bridge basically segmented a LAN into two collision domains which

- Reduced the number of collisions that occurred in a LAN segment
- Increased the available bandwidth

When switches arrived on the scene, these devices provided the same benefits of bridges, as well as the following:

- A larger number of interfaces to break up the collision domain into more segments
- Hardware-based switching instead of using software to make the decision

In a LAN where all nodes are connected directly to the switch, the throughput of the network increases dramatically. With each computer connected to a separate port on the switch, each is in a separate collision domain and has its own dedicated segment. The three primary reasons for this increase are the following:

- Dedicated bandwidth to each port
- Collision-free environment
- Full-duplex operation

Switching Logic

Ethernet switches selectively forward individual frames from a receiving port to the port where the destination node is connected. During this instant, the switch creates a full bandwidth, logical point-to-point connection between the two nodes.

Switches create this logical connection based on the source and destination Media Access Control (MAC) addresses in the Ethernet header. Specifically, the primary job of a LAN switch is to receive Ethernet frames and then make a decision: either forward the frame or ignore the frame. To accomplish this, the switch performs three actions:

1. Decides when to forward a frame or when to filter (not forward) a frame, based on the destination MAC address

2. Learns MAC addresses by examining the source MAC address of each frame received by the bridge

3. Creates a (Layer 2) loop-free environment with other bridges by using Spanning Tree Protocol (STP)

To make the forward or filter decision, the switch uses a dynamically built MAC address table stored in RAM. By comparing the frame's destination MAC address with the fields in the table, the switch decides how to forward and/or filter the frame.

For example, in Figure 27-1 the switch receives a frame from Host A with the destination MAC address OC. The switch looks in its MAC table and finds an entry for the MAC address and forwards the frame out port 6. The switch also filters the frame by not forwarding it out any other port, including the port on which the frame was received.

In addition to forwarding and filtering frames, the switch will also refresh the timestamp for the source MAC address of the frame. In Figure 27-1, the MAC address for Host A, OA, is already in the MAC table. So the switch refreshes the entry. Entries that are not refreshed will eventually be removed (after 300 seconds in Cisco IOS).

Continuing the example in Figure 27-1, assume another device, Host E, is attached to port 10. Host B then sends a frame to the new Host E. The switch does not yet know where Host E is located. So it forwards the frame out all active ports except for the port on which the frame was received. The new Host E will receive the frame. When it replies to Host B, the switch will learn Host E's MAC address and port for the first time and store it in the MAC address table. Subsequent frames destined for Host E will only be sent out port 10.

Figure 27-1   Switch Forwarding Based on MAC Address

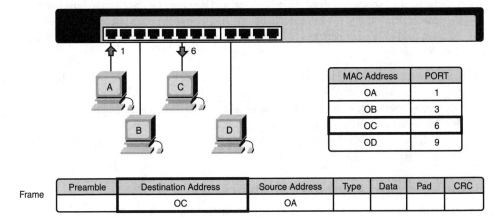

Finally, LAN switches must have a method for creating a loop-free path for frames to take within the LAN. STP provides loop prevention in Ethernet networks where redundant physical links exist. Day 24, "Switching Technologies and VLAN Concepts," reviews STP in more detail.

Collision and Broadcast Domains

A collision domain is the set of LAN interfaces whose frames could collide with each other. All shared media environments, such as those created by using hubs, are collision domains. When one host is attached to a switch port, the switch creates a dedicated connection thereby eliminating the potential for a collision. Switches reduce collisions and improve bandwidth use on network segments because they provide dedicated bandwidth to each network segment.

However, out of the box, a switch cannot provide relief from broadcast traffic. A collection of connected switches forms one large broadcast domain. If a frame with the destination address FFFF.FFFF.FFFF crosses a switch port, that switch must then flood the frame out all other active ports. Each attached device must then process the broadcast frame at least up to the network layer. Routers and VLANs are used to segment broadcast domains. Day 24 reviews the use of VLANs to segment broadcast domains.

Frame Forwarding

Switches operate in several ways to forward frames. They can differ in forwarding methods, port speeds, memory buffering, and the OSI layers used to make the forwarding decision. The sections that follow discuss these concepts in greater detail.

Switch Forwarding Methods

In the past, switches used one of the following forwarding methods for switching data between network ports:

- **Store-and-forward switching:** The switch stores received frames in its buffers, analyzes each frame for information about the destination, and evaluates the data integrity using the cyclic redundancy check (CRC) in the frame trailer. The entire frame is stored and the CRC calculated before any of the frame is forwarded. If the CRC passes, the frame is forwarded to the destination.

- **Cut-through switching:** The switch buffers just enough of the frame to read the destination MAC address so that it can determine to which port to forward the data. After the switch determines whether there is a match between the destination MAC address and an entry in the MAC address table, the frame is forwarded out the appropriate port(s). This happens as the rest of the initial frame is still being received. The switch does not perform any error checking on the frame.

Symmetric and Asymmetric Switching

Symmetric switching provides switched connections between ports with the same bandwidth, such as all 100 Mbps ports or all 1000 Mbps ports. An asymmetric LAN switch provides switched connections between ports of unlike bandwidth, such as a combination of 10 Mbps, 100 Mbps, and 1000 Mbps ports.

Memory Buffering

Switches store frames for a brief time in a memory buffer. There are two methods of memory buffering:

- **Port-based memory:** Frames are stored in queues that are linked to specific incoming ports.

- **Shared memory:** Frames are deposited into a common memory buffer, which all ports on the switch share.

Layer 2 and Layer 3 Switching

A Layer 2 LAN switch performs switching and filtering based only on MAC addresses. A Layer 2 switch is completely transparent to network protocols and user applications. A Layer 3 switch functions similarly to a Layer 2 switch. But instead of using only the Layer 2 MAC address information for forwarding decisions, a Layer 3 switch can also use IP address information. Layer 3 switches are also capable of performing Layer 3 routing functions, reducing the need for dedicated routers on a LAN. Because Layer 3 switches have specialized switching hardware, they can typically route data as quickly as they can switch data.

Accessing and Navigating Cisco IOS

By now, you are very familiar with connecting to Cisco devices and configuring them using the command-line interface (CLI). Here, we quickly review methods for accessing and navigating CLI.

Connecting to Cisco Devices

You can access a device directly or from a remote location. Figure 27-2 shows the many ways you can connect to Cisco devices.

Figure 27-2   Sources for Cisco Device Configuration

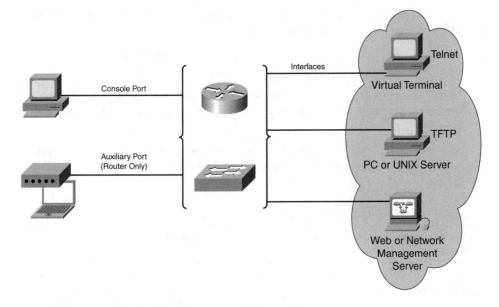

The two ways to configure Cisco devices are as follows:

- **Console terminal:** Use an RJ-45 to RJ-45 rollover cable and a computer with the terminal communications software (such as HyperTerminal, Tera Term, and so on) to establish a direct connection.

- **Remote terminal:** Use an external modem connected to the auxiliary port—routers only—to remotely configure the device.

Once configured, you can access the device using three additional methods:

- Establish a terminal (vty) session using Telnet.

- Configure the device through the current connection (console or auxiliary), or download a previously written startup-config file from a Trivial File Transfer Protocol (TFTP) server on the network.

- Download a configuration file using a network management software application such as CiscoWorks.

CLI EXEC Sessions

Cisco IOS separates the EXEC session into two basic access levels:

- **User EXEC mode:** Access to only a limited number of basic monitoring and troubleshooting commands, such as **show** and **ping**.

- **Privileged EXEC mode:** Full access to all device commands, including configuration and management.

Using the Help Facility

Cisco IOS has extensive command-line input help facilities, including context-sensitive help. The following summarizes the two types of help available:

- **Word help:** Enter a character sequence of an incomplete command immediately followed by a question mark (**sh?**) to get a list of available commands that start with the character sequence.

- **Command syntax help:** Enter the **?** command to get command syntax help to see all the available arguments to complete a command (**show ?**). IOS then displays a list of available arguments

As part of the help facility, IOS displays console error messages when incorrect command syntax is entered. Table 27-1 shows sample error messages, what they mean, and how to get help when they are displayed.

Table 27-1   Console Error Messages

Example Error Message	Meaning	How to Get Help
switch#**cl** % Ambiguous command: "cl"	You did not enter enough characters for your device to recognize the command.	Reenter the command followed by a question mark (?), without a space between the command and the question mark. The possible keywords that you can enter with the command are displayed.
switch#**clock** % Incomplete command.	You did not enter all the keywords or values required by this command.	Reenter the command followed by a question mark (?), with a space between the command and the question mark.
switch#**clock ste** ^ % Invalid input detected at '^' marker.	You entered the command incorrectly. The caret (^) marks the point of the error.	Enter a question mark (?) to display all the available commands or parameters.

CLI Navigation and Editing Shortcuts

Table 27-2 summarizes the shortcuts for navigating and editing commands in CLI. Although not specifically tested on the CCNA exam, these shortcuts may save you time when using the simulator during the exam.

Table 27-2   Hot Keys and Shortcuts

Keyboard Command	What Happens
Navigation Key Sequences	
Up arrow or Ctrl-P	This displays the most recently used command. If you press it again, the next most recent command appears, until the history buffer is exhausted. (The *P* stands for previous.)
Down arrow or Ctrl-N	If you have gone too far back into the history buffer, these keys take you forward to the more recently entered commands. (The *N* stands for next.)
Left arrow or Ctrl-B	This moves the cursor backward in the currently displayed command without deleting characters. (The *B* stands for back.)

Keyboard Command	What Happens
Navigation Key Sequences	
Right arrow or Ctrl-F	This moves the cursor forward in the currently displayed command without deleting characters. (The *F* stands for forward.)
Tab	Completes a partial command name entry.
Backspace	This moves the cursor backward in the currently displayed command, deleting characters.
Ctrl-A	This moves the cursor directly to the first character of the currently displayed command.
Ctrl-E	This moves the cursor directly to the end of the currently displayed command.
Ctrl-R	This redisplays the command line with all characters. It's useful when messages clutter the screen.
Ctrl-D	This deletes a single character.
Esc-B	This moves back one word.
Esc-F	This moves forward one word.
At the –More-- Prompt	
Enter key	Displays the next line.
Space Bar	Displays the next screen.
Any other alphanumeric key	Returns to the EXEC prompt.
Break Keys	
Ctrl-C	When in any configuration mode, this ends the configuration mode and returns to privileged EXEC mode. When in setup mode, aborts back to the command prompt.
Ctrl-Z	When in any configuration mode, this ends the configuration mode and returns to privileged EXEC mode. When in user or privileged EXEC mode, logs you out of the router.
Ctrl-Shift-6	All-purpose break sequence. Use to abort DNS lookups, traceroutes, pings.

Command History

Cisco IOS, by default, stores the last 10 commands you entered in a history buffer. This provides you with a quick way to move backward and forward in the history of commands, choose one, and then edit it before reissuing the command. To view or configure the command history buffer, use the commands shown in Table 27-3. Although the switch prompt is shown here, these commands are also appropriate for a router.

Table 27-3   Command History Buffer Commands

Command Syntax	Description
switch#**show history**	Displays the commands currently stored in the history buffer.
switch#**terminal history**	Enables terminal history. This command can be run from either user or privileged EXEC mode.

continues

Table 27-3   Command History Buffer Commands *continued*

Command Syntax	Description
switch#**terminal history size 50**	Configures the terminal history size. The terminal history can maintain 0 to 256 command lines.
switch#**terminal no history size**	Resets the terminal history size to the default value of 10 command lines.
switch#**terminal no history**	Disables terminal history.

IOS Examination Commands

To verify and troubleshoot network operation, you use **show** commands. Figure 27-3 delineates the different **show** commands, as follows:

- If they are applicable to IOS (stored in RAM)
- If they apply to the backup configuration file stored in NVRAM
- If they apply to flash or specific interfaces

Figure 27-3   Typical show Commands and the Information Provided

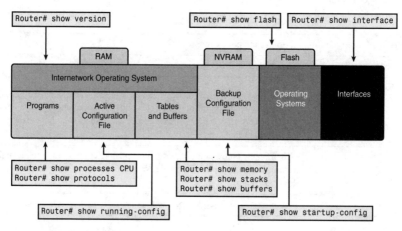

Subconfiguration Modes

To enter global configuration mode, enter the command **configure terminal**. From global configuration mode, IOS provides a multitude of subconfiguration modes. Table 27-4 summarizes the most common subconfiguration modes pertinent to the CCNA exam.

Table 27-4   Cisco Device Subconfiguration Modes

Prompt	Name of Mode	Examples of Commands Used to Reach This Mode
hostname(config)#	Global	**configure terminal**
hostname(config-line)#	Line	**line console 0** **line vty 0 15**
hostname(config-if)#	Interface	**interface fastethernet 0/0**
hostname(config-router)#	Router	**router rip** **router eigrp 100**

Storing and Erasing Configuration Files

When you configure a Cisco device, it needs to be able to retain the configuration in memory in case the switch or router loses power. Cisco devices have four main types of memory. Figure 27-4 shows these four memory types and the primary function of each.

Figure 27-4   Cisco Device Memory Types

RAM	Flash	ROM	NVRAM
(Working Memory and Running Configuration)	(Cisco IOS Software)	(Bootstrap Program)	(Startup Configuration)

Cisco devices use two configuration files—one file used when the device is powered on, and another file for the active, currently used running configuration in RAM. Table 27-5 list the names of these files, their purpose, and where they are stored in memory.

Table 27-5   Names and Purposes of the Two Main Cisco IOS Configuration Files

Configuration Filename	Purpose	Where It Is Stored
Startup-config	Stores the initial configuration used anytime the switch reloads Cisco IOS.	NVRAM
Running-config	Stores the currently used configuration commands. This file changes dynamically when someone enters commands in configuration mode.	RAM

Configuration files can also be stored on a TFTP server. The configuration files can be copied between RAM, NVRAM, and a TFTP server using the **copy** commands, as shown in Figure 27-5.

Figure 27-5   Configuration File copy Commands and Storage Locations

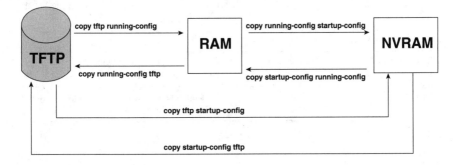

You can use three commands to erase the contents of NVRAM. The **write erase** and **erase start-up-config** commands are older, whereas the **erase nvram:** command is the more recent, and recommended, command. All three commands erase the contents of the NVRAM configuration file.

Study Resources

For today's exam topics, refer to the following resources for more study.

Resource	Chapter	Topic	Where to Find It
Foundational Resources			
CCNA Exploration Online Curriculum: Network Fundamentals	Chapter 9, "Ethernet" Chapter 11, "Configuring and Testing Your Network"	Hubs and Switches Configuring Cisco Devices—IOS Basics	Section 9.6 Section 11.1
CCNA Exploration Online Curriculum: LAN Switching and Wireless	Chapter 2, "Basic Switch Concepts and Configuration"	Introduction to Ethernet/802.3 LANs Forwarding Frames Using a Switch Switch Management Configuration	Sections 2.1.2–2.1.3 Section 2.2 Sections 2.3.1–2.3.5
CCNA Exploration Network Fundamentals Companion Guide	Chapter 9, "Ethernet" Chapter 11, "Configuring and Testing Your Network"	Hubs and Switches Configuring Cisco Devices: IOS Basics	pp. 347–354 pp. 410–429
CCNA Exploration LAN Switching and Wireless Companion Guide	Chapter 2, "Basic Switch Concepts and Configuration"	Introduction to Ethernet/802.3 LANs Forwarding Frames Using a Switch Switch Management Configuration	pp. 52–58 pp. 58–63 pp. 63–72
ICND1 Official Exam Certification Guide	Chapter 7, "Ethernet LAN Switching Concepts" Chapter 8, "Operating Cisco LAN Switches"	All topics within the chapter All topics within the chapter	pp. 171–193 pp. 200–225
ICND1 Authorized Self-Study Guide	Chapter 2, "Ethernet LANs"	Understanding the Challenges of Shared LANs Exploring the Packet Delivery Process Operating Cisco IOS Software Maximizing the Benefits of Switching	pp. 139–144 pp. 144–151 pp. 151–163 pp. 182–191
Supplemental Resources			
CCNA Flash Cards and Exam Practice Pack	ICND1, Section 4 ICND1, Section 5	LAN Network Technologies Operating Cisco IOS	pp. 88–112 pp. 114–126
CCNA Video Mentor	ICND1, Lab 1	Navigating a Router/Switch Command-Line Interface	pp. 3–5 and DVD

Basic Switch Configuration and Port Security

CCNA 640-802 Exam Topics

- Perform, save, and verify initial switch configuration tasks, including remote access management.

- Implement and verify basic switch security (including port security, unassigned ports, trunk access, and so on).

Key Topics

Today we review the commands necessary to perform a basic initial configuration of a switch. For basic switch security, we review changing default virtual local-area networks (VLANs), Secure Shell (SSH) configuration, and port security.

Basic Switch Configuration Commands

Table 26-1 reviews basic switch configuration commands.

Table 26-1   Basic Switch Configuration Commands

Command Description	Command Syntax
Enter global configuration mode.	Switch# **configure terminal**
Configure a name for the device.	Switch(config)# **hostname S1**
Enter the interface configuration mode for the VLAN 123 interface.	S1(config)# **interface vlan 123**
Configure the interface IP address.	S1(config-if)# **ip address 172.17.99.11 255.255.255.0**
Enable the interface.	S1(config-if)# **no shutdown**
Return to global configuration mode.	S1(config-if)# **exit**
Enter the interface to assign the VLAN.	S1(config)# **interface fastethernet 0/6**
Define the VLAN membership mode for the port.	S1(config-if)# **switchport mode access**
Assign the port to a VLAN.	S1(config-if)# **switchport access vlan 123**
Configure the interface duplex mode to enable AUTO duplex configuration.	S1(config-if)# **duplex auto**
Configure the interface duplex speed and enable AUTO speed configuration.	S1(config-if)# **speed auto**

continues

Table 26-1   Basic Switch Configuration Commands *continued*

Command Description	Command Syntax
Return to global configuration mode.	S1(config-if)# **exit**
Configure the default gateway on the switch.	S1(config)# **ip default-gateway 172.17.50.1**
Configure the HTTP server for authentication using the **enable** password, which is the default method of HTTP server user authentication.	S1(config)# **ip http authentication enable**
Enable the HTTP server.	S1(config)# **ip http server**
Switch from global configuration mode to line configuration mode for console 0.	S1(config)# **line console 0**
Set **cisco** as the password for the console 0 line on the switch.	S1(config-line)# **password cisco**
Set the console line to require the password to be entered before access is granted.	S1(config-line)# **login**
Return to global configuration mode.	S1(config-if)# **exit**
Switch from global configuration mode to line configuration mode for vty terminals 0 through 4.	S1(config)# **line vty 0 4**
Set **cisco** as the password for the vty lines on the switch.	S1(config-line)# **password cisco**
Set the vty line to require the password to be entered before access is granted.	S1(config-line)# **login**
Return to global configuration mode.	S1(config-line)# **exit**
Configure **cisco** as the enable password to enter privileged EXEC mode.	S1(config)# **enable password cisco**
Configure **class** as the enable secret password to enter privileged EXEC mode.	S1(config)# **enable secret class**
Encrypts all the system passwords that are stored in clear text.	S1(config)# **service password-encryption**
Configure a login banner. The # character delimits the beginning and end of the banner.	S1 (config)# **banner login #Authorized Personnel Only!#**
Configure a MOTD login banner. The # character delimits the beginning and end of the banner.	S1(config)# **banner motd #Device maintenance will be occurring on Friday!#**
Return to privileged EXEC mode.	S1(config)# **end**
Save the running configuration to the switch start-up configuration.	S1# **copy running-config startup –config**

In reference to the commands in Table 26-1, keep in mind the following:

- The default VLAN for all ports is VLAN 1. Because it is a best practice to use a VLAN other than the default VLAN 1 as the management VLAN, the command in the table uses VLAN 123.

- By default, the native VLAN assigned to 802.1Q trunks is also VLAN 1. It is a security best practice to define a dummy VLAN as the native VLAN—a VLAN that is distinct from all other VLANs. We discuss trunking configuration on Day 23, "VLAN and Trunking Configuration and Troubleshooting."

- Although the **enable password** command is shown in the table for completeness, this command is superseded by the **enable secret** command. If both are entered, IOS ignores the **enable password** command.

- To configure multiple ports with the same command, use the **interface range** command. For example, to configure ports 6 through 10 as access ports belonging to VLAN 10, you would enter the following:

```
Switch(config)#interface range FastEthernet 0/6 - 10
Switch(config-if-range)#switchport mode access
Switch(config-if-range)#switchport access vlan 10
```

Configuring SSH Access

Figure 26-1 graphically shows the steps to configure a switch (or a router) to support SSH.

Figure 26-1   SSH Configuration Steps

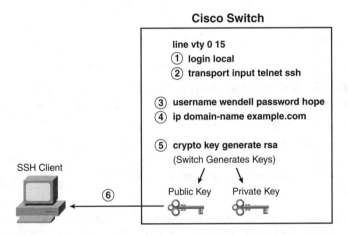

The following description details the steps shown in the figure:

Step 1   Change the vty lines to use usernames, with either locally configured usernames or an authentication, authorization, and accounting (AAA) server. In Figure 26-1, the **login local** subcommand defines the use of local usernames, replacing the **login** subcommand in vty configuration mode.

Step 2   Configure the switch to accept both Telnet and SSH connections with the **transport input telnet ssh** vty subcommand. (The default is **transport input telnet**, omitting the **ssh** parameter.)

Step 3   Add one or more **username** *name* **password** *pass-value* global configuration commands to configure username/password pairs.

Step 4   Configure a DNS domain name with the **ip domain-name** name global configuration command. This command is necessary only if you want to use a domain name instead of an IP address.

Step 5   Configure the switch to generate a matched public and private key pair, as well as a shared encryption key, using the **crypto key generate rsa** global configuration command.

Step 6   Although no switch commands are required, each SSH client needs a copy of the switch's public key before the client can connect.

Configuring Port Security

If you know which devices should be cabled and connected to particular interfaces on a switch, you can use port security to restrict that interface so that only the expected devices can use it. This reduces exposure to some types of attacks in which the attacker connects a laptop to the wall socket or uses the cable attached to another end device to gain access to the network.

Port security configuration involves several steps. Basically, you need to make the port an access port, which means that the port is not doing any VLAN trunking. You then need to enable port security and then configure the actual Media Access Control (MAC) addresses of the devices allowed to use that port. The following list outlines the steps, including the configuration commands used:

Step 1   Configure the interface for access mode using the **switchport mode access** interface subcommand.

Step 2   Enable port security using the **switchport port-security** interface subcommand.

Step 3   (Optional) Specify the maximum number of allowed MAC addresses associated with the interface using the **switchport port-security maximum** *number* interface subcommand. (Defaults to one MAC address.)

Step 4   (Optional) Define the action to take when a frame is received from a MAC address other than the defined addresses using the **switchport port-security violation** {**protect** | **restrict** | **shutdown**} interface subcommand. (The default action is to shut down the port.)

Step 5A   Specify the MAC address(es) allowed to send frames into this interface using the **switchport port-security mac-address** *mac-address* command. Use the command multiple times to define more than one MAC address.

Step 5B   Alternatively, instead of Step 5A, configure the interface to dynamically learn and configure the MAC addresses of currently connected hosts by configuring the **switchport port-security mac-address sticky** interface subcommand.

When an unauthorized device attempts to send frames to the switch interface, the switch can issue informational messages, discard frames from that device, or even discard frames from all devices by effectively shutting down the interface. Exactly what action the switch port takes depends on the option you configure in the **switchport port-security violation** command. Table 26-2 lists actions the switch will take based on whether you configure option **protect**, **restrict**, or **shutdown** (default).

Table 26-2   Actions When Port Security Violation Occurs

Option on the switchport port-security violation Command	Protect	Restrict	Shutdown
Discards offending traffic	Yes	Yes	Yes
Sends log and SNMP messages	No	Yes	Yes
Disables the interface, discarding all traffic	No	No	Yes

Example 26-1 shows a port security configuration where each access interface is allowed a maximum of three MAC address. If a fourth MAC is detected, only the offending device's traffic will be discarded. If the violation option is not explicitly configured, the traffic for devices that are allowed on the port would also be discarded because the port would be shut down by default.

Example 26-1   A Port Security Configuration Example

```
S1(config)#interface range fa 0/5 - fa 0/24
S1(config-if-range)#switchport mode access
S1(config-if-range)#switchport port-security
S1(config-if-range)#switchport port-security maximum 3
S1(config-if-range)#switchport port-security violation restrict
S1(config-if-range)#switchport port-security mac-address sticky
```

To verify port security configuration, use the more general **show port-security** command or the more specific **show port-security interface** *type number* command. Example 26-2 demonstrates the use of both commands. In the examples, notice that only one device is currently attached to an access port on S1.

Example 26-2   Port Security Verification Command Output Examples

```
S1#show port-security
Secure Port  MaxSecureAddr  CurrentAddr  SecurityViolation  Security Action
              (Count)        (Count)      (Count)
--------------------------------------------------------------------------
    Fa0/5         3             1              0             Restrict
    Fa0/6         3             0              0             Restrict
    Fa0/7         3             0              0             Restrict
    Fa0/8         3             0              0             Restrict
    Fa0/9         3             0              0             Restrict
    Fa0/10        3             0              0             Restrict
    Fa0/11        3             0              0             Restrict
    Fa0/12        3             0              0             Restrict
    Fa0/13        3             0              0             Restrict
    Fa0/14        3             0              0             Restrict
    Fa0/15        3             0              0             Restrict
    Fa0/16        3             0              0             Restrict
    Fa0/17        3             0              0             Restrict
```

```
        Fa0/18              3           0                 0        Restrict
        Fa0/19              3           0                 0        Restrict
        Fa0/20              3           0                 0        Restrict
        Fa0/21              3           0                 0        Restrict
        Fa0/22              3           0                 0        Restrict
        Fa0/23              3           0                 0        Restrict
        Fa0/24              3           0                 0        Restrict
    -------------------------------------------------------------------------
    Total Addresses in System (excluding one mac per port)    : 0
    Max Addresses limit in System (excluding one mac per port) : 8320
    S1#show port-security interface fastethernet 0/1
    Port Security               : Enabled
    Port Status                 : Secure-down
    Violation Mode              : Restrict
    Aging Time                  : 0 mins
    Aging Type                  : Absolute
    SecureStatic Address Aging  : Disabled
    Maximum MAC Addresses       : 3
    Total MAC Addresses         : 1
    Configured MAC Addresses    : 0
    Sticky MAC Addresses        : 1
    Last Source Address:Vlan    : 0014.22dd.37a3:1
    Security Violation Count    : 0
```

Shutting Down and Securing Unused Interfaces

Router interfaces, as you know, must be activated with the **no shutdown** command before they become operational. The exact opposite is true for the Cisco Catalyst switches. To provide out-of-the-box functionality, Cisco chose a default configuration that included interfaces that would work without any configuration, including automatically negotiating speed and duplex. In addition, all interfaces are assigned to the default VLAN 1.

This default configuration exposes switches to some security threats. The security best practices for unused interfaces are as follows:

- Administratively disable the interface using the **shutdown** interface subcommand.

- Prevent VLAN trunking and VTP by making the port a nontrunking interface using the **switchport mode access** interface subcommand.

- Assign the port to an unused VLAN using the **switchport access vlan** *number* interface subcommand.

Study Resources

For today's exam topics, refer to the following resources for more study.

Resource	Chapter	Topic	Where to Find It
Foundational Resources			
CCNA Exploration Online Curriculum: LAN Switching and Wireless	Chapter 2, "Basic Switch Concepts and Configuration"	Switch Management Configuration Configuring Switch Security	Sections 2.3.6–2.3.8 Section 2.4
CCNA Exploration LAN Switching and Wireless Companion Guide	Chapter 2, "Basic Switch Concepts and Configuration"	Switch Management Configuration Configuring Switch Security	pp. 63–85 pp. 85–110
ICND1 Official Exam Certification Guide	Chapter 9, "Ethernet Switch Configuration" Lab 3	All topics within the chapter Switch Basics: Learning, Forwarding/Filtering, and Interface Settings	pp. 231–260 Video Training CD
ICND1 Authorized Self-Study Guide	Chapter 2, "Ethernet LANs"	Starting a Switch Understanding Switch Security	pp. 163–174 pp. 174–182
ICND2 Authorized Self-Study Guide	Chapter 1, "Review of Cisco IOS for Routers and Switches" Chapter 2, "Medium-Sized Switched Network Construction"	All topics within the chapter Securing the Expanded Network	pp. 3–8 pp. 66–76
Supplemental Resources			
CCNA Flash Cards and Exam Practice Pack	ICND1, Section 6	Configuring a Cisco Switch	pp. 128–172
CCNA Video Mentor	ICND1, Lab 3	Switch Basics: Learning, Forwarding/Filtering, and Interface Settings	pp. 11–15 and DVD

Verifying and Troubleshooting Basic Switch Configurations

CCNA 640-802 Exam Topics

- Verify network status and switch operation using basic utilities (including ping, traceroute, telnet, SSH, ARP, ipconfig), and **show** and **debug** commands.

- Identify, prescribe, and resolve common switched network media issues, configuration issues, autonegotiation, and switch hardware failures.

- Interpret the output of various show and debug commands to verify the operational status of a Cisco switched network.

Key Points

In the days to come, we will review the configuration, verification, and troubleshooting tasks associated with VLANs, trunking, VLAN Trunking Protocol (VTP), Spanning Tree Protocol (STP) and inter-VLAN routing. Today we focus on troubleshooting skills associated with basic switch configuration including verifying network connectivity, interpreting commands that display the status of interfaces, and using Cisco Discovery Protocol (CDP).

Troubleshooting Methodology

Day 29, "Network Data Flow from End-to-End," discussed the three approaches to troubleshooting your network based on the layers of the OSI model: bottom up, top down, and divide and conquer. Regardless of the method you use, here are some general suggestions to make your troubleshooting more effective:

- **Understand normal switch operation:** No amount of studying can replace hands-on experience. Hopefully, you have already spent many hours configuring switches, at least in a lab environment or on a simulator. The configuration guides at Cisco.com will help fill in any gaps in your experience.

- **Create accurate physical and logical maps:** Because a switch can create different segments by implementing VLANs, the physical connections alone do not tell the whole story. You must know how the switches are configured to determine which segments (VLANs) exist and how they are logically connected.

- **Have a plan:** Before jumping to conclusions, try to verify in a structured way what is working and what is not. Because networks can be complex, it is helpful to isolate possible problem domains. For example, can all devices on the same LAN ping each other? Assuming that the switch is configured correctly, many of the problems you encounter will be related to physical layer issues (physical ports and cabling). Layer 2 issues could be the problem as well, however. The point is to have a plan for where to start—Layer 1 or Layer 2—and then solve all the problems at that layer before moving on.

- **Assume nothing:** Do not assume basic components are working correctly without testing them first. It usually takes only a minute to verify the basics (for example, that the ports are correctly connected and active), and it can save you valuable time.

The following steps outline a general troubleshooting method that can be used with any problem in the network. This is the method used in Wendell Odom's books in the *CCNA Official Exam Certification Library, Third Edition*:

Step 1   Analyzing/predicting normal operation.

Predict the details of what should happen if the network is working correctly, based on documentation, configuration, and **show** and **debug** command output.

Step 2   Problem isolation.

Determine how far along the expected path the frame/packet goes before it cannot be forwarded any further, again based on documentation, configuration, and **show** and **debug** command output.

Step 3   Root cause analysis.

Identify the underlying causes of the problems identified in the preceding step—specifically, the causes that have a specific action with which the problem can be fixed.

Following this process requires a variety of learned skills. You need to remember the theory of how networks should work, as well as how to interpret the **show** command output that confirms how the devices are currently behaving. This process requires the use of testing tools, such as **ping** and **traceroute**, to isolate the problem. Finally, this approach requires the ability to think broadly about everything that could affect a single component.

For our purposes today, we are going to assume that all the Layer 3 potential problems have been ruled out so we can focus on Layer 2 and Layer 1 issues. In a switched LAN, you will most likely need to determine some or all of the following:

- MAC addresses of devices involved (PCs and router interfaces)
- Switch interfaces that are in use
- Status of switch interfaces
- Expected behavior from source to destination

Verifying Network Connectivity

Using and interpreting the output of various testing tools is often the first step in isolating the cause of a network connectivity issue. The **ping** command can be used to systematically test connectivity in the following manner:

- Can an end device ping itself?
- Can an end device ping its default gateway?
- Can an end device ping the destination?

By using the **ping** command in this ordered sequence, you can isolate problems quicker. If local connectivity is not an issue—in other words, the end device can successfully ping its default gateway—using the **traceroute** utility can help isolate at what point in the path from source to destination that the traffic stops.

As a first step in the testing sequence, verify the operation of the TCP/IP stack on the local host by pinging the loopback address, 127.0.0.1, as demonstrated in Example 25-1.

Example 25-1   Testing the TCP/IP Stack on a Windows PC

```
C:\>ping 127.0.0.1

Pinging 127.0.0.1 with 32 bytes of data:

Reply from 127.0.0.1: bytes=32 time<1ms TTL=64
Reply from 127.0.0.1: bytes=32 time<1ms TTL=64
Reply from 127.0.0.1: bytes=32 time<1ms TTL=64
Reply from 127.0.0.1: bytes=32 time<1ms TTL=64

Ping statistics for 127.0.0.1:
    Packets: Sent = 4, Received = 4, Lost = 0 (0% loss),
Approximate round trip times in milli-seconds:
    Minimum = 0ms, Maximum = 0ms, Average = 0ms
```

Because this test should succeed regardless of whether the host is connected to the network, a failure indicates a software or hardware problem on the host itself. Either the network interface is not operating properly, or possibly support for the TCP/IP stack has been inadvertently removed from the operating system.

Next, verify connectivity to the default gateway. Determine the default gateway address using **ipconfig** and then attempt to ping it, as demonstrated in Example 25-2.

Example 25-2   Testing Connectivity to the Default Gateway on a Windows PC

```
C:\>ipconfig

Windows IP Configuration


Ethernet adapter Local Area Connection:

        Connection-specific DNS Suffix  . : cisco.com
        IP Address. . . . . . . . . . . : 192.168.1.25
        Subnet Mask . . . . . . . . . . : 255.255.255.0
        Default Gateway . . . . . . . . : 192.168.1.1

C:\>ping 192.168.1.1
```

```
Pinging 192.168.1.1 with 32 bytes of data:

Reply from 192.168.1.1: bytes=32 time=162ms TTL=255
Reply from 192.168.1.1: bytes=32 time=69ms TTL=255
Reply from 192.168.1.1: bytes=32 time=82ms TTL=255
Reply from 192.168.1.1: bytes=32 time=72ms TTL=255

Ping statistics for 192.168.1.1:
    Packets: Sent = 4, Received = 4, Lost = 0 (0% loss),
Approximate round trip times in milli-seconds:
    Minimum = 69ms, Maximum = 162ms, Average = 96ms
```

Failure here can indicate several problems, each of which will need to be checked in a systematic sequence. One possible order might be the following:

1. Is the cabling from the PC to the switch correct? Are link lights lit?

2. Is the configuration on the PC correct according to the logical map of the network?

3. Are the affected interfaces on the switch the cause of the problem? Is there a duplex or speed mismatch? VLAN misconfigurations?

4. Is the cabling from the switch to the router correct? Are link lights lit?

5. Is the configuration on the router interface correct according to the logical map of the network? Is the interface active?

Finally, verify connectivity to the destination by pinging it. Assume we are trying to reach a server at 192.168.3.100. Example 25-3 shows a successful ping test to the destination.

Example 25-3   Testing Connectivity to the Destination on a Windows PC

```
PC>ping 192.168.3.100

Pinging 192.168.3.100 with 32 bytes of data:

Reply from 192.168.3.100: bytes=32 time=200ms TTL=126
Reply from 192.168.3.100: bytes=32 time=185ms TTL=126
Reply from 192.168.3.100: bytes=32 time=186ms TTL=126
Reply from 192.168.3.100: bytes=32 time=200ms TTL=126

Ping statistics for 192.168.3.100:
    Packets: Sent = 4, Received = 4, Lost = 0 (0% loss),
Approximate round trip times in milli-seconds:
    Minimum = 185ms, Maximum = 200ms, Average = 192ms
```

Failure here would indicate a failure in the path beyond the default gateway interface because we already successfully tested connectivity to the default gateway. From the PC, the best tool to use to find the break in the path is the **tracert** command, as demonstrated in Example 25-4.

Example 25-4   Tracing the Route from a Windows PC

```
C:\>tracert 192.168.3.100

Tracing route to 192.168.3.100 over a maximum of 30 hops:

  1    97 ms      75 ms      72 ms     192.168.1.1
  2   104 ms     119 ms     117 ms     192.168.2.2
  3    *          *          *         Request timed out.
  4    *          *          *         Request timed out.
  5    *          *          *         Request timed out.
  6   ^C
C:\>
```

Note   The reason for failure at hops 3, 4, and 5 in Example 25-4 could be that these routers are configured to not send ICMP messages back to the source.

The last successful hop on the way to the destination was 192.168.2.2. If you have administrator rights to 192.168.2.2, you could continue your research by remotely accessing the command line on 192.168.2.2 and investigating why traffic will not go any further. Also, other devices between 192.168.2.2 and 192.168.3.100 could be the source of the problem. The point is, you want to use your **ping** and **tracert** tests as well as your network documentation to proceed in logical sequence from source to destination.

Regardless of how simple or complex your network is, using **ping** and **tracert** from the source to the destination is a simple, yet powerful, way to systematically test connectivity and locate breaks in a path from one source to one destination.

Interface Status and the Switch Configuration

Because today we are focusing on switch troubleshooting, let's look at the **show** commands that are helpful in troubleshooting your basic configuration.

Interface Status Codes

In general, interfaces are either "up" or "down." However, when an interface is "down" and you don't know why, the code in the **show interfaces** command provides more information to help you determine the reason. Table 25-1 lists the code combinations and some possible causes for the status indicated.

Table 25-1   LAN Switch Interface Status Codes

Line Status	Protocol Status	Interface Status	Typical Root Cause
Administratively Down	Down	disabled	The interface is configured with the **shutdown** command.
Down	Down	notconnect	No cable; bad cable; wrong cable pinouts; the speeds are mismatched on the two connected devices; the device on the other end of the cable is powered off or the other interface is shut down.

continues

Table 25-1   LAN Switch Interface Status Codes *continued*

Line Status	Protocol Status	Interface Status	Typical Root Cause
Up	Down	notconnect	An interface up/down state is not expected on LAN switch interfaces. This indicates a Layer 2 problem on Layer 3 devices.
Down	down (err-disabled)	err-disabled	Port security has disabled the interface. The network administrator must manually reenable the interface.
Up	Up	connect	The interface is working.

Duplex and Speed Mismatches

One of the more common problems is issues with speed and/or duplex mismatches. On switches and routers, the **speed {10 | 100 | 1000}** interface subcommand and the **duplex {half | full}** interface subcommand set these values. Note that configuring both speed and duplex on a switch interface disables the IEEE-standard autonegotiation process on that interface.

The **show interfaces status** and **show interfaces** commands list both the speed and duplex settings on an interface, as shown in Example 25-5.

Example 25-5   Commands to Verify Speed and Duplex Settings

```
S1#show interface status

Port        Name              Status        Vlan      Duplex  Speed Type
Fa0/1                         connected     trunk       full    100 10/100BaseTX
Fa0/2                         connected     1           half    100 10/100BaseTX
Fa0/3                         connected     1         a-full  a-100 10/100BaseTX
Fa0/4                         disabled      1           auto   auto 10/100BaseTX
Fa0/5                         disabled      1           auto   auto 10/100BaseTX
Fa0/6                         notconnect    1           auto   auto 10/100BaseTX
!Remaining output omitted
S1#show interface fa0/3
FastEthernet0/1 is up, line protocol is up (connected)
  Hardware is Fast Ethernet, address is 001b.5302.4e81 (bia 001b.5302.4e81)
  MTU 1500 bytes, BW 100000 Kbit, DLY 100 usec,
     reliability 255/255, txload 1/255, rxload 1/255
  Encapsulation ARPA, loopback not set
  Keepalive set (10 sec)
  Full-duplex, 100Mb/s, media type is 10/100BaseTX
  input flow-control is off, output flow-control is unsupported
  ARP type: ARPA, ARP Timeout 04:00:00
  Last input never, output 00:00:00, output hang never
  Last clearing of "show interface" counters never
  Input queue: 0/75/0/0 (size/max/drops/flushes); Total output drops: 0
  Queueing strategy: fifo
```

```
Output queue: 0/40 (size/max)
5 minute input rate 1000 bits/sec, 1 packets/sec
5 minute output rate 0 bits/sec, 0 packets/sec
    2745 packets input, 330885 bytes, 0 no buffer
    Received 1386 broadcasts (0 multicast)
    0 runts, 0 giants, 0 throttles
    0 input errors, 0 CRC, 0 frame, 0 overrun, 0 ignored
    0 watchdog, 425 multicast, 0 pause input
    0 input packets with dribble condition detected
    56989 packets output, 4125809 bytes, 0 underruns
    0 output errors, 0 collisions, 1 interface resets
    0 babbles, 0 late collision, 0 deferred
    0 lost carrier, 0 no carrier, 0 PAUSE output
    0 output buffer failures, 0 output buffers swapped out
```

Notice that both commands will show the duplex and speed settings of the interface. However, the **show interface status** command is preferred for troubleshooting duplex or speed mismatches because it shows exactly how the switch determined the duplex and speed of the interface. In the duplex column, **a-full** means the switch autonegotiated full duplex. The setting **full** or **half** means that the switch was configured at that duplex setting. Autonegotiation has been disabled. In the speed column, **a-100** means the switch autonegotiated 100 Mbps as the speed. The setting **10** or **100** means that the switch was configured at that speed setting.

Finding a duplex mismatch can be much more difficult than finding a speed mismatch, because if the duplex settings do not match on the ends of an Ethernet segment, the switch interface will still be in a connect (up/up) state. In this case, the interface works, but the network may work poorly, with hosts experiencing poor performance and intermittent communication problems. To identify duplex mismatch problems, check the duplex setting on each end of the link, and watch for incrementing collision and late collision counters.

Common Layer 1 Problems On "Up" Interfaces

When a switch interface is "up", it does not necessarily mean that the interface is operating in an optimal state. For this reason, IOS will track certain counters to help identify problems that can occur even though the interface is in a connect state. These counters are highlighted in the output in Example 25-5. Table 25-2 summarizes three general types of Layer 1 interface problems that can occur while an interface is in the "up," connected state.

Table 25-2   Common LAN Layer 1 Problem Indicators

Type of Problem	Counter Values Indicating This Problem	Common Root Causes
Excessive noise	Many input errors, few collisions	Wrong cable category (Cat 5, 5E, 6); damaged cables; EMI
Collisions	More than roughly .1% of all frames are collisions	Duplex mismatch (seen on the half-duplex side); jabber; DoS attack
Late collisions	Increasing late collisions	Collision domain or single cable too long; duplex mismatch

CDP as a Troubleshooting Tool

CDP discovers basic information about directly connected Cisco routers and switches by sending CDP messages. Example 25-6 shows the output from a switch that is directly connected to a Cisco router.

Example 25-6   Output from the show cdp Commands

```
S1#show cdp ?
  entry      Information for specific neighbor entry
  interface  CDP interface status and configuration
  neighbors  CDP neighbor entries
  traffic    CDP statistics
  ¦          Output modifiers
  <cr>


S1#show cdp neighbors
Capability Codes: R - Router, T - Trans Bridge, B - Source Route Bridge
                  S - Switch, H - Host, I - IGMP, r - Repeater, P - Phone

Device ID       Local Intrfce      Holdtme   Capability   Platform   Port ID
R1              Fas 0/3            124            R S I    1841       Fas 0/0
S1#show cdp neighbors detail
-------------------------
Device ID: R1
Entry address(es):
  IP address: 192.168.1.1
Platform: Cisco 1841,  Capabilities: Router Switch IGMP
Interface: FastEthernet0/3,  Port ID (outgoing port): FastEthernet0/0
Holdtime : 175 sec

Version :
Cisco IOS Software, 1841 Software (C1841-ADVIPSERVICESK9-M), Version 12.4(10b),
  RELEASE SO
FTWARE (fc3)
Technical Support: http://www.cisco.com/techsupport
Copyright (c) 1986-2007 by Cisco Systems, Inc.
Compiled Fri 19-Jan-07 15:15 by prod_rel_team

advertisement version: 2
VTP Management Domain: ''
Duplex: full
Management address(es):

S1#show cdp
Global CDP information:
        Sending CDP packets every 60 seconds
        Sending a holdtime value of 180 seconds
```

```
        Sending CDPv2 advertisements is  enabled

S1#show cdp interface
FastEthernet0/1 is up, line protocol is up
  Encapsulation ARPA
  Sending CDP packets every 60 seconds
  Holdtime is 180 seconds
FastEthernet0/2 is down, line protocol is down
  Encapsulation ARPA
  Sending CDP packets every 60 seconds
  Holdtime is 180 seconds
!
!Output is same for interface Fa0/3 through Gi0/1
!
GigabitEthernet0/2 is down, line protocol is down
  Encapsulation ARPA
  Sending CDP packets every 60 seconds
  Holdtime is 180 seconds
S1#
```

The **show cdp neighbors detail** output displays CDP messages that contain the following use-

ful information:

- **Device ID:** Typically the hostname

- **Entry address(es):** Network and data-link addresses

- **Platform:** The model and OS level running in the device

- **Capabilities:** Information on what type of device it is (for instance, a router or a switch)

- **Interface:** The interface on the router or switch issuing the **show cdp** command with which the neighbor was discovered

- **Port ID:** Text that identifies the port used by the neighboring device to send CDP messages to the local device

Also notice in the **show cdp interface** command that every interface on the switch is sending CDP messages every 60 seconds. CDP is enabled by default and, thus, creates a security issue because CDP messages can be intercepted and network information discovered. CDP can easily be disabled both globally for the entire device (**no cdp run**) or individually by interface (**no cdp enable**).

Study Resources

For today's exam topics, refer to the following resources for more study.

Resource	Chapter	Topic	Where to Find It
Foundational Resources			
CCNA Exploration Online Curriculum: Network Fundamentals	Chapter 11, "Configuring and Testing Your Network"	Verifying Connectivity Monitoring and Documenting Networks	Section 11.3 Section 11.4
CCNA Exploration Online Curriculum: Network Fundamentals	Chapter 11, "Configuring and Testing Your Network"	Verifying Connectivity Monitoring and Documenting Networks	pp. 444–458 pp. 458–463
ICND1 Official Exam Certification Guide	Chapter 10, "Ethernet Switch Troubleshooting"	All topics within the chapter	pp. 271–294
ICND1 Authorized Self-Study Guide	Chapter 2, "Ethernet LANs"	Troubleshooting Switch Issues	pp. 191–194
ICND2 Authorized Self-Study Guide	Chapter 2, "Medium-Sized Network Construction"	Troubleshooting Switched Networks	pp. 76–80
Supplemental Resources			
CCNA Flash Cards and Exam Practice Pack	ICND1, Section 6	Configuring a Cisco Switch	pp. 128–172

Switching Technologies and VLAN Concepts

CCNA 640-802 Exam Topics

- Describe enhanced switching technologies (VTP, RSTP, VLAN, PVSTP, 802.1Q).
- Describe how VLANs create logically separate networks and the need for routing between them.
- Configure, verify, and troubleshoot RSTP operation.

Key Points

Virtual local-area networks (VLANs) are a switching technology used to improve network performance by separating large broadcast domains into smaller ones. VLAN trunks provide a way for one physical interface to transport multiple VLANs. The IEEE 802.1Q trunking protocol is the recommended frame tagging method to use on trunk links. In larger networks where there are many switches to manage, VLAN Trunking Protocol (VTP) provides a way to automatically update switches with new or modified VLAN information. Spanning Tree Protocol (STP) and its variants allow redundant switched networks without worrying about switching loops. Although STP can be tweaked with a few commands, it runs by default and might not need any adjustment at all.

VLAN Concepts

Although a switch "out of the box" is configured to have only one VLAN, normally a switch will be configured to have two or more VLANs. Doing so creates multiple broadcast domains by putting some interfaces into one VLAN and other interfaces into other VLANs.

Reasons for using VLANs include the following:

- Grouping users by department instead of by physical location
- Segmenting devices into smaller LANs to reduce processing overhead for all devices on the LAN
- Reducing the workload of STP by limiting a VLAN to a single access switch
- Enforcing better security by isolating sensitive data to separate VLANs
- Separating IP voice traffic from data traffic

Benefits of using VLANs include the following:

- **Security:** Sensitive data can be isolated to one VLAN, separating it from the rest of the network.

- **Cost reduction:** Cost savings result from less need for expensive network upgrades and more efficient use of existing bandwidth and uplinks.

- **Higher performance:** Dividing flat Layer 2 networks into multiple logical broadcast domains reduces unnecessary traffic on the network and boosts performance.

- **Broadcast storm mitigation:** VLAN segmentation prevents a broadcast storm from propagating throughout the entire network.

- **Ease of management and troubleshooting:** A hierarchical addressing scheme groups network addresses contiguously. Because a hierarchical IP addressing scheme makes problem components easier to locate, network management and troubleshooting are more efficient.

Traffic Types

A key factor for VLAN deployment is understanding the traffic patterns and the various traffic types in the organization. Table 24-1 lists the common types of network traffic that you should evaluate before placing devices and configuring VLANs.

Table 24-1   Traffic Types

Traffic Type	Description
Network management	Many types of network management traffic can be present on the network. To make network troubleshooting easier, some designers assign a separate VLAN to carry certain types of network management traffic.
IP telephony	There are two types of IP telephony traffic: signaling information between end devices and the data packets of the voice conversation. Designers often configure the data to and from the IP phones on a separate VLAN designated for voice traffic so that they can apply quality of service measures to give high priority to voice traffic.
IP multicast	Multicast traffic can produce a large amount of data streaming across the network. Switches must be configured to keep this traffic from flooding to devices that have not requested it, and routers must be configured to ensure that multicast traffic is forwarded to the network areas where it is requested.
Normal data	Normal data traffic is typical application traffic that is related to file and print services, email, Internet browsing, database access, and other shared network applications.
Scavenger class	Scavenger class includes all traffic with protocols or patterns that exceed their normal data flows. Applications assigned to this class have little or no contribution to the organizational objectives of the enterprise and are typically entertainment oriented in nature.

Types of VLANs

Some VLAN types are defined by the type of traffic they support; others are defined by the specific functions they perform. The principal VLAN types and their descriptions follow:

- **Data VLAN:** Configured to carry only user-generated traffic, ensuring that voice and management traffic is separated from data traffic.

- **Default VLAN:** All the ports on a switch are members of the default VLAN when the switch is reset to factory defaults. The default VLAN for Cisco switches is VLAN 1. VLAN 1 has all the features of any VLAN, except that you cannot rename it and you cannot delete it. It is a security best practice to restrict VLAN 1 to serve as a conduit only for Layer 2 control traffic (for example, CDP or VTP), supporting no other traffic.

- **Black hole VLAN:** A security best practice is to define a black hole VLAN to be a dummy VLAN distinct from all other VLANs defined in the switched LAN. All unused switch ports are assigned to the black hole VLAN so that any unauthorized device connecting to an unused switch port will be prevented from communicating beyond the switch to which it is connected.

- **Native VLAN:** This VLAN type serves as a common identifier on opposing ends of a trunk link. A security best practice is to define a native VLAN to be a dummy VLAN distinct from all other VLANs defined in the switched LAN. The native VLAN is not used for any traffic in the switched network unless legacy bridging devices happen to be present in the network, or a multiaccess interconnection exists between switches joined by a hub.

- **Management VLAN:** A VLAN defined by the network administrator as a means to access the management capabilities of a switch. By default, VLAN 1 is the management VLAN. It is a security best practice to define the management VLAN to be a VLAN distinct from all other VLANs defined in the switched LAN. You do so by configuring and activating a new VLAN interface.

- **Voice VLANs:** The voice VLAN feature enables switch ports to carry IP voice traffic from an IP phone. The network administrator configures a voice VLAN and assigns it to access ports. Then when an IP phone is connected to the switch port, the switch sends CDP messages that instruct the attached IP phone to send voice traffic tagged with the voice VLAN ID.

Voice VLAN Example

Figure 24-1 shows an example of using one port on a switch to connect a user's IP phone and PC. The switch port is configured to carry data traffic on VLAN 20 and voice traffic on VLAN 150. The Cisco IP Phone contains an integrated three-port 10/100 switch to provide the following dedicated connections:

- Port 1 connects to the switch or other VoIP device.

- Port 2 is an internal 10/100 interface that carries the IP phone traffic.

- Port 3 (access port) connects to a PC or other device.

Figure 24-1   Cisco IP Phone Switching Voice and Data Traffic

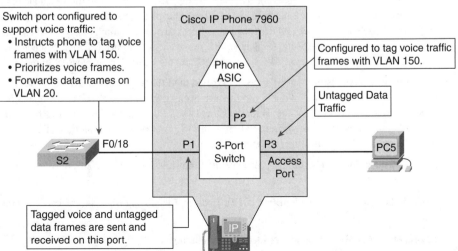

The traffic from the PC5 attached to the IP Phone passes through the IP Phone untagged. The link between S2 and the IP Phone act as a modified trunk to carry both the tagged voice traffic and the untagged data traffic.

Trunking VLANs

A VLAN trunk is an Ethernet point-to-point link between an Ethernet switch interface and an Ethernet interface on another networking device, such as a router or a switch, carrying the traffic of multiple VLANs over the singular link. A VLAN trunk allows you to extend the VLANs across an entire network. A VLAN trunk does not belong to a specific VLAN; rather, it serves as a conduit for VLANs between switches. Figure 24-2 shows a small switched network with a trunk link between S1 and S2 carrying multiple VLAN traffic.

Figure 24-2   Example of a VLAN Trunk

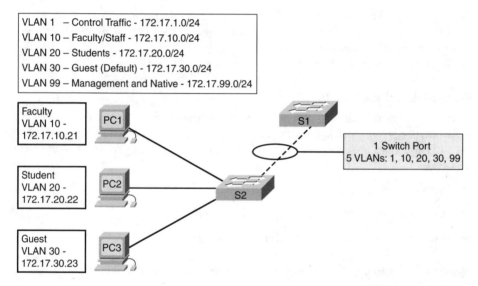

When a frame is placed on a trunk link, information about the VLAN it belongs to must be added to the frame. This is accomplished by using IEEE 802.1Q frame tagging. When a switch receives a frame on a port configured in access mode and destined for a remote device via a trunk link, the switch takes apart the frame and inserts a VLAN tag, recalculates the frame check sequence (FCS), and sends the tagged frame out the trunk port. Figure 24-3 shows the 802.1Q tag inserted in an Ethernet frame.

The VLAN tag field consists of a 16-bit Type field called the EtherType field and a Tag control information field. The EtherType field is set to the hexadecimal value of 0x8100. This value is called the tag protocol ID (TPID) value. With the EtherType field set to the TPID value, the switch receiving the frame knows to look for information in the Tag control information field. The Tag control information field contains the following:

- **3 bits of user priority:** Used to provide expedited transmission of Layer 2 frames, such as voice traffic.

- **1 bit of Canonical Format Identifier (CFI):** Enables Token Ring frames to be carried across Ethernet links easily.

- **12 bits of VLAN ID (VID):** VLAN identification numbers.

Figure 24-3   Fields of the 802.1Q Tag Inside an Ethernet Frame

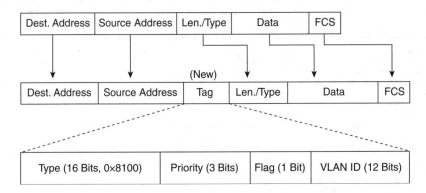

Although 802.1Q is the recommended method for tagging frames, you should be aware of Cisco's legacy trunking protocol called Inter-Switch link (ISL). You must specify the trunking protocol used on trunk interfaces on all Cisco Catalyst switches except the 29xx series.

Dynamic Trunking Protocol

Dynamic Trunking Protocol (DTP) is a Cisco proprietary protocol that negotiates both the status of trunk ports as well as the trunk encapsulation of trunk ports. DTP manages trunk negotiation only if the port on the other switch is configured in a trunk mode that supports DTP. A switch port on a Cisco Catalyst switch supports a number of trunking modes. The trunking mode defines how the port negotiates using DTP to set up a trunk link with its peer port. The following is a brief description of each trunking mode:

- If the switch is configured with the **switchport mode trunk** command, the switch port periodically sends DTP messages to the remote port advertising that it is in an unconditional trunking state.

- If the switch is configured with the **switchport mode trunk dynamic auto** command, the local switch port advertises to the remote switch port that it is able to trunk but does not request to go to the trunking state. After a DTP negotiation, the local port ends up in trunking state only if the remote port trunk mode has been configured so that the status is **on** or **desirable**. If both ports on the switches are set to **auto**, they do not negotiate to be in a trunking state. They negotiate to be in the access mode state.

- If the switch is configured with the **switchport mode dynamic desirable** command, the local switch port advertises to the remote switch port that it is able to trunk and asks the remote switch port to go to the trunking state. If the local port detects that the remote has been configured as **on**, **desirable**, or **auto** mode, the local port ends up in trunking state. If the remote switch port is in the **nonegotiate** mode, the local switch port remains as a nontrunking port.

- If the switch is configured with the **switchport nonegotiate** command, the local port is then considered to be in an unconditional trunking state. Use this feature when you need to configure a trunk with a switch from another switch vendor.

Table 24-2 summarizes the results of DTP negotiations based on the different DTP configuration commands.

Table 24-2   Trunk Negotiation Results Between a Local and a Remote Port

	Dynamic Auto	Dynamic Desirable	Trunk	Access
Dynamic Auto	Access	Trunk	Trunk	Access
Dynamic Desirable Trunk	Trunk	Trunk	Trunk	Access
Trunk	Trunk	Trunk	Trunk	Not Recommended
Access	Access	Access	Not Recommended	Access

VTP Concepts

The name for Cisco's proprietary VLAN Trunking Protocol (VTP) can be confusing. VTP does not provide a method for trunking between devices. Instead, VTP is a Layer 2 messaging protocol that maintains VLAN configuration consistency by managing the additions, deletions, and name changes of VLANs across networks. VTP helps with VLAN management and although it makes the configuration and troubleshooting of VLANs easier, it is not required.

The benefits of VTP include the following:

- VLAN configuration consistency across the network

- Accurate tracking and monitoring of VLANs

- Dynamic reporting of added VLANs across a network

Figure 24-4 shows an example of how VTP messages can be sent between the VTP server and VTP clients.

Figure 24-4   VTP Server Sends Updates to VTP Clients

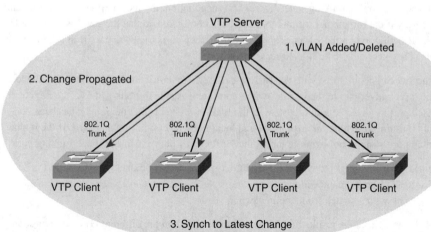

VTP Domain CCNA

Notice in the figure that the shaded area is named VTP Domain CCNA. A VTP domain is one switch or several interconnected switches that share VTP advertisements. A switch can be in only one VTP domain. A router or Layer 3 switch defines the boundary of each domain.

VTP Modes

VTP operates in one of three modes:

- **Server:** The server is where VLANs can be created, deleted, or renamed for the domain. VTP servers advertise VLAN information to other switches in the same VTP domain and store the VLAN information in NVRAM.

- **Client:** You cannot create, change, or delete VLANs on a VTP client. A switch reset deletes the VLAN information. You must configure a switch to change its VTP mode to client.

- **Transparent:** VTP transparent mode switches forward VTP advertisements to VTP clients and VTP servers, but do not originate or otherwise implement VTP advertisements. VLANs that are created, renamed, or deleted on a VTP transparent mode switch are local to that switch only.

VTP Operation

VTP advertisements are sent by the server every 5 minutes over the default VLAN using a multi-cast frame. A configuration revision number included in the frame is used by all VTP clients and servers to determine if there has been a change in the VLAN database. Figure 24-5 illustrates VTP operation.

Figure 24-5   VTP Operation

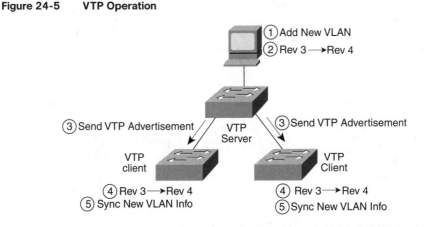

Figure 24-5 begins with all switches having the same VLAN configuration revision number, meaning that they have the same VLAN configuration database; this means that all switches know about the same VLAN numbers and VLAN names. The process begins with each switch knowing that the current configuration revision number is 3. The steps shown in Figure 24-5 are as follows:

1. Someone configures a new VLAN on the VTP server.

2. The VTP server updates its VLAN database revision number from 3 to 4.

3. The server sends VTP update messages out its trunk interfaces, stating revision number 4.

4. The two VTP client switches notice that the updates list a higher revision number (4) than their current revision numbers (3).

5. The two client switches update their VLAN databases based on the server's VTP updates.

VTP defines three types of messages:

- **Summary advertisement:** Sent every 5 minutes by the server; it lists the revision number, domain name, and other information, but no VLAN information.

- **Subset advertisement:** Follows a summary advertisement if something has changed in the VLAN database, indicated by a new larger revision number.

- **Advertisement request message:** Allows a switch to immediately request VTP messages from a neighboring switch as soon as a trunk comes up.

VTP Pruning

By default, a trunk connection carries traffic for all VLANs in the VTP management domain; however, every switch might not have ports assigned to every VLAN. VTP pruning uses VLAN advertisements to determine when a trunk connection is flooding VLAN traffic needlessly.

Pruning means that the appropriate switch trunk interfaces do not flood frames in that VLAN. Figure 24-6 shows an example, with the dashed-line rectangles denoting the trunks from which VLAN 10 has been automatically pruned.

Figure 24-6   VTP Pruning

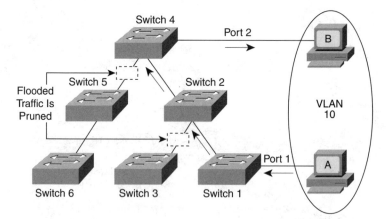

STP Concepts and Operation

One of the key characteristics of a well-built communications network is that it is resilient. This means that the network needs to be able to handle a device or link failure through redundancy. A redundant topology can eliminate a single point of failure by using multiple links, multiple devices, or both. Spanning Tree Protocol (STP) is used to prevent loops in a redundant switched network.

Without STP, redundancy in the switched network would introduce the following issues:

- **Broadcast storms:** Each switch floods broadcasts endlessly, called a broadcast storm.

- **Multiple frame transmission:** Multiple copies of unicast frames may be delivered to the destination causing unrecoverable errors.

- **MAC database instability:** Instability in the content of the MAC address table results from copies of the same frame being received on different ports of the switch.

STP is an IEEE committee standard defined as 802.1d. STP places certain ports in the blocking state so that they do not listen to, forward, or flood data frames. STP creates a tree that ensures there is only one path to each network segment at any one time. Then, if any segment experiences a disruption in connectivity, STP rebuilds a new tree by activating the previously inactive, but redundant, path.

The algorithm used by STP chooses the interfaces that should be placed into a Forwarding State. For any interfaces not chosen to be in a Forwarding State, STP places the interfaces in Blocking State.

Switches exchange STP configuration messages every 2 seconds by default using a multicast frame called the bridge protocol data unit (BPDU). One of the pieces of information included in the BPDU is the bridge ID (BID).

The BID is unique to each switch and is composed of a priority value (2 bytes) and the bridge MAC address (6 bytes). The default priority is 32,768. The root bridge is the bridge with the lowest BID. Therefore, if the default priority value is not changed, the switch with the lowest MAC address will become root.

To start the process, the STP algorithm elects a root switch and places all working interfaces on the root switch in Forwarding State. Then, each nonroot switch considers one of its ports to have the least administrative cost between itself and the root switch. STP places this least-root-cost interface, called that switch's root port (RP), in Forwarding State. Finally, many switches can attach to the same Ethernet segment. So the switch with the lowest administrative cost from itself to the root bridge, as compared with the other switches attached to the same segment, is placed in Forwarding State. The lowest-cost switch on each segment is called the designated bridge, and that bridge's interface, attached to that segment, is called the designated port (DP). Switches that are not designated bridges have their nondesignated ports placed in Blocking State.

Table 24-3 summarizes the reasons STP place a port in Forwarding or Blocking State.

Table 24-4   STP: Reasons for Forwarding or Blocking

Characterization of Port	STP State	Description
All the root switch's ports	Forwarding	The root switch is always the designated switch on all connected segments.
Each nonroot switch's root port	Forwarding	The port through which the switch has the least cost to reach the root switch.
Each LAN's designated port	Forwarding	The switch forwarding the lowest-cost BPDU onto the segment is the designated switch for that segment.
All other working ports	Blocking	The port is not used for forwarding frames, nor are any frames received on these interfaces considered for forwarding.

Port bandwidth is used to determine the cost to reach the root bridge. Table 24-4 lists the default port costs defined by IEEE, which had to be revised with the advent of 10 Gbps ports.

Table 24-4   Default IEEE Port Costs

Ethernet Speed	Original IEEE Cost	Revised IEEE Cost
10 Mbps	100	100
100 Mbps	10	19
1 Gbps	1	4
10 Gbps	1	2

STP uses the four states shown in Figure 24-7 as a port transitions from Blocking to Forwarding.

Figure 24-7   Spanning-Tree Port States

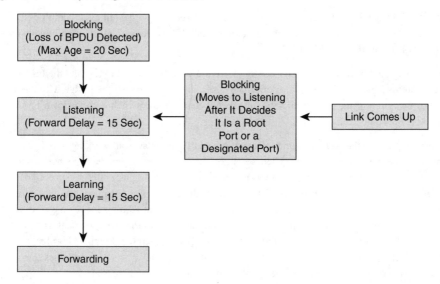

A fifth state, Disabled, occurs either when a network administrator manually disables the port or a security violation disables the port.

RSTP Concepts and Operation

IEEE improved the convergence performance of STP from 50 seconds to less than 10 seconds with its definition of Rapid STP (RSTP) in the standard 802.1w. RSTP is identical to STP in the following ways:

- It elects the root switch using the same parameters and tiebreakers.

- It elects the root port on nonroot switches with the same rules.

- It elects designated ports on each LAN segment with the same rules.

- It places each port in either Forwarding or Blocking State, although RSTP calls the Blocking State the Discarding State.

The main changes with RSTP can be seen when changes occur in the network. RSTP acts differently on some interfaces based on what is connected to the interface.

- **Edge-Type Behavior and PortFast:** RSTP improves convergence for edge-type connections by immediately placing the port in Forwarding State when the link is physically active.

- **Link-Type Shared:** RSTP doesn't do anything differently from STP on link-type shared links. However, because most of the links between switches today are not shared, but are typically full-duplex point-to-point links, it doesn't matter.

- **Link-Type Point-to-Point:** RSTP improves convergence over full-duplex links between switches. RSTP recognizes the loss of the path to the root bridge, through the root port, in 3 times the Hello timer, or 6 seconds with a default Hello timer value of 2 seconds. So RSTP recognizes a lost path to the root much more quickly.

RSTP uses different terminology to describe port states. Table 24-5 lists the port states for RSTP and STP.

Table 24-5   RSTP and STP Port States

Operational State	STP State (802.1d)	RSTP State (802.1w)	Forwards Data Frames in This State?
Enabled	Blocking	Discarding	No
Enabled	Listening	Discarding	No
Enabled	Learning	Learning	No
Enabled	Forwarding	Forwarding	Yes
Disabled	Disabled	Discarding	No

RSTP removes the need for Listening State and reduces the time required for Learning State by actively discovering the network's new state. STP passively waits on new BPDUs and reacts to them during the Listening and Learning States. With RSTP, the switches negotiate with neighboring switches by sending RSTP messages. The messages enable the switches to quickly determine whether an interface can be immediately transitioned to a Forwarding State. In many cases, the process takes only a second or two for the entire RSTP domain.

RSTP also adds three more port roles to the root port and designated port roles defined in STP. Table 24-6 lists and defines the port roles.

Table 24-6   RSTP and STP Port Roles

RSTP Role	STP Role	Definition
Root port	Root port	A single port on each nonroot switch in which the switch hears the best BPDU out of all the received BPDUs
Designated port	Designated port	Of all switch ports on all switches attached to the same segment/collision domain, the port that advertises the "best" BPDU
Alternate port	–	A port on a switch that receives a suboptimal BPDU
Backup port	–	A nondesignated port on a switch that is attached to the same segment/collision domain as another port on the same switch
Disabled	–	A port that is administratively disabled or is not capable of working for other reasons

Configuring and Verifying STP

By default, all Cisco switches use STP without any configuration by the network administrator. However, because STP runs on a per-VLAN basis—creates a separate spanning-tree instance for every VLAN—you can take advantage of several options to load-balance traffic across redundant links.

PVST+, PVRST, and MIST

802.1d does not support a spanning-tree instance for each VLAN because VLANs did not exist when the standard was first introduced. Cisco switches include a proprietary feature called Per-VLAN Spanning Tree Plus (PVST), which creates a separate instance of STP for each VLAN.

Again, when IEEE introduced 802.1w, there still was no support for multiple instances of STP. So Cisco implemented another proprietary solution called either Rapid Per-VLAN Spanning Tree (RPVST) or Per-VLAN Rapid Spanning Tree (PVRST). Later, IEEE created the 802.1s standard called Multiple Instances of Spanning Tree (MIST). Table 24-7 summarizes these three options for using multiple spanning trees to load balance traffic.

Table 24-7   Comparing Three Options for Multiple Spanning Trees

Option	Supports STP	Supports RSTP	Configuration Effort	Only One Instance Required for Each Redundant Path
PVST+	Yes	No	Small	No
PVRST	No	Yes	Small	No
MIST	No	Yes	Medium	Yes

Configuring and Verifying the BID

Regardless of the which per-VLAN Spanning Tree is used, two main configuration options can be used to achieve load-balancing—bridge ID and port cost manipulation. The bridge ID influences the choice of root switch and can be configured per VLAN. Each interface's (per-VLAN) STP cost to reach the root influences the choice of designated port on each LAN segment. Because PVST requires that a separate instance of spanning tree run for each VLAN, the BID field is required to carry VLAN ID (VID) information. This is accomplished by reusing a portion of the Priority field as the extended system ID to carry a VID.

Table 24-8 summarizes the default settings for both BID and port costs.

Table 24-8   STP Defaults and Configuration Options

Setting	Default	Command(s) to Change Default
Bridge ID	Priority: 32,768 + VLAN ID System:A burned-in MAC on the switch	spanning-tree vlan *vlan-id* root {primary | secondary} spanning-tree vlan *vlan-id* priority *priority*
Interface cost	100 for 10 Mbps, 19 for 100 Mbps, 4 for 1 Gbps, 2 for 10 Gbps	spanning-tree vlan *vlan-id* cost *cost*

Figure 24-8 shows a simple three-switch STP topology.

Figure 24-8   STP Topology

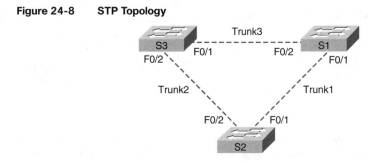

The network administrator wants to ensure that S1 is always the root bridge and S2 is the backup root bridge. The following commands achieve this objective.

```
S1(config)# spanning-tree vlan 1 root primary
S2(config)# spanning-tree vlan 1 root secondary
```

The **primary** keyword sets the priority to 24576 or to the next 4096 increment value below the lowest bridge priority detected on the network.

The **secondary** keyword sets the priority to 28672, assuming the rest of the network is set to the default priority of 32768.

Alternatively, the network administrator can configure the priority value in increments of 4096 between 0 and 65536 using the following command.

```
S1(config)# spanning-tree vlan 1 priority 24576
S2(config)# spanning-tree vlan 1 priority 28672
```

Note   These commands changed the priority values only for VLAN 1. Additional commands must be entered for each VLAN to take advantage of load balancing.

To verify the current spanning-tree instances and root bridges, use the **show spanning-tree** command as shown in Example 24-1.

Example 24-1   Verifying Spanning-Tree Configurations

```
S1# show spanning-tree

VLAN0001
  Spanning tree enabled protocol ieee
  Root ID    Priority    24577
             Address     001b.5302.4e80
             This bridge is the root
             Hello Time   2 sec  Max Age 20 sec  Forward Delay 15 sec

  Bridge ID  Priority    24577  (priority 24576 sys-id-ext 1)
             Address     001b.5302.4e80
             Hello Time   2 sec  Max Age 20 sec  Forward Delay 15 sec
             Aging Time 300
```

```
Interface        Role Sts Cost      Prio.Nbr Type
---------------- ---- --- --------- -------- --------------------------------
Fa0/1            Desg FWD 19        128.1    P2p
Fa0/2            Desg FWD 19        128.2    P2p
```

Because an extended system ID is used in the BID, the value of the priority includes the addition of the VLAN ID. So, a priority of 24576 plus a VLAN of 1 results in an priority output of 24577.

PortFast

To speed up convergence for access ports when they become active, you can use Cisco's proprietary PortFast technology. After PortFast is configured and a port is activated, the port immediately transitions from the blocking state to the forwarding state. Example 24-2 shows the interface command to configure PortFast.

Example 24-2   Configuring PortFast

```
Switch# configure terminal
Enter configuration commands, one per line. End with CNTL/Z.
Switch(config)# interface f0/11
Switch(config)# switchport mode access
Switch(config-if)# spanning-tree portfast
```

Alternatively, you can configure the global command **spanning-tree portfast default**, which enables PortFast by default on all access ports.

Configuring RSTP

Remember, STP is the default operation of Cisco switches. To change to RSTP and PVRST, use a single global command on all switches: **spanning-tree mode rapid-pvst**.

Troubleshooting STP

STP runs by default on switches and rarely causes problems in small- to medium-sized networks. However, you might encounter STP troubleshooting problems on the exam. Use the following steps to analyze an STP problem:

Step 1   Determine the root switch.

Step 2   For each nonroot switch, determine its one root port (RP) and cost to reach the root switch through that RP.

Step 3   For each segment, determine the designated port (DP) and the cost advertised by the DP onto that segment.

The information requested in each of the steps can be obtained from variations of the **show spanning-tree** command.

Study Resources

For today's exam topics, refer to the following resources for more study.

Resource	Chapter	Topic	Where to Find It
Foundational Resources			
CCNA Exploration Online Curriculum: LAN Switching and Wireless	Chapter 3, "VLANs" Chapter 4, "VTP" Chapter 5, "STP"	Introducing VLANs VLAN Trunking VTP Concepts VTP Operation All topics within the chapter	Section 3.1 Section 3.2 Section 4.1 Section 4.2 All Sections
CCNA Exploration LAN Switching and Wireless Companion Guide	Chapter 3, "VLANs" Chapter 4, "VTP" Chapter 5, "STP"	Introducing VLANs VLAN Trunking VTP Concepts VTP Operation All topics within the chapter	pp. 122–143 pp. 143–151 pp. 182–186 pp. 186–204 pp. 229–319
ICND1 Official Exam Certification Guide	Chapter 7, "Ethernet LAN Switching Concepts"	Virtual LANs (VLANs)	pp. 187–188
ICND2 Official Exam Certification Guide	Chapter 1, "Virtual VLANs" Chapter 2, "Spanning Tree Protocol"	Virtual LAN Concepts All topics within the chapter	pp. 9–23 pp. 61–104
ICND1 Authorized Self-Study Guide	Chapter 2, "Ethernet LANs"	Maximizing the Benefits of Switching	pp. 182–191
ICND2 Authorized Self-Study Guide	Chapter 2, "Medium-Sized Network Construction"	Implementing VLANs and Trunks Improving Performance with Spanning Tree Troubleshooting Spanning Tree	pp. 13–30 pp. 40–64 pp. 85–87
Supplemental Resources			
CCNA Flash Cards and Exam Practice Pack	ICND1, Section 6 ICND2, Section 1 ICND2, Section 2	Configuring a Cisco Switch Implementing VLANS and Trunks Redundant Switching and STP	pp. 128–172 pp. 346–379 pp. 380–409

VLAN and Trunking Configuration and Troubleshooting

CCNA 640-802 Exam Topics

- Configure, verify, and troubleshoot VLANs
- Configure, verify, and troubleshoot trunking on Cisco switches

Key Points

The following sections present a sample topology and the commands to configure, verify, and troubleshoot VLANs and trunking. The review for today is brief so that you can spend your time practicing your configuration, verification, and troubleshooting skills.

Sample Topology

For today's exam topics, we will use the topology shown in Figure 23-1 to review the commands for configuring, verifying, and troubleshooting VLAN and trunking. I strongly recommend that you build and configure this topology—either using real equipment or a network simulator—as part of your review for the CCNA exam.

Figure 23-1   Day 23 Sample Topology

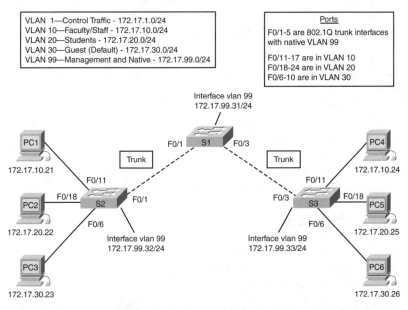

VLAN Configuration and Verification Commands

The default configuration of a Cisco switch is to put all interfaces in VLAN 1, which can be verified with the **show vlan brief** command, as demonstrated for S2 in Example 23-1.

Example 23-1   Default VLAN Configuration

```
S2#show vlan brief

VLAN Name                             Status    Ports
---- -------------------------------- --------- -------------------------------
1    default                          active    Fa0/1, Fa0/2, Fa0/3, Fa0/4
                                                Fa0/5, Fa0/6, Fa0/7, Fa0/8
                                                Fa0/9, Fa0/10, Fa0/11, Fa0/12
                                                Fa0/13, Fa0/14, Fa0/15, Fa0/16
                                                Fa0/17, Fa0/18, Fa0/19, Fa0/20
                                                Fa0/21, Fa0/22, Fa0/23, Fa0/24
                                                Gig1/1, Gig1/2
1002 fddi-default                     active
1003 token-ring-default               active
1004 fddinet-default                  active
1005 trnet-default                    active
```

A VLAN can be created in one of two ways: either in global configuration mode or directly under the interface. The advantage to configuring in global configuration mode is that you can then assign a name with the **name** *vlan-name* command. The advantage to configuring the VLAN in interface configuration mode is that you assign the VLAN to the interface and create the VLAN with just one command. However, to name the VLAN, you still have to go back to the global configuration method. Example 23-2 shows the creation of VLANs 10 and 20 using these two methods. VLAN 20 is then named, and the remaining VLANs are created in global configuration mode.

Example 23-2   Creating VLANs

```
S2#config t
Enter configuration commands, one per line.  End with CNTL/Z.
S2(config)#vlan 10
S2(config-vlan)#name Faculty/Staff
S2(config-vlan)#interface fa 0/18
S2(config-if)#switchport access vlan 20
% Access VLAN does not exist. Creating vlan 20
S2(config-if)#vlan 20
S2(config-vlan)#name Students
S2(config-vlan)#vlan 30
S2(config-vlan)#name Guest(Default)
S2(config-vlan)#vlan 99
S2(config-vlan)#name Management&Native
```

```
S2(config-vlan)#end
%SYS-5-CONFIG_I: Configured from console by console
S2#
```

Notice in Example 23-3 that all the VLANs are created. But only VLAN 20 is assigned to an interface.

Example 23-3   Verifying VLAN Creation

```
S2#show vlan brief

VLAN Name                             Status    Ports
---- -------------------------------- --------- -------------------------------
1    default                          active    Fa0/1, Fa0/2, Fa0/3, Fa0/4
                                                Fa0/5, Fa0/6, Fa0/7, Fa0/8
                                                Fa0/9, Fa0/10, Fa0/11, Fa0/12
                                                Fa0/13, Fa0/14, Fa0/15, Fa0/16
                                                Fa0/17, Fa0/19, Fa0/20, Fa0/21
                                                Fa0/22, Fa0/23, Fa0/24, Gig1/1
                                                Gig1/2
10   Faculty/Staff                    active
20   Students                         active    Fa0/18
30   Guest(Default)                   active
99   Management&Native                active
1002 fddi-default                     active
1003 token-ring-default               active
1004 fddinet-default                  active
1005 trnet-default                    active
S2#
```

To assign the remaining interfaces to the VLANs specified in Figure 23-1, you can configure one interface at a time, or you can use the **range** command to configure all the interfaces that belong to a VLAN with one command, as shown in Example 23-4.

Example 23-4   Assigning VLANs to Interfaces

```
S2#config t
Enter configuration commands, one per line.  End with CNTL/Z.
S2(config)#interface range fa 0/11 - 17
S2(config-if-range)#switchport access vlan 10
S2(config-if-range)#interface range fa 0/18 - 24
S2(config-if-range)#switchport access vlan 20
S2(config-if-range)#interface range fa 0/6 - 10
S2(config-if-range)#switchport access vlan 30
S2(config-if-range)#end
%SYS-5-CONFIG_I: Configured from console by console
S2#
```

The **show vlan brief** command in Example 23-5 verifies that all interfaces specified in Figure 23-1 have been assigned to the appropriate VLAN. Notice that unassigned interfaces still belong to the default VLAN 1.

Example 23-5   Verifying VLAN Assignments to Interfaces

```
S2#show vlan brief

VLAN Name                             Status    Ports
---- -------------------------------- --------- -------------------------------
1    default                          active    Fa0/1, Fa0/2, Fa0/3, Fa0/4
                                                Fa0/5, Gig1/1, Gig1/2
10   Faculty/Staff                    active    Fa0/11, Fa0/12, Fa0/13, Fa0/14
                                                Fa0/15, Fa0/16, Fa0/17
20   Students                         active    Fa0/18, Fa0/19, Fa0/20, Fa0/21
                                                Fa0/22, Fa0/23, Fa0/24
30   Guest(Default)                   active    Fa0/6, Fa0/7, Fa0/8, Fa0/9
                                                Fa0/10
99   Management&Native                active
1002 fddi-default                     active
1003 token-ring-default               active
1004 fddinet-default                  active
1005 trnet-default                    active
S2#
```

You can also verify a specific interface's VLAN assignment with the **show interfaces** *type number* **switchport** command, as shown for FastEthernet 0/11 in Example 23-6.

Example 23-6   Verifying an Interface's VLAN Assignment

```
S2#show interfaces fastethernet 0/11 switchport
Name: Fa0/11
Switchport: Enabled
Administrative Mode: dynamic auto
Operational Mode: static access
Administrative Trunking Encapsulation: dot1q
Operational Trunking Encapsulation: native
Negotiation of Trunking: On
Access Mode VLAN: 10 (Faculty/Staff)
Trunking Native Mode VLAN: 1 (default)
Voice VLAN: none
Administrative private-vlan host-association: none
Administrative private-vlan mapping: none
Administrative private-vlan trunk native VLAN: none
Administrative private-vlan trunk encapsulation: dot1q
Administrative private-vlan trunk normal VLANs: none
Administrative private-vlan trunk private VLANs: none
```

```
Operational private-vlan: none
Trunking VLANs Enabled: ALL
Pruning VLANs Enabled: 2-1001
Capture Mode Disabled
Capture VLANs Allowed: ALL
Protected: false
Appliance trust: none
S2#
```

For the sample topology shown in Figure 23-1, you would configure the VLANs on S1 and S3 as well, but only S3 needs VLANs assigned to interfaces.

Configuring and Verifying Trunking

Following security best practices, we are configuring a different VLAN for the management and default VLAN. In a production network, you would want to use a different one for each: one for the management VLAN and one for the native VLAN. However, for expediency we are using VLAN 99 for both.

To begin, we must first define a new management interface for VLAN 99, as shown in Example 23-7.

Example 23-7   Defining a New Management Interface

```
S1#config t
Enter configuration commands, one per line.  End with CNTL/Z.
S1(config)#interface vlan 99
%LINK-5-CHANGED: Interface Vlan99, changed state to up
S1(config-if)#ip address 172.17.99.31 255.255.255.0
S1(config-if)#end
%SYS-5-CONFIG_I: Configured from console by console
S1#
```

Repeat the configuration on S2 and S3. The IP address is used for testing connectivity to the switch as well as the IP address the network administrator uses for remote access (Telnet, SSH, SDM, HTTP, etc.).

Depending on the switch model and IOS version, DTP may have already established trunking between two switches that are directly connected. For example, the default trunk configuration for 2950 switches is **dynamic desirable**. Therefore, a 2950 will initiate trunk negotiations. For our purposes, we will assume the switches are all 2960s. The 2960 default trunk configuration is **dynamic auto,** in which the interface will not initiate trunk negotiations.

In Example 23-8, the first five interfaces on S1 are configured for trunking. Also, notice that the native VLAN is changed to VLAN 99.

Example 23-8   Trunk Configuration and Native VLAN Assignment

```
S1#config t
Enter configuration commands, one per line.  End with CNTL/Z.
S1(config)#interface range fa0/1 - 5
S1(config-if-range)#switchport mode trunk
S1(config-if-range)#switchport trunk native vlan 99
S1(config-if-range)#end
%SYS-5-CONFIG_I: Configured from console by console
S1#
%CDP-4-NATIVE_VLAN_MISMATCH: Native VLAN mismatch discovered on FastEthernet0/1
(99), with S2 FastEthernet0/1 (1).
%CDP-4-NATIVE_VLAN_MISMATCH: Native VLAN mismatch discovered on FastEthernet0/3
(99), with S3 FastEthernet0/3 (1).
```

If you wait for the next round of CDP messages, you should get the error message shown in
Example 23-8. Although the trunk is working between S1 and S2 and between S1 and S3, the
switches do not agree on the native VLAN. Repeat the trunking commands on S2 and S3 to correct
the native VLAN mismatch.

Note   The encapsulation type—**dot1q** or **isl**—might need to be configured depending on
the switch model. If so, the syntax for configuring the encapsulation type is as follows:

```
Switch(config-if)#switchport trunk encapsulation { dot1q ¦ isl ¦ negotiate }
```

The 2960 series supports only 802.1Q, so this command is not available.

To verify that trunking is operational, use the commands shown in Example 23-9.

Example 23-9   Verifying Trunk Configuration

```
S1#show interfaces trunk
Port        Mode         Encapsulation Status         Native vlan
Fa0/1       on           802.1q        trunking       99
Fa0/3       on           802.1q        trunking       99


Port        Vlans allowed on trunk
Fa0/1       1-1005
Fa0/3       1-1005


Port        Vlans allowed and active in management domain
Fa0/1       1,10,20,30,99,1002,1003,1004,1005
Fa0/3       1,10,20,30,99,1002,1003,1004,1005


Port        Vlans in spanning tree forwarding state and not pruned
Fa0/1       1,10,20,30,99,1002,1003,1004,1005
Fa0/3       1,10,20,30,99,1002,1003,1004,1005
S1#show interface fa 0/1 switchport
Name: Fa0/1
Switchport: Enabled
```

```
Administrative Mode: trunk
Operational Mode: trunk
Administrative Trunking Encapsulation: dot1q
Operational Trunking Encapsulation: dot1q
Negotiation of Trunking: On
Access Mode VLAN: 1 (default)
Trunking Native Mode VLAN: 99 (Management&Native)
Voice VLAN: none
Administrative private-vlan host-association: none
Administrative private-vlan mapping: none
Administrative private-vlan trunk native VLAN: none
Administrative private-vlan trunk encapsulation: dot1q
Administrative private-vlan trunk normal VLANs: none
Administrative private-vlan trunk private VLANs: none
Operational private-vlan: none
Trunking VLANs Enabled: ALL
Pruning VLANs Enabled: 2-1001
Capture Mode Disabled
Capture VLANs Allowed: ALL
Protected: false
Appliance trust: none
S1#
```

Remember, hosts on the same VLAN must be configured with an IP address and subnet mask on the same subnet. So the ultimate test of your configuration is to verify that end devices on the same VLAN can now ping each other. If not, use the verification commands to systematically track down the problem with your configuration, as discussed in the next section.

Troubleshooting VLAN and Trunking Problems

In Wendell Odom's book, *CCNA ICND2 Official Exam Certification Guide Second Edition*, he details a methodology for troubleshooting a switched network from the physical layer up to and including VLAN and trunk configurations. Although today we are focusing on VLAN and trunk configuration, verification, and troubleshooting, a quick review of troubleshooting other switch problems is included in this very brief summary of the steps delineated by Odom.

Step 1   **Confirm the network diagram using CDP.**

Network diagrams are often outdated or incomplete. Use the CDP commands **show cdp neighbors** and **show cdp neighbors detail** to gain more information about direct-ly connected neighbors.

Step 2   **Isolate interface problems.**

    a. Determine interface status code(s) for each required interface, and if not in a con-nect or up/up state, resolve the problems until the interface reaches the connect or up/up state.

b. For interfaces in a connect (up/up) state, also check for two other problems: duplex mismatches and some variations of port security purposefully dropping frames.

Helpful commands include **show interfaces** and **show interfaces status**.

Step 3   **Isolate filtering and port security problems.**

a. Identify all interfaces on which port security is enabled (**show running-config** or **show port-security**).

b. Determine whether a security violation is currently occurring based in part on the *violation mode* of the interface's port security configuration, as follows:

— **shutdown**: The interface will be in an **err-disabled** state.

— **restrict**: The interface will be in a connect state, but the **show portsecurity interface** command will show an incrementing violations counter.

— **protect**: The interface will be in a connect state, and the **show portsecurity interface** command will not show an incrementing violations counter.

c. In all cases, compare the port security configuration to the diagram as well as the "last source address" field in the output of the **show portsecurity interface** command.

Step 4   Isolate VLAN and trunking problems.

a. Identify all access interfaces and their assigned access VLANs, and reassign into the correct VLANs as needed.

b. Determine whether the VLANs both exist (configured or learned with VTP) and are active on each switch. If not, configure and activate the VLANs to resolve problems as needed.

c. Identify the operationally trunking interfaces on each switch, and determine the VLANs that can be forwarded over each trunk.

Study Resources

For today's exam topics, refer to the following resources for more study.

Resource	Chapter	Topic	Where to Find It
Foundational Resources			
CCNA Exploration Online Curriculum: LAN Switching and Wireless	Chapter 3, "VLANs"	Configure VLANs and Trunks Troubleshooting VLANs and Trunks	Section 3.3 Section 3.4
CCNA Exploration LAN Switching and Wireless Companion Guide	Chapter 3, "VLANs"	Configure VLANs and Trunks Troubleshooting VLANs and Trunks	pp. 151–164 pp. 164–172
ICND2 Official Exam Certification Guide	Chapter 1, "Virtual VLANs" Chapter 3, "Troubleshooting LAN Switching"	VLAN and VLAN Trunking Configuration and Verification Troubleshooting the LAN Switching Data Plane	pp. 23–38 pp. 117–147
ICND2 Authorized Self-Study Guide	Chapter 2, "Medium-Sized Network Construction"	Implementing VLANs and Trunks Troubleshooting VLANs and Trunking	pp. 30–39 pp. 80–82
Supplemental Resources			
CCNA Flash Cards and Exam Practice Pack	ICND2, Section 1 ICND2, Section 3	Implementing VLANS and Trunks Troubleshooting Switched Networks	pp. 346–378 pp. 410–422
CCNA Video Mentor	ICND2, Lab 1	Configuring VLANs	pp. 45–48 and DVD

VTP and InterVLAN Routing Configuration and Troubleshooting

CCNA 640-802 Exam Topics

- Configure, verify, and troubleshoot VTP.

- Configure, verify, and troubleshoot inter-VLAN routing.

Key Points

Today we review the commands and tasks necessary to configure, verify, and troubleshoot VLAN Trunking Protocol (VTP). Also, we review inter-VLAN routing and router commands for a router-on-a-stick implementation.

VTP Configuration and Verification

VTP is a Layer 2 messaging protocol that maintains VLAN configuration consistency by managing the additions, deletions, and name changes of VLANs across networks. This section uses the sample topology in Figure 22-1, which is the same topology used for Day 23. You should build and configure this topology as part of your review for the CCNA exam.

Figure 22-1   Day 22 Sample Topology for VTP

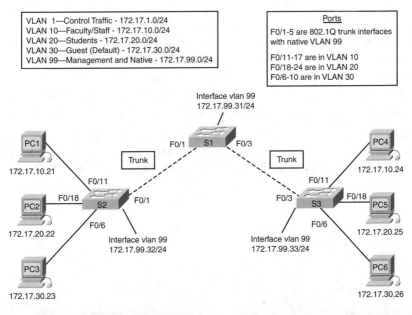

VLAN 1—Control Traffic - 172.17.1.0/24
VLAN 10—Faculty/Staff - 172.17.10.0/24
VLAN 20—Students - 172.17.20.0/24
VLAN 30—Guest (Default) - 172.17.30.0/24
VLAN 99—Management and Native - 172.17.99.0/24

Ports
F0/1-5 are 802.1Q trunk interfaces with native VLAN 99

F0/11-17 are in VLAN 10
F0/18-24 are in VLAN 20
F0/6-10 are in VLAN 30

Interface vlan 99
172.17.99.31/24

PC1
172.17.10.21

F0/1 S1 F0/3

Trunk

F0/11

PC2
172.17.20.22

F0/18

F0/1

S2

F0/6

Interface vlan 99
172.17.99.32/24

PC3
172.17.30.23

PC4
172.17.10.24

Trunk

F0/11

F0/3

S3

F0/18

PC5

F0/6

Interface vlan 99
172.17.99.33/24

172.17.20.25

PC6
172.17.30.26

After choosing which switch will be the server and which switches will be clients, use the following steps to configure VTP:

Step 1   Configure the VTP mode using the **vtp mode {server | client}** global configuration command.

Step 2   (Optional, but recommended) On both clients and servers, configure the same case-sensitive password using the **vtp password** *password-value* global configuration command.

Step 3   Configure the VTP (case-sensitive) domain name using the **vtp domain** *domain-name* global configuration command.

Step 4   (Optional) Configure VTP pruning on the VTP servers using the **vtp pruning** global configuration command.

Step 5   (Optional) Enable VTP version 2 with the **vtp version 2** global configuration command.

Step 6   Bring up trunks between the switches.

Before configuring VTP, look at the default VTP state of S1. To do so, use the command **show vtp status** as shown in Example 22-1.

Example 22-1   Default VTP Configuration on S1

```
S1#show vtp status
VTP Version                    : 2
Configuration Revision         : 0
Maximum VLANs supported locally : 64
Number of existing VLANs       : 5
VTP Operating Mode             : Server
VTP Domain Name                :
VTP Pruning Mode               : Disabled
VTP V2 Mode                    : Disabled
VTP Traps Generation           : Disabled
MD5 digest                     : 0x7D 0x5A 0xA6 0x0E 0x9A 0x72 0xA0 0x3A
Configuration last modified by 0.0.0.0 at 0-0-00 00:00:00
Local updater ID is 0.0.0.0 (no valid interface found)
```

Notice the configuration revision number is 0 and that the number of existing VLANs is 5—the five default VLANs that always exist on the switch. Also notice that S1 is already a VTP server.

The commands in Example 22-2 configure S1 as the server using **cisco** as the VTP password and **CCNA** as the VTP domain name. Because S2 and S3 share all the same VLANs, we are not configuring VTP pruning (enabled globally with the command **vtp pruning**). We will also leave VTP in the default version 1 mode (enabled globally with the command **vtp version 2**).

Example 22-2   Configuring the VTP Server

```
S1#config t
Enter configuration commands, one per line.  End with CNTL/Z.
S1(config)#vtp mode server
Device mode already VTP SERVER.
S1(config)#vtp password cisco
Setting device VLAN database password to cisco
S1(config)#vtp domain CCNA
Changing VTP domain name from NULL to CCNA
S1(config)#end
%SYS-5-CONFIG_I: Configured from console by console
S1#
```

Note   We configured the VTP password before the VTP domain name for a specific reason. As soon as the VTP domain name is configured, S1 will begin sending out VTP messages on all trunk links that are active. If switches on the other end of the trunk are using the
default VTP configuration (server mode, null as the domain name, and no password), they
will start using the domain name sent in the VTP messages. This can cause VLAN database
corruption if the receiving switch has a higher configuration revision number than the configured server. The receiving switch is also a VTP server and will send out its VLAN database
to the configured VTP server. By configuring the password first, we avoid the potential for
this to happen. After the switches on the other end of the trunks are configured as clients,
their configuration revision number is reset to 0. Then when the domain name and password
are configured, VTP updates will be requested from the VTP server.

We explicitly configured S1 as a VTP server instead of assuming it is in the default VTP server
mode. Example 22-3 shows the commands used to verify the configuration.

Example 22-3   Verifying the VTP Configuration

```
S1#show vtp status
VTP Version                    : 2
Configuration Revision         : 0
Maximum VLANs supported locally : 64
Number of existing VLANs       : 5
VTP Operating Mode             : Server
VTP Domain Name                : CCNA
VTP Pruning Mode               : Disabled
VTP V2 Mode                    : Disabled
VTP Traps Generation           : Disabled
MD5 digest                     : 0x8C 0x29 0x40 0xDD 0x7F 0x7A 0x63 0x17
Configuration last modified by 0.0.0.0 at 0-0-00 00:00:00
Local updater ID is 0.0.0.0 (no valid interface found)
S1#show vtp password
VTP Password: cisco
S1#
```

Example 22-4 shows the commands to configure S2 as a client with the same password and domain name as S1. Repeat the same commands on S3.

Example 22-4   Configure the VTP Clients

```
S2#config t
Enter configuration commands, one per line.  End with CNTL/Z.
S2(config)#vtp mode client
Setting device to VTP CLIENT mode.
S2(config)#vtp password cisco
Setting device VLAN database password to cisco
S2(config)#vtp domain CCNA
Changing VTP domain name from NULL to CCNA
S2(config)#end
%SYS-5-CONFIG_I: Configured from console by console
S2#
```

Again, verify the configuration with the **show vtp status** and **show vtp password** commands.

At this point, configure the VLANs on the VTP server, S1. You will not be able to create VLANs on S2 or S3. If you try, you will get the following console message:

```
S3(config)#vlan 10
VTP VLAN configuration not allowed when device is in CLIENT mode.
S3(config)#
```

Remember, however, that on the client switches you will still be able to assign switch ports to specific VLANs.

After configuring the VLANs, notice that the configuration revision number is incremented for each modification to the VLAN database. If you made no errors in your configuration, the configuration revision number should be 8, as shown in Example 22-5—one increment for each time you added one of the four VLANs and one increment for each time you named one of the VLANs. There are now a total of nine VLANs on the server.

Example 22-5   Verifying the VLAN Configuration on the VTP Server

```
S1#show vtp status
VTP Version                    : 2
Configuration Revision         : 8
Maximum VLANs supported locally : 64
Number of existing VLANs       : 9
VTP Operating Mode             : Server
VTP Domain Name                : CCNA
VTP Pruning Mode               : Disabled
VTP V2 Mode                    : Disabled
VTP Traps Generation           : Disabled
MD5 digest                     : 0x61 0x2A 0x9A 0xC3 0xCF 0xDD 0x2C 0x10
Configuration last modified by 0.0.0.0 at 3-1-93 00:25:46
```

```
Local updater ID is 0.0.0.0 (no valid interface found)
S1#show vlan brief

VLAN Name                             Status    Ports
---- -------------------------------- --------- ------------------------------
1    default                          active    Fa0/1, Fa0/2, Fa0/3, Fa0/4
                                                Fa0/5, Fa0/6, Fa0/7, Fa0/8
                                                Fa0/9, Fa0/10, Fa0/11, Fa0/12
                                                Fa0/13, Fa0/14, Fa0/15, Fa0/16
                                                Fa0/17, Fa0/18, Fa0/19, Fa0/20
                                                Fa0/21, Fa0/22, Fa0/23, Fa0/24
                                                Gig1/1, Gig1/2
10   Faculty/Staff                    active
20   Students                         active
30   Guest(Default)                   active
99   Management&Native                active
1002 fddi-default                     active
1003 token-ring-default               active
1004 fddinet-default                  active
1005 trnet-default                    active
S1#
```

S2 and S3 have not received the VLANs yet because the trunks are not active between the switches and S1. In this case, configure the appropriate S1 interfaces to trunk and assign VLAN 99 as the native VLAN. In some cases, DTP will autonegotiate the trunk links on S2 and S3. Now both client switches should have received VTP advertisements for S1. As shown in Example 22-6, both S2 and S3 have synchronized VLAN databases.

Example 22-6   Verifying S2 and S3 Now Have Synchronized VLAN Databases

```
S2#show vtp status
VTP Version                     : 2
Configuration Revision          : 8
Maximum VLANs supported locally : 64
Number of existing VLANs        : 9
VTP Operating Mode              : Client
VTP Domain Name                 : CCNA
VTP Pruning Mode                : Disabled
VTP V2 Mode                     : Disabled
VTP Traps Generation            : Disabled
MD5 digest                      : 0x43 0x68 0xD5 0x3B 0x58 0x79 0x68 0x0E
Configuration last modified by 172.17.99.31 at 3-1-93 00:33:01
S2#
```

```
S3#show vtp status
VTP Version                     : 2
Configuration Revision          : 8
Maximum VLANs supported locally : 64
Number of existing VLANs        : 9
VTP Operating Mode              : Client
VTP Domain Name                 : CCNA
VTP Pruning Mode                : Disabled
VTP V2 Mode                     : Disabled
VTP Traps Generation            : Disabled
MD5 digest                      : 0x43 0x68 0xD5 0x3B 0x58 0x79 0x68 0x0E
Configuration last modified by 172.17.99.31 at 3-1-93 00:33:01
S3#
```

Note Although configuring VTP does help manage the VLAN configuration in your networks, it is not required to create VLANs. In addition, VTP does not assign VLANs to switch ports. You must manually assign VLANs to switch ports on each switch.

To avoid using VTP on a switch, configure it to use transparent mode:

    Switch(config)#vtp mode transparent

The switch will not update its VLAN database from VTP messages but will still forward the VTP messages out trunk interfaces. In addition, you can configure local VLANs on a switch in VTP transparent mode.

VTP Troubleshooting

Although VTP provides a level of efficiency to your switched network by allowing you to configure your VLAN database on a VTP server, VTP also has the potential to cause serious problems. To combat the misuse of VTP in production networks, Cisco created the following training tutorial on Cisco.com, which you should review as part of your preparation for the CCNA exam:

    http://www.cisco.com/warp/public/473/vtp_flash/

The following steps are a systematic way to determine why VTP is not currently working as expected.

Step 1   Confirm the switch names, topology (including which interfaces connect which switches), and switch VTP modes.

Step 2   Identify sets of two neighboring switches that should be either VTP clients or servers whose VLAN databases differ with the **show vlan** command.

Step 3   On each pair of two neighboring switches whose databases differ, verify the following:

a. At least one operational trunk should exist between the two switches (use the **show interfaces trunk**, **show interfaces switchport**, or **show cdp neighbors** command).

b. The switches must have the same (case-sensitive) VTP domain name (**show vtp status**).

c. If configured, the switches must have the same (case-sensitive) VTP password (**show vtp password**).

d. Although VTP pruning should be enabled or disabled on all servers in the same domain, having two servers configured with opposite pruning settings does not prevent the synchronization process.

Step 4 For each pair of switches identified in Step 3, solve the problem by either troubleshooting the trunking problem or reconfiguring a switch to correctly match the domain name or password.

To avoid the potential for VTP problems, implement the following best practices.

- Reset the configuration revision number before installing a new switch. This can be done in one of the following ways:

  — Change the switch to VTP transparent mode.

  — Change the domain name to something other than the existing domain name.

  — Delete the **vlan.dat** file and reload the switch.

- If you do not intend to use VTP at all, configure each switch to use transparent mode.

- If using VTP server or client mode, always use a VTP password.

- Prevent VTP attacks by disabling the potential for dynamic trunking negotiation on all interfaces except known trunks with either the **switchport mode access** or **switchport nonegotiate** commands.

Inter-VLAN Routing Configuration and Verification

Cisco switches support two trunking protocols: Inter-Switch Link (ISL) and IEEE 802.1Q. Cisco created ISL many years before the IEEE created the 802.1Q standard VLAN trunking protocol. Because ISL is Cisco proprietary, it can be used only between two Cisco switches that support ISL. ISL fully encapsulates each original Ethernet frame in an ISL header and trailer.

Years after Cisco created ISL, the IEEE completed work on the 802.1Q standard, which defines a different way to do trunking. Today, 802.1Q has become the more popular trunking protocol, with Cisco not even supporting ISL in some of its newer models of LAN switches, including the 2960 switches used in the examples in this book. 802.1Q does not actually encapsulate the original frame in another Ethernet header and trailer. Instead, 802.1Q inserts an extra 4-byte VLAN header into the original frame's Ethernet header. For more details on the differences and similarities between ISL and 802.1Q, see your study resources.

Configuring inter-VLAN routing is pretty straightforward. Refer to the sample topology shown in Figure 22-2 to review the commands.

Figure 22-2   Day 22 Sample Topology for Inter-VLAN Routing

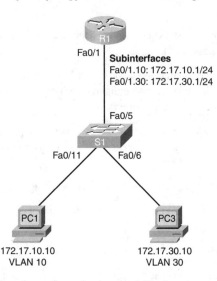

This router-on-a-stick topology is configured using the following steps on the router:

Step 1   Activate the physical interface that is trunking with the switch using the **no shutdown** command.

Step 2   Enter subinterface configuration mode for the first VLAN that needs routing. One convention is to use the VLAN number as the subinterface number. For example, the command **interface fa0/1.10** enters subinterface configuration mode for VLAN 10.

Step 3   Configure the trunking encapsulation type using the subinterface configuration command **encapsulation** {**dot1q** | **isl**} *vlan-number* [**native**]. Set the encapsulation—either **dot1q** or **isl**—to the type used by the switch. On some routers, the optional keyword **native** must be configured for the native VLAN before the router will route the native VLAN.

Step 4   Configure the IP address and subnet mask.

Step 5   Repeat Steps 2 through 4 for each additional VLAN that needs routing.

Assuming the switch is already configured with VLANs and trunking, Example 22-7 shows the commands to configure R1 to provide routing between VLAN 10 and VLAN 30.

Example 22-7   Configuring R1 to Route Between VLANs

```
R1#config t
Enter configuration commands, one per line.  End with CNTL/Z.
R1(config)#interface fa0/0
R1(config-if)#no shutdown
R1(config-if)#interface fa0/1.10
R1(config-subif)#encapsulation dot1q 10
R1(config-subif)#ip add 172.17.10.1 255.255.255.0
R1(config-subif)#interface fa0/1.30
R1(config-subif)#encapsulation dot1q 30
R1(config-subif)#ip add 172.17.30.1 255.255.255.0
R1(config-subif)#
```

To verify the configuration, use the **show ip route** and **show ip interface brief** commands to make sure the new networks are in the routing table and the subinterfaces are "up" and "up" as shown in Example 22-8.

Example 22-8   Verifying the Inter-VLAN Routing Configuration

```
R1#show ip route
<output omitted>


Gateway of last resort is not set

     172.17.0.0/24 is subnetted, 2 subnets
C       172.17.10.0 is directly connected, FastEthernet0/1.10
C       172.17.30.0 is directly connected, FastEthernet0/1.30
R1#show ip interface brief
Interface            IP-Address      OK? Method Status                Protocol
FastEthernet0/0      unassigned      YES manual administratively down down
FastEthernet0/1      unassigned      YES manual up                    up
FastEthernet0/1.10   172.17.10.1     YES manual up                    up
FastEthernet0/1.30   172.17.30.1     YES manual up                    up
Serial0/0/0          unassigned      YES manual administratively down down
Serial0/0/1          unassigned      YES manual administratively down down
Vlan1                unassigned      YES manual administratively down down
R1#
```

Assuming that the switch and PCs are configured correctly, the two PCs should now be able to ping each other. R1 will route the traffic between VLAN 10 and VLAN 30.

Troubleshooting Inter-VLAN Routing

To troubleshoot problems with inter-VLAN routing that are directly related to the router's configuration, confirm the following:

- Is the physical cabling to the switch correct?
- Is the physical interface activated?
- Is the encapsulation set to the right type?
- Is the IP addressing correct?

If you answer "no" to any of these questions, isolate and correct the problem.

Study Resources

For today's exam topics, refer to the following resources for more study.

Resource	Chapter	Topic	Where to Find It
Foundational Resources			
CCNA Exploration Online Curriculum: LAN Switching and Wireless	Chapter 4, "VTP" Chapter 6, "Inter-VLAN Routing"	Configure VTP All topics within the chapter	Section 4.3 All Sections
CCNA Exploration LAN Switching and Wireless Companion Guide	Chapter 4, "VTP" Chapter 6, "Inter-VLAN Routing"	Configure VTP All topics within the chapter	pp. 204–218 pp. 332–365
ICND2 Official Exam Certification Guide	Chapter 1, "Virtual VLANs" Chapter 4, "IP Routing: Static and Connected Routes"	Trunking with ISL and 802.1Q VTP Configuration and Verification ISL and 802.1Q Configuration on Routers	pp. 11–15 pp. 38–52 pp. 178–180
ICND2 Authorized Self-Study Guide	Chapter 2, "Medium-Sized Network Construction"	Implementing VLANs and Trunks Routing Between VLANs Troubleshooting VTP	pp. 24–32 pp. 64–66 pp. 80–82
Supplemental Resources			
CCNA Flash Cards and Exam Practice Pack	ICND2, Section 1 ICND2, Section 3	Implementing VLANS and Trunks Troubleshooting Switched Networks	pp. 346–378 pp. 410–422
CCNA Video Mentor	ICND2, Lab 2	VTP Servers and Clients	pp. 49–52 and DVD

Part III

Addressing the Network

Day 21:   IPv4 Address Subnetting

Day 20:   Host Addressing, DHCP, and DNS

Day 19:   Basic IPv6 Concepts

IPv4 Address Subnetting

CCNA 640-802 Exam Topics

- Calculate and apply an addressing scheme, including VLSM IP addressing design to a network.

- Determine the appropriate classless addressing scheme using VLSM and summarization to satisfy addressing requirements in a LAN/WAN environment.

- Describe the operation and benefits of using private and public IP addressing.

Key Topics

By now, you should be able to subnet very quickly. For example, you should be able to quickly answer a question such as: If you are given a /16 network, what subnet mask would you use that would maximize the total number of subnets while still providing enough addresses for the largest subnet with 500 hosts? The answer would be 255.255.254.0 or /23. This would give you 128 subnets with 510 usable hosts per subnet. You should be able to calculate this information in very short order.

The CCNA exam promises to contain lots of subnetting and subnetting-related questions. Today we focus on this necessary skill as well as designing addressing schemes using variable-length subnet masking (VLSM) and summarization to optimize your network routing traffic. We also review the difference between public and private addressing.

IPv4 Addressing

Although IPv6 is rapidly being deployed on the Internet backbone, and all U.S. government networks were required to be IPv6-capable by June 30, 2008, migration away from IPv4 will take years to complete. Even though U.S. government networks are now IPv6 capable, this does not mean they are actually *running* IPv6. So IPv4 and your skill in its use is still in demand.

Header Format

To facilitate the routing of packets over a network, the TCP/IP protocol suite uses a 32-bit logical address known as an IP address. This address must be unique for each device in the internetwork.

Figure 21-1 shows the layout of the IPv4 header.

Note that each IP packet carries this header, which includes a source IP address and destination IP address.

Figure 21-1   IPv4 Header Format

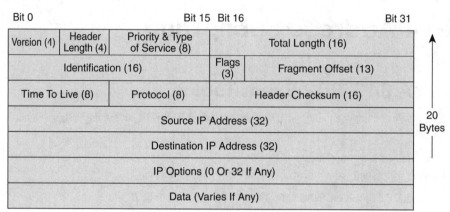

An IP address consists of two parts:

- The high order, or left-most, bits specify the network address component (network ID) of the address.

- The low order, or right-most, bits specify the host address component (host ID) of the address.

Classes of Addresses

From the beginning, IPv4 was designed with class structure: Class A, B, C, D and E. Class D is used for multicasting addresses and Class E is reserved for experimentation. Classes A, B, and C are assigned to network hosts. To provide a hierarchical structure, these classes are divided into network and host portions, as shown in Figure 21-2. The high-order bits specify the network ID, and the low order bits specify the host ID.

Figure 21-2   The Network/Host Boundary for Each Class of IPv4 Address

	8 Bits	8 Bits	8 Bits	8 Bits
Class A:	Network	Host	Host	Host
Class B:	Network	Network	Host	Host
Class C:	Network	Network	Network	Host
Class D:	Multicast			
Class E:	Research			

Note Today your ISP assigns you a block of addresses that has no relationship to the original classes. Based on your needs, you could be assigned one or more addresses. But with the use of NAT and private addresses inside your network, rarely will you need more than a handful of public IP addresses.

In a classful addressing scheme, devices that operate at Layer 3 can determine the address class of an IP address from the format of the first few bits in the first octet. Initially, this was important so that a networking device could apply the default subnet mask for the address and determine the host address. Table 21-1 summarizes how addresses are divided into classes, the default subnet mask, the number of networks per class, and the number of hosts per classful network address.

Table 21-1   IP Address Classes

Address Class	First Octet Range (Decimal)	First Octet Bits (Highlighted Bits Do Not Change)	Network (N) and Host (H) Portions of Address	Default Subnet Mask (Decimal and Binary)	Number of Possible Networks and Hosts Per Network
A	1–127	00000000–01111111	N.H.H.H	255.0.0.0 11111111.00000000.00000000.00000000	2^7 or 127 networks $2^{24}-2$ or 16,777,214 hosts per network
B	128–191	10000000–10111111	N.N.H.H	255.255.0.0 11111111.11111111.00000000.00000000	2^{14} or 16,384 networks $2^{16}-2$ or 65,534 hosts per network
C	192–223	11000000–11011111	N.N.N.H	255.255.255.0 11111111.11111111.11111111.00000000	2^{21} or 2,097,152 networks 2^8-2 or 254 hosts per network
D	224–239	11100000–11101111	Not used for host addressing		
E	240–255	11110000–11111111	Not used for host addressing		

In the last column, the "minus 2" for hosts per network is to account for the reserved network and broadcast addresses for each network. These two addresses cannot be assigned to hosts.

Note We are not reviewing the process of converting between binary and decimal. At this point in your studies, you should be very comfortable moving between the two numbering systems. If not, take some time to practice this necessary skill. Refer to the "Study Resources" section. You can also search the Internet for binary conversion tricks, tips, and games to help you practice.

Purpose of the Subnet Mask

Subnet masks are always a series of one bits followed by a series of zero bits. The boundary where the series changes from ones to zeros is the boundary between network and host. This is how a device that operates at Layer 3 determines the network address for a packet—by finding the bit boundary where the series of one bits ends and the series of zero bits begins. The bit boundary for subnet masks break on the octet boundary. Determining the network address for an IP address that uses a default mask is easy.

For example, a router receives a packet destined for 192.168.1.51. By "ANDing" the IP address and the subnet mask, the router determines the network address for the packet. By the "ANDing" rules, a one AND a one equals one. All other possibilities equal zero. Table 21-2 shows the results of the "ANDing" operation. Notice that the host bits in the last octet are ignored.

Table 21-2   "ANDing" an IP Address and Subnet Mask to Find the Network Address

Destination Address	192.168.1.51	11000000.10101000.00000001.00110011
Subnet Mask	255.255.255.0	11111111.11111111.11111111.00000000
Network Address	192.168.1.0	11000000.10101000.00000001.00000000

With the advent of CIDR using VLSM, the bit boundary can now occur in just about any place in the 32 bits. Table 21-3 summarizes the values for the last nonzero octet in a subnet mask.

Table 21-3   Subnet Mask Binary Values

Mask (Decimal)	Mask (Binary)	Network Bits	Host Bits
0	00000000	0	8
128	10000000	1	7
192	11000000	2	6
224	11100000	3	5
240	11110000	4	4
248	11111000	5	3
252	11111100	6	2
254	11111110	7	1
255	11111111	8	0

Subnetting in Four Steps

Everyone has a preferred method of subnetting. Each teacher will use a slightly different strategy to help students master this crucial skill. Each of the suggested "Study Resources" has a slightly different way of approaching this subject.

The method I prefer can be broken down into four steps:

Step 1   Determine how many bits to borrow based on the network requirements.

Step 2   Determine the new subnet mask.

Step 3   Determine the subnet multiplier.

Step 4   List the subnets including subnetwork address, host range, and broadcast address.

The best way to demonstrate this method is to use an example. Let's assume you are given the network address 192.168.1.0 with the default subnet mask 255.255.255.0. The network address and subnet mask can be written as 192.168.1.0/24. The "slash 24" represents the subnet mask in a shorter notation and means the first 24 bits are network bits.

Let's further assume you need 30 hosts per network and want to create as many subnets for the given address space as possible. With these network requirements, let's subnet the address space.

Determine How Many Bits to Borrow

To determine the number of bits you can borrow, you first must know how many host bits you have to start with. Because the first 24 bits are network bits in our example, the remaining 8 bits are host bits.

Because our requirement specifies 30 host addresses per subnet, we need to first determine the minimum number of host bits to leave. The remaining bits can be borrowed:

Host Bits = Bits Borrowed + Bits Left

To provide enough address space for 30 hosts, we need to leave 5 bits. Use the following formula:

$2^{BL} - 2$ = number of host addresses

where the exponent BL is bits left in the host portion.

Remember, the "minus 2" is to account for the network and broadcast addresses that cannot be assigned to hosts.

In this example, leaving 5 bits in the host portion will provide the right amount of host address: $2^5 - 2 = 30$.

Because we have 3 bits remaining in the original host portion, we borrow all these bits to satisfy the requirement to "create as many subnets as possible." To determine how many subnets we can create, use the following formula:

2^{BB} = number of subnets

where the exponent BB is bits borrowed from the host portion.

In this example, borrowing 3 bits from the host portion will create 8 subnets: $2^3 = 8$.

As shown in Table 21-4, the 3 bits are borrowed from the left-most bits in the host portion. The highlighted bits in the table show all possible combinations of manipulating the 8 bits borrowed to create the subnets.

Table 21-4   Binary and Decimal Value of the Subnetted Octet

Subnet Number	Last Octet Binary Value	Last Octet Decimal Value
0	00000000	.0
1	00100000	.32
2	01000000	.64
3	01100000	.96
4	10000000	.128
5	10100000	.160
6	11000000	.192
7	11100000	.224

Determine the New Subnet Mask

Notice in Table 21-4 that the network bits now include the 3 borrowed host bits in the last octet. Add these 3 bits to the 24 bits in the original subnet mask and you have a new subnet mask, /27. In decimal format, you turn on the 128, 64, and 32 bits in the last octet for a value of 224. So the new subnet mask is 255.255.255.224.

Determine the Subnet Multiplier

Notice in Table 21-4 that the last octet decimal value increments by 32 with each subnet number. The number 32 is the subnet multiplier. You can quickly find the subnet multiplier using one of two methods:

- **Method 1:** Subtract the last nonzero octet of the subnet mask from 256. In this example, the last nonzero octet is 224. So the subnet multiplier is 256 – 224 = 32.

- **Method 2:** The decimal value of the last bit borrowed is the subnet multiplier. In this example, we borrowed the 128 bit, the 64 bit, and the 32 bit. The 32 bit is the last bit we borrowed and is, therefore, the subnet multiplier.

By using the subnet multiplier, you no longer have to convert binary subnet bits to decimal.

List the Subnets, Host Ranges, and Broadcast Addresses

Listing the subnets, host ranges, and broadcast addresses helps you see the flow of addresses within one address space. Table 21-5 documents our subnet addressing scheme for the 192.168.1.0/24 address space.

Table 21-5   Subnet Addressing Scheme for 192.168.1.0/24: 30 Hosts Per Subnet

Subnet Number	Subnet Address	Host Range	Broadcast Address
0	192.168.1.0	192.168.1.1–192.168.1.30	192.168.1.31
1	192.168.1.32	192.168.1.33–192.168.1.62	192.168.1.63
2	192.168.1.64	192.168.1.65–192.168.1.94	192.168.1.95
3	192.168.1.96	192.168.1.97–192.168.1.126	192.168.1.127
4	192.168.1.128	192.168.1.129–192.168.1.158	192.168.1.159
5	192.168.1.160	192.168.1.161–192.168.1.190	192.168.1.191
6	192.168.1.192	192.168.1.193–192.168.1.222	192.168.1.223
7	192.168.1.224	192.168.1.225–192.168.1.254	192.168.1.255

The following are three examples using the four subnetting steps. For brevity, only the first three subnets are listed in step 4.

Subnetting Example 1

Subnet the address space 172.16.0.0/16 to provide at least 80 host addresses per subnet while creating as many subnets as possible.

1. There are 16 host bits. Leave 7 bits for host addresses ($2^7 - 2 = 126$ host addresses per subnet). Borrow the first 9 host bits to create as many subnets as possible ($2^9 = 512$ subnets).

2. The original subnet mask is /16 or 255.255.0.0. Turn on the next 9 bits starting in the second octet for a new subnet mask of /25 or 255.255.255.128.

3. The subnet multiplier is 128, which can be found as $256 - 128 = 128$ or because the 128 bit is the last bit borrowed.

4. Table 21-6 lists the first three subnets, host ranges, and broadcast addresses.

Table 21-6   Subnet Addressing Scheme for Example 1

Subnet Number	Subnet Address	Host Range	Broadcast Address
0	172.16.0.0	172.16.0.1–172.16.0.126	172.16.0.127
1	172.16.0.128	172.16.0.129–172.16.0.254	172.16.0.255
2	172.16.1.0	172.16.1.1–172.16.1.126	172.16.1.127

Subnetting Example 2

Subnet the address space 172.16.0.0/16 to provide at least 80 subnet addresses.

1. There are 16 host bits. Borrow the first 7 host bits to create at least 80 subnets ($2^7 = 126$ subnets). That leaves 9 bits for host addresses or $2^9 - 2 = 510$ host addresses per subnet.

2. The original subnet mask is /16 or 255.255.0.0. Turn on the next 7 bits starting in the second octet for a new subnet mask of /23 or 255.255.254.0.

3. The subnet multiplier is 2, which can be found as $256 - 254 = 2$ or because the 2 bit is the last bit borrowed.

4. Table 21-7 lists the first three subnets, host ranges, and broadcast addresses.

Table 21-7   Subnet Addressing Scheme for Example 2

Subnet Number	Subnet Address	Host Range	Broadcast Address
0	172.16.0.0	172.16.0.1–172.16.1.254	172.16.1.255
1	172.16.2.0	172.16.2.1–172.16.3.254	172.16.3.255
2	172.16.4.0	172.16.4.1–172.16.5.254	172.16.5.255

Subnetting Example 3

Subnet the address space 172.16.10.0/23 to provide at least 60 host addresses per subnet while creating as many subnets as possible.

1. There are 9 host bits. Leave 6 bits for host addresses ($2^6 - 2 = 62$ host addresses per subnet). Borrow the first 3 host bits to create as many subnets as possible ($2^3 = 8$ subnets).

2. The original subnet mask is /23 or 255.255.254.0. Turn on the next 3 bits starting with the last bit in the second octet for a new subnet mask of /26 or 255.255.255.192.

3. The subnet multiplier is 64, which can be found as 256 − 192 = 64 or because the 64 bit is the last bit borrowed.

4. Table 21-7 lists the first three subnets, host ranges, and broadcast addresses.

Table 21-7   Subnet Addressing Scheme for Example 3

Subnet Number	Subnet Address	Host Range	Broadcast Address
0	172.16.10.0	172.16.10.1–172.16.10.62	172.16.10.63
1	172.16.10.64	172.16.10.65–172.16.10.126	172.16.10.127
2	172.16.10.128	172.16.10.129–172.16.10.190	172.16.10.191

VLSM

You probably noticed that the starting address space in Subnetting Example 3 is not an entire classful address. In fact, it is subnet 5 from Subnetting Example 2. So in Subnetting Example 3, we "subnetted a subnet." That is what VLSM is in a nutshell—subnetting a subnet.

With VLSM, you can customize your subnets to fit your network. Subnetting works the same way. You just have to do it more than once to complete your addressing scheme. To avoid overlapping address spaces, start with your largest host requirement, create a subnet for it, and then continue with the next largest host requirement.

Let's use a small example. Given the address space 172.30.4.0/22 and the network requirements shown in Figure 21-3, apply an addressing scheme that conserves the most amount of addresses for future growth.

Figure 21-3   VLSM Example Topology

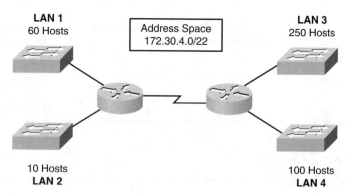

We need five subnets: four LAN subnets and one WAN subnet. Starting with the largest host requirement on LAN 3, begin subnetting the address space.

To satisfy the 250 hosts requirement, we leave 8 hosts bits ($2^8 − 2 = 252$ hosts per subnet). Because we have 10 host bits total, we borrow 2 bits to create the first round of subnets ($2^2 = 4$ subnets). The starting subnet mask is /22 or 255.255.252.0. We turn on the next two bits in the subnet mask to get /24 or 255.255.255.0. The multiplier is 1. The four subnets are as follows:

- **Subnet 0**: 172.30.4.0/24

- **Subnet 1**: 172.30.5.0/24

- **Subnet 2**: 172.30.6.0/24

- **Subnet 3**: 172.30.7.0/24

Assigning Subnet 0 to LAN 3, we are left with three /24 subnets. Continuing on to the next largest host requirement on LAN 4, we take Subnet 1, 172.30.5.0/24, and subnet it further.

To satisfy the 100 hosts requirement, we leave 7 bits ($2^7 - 2 = 128$ hosts per subnet). Because we have 8 host bits total, we can borrow only 1 bit to create the subnets ($2^1 = 2$ subnets). The starting subnet mask is /24 or 255.255.255.0. We turn on the next bit in the subnet mask to get /25 or 255.255.255.128. The multiplier is 128. The two subnets are as follows:

- **Subnet 0**: 172.30.4.0/25

- **Subnet 1**: 172.30.4.128/25

Assigning Subnet 0 to LAN 4, we are left with one /25 subnet and two /24 subnets. Continuing on to the next largest host requirement on LAN 1, we take Subnet 1, 172.30.4.128/24, and subnet it further.

To satisfy the 60 hosts requirement, we leave 6 bits ($2^6 - 2 = 62$ hosts per subnet). Because we have 7 host bits total, we borrow 1 bit to create the subnets ($2^1 = 2$ subnets). The starting subnet mask is /25 or 255.255.255.128. We turn on the next bit in the subnet mask to get /26 or 255.255.255.192. The multiplier is 64. The two subnets are as follows:

- **Subnet 0**: 172.30.4.128/26

- **Subnet 1**: 172.30.4.192/26

Assigning Subnet 0 to LAN 1, we are left with one /26 subnet and two /24 subnets. Finishing our LAN subnetting with LAN 2, we take Subnet 1, 172.30.4.192/26, and subnet it further.

To satisfy the 10 hosts requirement, we leave 4 bits ($2^4 - 2 = 14$ hosts per subnet). Because we have 6 host bits total, we borrow 2 bits to create the subnets ($2^2 = 4$ subnets). The starting subnet mask is /26 or 255.255.255.192. We turn on the next two bits in the subnet mask to get /28 or 255.255.255.240. The multiplier is 16. The four subnets are as follows:

- **Subnet 0**: 172.30.4.192/28

- **Subnet 1**: 172.30.4.208/28

- **Subnet 2**: 172.30.4.224/28

- **Subnet 3**: 172.30.4.240/28

Assigning Subnet 0 to LAN 2, we are left with three /28 subnets and two /24 subnets. To finalize our addressing scheme, we need to create a subnet only for the WAN link, which needs only 2 host addresses. We take Subnet 1, 172.30.4.208/28, and subnet it further.

To satisfy the 2 host requirement, we leave 2 bits ($2^2 - 2 = 2$ hosts per subnet). Because we have 4 host bits total, we borrow 2 bits to create the subnets ($2^2 = 4$ subnets). The starting subnet mask is /28 or 255.255.255.240. We turn on the next two bits in the subnet mask to get /30 or 255.255.255.252. The multiplier is 4. The four subnets are as follows:

- **Subnet 0**: 172.30.4.208/30

- **Subnet 1**: 172.30.4.212/30

- **Subnet 2**: 172.30.4.216/30

- **Subnet 3**: 172.30.4.220/30

We assign Subnet 0 to the WAN link. We are left with three /30 subnets, two /28 subnets, and two /24 subnets.

Summarizing Subnet Addresses

When a network's addressing scheme is designed hierarchically, summarizing addresses to upstream routers makes routing much more efficient. Instead of sending a collection of various subnets, a border router can send one summary route to the next router.

If you are using static routing or configuring a summary route for EIGRP, you might need to calculate the right network prefix and subnet mask.

Referring to Figure 21-4, what summary route would R1 send to the upstream router, BBR (Backbone Router) for the four subnets?

Figure 21-4   Summarizing Subnets: Example 1

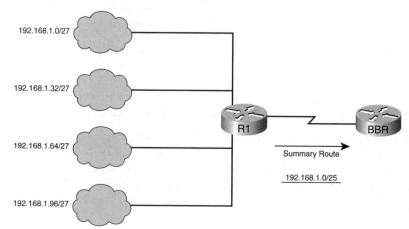

Use the following steps to calculate a summary route:

Step 1   Write out the networks that you want to summarize in binary, as shown following Step 4.

Step 2   To find the subnet mask for summarization, start with the left-most bit.

Step 3   Work your way to the right, finding all the bits that match consecutively.

Step 4   When you find a column of bits that do not match, stop. You are at the summary boundary.

```
11000000.10101000.00000001.00000000
11000000.10101000.00000001.00100000
11000000.10101000.00000001.01000000
11000000.10101000.00000001.01100000
```

Step 5   Count the number of left-most matching bits, which in this example is 25. This number becomes your subnet mask for the summarized route, /25 or 255.255.255.128.

Step 6   To find the network address for summarization, copy the matching 25 bits and add all 0 bits to the end to make 32 bits. In this example, the network address is 192.168.1.0.

In production networks, the subnets to be summarized most likely will not have the same subnet mask. For example, the subnets in Figure 21-5 are using three different subnet masks. What summary route would R1 send to BBR for the four subnets?

Figure 21-5   Summarizing Subnets: Example 2

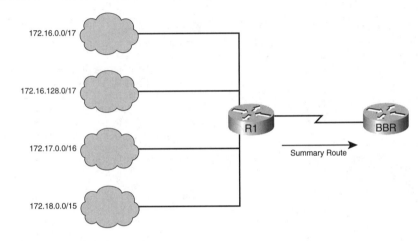

Use the same steps to calculate the summary.

```
10101100.00010000.00000000.00000000
10101100.00010000.10000000.00000000
10101100.00010001.00000000.00000000
10101100.00010010.00000000.00000000
```

Summary Route: 172.16.0.0/14

Private and Public IP Addressing

RFC 1918, "Address Allocation for Private Internets," eased the demand for IP addresses by reserving the following addresses for use in private internetworks.

- **Class A**: 10.0.0.0/8 (10.0.0.0 to 10.255.255.255)

- **Class B**: 172.16.0.0/12 (172.16.0.0 to 172.31.255.255)

- **Class C**: 192.168.0.0/16 (192.168.0.0 to 192.168.255.255)

If you are addressing a nonpublic intranet, these private addresses can be used instead of globally unique public addresses. This provides flexibility in your addressing design. Any organization can take full advantage of an entire Class A address (10.0.0.0/8). Forwarding traffic to the public Internet requires translation to a public address using network address translation (NAT). But by overloading an Internet routable address with many private addresses, a company needs only a handful of public addresses. Day 5, "NAT Concepts, Configuration, and Troubleshooting," reviews NAT operation and configuration in greater detail.

Study Resources

For today's exam topics, refer to the following resources for more study.

Resource	Chapter	Topic	Where to Find It
Foundational Resources			
CCNA Exploration Online Curriculum: Network Fundamentals	Chapter 6, "Addressing the Network—IPv4"	IPv4 Addresses Addresses for Different Purposes Assigning Addresses Is It On My Network? Calculating Addresses	Section 6.1 Section 6.2 Sections 6.3.1–6.3.5 Section 6.4 Section 6.5
	Chapter 10, "Planning and Cabling Networks"	Developing an Addressing Scheme Calculating the Subnets	Section 10.3 Section 10.4
CCNA Exploration Online Curriculum: Routing Protocols and Concepts	Chapter 3, "Introduction to Routing and Packet Forwarding" Chapter 6, "VLSM and CIDR"	Routing Protocols and Subnetting Activities All topics within the chapter	Sections 3.5.2–3.5.4 All sections
CCNA Exploration Network Fundamentals Companion Guide	Chapter 6, "Addressing the Network—IPv4"	IPv4 Addresses IPv4 Addresses for Different Purposes Assigning Addresses Calculating Addresses	pp. 173–188 pp. 188–198 pp. 198–206 pp. 206–227
	Chapter 10, "Planning and Cabling Networks"	Developing an Addressing Scheme Calculating the Subnets	pp. 388–391 pp. 391–398
CCNA Exploration Routing Protocols and Concepts Companion Guide	Chapter 6, "VLSM and CIDR"	All topics within the chapter	pp. 264–280
ICND1 Official Exam Certification Guide	Chapter 5, "Fundamentals of IP Addressing and Routing" Chapter 12, "IP Addressing and Subnetting CCNA Subnetting Video" Printable Appendices Cisco Binary Game	IP Addressing All topics within the chapter All eight examples Appendixes D–G Practice your binary skills	pp. 105–114 pp. 336–393 DVD-ROM in front of book CD-ROM in back of book CD-ROM in back of book

Resource	Chapter	Topic	Where to Find It
ICND2 Official Exam Certification Guide	Chapter 5, "VLSM and Route Summarization CCNA Subnetting Video"	All topics within the chapter All eight examples	pp. 202–223 DVD-ROM in front of book
	Printable Appendices	Appendices D–G	CD-ROM in back of book
	Cisco Binary Game	Practice your binary skills	CD-ROM in back of book
ICND1 Authorized Self-Study Guide	Chapter 1, "Building a Simple Network" Chapter 4, "LAN Connections"	IP Network Addressing Understanding Binary Numbering Constructing a Network Addressing Scheme	pp. 44–57 pp. 246–252 pp. 252–270
ICND2 Authorized Self-Study Guide	Chapter 3, "Medium-Sized Routed Network Construction"	Implementing Variable-Length Subnet Masks	pp. 123–132
Supplemental Resources			
CCNA Flash Cards and Exam Practice Pack	ICND1, Section 2 ICND2, Section 4	Understanding TCP/IP Routing Operations and VLSM	pp. 38–68 pp. 426–450
CCNA Video Mentor	ICND1, Lab4	Finding the Subnet Number	pp. 17–18 and DVD
	ICND1, Lab5	Finding the Broadcast Address and Range of Addresses in a Subnet	pp. 19–22 and DVD
	ICND1, Lab6	Finding All Subnets of a Network with Less Than Eight Subnet Bits	pp. 23–26 and DVD
	ICND1, Lab7	IP Subnet Design and Implementation	pp. 27–32 and DVD

Host Addressing, DHCP, and DNS

CCNA 640-802 Exam Topics

- Implement static and dynamic addressing services for hosts in a LAN environment.
- Identify and correct common problems associated with IP addressing and host configurations.
- Explain the operation and benefits of using DHCP and DNS.
- Configure, verify and troubleshoot DHCP and DNS operation on a router (CLI/SDM).

Key Topics

Today we review static and dynamic IP addressing for end devices as well as the protocols surrounding host-to-host communications including Address Resolution Protocol (ARP), Domain Name System (DNS), and Dynamic Host Configuration Protocol (DHCP). Because a Cisco router can also be a DHCP server, we will review those commands. Also, because an IP addressing implementation is not always perfect, we review the testing tools at your disposal to track down and solve connectivity problems related to host addressing.

Addressing Devices

Addresses in the network can be assigned to hosts statically or dynamically. Static addresses have some advantages over dynamic addresses. For example, if hosts normally access a server, a printer, or other devices at a particular IP address, it might cause problems if that address changed. Additionally, static assignment of addressing information can provide increased control of network resources. However, it can be time consuming to enter the information on each host, and because a duplicated address affects the host operation, care must be taken not to reuse an address.

To configure a static address on a PC running Windows XP, access the Internet Protocol (TCP/IP) Properties dialog box as shown in Figure 20-1 and enter all the necessary IP configuration information.

Because of the challenges associated with static address management, end-user devices often have addresses dynamically assigned, using DHCP.

To configure a Windows PC to use DHCP, access the Internet Protocol (TCP/IP) Properties dialog box as shown in Figure 20-2 and click both radio buttons for obtaining addressing information automatically.

Figure 20-1   Statically Configure IP Addressing in Windows

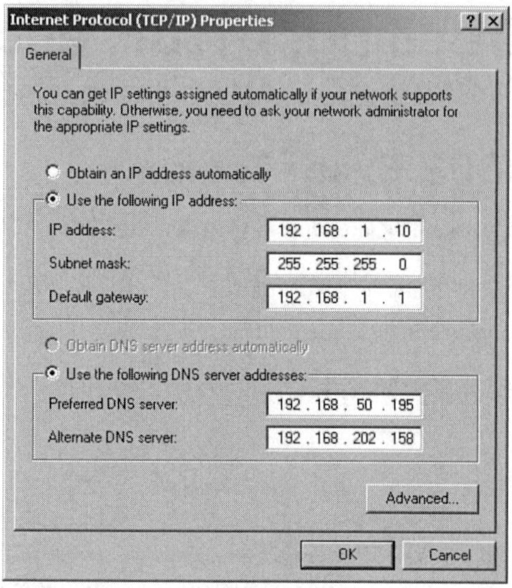

Figure 20-2   Configure Windows to Use DHCP

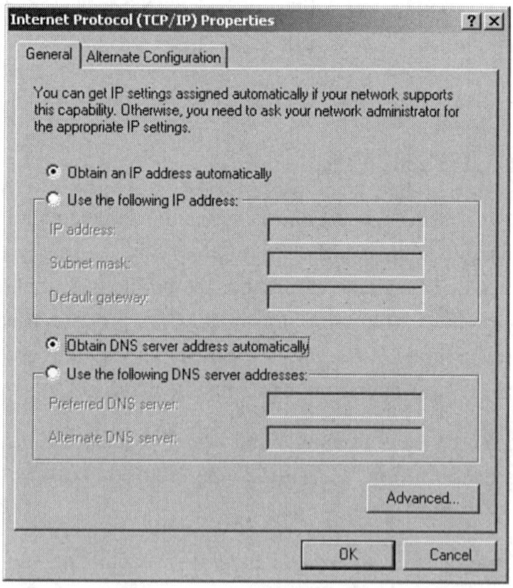

ARP

For IP communication on Ethernet-connected networks to take place, the logical (IP) address needs to be bound to the physical (MAC) address of its destination. This process is carried out using ARP. Figure 20-3 shows an example of mapping a Layer 2 address to a Layer 3 address.

Figure 20-3   ARP Maps Layer 2 to Layer 3

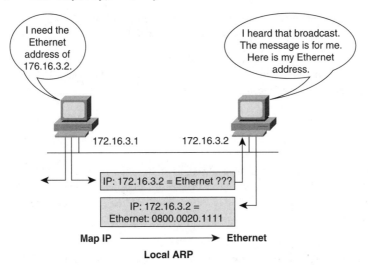

To send data to a destination, a host on an Ethernet network must know the physical (MAC) address of the destination. ARP provides the essential service of mapping IP addresses to physical addresses on a network.

The resulting mappings or address bindings are kept in a table and depending upon the operating system can be anywhere from 2 to 20 minutes, or even longer before the entry expires. Every networking device that sends IP packets on an Ethernet network segment maintains an ARP table in memory similar to the table shown in Example 20-1.

Example 20-1   ARP Table for a Windows PC

```
C:\>arp -a

Interface: 10.10.10.102 --- 0x2
  Internet Address       Physical Address      Type
  10.10.10.1             00-18-39-b1-9b-b7     dynamic
  10.10.10.100           00-18-fe-2c-40-c8     dynamic

C:\>
```

Example 20-2 shows what an ARP table looks like on a Cisco device.

Example 20-2   ARP Table for a Cisco Device

```
Router#show ip arp
Protocol  Address          Age (min)  Hardware Addr   Type   Interface
Internet  10.10.10.1              -    001b.530c.f098  ARPA   FastEthernet0/0
Internet  10.10.10.100           2    001b.5302.4ec0  ARPA   FastEthernet0/0
Internet  10.10.10.101           4    001b.5302.4ec0  ARPA   FastEthernet0/0
Router#
```

Regardless of the format of the output, the ARP table shows the IP to MAC address bindings.

ARP helps end devices communicate on the same LAN. But what happens when an end device wants to communicate with another device on a remote LAN?

If the destination host is not on the local network, the source sends the frame to the local router. To do this, the source will use the default gateway's MAC address in the frame. The default gateway (the local router), will then take care of routing the packet to the next hop.

DNS

IP packets require destination and source IP addresses. But most humans would have a hard time remembering all the IP addresses for their favorite destinations. Hence, the Domain Name System (DNS) was created to convert recognizable names into IP addresses so that end devices can then encapsulate a packet with the necessary addressing information.

The DNS server acts as the phone book for the Internet: It translates human-readable computer hostnames—for example, http://www.cisco.com—into the IP addresses that networking equipment needs for delivering information. To see this "phone book" in action on a Windows machine, enter the command **nslookup** as shown in Example 20-3. Then enter the name for a website.

Example 20-3   Using nslookup to Find an IP Address

```
C:\>nslookup
Default Server:  dns-rtp.cisco.com
Address:  64.102.6.247


> www.cisco.com
Server:  dns-rtp.cisco.com
Address:  64.102.6.247


Name:    www.cisco.com
Address:  198.133.219.25


> exit


C:\>
```

Notice that the DNS server, which is located at IP address 64.102.6.247, returned the IP address 198.133.219.25 for www.cisco.com.

DNS uses a hierarchical system to create a name database to provide name resolution. At the top of the hierarchy, the root servers maintain records about how to reach the top-level domain servers, which in turn have records that point to the secondary-level domain servers, and so on.

The different top-level domains represent either the type of organization or the country of origin. The following are examples of top-level domains:

- **.au**: Australia

- **.co**: Colombia

- **.com**: A business or industry

- **.jp**: Japan

- **.org**: A nonprofit organization

DHCP

DHCP allows a host to obtain an IP address dynamically when it connects to the network. The DHCP server is contacted by sending a request, and an IP address is requested. The DHCP server chooses an address from a configured range of addresses called a pool and assigns it to the host client for a set period. Figure 20-4 graphically shows the process for how a DHCP server allocates IP addressing information to a DHCP client.

Figure 20-4   Allocating IP Addressing Information Using DHCP

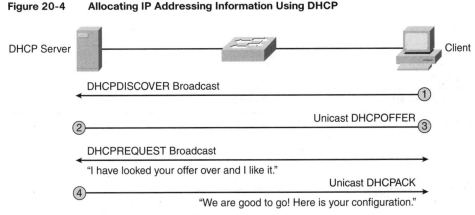

When a DHCP-configured device boots up or connects to the network, the client broadcasts a DHCPDISCOVER packet to identify any available DHCP servers on the network. A DHCP server replies with a DHCPOFFER, which is a lease offer message with an assigned IP address, subnet mask, DNS server, and default gateway information, as well as the duration of the lease.

The client can receive multiple DHCPOFFER packets if the local network has more than one DHCP server. The client must choose between them and broadcast a DHCPREQUEST packet that identifies the explicit server and lease offer that it is accepting.

Assuming that the IP address is still valid, the chosen server returns a DHCPACK (acknowledgment) message finalizing the lease. If the offer is no longer valid for some reason, the chosen server responds to the client with a DHCPNAK (negative acknowledgment) message. After it is leased, the client will renew prior to the lease expiration through another DHCPREQUEST. If the client is powered down or taken off the network, the address is returned to the pool for reuse.

Configuring on a Cisco Router as a DHCP Server

Note   Because of space limitations, only the CLI method for configuring DHCP is reviewed here. However, because the exam topic includes both the CLI and Security Device Manager (SDM) methods, review the SDM method by consulting your study resources.

The steps to configure a router as a DHCP server are as follows:

Step 1   Use the **ip dhcp excluded-address** *low-address* [*high-address*] command to identify an address or range of addresses to exclude from the DHCP pool. For example:

```
R1(config)# ip dhcp excluded-address 192.168.10.1 192.168.10.9
R1(config)# ip dhcp excluded-address 192.168.10.254
```

Step 2   Create the DHCP pool using the **ip dhcp pool** *pool-name* command, which will then place you in DHCP config mode, as demonstrated here:

```
R1(config)# ip dhcp pool LAN-POOL-10
R1(dhcp-config)#
```

Step 3   Finally, configure the IP addressing parameter you need to automatically assign to requesting clients. Table 20-1 lists the required commands.

Table 20-1   Required DHCP Configuration Commands

Required Task	Command
Define the address pool	**network** *network-number* [*mask*	/*prefix-length*]
Define the default router or gateway	**default-router** *address* [*address2...address8*]

Table 20-2 lists some of the more common optional DHCP tasks.

Table 20-2   Optional DHCP Configuration Commands

Optional Task	Command
Define a DNS server	**dns-server** *address* [*address2...address8*]
Define the domain name	**domain-name** *domain*
Define the duration of the DHCP lease	**lease** {*days* [*hours*] [*minutes*]	**infinite**}
Define the NetBIOS WINS server	**netbios-name-server** *address* [*address2...address8*]

Figure 20-5 shows a sample DHCP topology.

Figure 20-5   DHCP Sample Topology

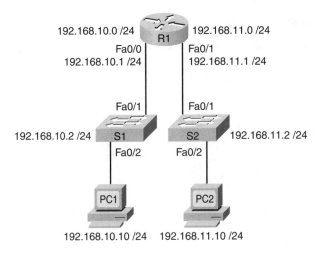

192.168.10.0 /24   R1   192.168.11.0 /24
Fa0/0   Fa0/1
192.168.10.1 /24   192.168.11.1 /24

Fa0/1   Fa0/1

192.168.10.2 /24   S1   S2   192.168.11.2 /24
Fa0/2   Fa0/2

PC1   PC2

192.168.10.10 /24   192.168.11.10 /24

Example 20-4 shows DHCP required and optional commands to configure R1 as the DHCP server for both LANs.

Example 20-4   DHCP Configuration Example

```
R1(config)#ip dhcp excluded-address 192.168.10.1 192.168.10.9
R1(config)#ip dhcp excluded-address 192.168.10.254
R1(config)#ip dhcp excluded-address 192.168.11.1 192.168.11.9
R1(config)#ip dhcp excluded-address 192.168.11.254
R1(config)#ip dhcp pool LAN-POOL-10
R1(dhcp-config)#network 192.168.10.0 255.255.255.0
R1(dhcp-config)#default-router 192.168.10.1
R1(dhcp-config)#dns-server 192.168.50.195 209.165.202.158
R1(dhcp-config)#domain-name cisco.com
R1(dhcp-config)#lease 2
R1(dhcp-config)#netbios-name-server 192.168.10.254
R1(dhcp-config)#ip dhcp pool LAN-POOL-11
R1(dhcp-config)#network 192.168.11.0 255.255.255.0
R1(dhcp-config)#default-router 192.168.11.1
R1(dhcp-config)#dns-server 192.168.50.195 209.165.202.158
R1(dhcp-config)#domain-name cisco.com
R1(dhcp-config)#lease 2
R1(dhcp-config)#netbios-name-server 192.168.11.254
R1(dhcp-config)#end
```

Cisco IOS Software supports DHCP service by default. To disable it, use the global command **no service dhcp**.

To verify DHCP operations on the router, use the commands shown in Example 20-5.

Example 20-5   Verifying DHCP Operation

```
R1#show ip dhcp binding
Bindings from all pools not associated with VRF:
IP address              Client-ID/              Lease expiration        Type
                        Hardware address/
                        User name
192.168.10.10           0100.1641.aea5.a7       Jul 18 2008 08:17 AM    Automatic
192.168.11.10           0100.e018.5bdd.35       Jul 18 2008 08:17 AM    Automatic

R1#show ip dhcp server statistics
Memory usage           26455
Address pools          2
Database agents        0
Automatic bindings     2
Manual bindings        0
Expired bindings       0
Malformed messages     0
Secure arp entries     0

Message                Received
BOOTREQUEST            0
DHCPDISCOVER           2
DHCPREQUEST            2
DHCPDECLINE            0
DHCPRELEASE            0
DHCPINFORM             0

Message                Sent
BOOTREPLY              0
DHCPOFFER              2
DHCPACK                2
DHCPNAK                0
R1#
```

Because PC1 and PC2 are connected to the LANs, each automatically receives its IP addressing information from the router's DHCP server. Example 20-6 shows the output from the **ipconfig/all** command on PC1.

Example 20-6   DHCP Client Configuration

```
C:\>ipconfig/all

Windows IP Configuration

        Host Name . . . . . . . . . . . . : ciscolab
```

```
        Primary Dns Suffix  . . . . . . . :
        Node Type . . . . . . . . . . . . : Hybrid
        IP Routing Enabled. . . . . . . . : No
        WINS Proxy Enabled. . . . . . . . : No

Ethernet adapter Local Area Connection:

        Connection-specific DNS Suffix  . : cisco.com
        Description . . . . . . . . . . . : Intel(R) PRO/1000 PL
        Physical Address. . . . . . . . . : 00-16-41-AE-A5-A7
        Dhcp Enabled. . . . . . . . . . . : Yes
        Autoconfiguration Enabled . . . . : Yes
        IP Address. . . . . . . . . . . . : 192.168.10.11
        Subnet Mask . . . . . . . . . . . : 255.255.255.0
        Default Gateway . . . . . . . . . : 192.168.10.1
        DHCP Server . . . . . . . . . . . : 192.168.10.1
        DNS Servers . . . . . . . . . . . : 192.168.50.195
                                            209.165.202.158
        Primary WINS Server . . . . . . . : 192.168.10.254
        Lease Obtained. . . . . . . . . . : Wednesday, July 16, 2008 8:16:59 AM
        Lease Expires . . . . . . . . . . : Friday, July 18, 2008 8:16:59 AM

C:\>
```

To release the DHCP configuration on a Windows-based client, enter the command
ipconfig/release. To renew the DHCP configuration, enter the command **ipconfig/renew**.

In a complex network, the DHCP servers are usually contained in a server farm. Therefore, clients
typically are not on the same subnet as the DHCP server, as shown in the previous example. To
ensure broadcasted DHCPDISCOVER messages are sent to the remote DHCP server, use the **ip
helper-address** *address* command.

For example, in Figure 20-6 the DHCP server is located on the 192.168.11.0/24 LAN and is serving IP addressing information for both LANs.

Without the **ip helper-address** command, R1 would discard any broadcasts from PC1 requesting
DHCP services. To configure R1 to relay DHCPDISCOVER messages, enter the following command:

```
R1(config)#interface fastethernet 0/0
R1(config-if)#ip helper-address 192.168.11.5
```

Notice the command is entered on the interface that will receive DHCP broadcasts. R1 then forwards DHCP broadcast messages as a unicast to 192.168.11.5. The **ip helper-address** command
by default forwards the following eight UDP services:

- **Port 37**: Time

- **Port 49**: TACACS

- **Port 53**: DNS

- **Port 67**: DHCP/BOOTP client

- **Port 68**: DHCP/BOOTP server

- **Port 69**: TFTP

- **Port 137**: NetBIOS name service

- **Port 138**: NetBIOS datagram service

Figure 20-6   DHCP Relay Topology

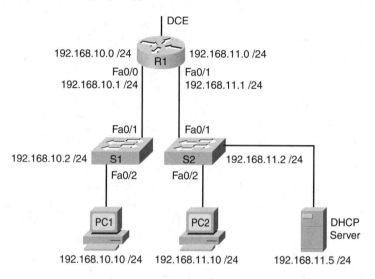

To specify additional ports, use the global command **ip forward-protocol udp** [*port-number | protocol*]. To disable broadcasts of a particular protocol, use the **no** form of the command.

Network Layer Testing Tools

The **ping** and **tracert** (**traceroute** for Cisco IOS) are commonly used to test connectivity and identify problems with host addressing.

Ping

For testing end-to-end connectivity between hosts, use the **ping** command. If the ping is successful, as shown in Examples 20-7 and 20-8, you know that at least one path exists to route traffic between the source and destination.

Example 20-7   Ping Output on a Windows PC

```
C:\>ping 192.168.10.1

Pinging 192.168.10.1 with 32 bytes of data:

Reply from 192.168.10.1: bytes=32 time<1ms TTL=64
Reply from 192.168.10.1: bytes=32 time<1ms TTL=64
```

```
Reply from 192.168.10.1: bytes=32 time<1ms TTL=64
Reply from 192.168.10.1: bytes=32 time<1ms TTL=64

Ping statistics for 192.168.10.1:
    Packets: Sent = 4, Received = 4, Lost = 0 (0% loss),
Approximate round trip times in milli-seconds:
    Minimum = 0ms, Maximum = 0ms, Average = 0ms

C:\>
```

Example 20-8   Ping Output in the Cisco IOS

```
R1#ping 192.168.10.10

Type escape sequence to abort.
Sending 5, 100-byte ICMP Echos to 192.168.10.10, timeout is 2 seconds:
.!!!!
Success rate is 100 percent (5/5), round-trip min/avg/max = 1/2/4 ms
R1#
```

Notice that the first ping failed (.). Most likely, this was due to a timeout while R1 initiated an ARP request to 192.168.10.10. After R1 had the MAC address for 192.168.10.10, it could then send the ICMP requests. The next four pings succeed (!). If the ping test fails for end-to-end connectivity, you might want to back up to the local machine to test your TCP/IP stack by pinging the 127.0.0.1 address. If this ping succeeds, test your connectivity to the default gateway. If this ping fails, check your physical connectivity and IP configuration.

If the ping succeeds to the default gateway, use **traceroute** to find where there is failure. Traceroute (**tracert**) allows you to observe the path between these hosts. The trace generates a list of hops that were successfully reached along the path, as shown in Example 20-9. This list can provide you with important verification and troubleshooting information.

Example 20-9   Sample tracert Output

```
C:\> tracert www.cisco.com
Tracing route to www.cisco.com [198.133.219.25]
over a maximum of 30 hops:
1 87 ms 87 ms 89 ms sjck-access-gw2-vla30.cisco.com [10.20.0.94]
2 89 ms 88 ms 87 ms sjce-sbb1-gw1-gig3-7.cisco.com [171.69.14.245]
3 88 ms 87 ms 88 ms sjck-rbb-gw2-ten7-1.cisco.com [171.69.14.45]
4 90 ms 87 ms 95 ms sjck-corp-gw1-gig1-0-0.cisco.com [171.69.7.174]
5 90 ms 88 ms 92 ms sjce-dmzbb-gw1.cisco.com [128.107.236.38]
6 * * * Request timed out.
7 * * ^C
C:\>
```

The **tracert** to www.cisco.com shows responses from the routers along the path. The local host sends a packet to the designation address of 198.133.219.2. The first response is a response from the host's default gateway, 10.20.0.94.

When the final destination is reached, the host responds with either an ICMP Port Unreachable message or an ICMP Echo Reply message. In the case of Example 20-8, the asterisk (*) indicates the ICMP Time Exceeded message that there were no responses from the destination.

Study Resources

For today's exam topics, refer to the following resources for more study.

Resource	Chapter	Topic	Where to Find It
Foundational Resources			
CCNA Exploration Online Curriculum: Network Fundamentals	Chapter 3, "Application Layer Functionality and Protocols"	DNS Services and Protocol	Section 3.3.1
		DHCP	Section 3.3.5
	Chapter 6, "Addressing the Network—IPv4"	Static or Dynamic Addressing for End User Devices	Section 6.3.2
		Testing the Network Layer	Section 6.6
	Chapter 9, "Ethernet"	Address Resolution Protocol (ARP)	Section 9.7
CCNA Exploration Online Curriculum: Routing Protocols and Concepts	Chapter 1, "Introduction to Routing and Packet Forwarding"	Implementing Basic Addressing Schemes	Section 1.2.1
CCNA Exploration Online Curriculum: Accessing the WAN	Chapter 7, "IP Addressing Services"	DHCP	Section 7.1
CCNA Exploration Network Fundamentals Companion Guide	Chapter 3, "Application Layer Functionality and Protocols"	DNS Services and Protocol	pp. 77–81
		DHCP	pp. 87–89
	Chapter 6, "Addressing the Network: IPv4"	Static or Dynamic Addressing for End User Devices	pp. 200–201
		Testing the Network Layer	pp. 228–235
	Chapter 9, "Ethernet"	Address Resolution Protocol (ARP)	pp. 355–361
CCNA Exploration Routing Protocols and Concepts Companion Guide	Chapter 1, "Introduction to Routing and Packet Forwarding"	Implementing Basic Addressing Schemes	pp. 24–25
CCNA Exploration Accessing the WAN Companion Guide	Chapter 7, "IP Addressing Services"	DHCP	pp. 431–460
ICND1 Official Exam Certification Guide	Chapter 5, "Fundamentals of IP Addressing and Routing"	Network Layer Utilities	pp. 121–125

Resource	Chapter	Topic	Where to Find It
ICND1 Authorized Self-Study Guide	Chapter 1, "Building a Simple Network"	IP Network Addressing	pp. 58–62
		Exploring the Packet Delivery Process	pp. 86–99
	Chapter 4, "LAN Connections"	Exploring the Packet Delivery Process	pp. 295–305
		Using a Cisco Router as a DHCP Server	pp. 317–323
Supplemental Resources			
CCNA Flash Cards and Exam Practice Pack	ICND1, Section 2	Understanding TCP/IP	pp. 38–68

Basic IPv6 Concepts

CCNA 640-802 Exam Topics

- Describe IPv6 addresses.
- Describe the technological requirements for running IPv6 in conjunction with IPv4 (including protocols, dual stack, tunneling).

Key Topics

In the early 1990s, the Internet Engineering Task Force (IETF) grew concerned about the exhaustion of the IPv4 network addresses and began to look for a replacement for this protocol. This activity led to the development of what is now known as IPv6. Today's review focuses on the rapidly emerging replacement for IPv4.

> **Note** The study resources detail basic IPv6 addressing and routing configuration. Although interesting to read and practice on real equipment, IPv6 configuration is not a CCNA objective. Therefore, it will not be a part of our Key Topics. However, by practicing configuration tasks you will also be reinforcing basic IPv6 concepts.

Overview of IPv6

The capability to scale networks for future demands requires a limitless supply of IP addresses and improved mobility that private addressing and NAT alone cannot meet. IPv6 satisfies the increasingly complex requirements of hierarchical addressing that IPv4 does not provide.

Table 19-1 compares the binary and alphanumeric representations of IPv4 and IPv6 addresses.

Table 19-1   IPv4 and IPv6 Address Comparison

	IPv4 (4 octets)	IPv6 (16 octets)
Binary Representation	11000000.10101000. 00001010.01100101	10100101.00100100. 01110010.11010011. 00101100.10000000 11011101.00000010 00000000.00101001 11101100.01111010 00000000.00101011 11101010.01110011
Alphanumeric Representation	192.168.10.101	A524:72D3:2C80:DD02: 0029:EC7A:002B:EA73
Total IP Addresses	4,294,467,295 or 2^{32}	$3.4 * 10^{38}$ or 2^{128}

An IPv6 address is a 128-bit binary value, which can be displayed as 32 hexadecimal digits. IPv6 should provide sufficient addresses for future Internet growth needs for many years to come.

IPv6 is a powerful enhancement to IPv4. Several features in IPv6 offer functional improvements.

- **Larger address space:** Larger address space includes several enhancements:
  - Improved global reachability and flexibility
  - The aggregation of prefixes that are announced in routing tables
  - Multihoming to several ISPs
  - Autoconfiguration that can include data-link layer addresses in the address space
  - Plug-and-play options
  - Public-to-private readdressing end to end without address translation
  - Simplified mechanisms for address renumbering and modification

- **Simpler header:** A simpler header offers several advantages over IPv4:
  - Better routing efficiency for performance and forwarding-rate scalability
  - No broadcasts and thus no potential threat of broadcast storms
  - No requirement for processing checksums
  - Simpler and more efficient extension header mechanisms
  - Flow labels for per-flow processing with no need to open the transport inner packet to identify the various traffic flows

- **Mobility and security:** Mobility and security help ensure compliance with mobile IP and IPsec standards functionality. Mobility enables people with mobile network devices—many with wireless connectivity—to move around in networks:
  - IPv4 does not automatically enable mobile devices to move without breaks in established network connections.
  - In IPv6, mobility is built in, which means that any IPv6 node can use mobility when necessary.
  - IPsec is enabled on every IPv6 node and is available for use, making the IPv6 Internet more secure.

- **Transition strategies:** You can incorporate existing IPv4 capabilities with the added features of IPv6 in several ways:
  - You can implement a dual-stack method, with both IPv4 and IPv6 configured on the interface of a network device.
  - You can use tunneling, which will become more prominent as the adoption of IPv6 grows.
  - Cisco IOS Software Release 12.3(2)T and later include Network Address Translation-Protocol Translation (NAT-PT) between IPv6 and IPv4.

IPv6 Address Structure

You know the 32-bit IPv4 address as a series of four 8-bit fields, separated by dots. However, larger 128-bit IPv6 addresses need a different representation because of their size.

Conventions for Writing IPv6 Addresses

IPv6 conventions use 32 hexadecimal numbers, organized into 8 quartets of 4 hex digits separated by a colon, to represent a 128-bit IPv6 address. For example:

> 2340:1111:AAAA:0001:1234:5678:9ABC

To make things a little easier, two conventions allow you to shorten what must be typed for an IPv6 address:

- Omit the leading 0s in any given quartet.

- Represent 1 or more consecutive quartets of all hex 0s with a double colon (::), but only for one such occurrence in a given address.

Note   The term quartet comes from Wendell Odom's book *CCNA ICND2 Official Exam Certification Guide Second Edition*. For IPv6, a quartet is one set of four hex digits. Eight quartets are in each IPv6 address.

For example, consider the following address. The bold digits represent digits in which the address could be abbreviated.

> FE00:**0000:0000:0001**:**0000:0000:0000:0056**

This address has two locations in which one or more quartets have four hex 0s, so two main options exist for abbreviating this address, using the :: abbreviation in one or the other location. The following two options show the two briefest valid abbreviations:

- FE00::1:0:0:56

- FE00:0:0:1::56

In the first example, the second and third quartets preceding 0001 were replaced with ::. In the second example, the fifth, sixth, and seventh quartets were replaced with ::. In particular, note that the :: abbreviation, meaning "one or more quartets of all 0s," cannot be used twice, because that would be ambiguous. So, the abbreviation FE00::1::56 would not be valid.

Conventions for Writing IPv6 Prefixes

IPv6 prefixes represent a range or block of consecutive IPv6 addresses. The number that represents the range of addresses, called a *prefix*, is usually seen in IP routing tables, just like you see IP subnet numbers in IPv4 routing tables.

As with IPv4, when writing or typing a prefix in IPv6, the bits past the end of the prefix length are all binary 0s. The following IPv6 address is an example of an address assigned to a host:

> 2000:1234:5678:9ABC:1234:5678:9ABC:1111/64

The prefix in which this address resides would be as follows:

> 2000:1234:5678:9ABC:**0000:0000:0000:0000**/64

When abbreviated, this would be

> 2000:1234:5678:9ABC::/64

If the prefix length does not fall on a quartet boundary (is not a multiple of 16), the prefix value should list all the values in the last quartet. For example, assume the prefix length in the previous example is /56. So, by convention, the rest of the fourth quartet should be written, after being set to binary 0s, as follows:

> 2000:1234:5678:9A**00**::/56

The following list summarizes some key points about how to write IPv6 prefixes:

- The prefix has the same value as the IP addresses in the group for the first number of bits, as defined by the prefix length.

- Any bits after the prefix-length number of bits are binary 0s.

- The prefix can be abbreviated with the same rules as IPv6 addresses.

- If the prefix length is not on a quartet boundary, write down the value for the entire quartet.

Table 19-2 shows several sample prefixes, their format, and a brief explanation.

Table 19-2   Example IPv6 Prefixes and Their Meanings

Prefix	Explanation	Incorrect Alternative
2000::/3	All addresses whose first 3 bits are equal to the first 3 bits of hex number 2000 (bits are 001)	2000/3 (omits ::) 2::/3 (omits the rest of the first quartet)
2340:1140::/26	All addresses whose first 26 bits match the listed hex number	2340:114::/26 (omits the last digit in the second quartet)
2340:1111::/32	All addresses whose first 32 bits match the listed hex number	2340:1111/32 (omits ::)

IPv6 Global Unicast Address

IPv6 has an address format that enables aggregation upward eventually to the ISP. An IPv6 global unicast address is globally unique. Similar to a public IPv4 address, it can be routed in the Internet without any modification. An IPv6 global unicast address consists of a 48-bit global routing prefix and a 16-bit subnet ID, as shown in Figure 19-1.

Figure 19-1   Global Unicast Address

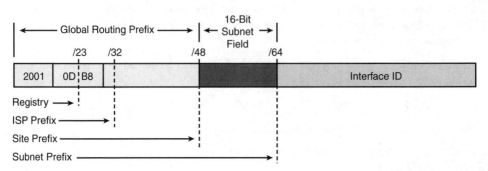

The current global unicast address that is assigned by the IANA uses the range of addresses that start with binary value 001 (2000::/3), which is one-eighth of the total IPv6 address space and is the largest block of assigned addresses.

Reserved, Private, and Loopback Addresses

The IETF reserves a portion of the IPv6 address space for various uses, both present and future. Reserved addresses represent 1/256 of the total IPv6 address space. Some of the other types of IPv6 addresses come from this block.

A block of IPv6 addresses is set aside for private addresses, just as is done in IPv4. These private addresses are local only to a particular link or site and therefore are never routed outside a particular company network. Private addresses have a first-octet value of FE in hexadecimal notation, with the next hexadecimal digit being a value from 8 to F.

These addresses are further divided into two types, based on their scope:

- **Site-local addresses**: These are for an entire site or organization. However, the use of site-local addresses is problematic and is being deprecated as of 2003 by RFC 3879. In hexadecimal, site-local addresses begin with FE and then C to F for the third hexadecimal digit. So, these addresses begin with FEC, FED, FEE, or FEF.

- **Link-local addresses**: These have a smaller scope than site-local addresses; they refer to only a particular physical link (physical network). Routers do not forward datagrams using link-local addresses, not even within the organization; they are only for local communication on a particular physical network segment. They are used for link communications such as automatic address configuration, neighbor discovery, and router discovery. Many IPv6 routing protocols also use link-local addresses. Link-local addresses begin with FE and then have a value from 8 to B for the third hexadecimal digit. So, these addresses start with FE8, FE9, FEA, or FEB.

Just as in IPv4, a provision has been made for a special loopback IPv6 address for testing. The loopback address is 0:0:0:0:0:0:0:1, which normally is expressed using zero compression as ::1.

The IPv6 Interface ID and EUI-64 Format

Figure 19-1 showed the format of an IPv6 global unicast address, with the second half of the address called the host or interface ID. The value of the interface ID portion of a global unicast address can be set to any value, as long as no other host in the same subnet attempts to use the same value. However, the size of the interface ID was chosen to allow easy autoconfiguration of IP addresses by plugging the MAC address of a network card into the interface ID field in an IPv6 address.

MAC addresses are 6 bytes (48 bits) in length. So to complete the 64-bit interface ID, IPv6 fills in 2 more bytes by separating the MAC address into two 3-byte halves. It then inserts hex FFFE in between the halves and sets the seventh bit in the first byte to binary 1 to form the interface ID field. Figure 19-2 shows this format, called the EUI-64 format (EUI stands for Extended Unique Identifier).

Figure 19-2   IPv6 Address Format with Interface ID and EUI-64

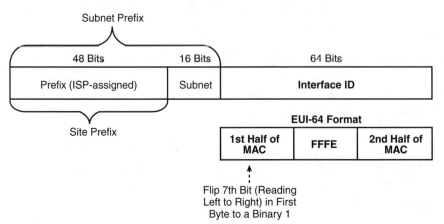

For example, the following two lines list a host's MAC address and corresponding EUI-64 format interface ID, assuming the use of an address configuration option that uses the EUI-64 format:

- **MAC Address:** 0034:5678:9ABC

- **EUI-64 Interface ID:** 0234:56FF:FE78:9ABC

Note   To change the seventh bit (reading left to right) in the example, convert hex 00 to binary 00000000, change the seventh bit to 1 (00000010), and then convert back to hex, for hex 02 as the first two digits.

IPv6 Address Management

Two options exist for static IPv6 address configuration for both routers and hosts:

- Static configuration of the entire address

- Static configuration of a /64 prefix with the host calculating its EUI-64 interface ID to complete the IP address.

IPv6 supports two methods of dynamic configuration of IPv6 addresses:

- **DHCPv6:** Works the same conceptually as DHCP in IPv4.

- **Stateless autoconfiguration:** A host dynamically learns the /64 prefix through the IPv6 Neighbor Discovery Protocol (NDP) and then calculates the rest of its address by using an EUI-64 interface ID based on its network interface card (NIC) MAC address.

Transitioning to IPv6

The transition from IPv4 to IPv6 does not require upgrades on all nodes at the same time. Many transition mechanisms enable smooth integration of IPv4 and IPv6. Other mechanisms that allow IPv4 nodes to communicate with IPv6 nodes are available. Different situations demand different strategies. Different transition mechanisms include the following:

- **Dual stacking:** An integration method in which a node has implementation and connectivity to both an IPv4 and IPv6 network. This is the recommended option and involves running IPv4 and IPv6 at the same time.

- **Tunneling:** Several tunneling techniques are available:

  - **Manually configured tunnels (MCT):** An IPv6 packet is encapsulated within the IPv4 protocol. This method requires dual-stack routers.

  - **Dynamic 6to4 tunnels:** This term refers to a specific type of dynamically created tunnel, typically done on the IPv4 Internet, in which the IPv4 addresses of the tunnel endpoints can be dynamically found based on the destination IPv6 address.

  - **Intrasite Automatic Tunnel Addressing Protocol (ISATAP):** Another dynamic tunneling method, typically used inside an enterprise. Unlike 6to4 tunnels, ISATAP tunnels do not work if IPv4 NAT is used between the tunnel endpoints.

  - **Teredo tunneling:** This method allows dual-stack hosts to create a tunnel to another host, with the host itself both creating the IPv6 packet and encapsulating the packet inside an IPv4 header.

- **NAT-Protocol Translation (NAT-PT):** This transition option allows direct communication between IPv4-only hosts and IPv6-only hosts. These translations are more complex than IPv4 NAT. At this time, this translation technique is the least favorable option and should be used as a last resort.

Remember this advice: "Dual stack where you can; tunnel where you must." These two methods are the most common techniques to transition from IPv4 to IPv6.

Table 19-3 summarizes the transition options for IPv6.

Table 19-3   Summary of IPv6 Transition Options

Name	Particular Type	Description
Dual stack	N/A	Supports both protocols and sends IPv4 to IPv4 hosts and IPv6 to IPv6 hosts.
Tunnel	MCT	Tunnel is manually configured; sends IPv6 through IPv4 network, typically between routers.
Tunnel	6to4	Tunnel endpoints are dynamically discovered; sends IPv6 through IPv4 network, typically between routers.
Tunnel	ISATAP	Tunnel endpoints are dynamically discovered; sends IPv6 through IPv4 network between routers; does not support IPv4 NAT.
Tunnel	Teredo	Typically used by hosts; host creates IPv6 packet and encapsulates in IPv4.
NAT-PT	N/A	Router translates between IPv4 and IPv6; allows IPv4 hosts to communicate with IPv6 hosts.

Study Resources

For today's exam topics, refer to the following resources for more study.

Resource	Chapter	Topic	Where to Find It
Foundational Resources			
CCNA Exploration Online Curriculum: Network Fundamentals	Chapter 6, "Addressing the Network—IPv4"	Overview of IPv6	Section 6.3.6
CCNA Exploration Online Curriculum: Accessing the WAN	Chapter 7, "IP Addressing Services"	IPv6	Section 7.3
CCNA Exploration Network Fundamentals Companion Guide	Chapter 6, "Addressing the Network: IPv4"	Overview of IPv6	pp. 235–236
CCNA Exploration Accessing the WAN Companion Guide	Chapter 7, "IP Addressing Services"	IPv6	pp. 485–511
ICND2 Official Exam Certification Guide	Chapter 17, "IP Version 6"	All topics within the	pp. 580–612
ICND2 Authorized Self-Study Guide	Chapter 6, "Managing Address Space with NAT and IPv6"	Transitioning to IPv6	pp. 270–287
Supplemental Resources			
CCNA Flash Cards and Exam Practice Pack	ICND2, Section 8	Managing Address Space with NAT and IPv6	pp. 538–568
CCNA Video Mentor	ICND2, Lab8	IPv6 Subnetting and Address Configuration	pp. 83–86 and DVD

Part IV

Routing Concepts and Configuration

Day 18:   Basic Routing Concepts

Day 17:   Connecting and Booting Routers

Day 16:   Basic Router Configuration and Verification

Day 15:   Managing Cisco IOS and Configuration Files

Day 14:   Static, Default, and RIP Routing

Day 13:   EIGRP Routing

Day 12:   OSPF Routing

Day 11:   Troubleshooting Routing

Basic Routing Concepts

- Describe basic routing concepts (including packet forwarding, router lookup process).
- Compare and contrast methods of routing and routing protocols.

Key Topics

Today we review basic routing concepts, including exactly how a packet is processed by intermediary devices (routers) on its way from source to decision. We then review the basic routing methods, including connected, static, and dynamic routes. Because dynamic routing is such a large CCNA topic area, we spend some time discussing classifications as well as the basic features of distance vector and link-state routing protocols.

> **Note** The CCNA Exploration material for today's exam topics is rather extensive. In most cases, the material takes the student way beyond the scope of the CCNA. In particular, Chapter 8, "The Routing Table: A Closer Look," should not be a top priority for your review today. However, if you are using Exploration material to review, scan all the relevant chapters and focus on those topics you are weak in.

Packet Forwarding

Packet forwarding by routers is accomplished through path determination and switching functions. The path determination function is the process of how the router determines which path to use when forwarding a packet. To determine the best path, the router searches its routing table for a network address that matches the packet's destination IP address.

One of three path determinations results from this search:

- **Directly connected network:** If the destination IP address of the packet belongs to a device on a network that is directly connected to one of the router's interfaces, that packet is forwarded directly to that device. This means that the destination IP address of the packet is a host address on the same network as this router's interface.
- **Remote network:** If the destination IP address of the packet belongs to a remote network, the packet is forwarded to another router. Remote networks can be reached only by forwarding packets to another router.
- **No route determined:** If the destination IP address of the packet does not belong to either a connected or remote network, and the router does not have a default route, the packet is discarded. The router sends an Internet Control Message Protocol (ICMP) Unreachable message to the source IP address of the packet.

In the first two results, the router completes the process by switching the packet out the correct interface. It does this by reencapsulating the IP packet into the appropriate Layer 2 data-link frame format for the exit interface. The type of Layer 2 encapsulation is determined by the type of interface. For example, if the exit interface is Fast Ethernet, the packet is encapsulated in an Ethernet frame. If the exit interface is a serial interface configured for PPP, the IP packet is encapsulated in a PPP frame.

Path Determination and Switching Function Example

Most of the study resources have detailed examples with excellent graphics that explain the path deter-mination and switching functions performed by routers as a packet travels from source to destination.

Although we do not have an abundance of room here to repeat those graphics, we can textually review an example using one graphic, shown in Figure 18-1.

Figure 18-1   Packet Forwarding Sample Topology

For brevity, only the last two octets of the MAC address are shown in the figure.

1. PC1 has a packet to be sent to PC2.

   Using the AND operation on the destination's IP address and PC1's subnet mask, PC1 has determined that the IP source and IP destination addresses are on different networks. Therefore, PC1 checks its Address Resolution Protocol (ARP) table for the IP address of the default gateway and its associated MAC address. It then encapsulates the packet in an Ethernet header and forwards it to R1.

2. Router R1 receives the Ethernet frame.

   Router R1 examines the destination MAC address, which matches the MAC address of the receiving interface, FastEthernet 0/0. R1 will therefore copy the frame into its buffer.

   R1 decapsulates the Ethernet frame and reads the destination IP address. Because it does not match any of R1's directly connected networks, the router consults its routing table to route this packet.

   R1 searches the routing table for a network address and subnet mask that would include this packet's destination IP address as a host address on that network. The entry with the longest match (longest prefix) is selected. R1 then encapsulates the packet in the appropriate frame format for the exit interface and switches the frame to the interface (FastEthernet 0/1 in our example). The interface then forwards it to the next hop.

3. Packet arrives at Router R2.

   R2 performs the same functions as R1, except this time the exit interface is a serial interface—not Ethernet. Therefore, R2 encapsulates the packet in the appropriate frame format used by the serial interface and sends it to R3. For our example, assume the interface is using High-Level Data Link Control (HDLC), which uses the data-link address 0x8F. Remember, there are no MAC addresses on serial interfaces.

4. Packet arrives at R3.

   R3 decapsulates the data-link HDLC frame. The search of the routing table results in a net-work that is one of R3's directly connected networks. Because the exit interface is a directly connected Ethernet network, R3 needs to resolve the destination IP address of the packet with a destination MAC address.

   R3 searches for the packet's destination IP address of 192.168.4.10 in its ARP cache. If the entry is not in the ARP cache, R3 sends an ARP request out its FastEthernet 0/0 interface.

PC2 sends back an ARP reply with its MAC address. R3 updates its ARP cache with an entry for 192.168.4.10 and the MAC address returned in the ARP reply.

The IP packet is encapsulated into a new data-link Ethernet frame and sent out R3's FastEthernet 0/0 interface.

5. Ethernet frame with encapsulated IP packet arrives at PC2.

PC2 examines the destination MAC address, which matches the MAC address of the receiving interface—that is, its own Ethernet NIC. PC2 will therefore copy the rest of the frame. PC2 sees that the Ethernet Type field is 0x800, which means that the Ethernet frame contains an IP packet in the data portion of the frame. PC2 decapsulates the Ethernet frame and passes the IP packet to its operating system's IP process.

Routing Methods

A router can learn routes from three basic sources:

- **Directly connected routes**: Automatically entered in the routing table when an interface is activated with an IP address

- **Static routes**: Manually configured by the network administrator and are entered in the routing table if the exit interface for the static route is active

- **Dynamic routes**: Learned by the routers through sharing routes with other routers that use the same routing protocol.

In many cases, the complexity of the network topology, the number of networks, and the need for the network to automatically adjust to changes require the use of a dynamic routing protocol. Dynamic routing certainly has several advantages over static routing; however, static routing is still used in networks today. In fact, networks typically use a combination of both static and dynamic routing.

Table 18-1 compares dynamic and static routing features. From this comparison, you can list the advantages of each routing method. The advantages of one method are the disadvantages of the other.

Table 18-1   Dynamic Versus Static Routing

Feature	Dynamic Routing	Static Routing
Configuration complexity	Generally independent of the network size	Increases with network size
Required administrator knowledge	Advanced knowledge required	No extra knowledge required
Topology changes	Automatically adapts to topology changes	Administrator intervention required
Scaling	Suitable for simple and complex topologies	Suitable for simple topologies
Security	Less secure	More secure
Resource usage	Uses CPU, memory, and link bandwidth	No extra resources needed
Predictability	Route depends on the current topology	Route to destination is always the same

Classifying Dynamic Routing Protocols

Figure 18-2 shows a timeline of IP routing protocols along with a chart that will help you memorize the various ways to classify routing protocols.

Figure 18-2   Routing Protocols' Evolution and Classification

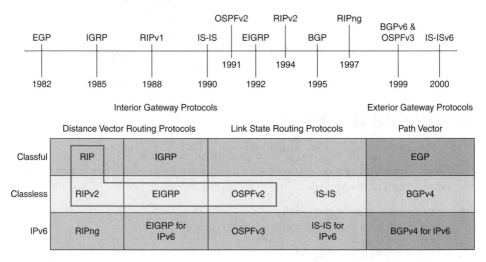

The highlighted routing protocols in the figure are the focus of the CCNA exam.

Routing protocols can be classified into different groups according to their characteristics:

- IGP or EGP
- Distance vector or link-state
- Classful or classless

IGP and EGP

An autonomous system (AS) is a collection of routers under a common administration that presents a common, clearly defined routing policy to the Internet. Typical examples are a large company's internal network and an ISP's network. Most company networks are not autonomous systems, only a network within their own ISP's autonomous system. Because the Internet is based on the autonomous system concept, two types of routing protocols are required:

- **Interior Gateway Protocols (IGP):** Used for intra-AS routing—that is, routing inside an AS
- **Exterior Gateway Protocols (EGP):** Used for inter-AS routing—that is, routing between autonomous systems

Distance Vector Routing Protocols

Distance vector means that routes are advertised as vectors of distance and direction. Distance is defined in terms of a metric such as hop count, and direction is the next-hop router or exit interface. Distance vector protocols typically use the Bellman-Ford algorithm for the best-path route determination.

Some distance vector protocols periodically send complete routing tables to all connected neighbors. In large networks, these routing updates can become enormous, causing significant traffic on the links.

Although the Bellman-Ford algorithm eventually accumulates enough knowledge to maintain a database of reachable networks, the algorithm does not allow a router to know the exact topology of an internetwork. The router knows only the routing information received from its neighbors.

Distance vector protocols use routers as signposts along the path to the final destination. The only information a router knows about a remote network is the distance or metric to reach that network and which path or interface to use to get there. Distance vector routing protocols do not have an actual map of the network topology.

Distance vector protocols work best in situations where

- The network is simple and flat and does not require a hierarchical design.

- The administrators do not have enough knowledge to configure and troubleshoot link-state protocols.

- Specific types of networks, such as hub-and-spoke networks, are being implemented.

- Worst-case convergence times in a network are not a concern.

Link-State Routing Protocols

In contrast to distance vector routing protocol operation, a router configured with a link-state routing protocol can create a "complete view," or topology, of the network by gathering information from all the other routers. Think of a link-state routing protocol as having a complete map of the network topology. The signposts along the way from source to destination are not necessary, because all link-state routers are using an identical "map" of the network. A link-state router uses the link-state information to create a topology map and to select the best path to all destination networks in the topology.

With some distance vector routing protocols, routers send periodic updates of their routing information to their neighbors. Link-state routing protocols do not use periodic updates. After the network has converged, a link-state update is sent only when there is a change in the topology.

Link-state protocols work best in situations where

- The network design is hierarchical, usually occurring in large networks.

- The administrators have a good knowledge of the implemented link-state routing protocol.

- Fast convergence of the network is crucial.

Classful Routing Protocols

Classful routing protocols do not send subnet mask information in routing updates. The first routing protocols, such as Routing Information Protocol (RIP), were classful. This was at a time when network addresses were allocated based on classes: Class A, B, or C. A routing protocol did not need to include the subnet mask in the routing update because the network mask could be determined based on the first octet of the network address.

Classful routing protocols can still be used in some of today's networks, but because they do not include the subnet mask, they cannot be used in all situations. Classful routing protocols cannot be used when a network is subnetted using more than one subnet mask. In other words, classful routing protocols do not support variable-length subnet masking (VLSM).

Other limitations exist to classful routing protocols, including their inability to support discontiguous networks and supernets. Classful routing protocols include Routing Information Protocol version 1 (RIPv1) and Interior Gateway Routing Protocol (IGRP).

Classless Routing Protocols

Classless routing protocols include the subnet mask with the network address in routing updates. Today's networks are no longer allocated based on classes, and the subnet mask cannot be determined by the value of the first octet. Classless routing protocols are required in most networks today because of their support for VLSM and discontiguous networks and supernets. Classless routing protocols are Routing Information Protocol version 2 (RIPv2), Enhanced IGRP (EIGRP), Open Shortest Path First (OSPF), Intermediate System-to-Intermediate System (IS-IS), and Border Gateway Protocol (BGP).

Dynamic Routing Metrics

There are cases when a routing protocol learns of more than one route to the same destination from the same routing source. To select the best path, the routing protocol must be able to evaluate and differentiate among the available paths. A *metric* is used for this purpose. Two different routing protocols might choose different paths to the same destination because of using different metrics. Metrics used in IP routing protocols include the following:

- **RIP—Hop count:** Best path is chosen by the route with the lowest hop count.

- **IGRP and EIGRP—Bandwidth, delay, reliability, and load:** Best path is chosen by the route with the smallest composite metric value calculated from these multiple parameters. By default, only bandwidth and delay are used.

- **IS-IS and OSPF—Cost:** Best path is chosen by the route with the lowest cost. The Cisco implementation of OSPF uses bandwidth to determine the cost.

The metric associated with a certain route can be best viewed using the **show ip route** command. The metric value is the second value in the brackets for a routing table entry. In Example 18-1, R2 has a route to the 192.168.8.0/24 network that is two hops away.

Example 18-1   Routing Table for R2

```
R2#show ip route

<output omitted>

Gateway of last resort is not set

R 192.168.1.0/24 [120/1] via 192.168.2.1, 00:00:24, Serial0/0/0
```

```
C 192.168.2.0/24 is directly connected, Serial0/0/0
C 192.168.3.0/24 is directly connected, FastEthernet0/0
C 192.168.4.0/24 is directly connected, Serial0/0/1
R 192.168.5.0/24 [120/1] via 192.168.4.1, 00:00:26, Serial0/0/1
R 192.168.6.0/24 [120/1] via 192.168.2.1, 00:00:24, Serial0/0/0
                 [120/1] via 192.168.4.1, 00:00:26, Serial0/0/1
R 192.168.7.0/24 [120/1] via 192.168.4.1, 00:00:26, Serial0/0/1
R 192.168.8.0/24 [120/2] via 192.168.4.1, 00:00:26, Serial0/0/1
```

Notice in the output that one network, 192.168.6.0/24, has two routes. RIP will load balance between these equal-cost routes. All the other routing protocols are capable of automatically load-balancing traffic for up to four equal-cost routes by default. EIGRP is also capable of load-balancing across unequal-cost paths.

Administrative Distance

There can be times when a router learns a route to a remote network from more than one routing source. For example, a static route might have been configured for the same network/subnet mask that was learned dynamically by a dynamic routing protocol, such as RIP. The router must choose which route to install.

Although less common, more than one dynamic routing protocol can be deployed in the same network. In some situations, it might be necessary to route the same network address using multiple routing protocols such as RIP and OSPF. Because different routing protocols use different metrics—RIP uses hop count and OSPF uses bandwidth—it is not possible to compare metrics to determine the best path.

Administrative distance (AD) defines the preference of a routing source. Each routing source—including specific routing protocols, static routes, and even directly connected networks—is prioritized in order of most to least preferable using an AD value. Cisco routers use the AD feature to select the best path when they learn about the same destination network from two or more different routing sources.

The AD value is an integer value from 0 to 255. The lower the value, the more preferred the route source. An administrative distance of 0 is the most preferred. Only a directly connected network has an AD of 0, which cannot be changed. An AD of 255 means the router will not believe the source of that route, and it will not be installed in the routing table.

In the routing table shown in Example 18-1, the AD value is the first value listed in the brackets. You can see that the AD value for RIP routes is 120. You can also verify the AD value with the **show ip protocols** command as demonstrated in Example 18-2.

Example 18-2   Verifying the AD Value with the show ip protocols Command

```
R2#show ip protocols

Routing Protocol is "rip"
  Sending updates every 30 seconds, next due in 12 seconds
  Invalid after 180 seconds, hold down 180, flushed after 240
  Outgoing update filter list for all interfaces is not set
```

```
Incoming update filter list for all interfaces is not set
Redistributing: rip
Default version control: send version 1, receive any version
  Interface           Send  Recv  Triggered RIP  Key-chain
  Serial0/0/1          1     2 1
  FastEthernet0/0      1     2 1
Automatic network summarization is in effect
Maximum path: 4
Routing for Networks:
  192.168.3.0
  192.168.4.0
Passive Interface(s):
Routing Information Sources:
  Gateway         Distance      Last Update
  192.168.4.1        120
Distance: (default is 120)
```

Table 18-2 shows a chart of the different administrative distance values for various routing protocols.

Table 18-2   Default Administrative Distances

Route Source	AD
Connected	0
Static	1
EIGRP summary route	5
External BGP	20
Internal EIGRP	90
IGRP	100
OSPF	110
IS-IS	115
RIP	120
External EIGRP	170
Internal BGP	200

IGP Comparison Summary

Table 18-3 compares several features of the currently most popular IGPs: RIPv2, OSPF, and EIGRP.

Table 18-3   Comparing Features of IGPs: RIPv2, OSPF, and EIGRP

Features	RIPv2	OSPF	EIGRP
Metric	Hop count	Bandwidth	Function of bandwidth, delay
Sends periodic updates	Yes (30 seconds)	No	No
Full or partial routing updates	Full	Partial	Partial
Where updates are sent	(224.0.0.9)	(224.0.0.5, 224.0.0.6)	(224.0.0.10)
Route considered to unreachable	16 hops	Depends on MaxAge of LSA, which is never incremented past 3,600 seconds	A delay of all 1s
Supports unequal-cost load balancing	No	No	Yes

Routing Loop Prevention

Without preventive measures, distance vector routing protocols could cause severe routing loops in the network. A routing loop is a condition in which a packet is continuously transmitted within a series of routers without ever reaching its intended destination network. A routing loop can occur when two or more routers have inaccurate routing information to a destination network.

A number of mechanisms are available to eliminate routing loops, primarily with distance vector routing protocols. These mechanisms include the following:

- **Defining a maximum metric to prevent count to infinity:** To eventually stop the incrementing of a metric during a routing loop, "infinity" is defined by setting a maximum metric value. For example, RIP defines infinity as 16 hops—an"unreachable" metric. When the routers "count to infinity," they mark the route as unreachable.

- **Hold-down timers:** Used to instruct routers to hold any changes that might affect routes for a specified period of time. If a route is identified as down or possibly down, any other information for that route containing the same status, or worse, is ignored for a predetermined amount of time (the hold-down period) so that the network has time to converge.

- **Split horizon:** Used to prevent a routing loop by not allowing advertisements to be sent back through the interface they originated from. The split horizon rule stops a router from incrementing a metric and then sending the route back to its source.

- **Route poisoning or poison reverse:** Used to mark the route as unreachable in a routing update that is sent to other routers. Unreachable is interpreted as a metric that is set to the maximum.

- **Triggered updates:** A routing table update that is sent immediately in response to a routing change. Triggered updates do not wait for update timers to expire. The detecting router immediately sends an update message to adjacent routers.

- **TTL Field in the IP Header:** The purpose of the Time to Live (TTL) field is to avoid a situation in which an undeliverable packet keeps circulating on the network endlessly. With TTL, the 8-bit field is set with a value by the source device of the packet. The TTL is decreased by 1 by every router on the route to its destination. If the TTL field reaches 0 before the packet arrives at its destination, the packet is discarded and the router sends an ICMP error message back to the source of the IP packet.

Link-State Routing Protocol Features

Like distance vector protocols that send routing updates to their neighbors, link-state protocols send link-state updates to neighboring routers, which in turn forward that information to their neighbors, and so on. At the end of the process, like distance vector protocols, routers that use link-state protocols add the best routes to their routing tables, based on metrics. However, beyond this level of explanation, these two types of routing protocol algorithms have little in common.

Building the LSDB

Link-state routers flood detailed information about the internetwork to all the other routers so that every router has the same information about the internetwork. Routers use this link-state database (LSDB) to calculate the currently best routes to each subnet.

OSPF, the most popular link-state IP routing protocol, advertises information in routing update messages of various types, with the updates containing information called link-state advertisements (LSAs).

Figure 18-3 shows the general idea of the flooding process, with R8 creating and flooding its router LSA. Note that Figure 18-3 shows only a subset of the information in R8's router LSA.

Figure 18-3   Flooding LSAs Using a Link-State Routing Protocol

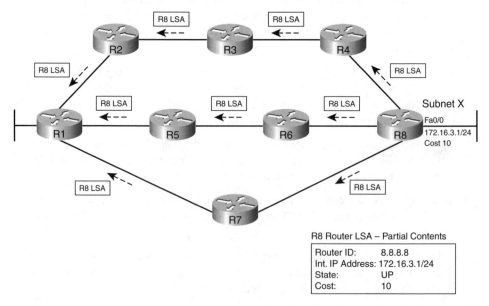

R8 Router LSA – Partial Contents

Router ID:	8.8.8.8
Int. IP Address:	172.16.3.1/24
State:	UP
Cost:	10

Figure 18-3 shows the rather basic flooding process, with R8 sending the original LSA for itself, and the other routers flooding the LSA by forwarding it until every router has a copy.

After the LSA has been flooded, even if the LSAs do not change, link-state protocols do require periodic reflooding of the LSAs by default every 30 minutes. However, if an LSA changes, the router immediately floods the changed LSA. For example, if Router R8's LAN interface failed, R8 would need to reflood the R8 LSA, stating that the interface is now down.

Calculating the Dijkstra Algorithm

The flooding process alone does not cause a router to learn what routes to add to the IP routing table. Link-state protocols must then find and add routes to the IP routing table using the Dijkstra Shortest Path First (SPF) algorithm.

The SPF algorithm is run on the LSDB to create the SPF tree. The LSDB holds all the information about all the possible routers and links. Each router must view itself as the starting point, and each subnet as the destination, and use the SPF algorithm to build its own SPF tree to pick the best route to each subnet.

Figure 18-4 shows a graphical view of the results of the SPF algorithm run by router R1 when trying to find the best route to reach subnet 172.16.3.0/24 (based on Figure 18-3).

Figure 18-4   SPF Tree to Find R1's Route to 172.16.3.0/24

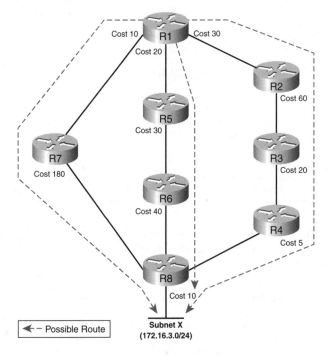

To pick the best route, a router's SPF algorithm adds the cost associated with each link between itself and the destination subnet, over each possible route. Figure 18-4 shows the costs associated with each route beside the links, with the dashed lines showing the three routes R1 finds between itself and subnet X (172.16.3.0/24).

Table 18-4 lists the three routes shown in Figure 18-4, with their cumulative costs, showing that R1's best route to 172.16.3.0/24 starts by going through R5.

Table 18-4   Comparing R1's Three Alternatives for the Route to 172.16.3.0/24

Route	Location in Figure 18-4	Cumulative Cost
R1–R7–R8	Left	10 + 180 + 10 = 200
R1–R5–R6–R8	Middle	20 + 30 + 40 + 10 = 100
R1–R2–R3–R4–R8	Right	30 + 60 + 20 + 5 + 10 = 125

As a result of the SPF algorithm's analysis of the LSDB, R1 adds a route to subnet 172.16.3.0/24 to its routing table, with the next-hop router of R5.

Convergence with Link-State Protocols

Remember, when an LSA changes, link-state protocols react swiftly, converging the network and using the currently best routes as quickly as possible. For example, imagine that the link between R5 and R6 fails in the internetwork of Figures 18-3 and 18-4. The following list explains the process R1 uses to switch to a different route.

1. R5 and R6 flood LSAs that state that their interfaces are now in a "down" state.

2. All routers run the SPF algorithm again to see if any routes have changed.

3. All routers replace routes, as needed, based on the results of SPF. For example, R1 changes its route for subnet X (172.16.3.0/24) to use R2 as the next-hop router.

These steps allow the link-state routing protocol to converge quickly—much more quickly than distance vector routing protocols.

Study Resources

For today's exam topics, refer to the following resources for more study.

Resource	Chapter	Topic	Where to Find It
Foundational Resources			
CCNA Exploration Online Curriculum: Network Fundamentals	Chapter 5, "OSI Network Layer"	Routing—How Data Packets Are Handled	Section 5.3
		Routing Processes— How Routes Are Learned	Section 5.4
CCNA Exploration Online Curriculum: Routing Protocols and Concepts	Chapter 1, "Introduction to Routing and Packet Forwarding"	Building the Routing Table	Sections 1.3.3–1.3.4
		Path Determination and Switching Function	Sections 1.4.4–1.4.5
	Chapter 3, "Introduction to Dynamic Routing Protocols"	All sections within the chapter excluding Section 3.5	Sections 3.1–3.4
	Chapter 4, "Distance Vector Routing Protocols"	All sections within the chapter	Sections 4.1–4.5
	Chapter 8, "The Routing Table: A Closer Look"	All sections within the chapter	Sections 8.1–8.3

Resource	Chapter	Topic	Where to Find It
	Chapter 10, "Link-State Routing Protocols"	All sections within the chapter	Sections 10.1–10.2
CCNA Exploration Network Fundamentals Companion Guide	Chapter 5, "OSI Network Layer"	Routing: How Data Packets Are Handled	pp. 153–163
		Routing Processes: How Routes Are Learned	pp. 163–165
CCNA Exploration Routing Protocols and Concepts Companion Guide	Chapter 1, "Introduction to Routing and Packet Forwarding"	Building the Routing Table	pp. 40–44
		Path Determination and Switching Function	pp. 50–57
	Chapter 3, "Introduction to Dynamic Routing Protocols"	All topics within the chapter	pp. 148–173
	Chapter 4, "Distance Vector Routing Protocols"	All topics within the chapter	pp. 182–212
	Chapter 8, "The Routing Table: A Closer Look"	All topics within the chapter	pp. 338–381
	Chapter 10, "Link-State Routing Protocols"	All topics within the chapter	pp. 470–492
ICND1 Official Exam Certification Guide	Chapter 5, "Fundamentals of IP Addressing and Routing"	Overview of Network Layer Functions	pp. 98–105
		IP Routing	pp. 114–118
		IP Routing Protocols	pp. 118–121
ICND2 Official Exam Certification Guide	Chapter 8, "Routing Protocol Theory"	All topics within the chapter	pp. 309–338
ICND1 Authorized Self-Study Guide	Chapter 4, "LAN Connections"	Exploring the Functions of Routing	pp 238–246
ICND2 Authorized Self-Study Guide	Chapter 3, "Medium-Sized Routed Network Construction"	Reviewing Dynamic Routing	pp. 98–123
Supplemental Resources			
CCNA Flash Cards and Exam Practice Pack	ICND1, Section 8 ICND2, Section 4	Exploring the Functions of Routing	pp. 192–216
		Routing Operations and VLSM	pp. 426–450
CCNA Video Mentor	ICND2, Lab3	RIP with Split Horizon, Route Poisoning, and Poison Reverse	pp. 53–57

Connecting and Booting Routers

CCNA 640-802 Exam Topics

- Select the appropriate media, cables, ports, and connectors to connect routers to other network devices and hosts.

- Describe the operation of Cisco routers (including router bootup process, POST, router components).

Key Topics

Today we review basic router components, the router bootup process, router interfaces, and connecting to routers. The content for today's review is rather light. Take this opportunity to review more difficult material from previous days or move on to the next day when you're done here. You might also simply take a break.

Router Internal Components

Similar to a PC, a router also includes the following internal components:

- **CPU:** Executes the operating system instructions, such as system initialization, routing functions, and network interface control.

- **RAM:** Volatile memory that stores data structures needed by the CPU while the router is powered, including

  - **Operating system:** Cisco IOS Software is copied into RAM during bootup.

  - **Running configuration file:** Stores the configuration commands that the router's IOS is currently using.

  - **IP routing table:** Stores information about directly connected and remote networks.

  - **ARP cache:** Similar to the ARP cache on a PC.

  - **Packet buffering:** Packets are temporarily stored in a buffer when received on an interface or before they exit an interface.

- **ROM:** A form of permanent storage used to store

  - Bootstrap instructions

  - Basic diagnostic software

  - Scaled-down version of IOS

- **Flash memory:** Flash memory is nonvolatile computer memory that can be electrically erased and reprogrammed. Flash is used as permanent storage for the Cisco IOS.

- **NVRAM:** Nonvolatile random-access memory, which does not lose its information when the power is turned off. NVRAM is used by Cisco IOS Software as permanent storage for the startup configuration file.

IOS

The operating system software used in Cisco routers is known as Cisco Internetwork Operating System (IOS). Like any operating system on any other computer, Cisco IOS Software is responsible for managing the hardware and software resources of the router, including allocating memory, managing processes and security, and managing file systems. Cisco IOS is a multitasking operating system that is integrated with routing, switching, internetworking, and telecommunications functions. Although Cisco IOS Software might appear to be the same on many routers, there are many different IOS images. Cisco creates many IOS images, depending on the model and the features within IOS. Typically, additional features require more flash and RAM to store and load IOS.

As with other operating systems, Cisco IOS has its own user interface. Although some routers provide a graphical user interface (GUI), the command-line interface (CLI) is a much more common method of configuring Cisco routers.

Router Bootup Process

Like all computers, a router uses a systematic process to boot. This involves testing the hardware, loading the operating system software, and performing any saved configuration commands in the saved startup configuration file. Some of the details of this process have been excluded and are examined more completely in a later course.

Figure 17-1 shows the six major phases in the bootup process:

1. Power-On Self Test (POST): Testing the router hardware
2. Loading the bootstrap program
3. Locating Cisco IOS
4. Loading Cisco IOS
5. Locating the configuration file
6. Loading the startup configuration file or entering setup mode

Use the **show version** command to verify and troubleshoot some of the basic hardware and software components of a router. The **show version** command in Example 17-1 displays information about the version of Cisco IOS Software currently running on the router, the version of the bootstrap program, and information about the hardware configuration, including the amount of system memory.

Figure 17-1   How a Router Boots

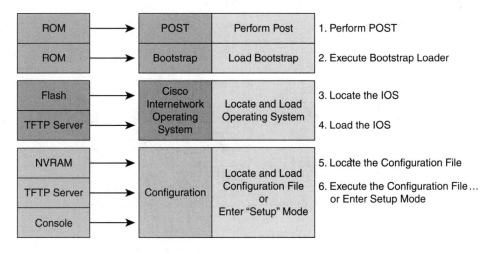

Example 17-1   show version Command Output

```
Router#show version

Cisco Internetwork Operating System Software
IOS (tm) C2600 Software (C2600-I-M), Version 12.2(28), RELEASE SOFTWARE (fc5)
Technical Support: http://www.cisco.com/techsupport
Copyright (c) 1986-2005 by cisco Systems, Inc.
Compiled Wed 27-Apr-04 19:01 by miwang
Image text-base: 0x8000808C, data-base: 0x80A1FECC

ROM: System Bootstrap, Version 12.1(3r)T2, RELEASE SOFTWARE (fc1)
Copyright (c) 2000 by cisco Systems, Inc.
ROM: C2600 Software (C2600-I-M), Version 12.2(28), RELEASE SOFTWARE (fc5)

System returned to ROM by reload
System image file is "flash:c2600-i-mz.122-28.bin"

cisco 2621 (MPC860) processor (revision 0x200) with 60416K/5120K bytes of memory.
Processor board ID JAD05190MTZ (4292891495)
M860 processor: part number 0, mask 49
Bridging software.
X.25 software, Version 3.0.0.
2 FastEthernet/IEEE 802.3 interface(s)
2 Low-speed serial(sync/async) network interface(s)
32K bytes of non-volatile configuration memory.
16384K bytes of processor board System flash (Read/Write)

Configuration register is 0x2102
```

Router Ports and Interfaces

Figure 17-2 shows the back side of a 2621 router with management ports and interfaces labeled.

Figure 17-2   Router Ports and Interfaces

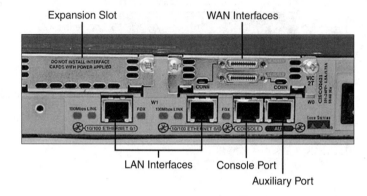

Each interface connects to a different network;
thus, each interface has an IP address/mask from that network.

Management ports are not used for packet forwarding like Ethernet and serial interfaces, but are used to connect a terminal to the router and configure it without network access. The console port must be used during initial configuration of the router. The auxiliary port can provide remote management if a modem is attached.

Routers have multiple interfaces used to connect to multiple networks. For example, a router will most likely have Fast Ethernet interfaces for connections to different LANs and also have different types of WAN interfaces used to connect a variety of serial links, including T1, DSL, and ISDN.

Router Connections

Connecting a router to a network requires a router interface connector to be coupled with a cable connector. As you can see in Figure 17-3, Cisco routers support many serial connectors including EIA/TIA-232, EIA/TIA-449, V.35, X.21, and EIA/TIA-530 standards.

For Ethernet-based LAN connections, an RJ-45 connector for the unshielded twisted-pair (UTP) cable is most commonly used.

Two types of cables can be used with Ethernet LAN interfaces:

- A straight-through, or patch, cable, with the order of the colored pins the same on each end of the cable

- A crossover cable, with pin 1 connected to pin 3 and pin 2 connected to pin 6

Figure 17-3   WAN Connections and Connectors

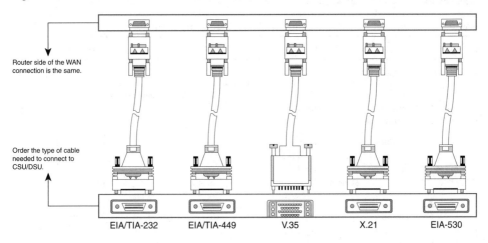

Router side of the WAN
connection is the same.

Order the type of cable
needed to connect to
CSU/DSU.

EIA/TIA-232   EIA/TIA-449   V.35   X.21   EIA-530

Straight-through cables are used for the following connections:

- Switch-to-router

- Hub-to-router

- Switch-to-PC/server

- Hub-to-PC/server

Crossover cables are used for the following connections:

- Switch-to-switch

- PC/server-to-PC/server

- Switch-to-hub

- Hub-to-hub

- Router-to-router

- Router-to-PC/server

Connecting to a router through its wireless interface will be reviewed on Day 9, "Configuring and Troubleshooting Wireless Networks."

Study Resources

For today's exam topics, refer to the following resources for more study.

Resource	Chapter	Topic	Where to Find It
Foundational Resources			
CCNA Exploration Online Curriculum: Network Fundamentals	Chapter 10, "Planning and Cabling Networks"	Making LAN Connections	Section 10.2.2
CCNA Exploration Online Curriculum: Routing Protocols and Concepts	Chapter 1, "Introduction to Routing and Packet Forwarding" Chapter 2, "Static Routing"	Inside the Router Examining the Connections to Router	Section 1.1 Section 2.1.3
CCNA Exploration Network Fundamentals Companion Guide	Chapter 10, "Planning and Cabling Networks"	Making LAN Connections	pp. 380–384
CCNA Exploration Routing Protocols and Concepts Companion Guide	Chapter 1, "Introduction to Routing and Packet Forwarding" Chapter 2, "Static Routing"	Inside the Router Examining the Connections to Router	pp. 3–24 pp. 68–71
ICND1 Official Exam Certification Guide	Chapter 13, "Operating Cisco Routers"	Installing Cisco Routers The Cisco IOS Software Boot Sequence	pp. 403–409 pp. 423–430
ICND1 Authorized Self-Study Guide	Chapter 4, "LAN Connections" Chapter 6, "Network Environment Management"	Starting a Cisco Router Discovering Neighbors on the Network	pp. 271–283 pp. 425–433
Supplemental Resources			
CCNA Flash Cards and Exam Practice Pack	ICND1, Section 9	Configuring a Cisco Router	pp. 218–250

Basic Router Configuration and Verification

CCNA 640-802 Exam Topics

- Access and utilize the router to set basic parameters (CLI/SDM).
- Connect, configure, and verify operation status of a device interface.
- Implement basic router security.
- Verify device configuration and network connectivity using ping, traceroute, telnet, SSH, or other utilities.
- Verify network connectivity (using ping, traceroute, and telnet or SSH).

Key Topic

Today we review the basic router configuration and verification commands as well as testing using the **ping**, **traceroute**, and **telnet** commands. Most of this should be very familiar to you at this point in your studies because these skills are fundamental to all other router configuration tasks.

> **Note** Cisco Security Device Manager (SDM) is a GUI-based method to access and configure the router. Reviewing SDM here would take up too much space because we would need to repeat dozens of screenshots. So for your SDM review today, refer to your Study Resources. Each has an extensive review of basic router configuration using SDM.

Basic Router Configuration

Figure 16-1 shows the topology and addressing scheme we will use to review basic router configuration and verification tasks.

When configuring a router, certain basic tasks are performed, including the following:

- Naming the router
- Setting passwords
- Configuring interfaces
- Configuring a banner
- Saving changes on a router
- Verifying basic configuration and router operations

Figure 16-1   Basic Router Configuration Topology

Device	Interface	IP Address	Subnet Mask	Default Gateway
R1	Fa0/0	192.168.1.1	255.255.255.0	N/A
R1	S0/0/0	192.168.2.1	255.255.255.0	N/A
R2	Fa0/0	192.168.3.1	255.255.255.0	N/A
R2	S0/0/0	192.168.2.2	255.255.255.0	N/A
PC1	N/A	192.168.1.10	255.255.255.0	192.168.1.1
PC2	N/A	192.168.3.10	255.255.255.0	192.168.3.1

Table 16-1 shows the basic router configuration command syntax used to configure R1 in the following example.

Table 16-1   Basic Router Configuration Command Syntax

Naming the router	Router(config)#**hostname** *name*
Setting passwords	Router(config)#**enable secret** *password*
	Router(config)#**line console 0**
	Router(config-line)#**password** *password*
	Router(config-line)#**login**
	Router(config)#**line vty 0 4**
	Router(config-line)#**password** *password*
	Router(config-line)#**login**
Configuring a message-of-the-day banner	Router(config)#**banner motd** # *message* #
Configuring an interface	Router(config)#**interface** *type number*
	Router(config-if)#**ip address** *address mask*
	Router(config-if)#**description** *description*
	Router(config-if)#**no shutdown**
Saving changes on a router	Router#**copy running-config startup-config**
Examining the output of **show** commands	Router#**show running-config**
	Router#**show ip route**
	Router#**show ip interface brief**
	Router#**show interfaces**

Let's walk through a basic configuration for R1. First, we enter privileged EXEC mode and then we enter global configuration mode:

```
Router>enable
Router#config t
```

Next, name the router and enter the encrypted password for entering privileged EXEC mode. This command overrides the older **enable password** *password* command so we are not entering that one:

```
Router(config)#hostname R1
R1(config)#enable secret class
```

Next, configure the console password and require it be entered with the **login** password:

```
R1(config)#line console 0
R1(config-line)#password cisco
R1(config-line)#login
```

Then configure the password for the Telnet lines and require it to be entered with the **login** password:

```
R1(config)#line vty 0 4
R1(config-line)#password cisco
R1(config-line)#login
```

Configure the message-of-the-day (MOTD) banner. A delimiting character such as a # is used at the beginning and at the end of the message. At a minimum, a banner should warn against unauthorized access. A good security policy would prohibit configuring a banner that "welcomes" an unauthorized user:

```
R1(config)#banner motd #
Enter TEXT message.  End with the character '#'.
******************************************
WARNING!! Unauthorized Access Prohibited!!
******************************************
#
```

Now configure the individual router interfaces with IP addresses and other information. First, enter interface configuration mode by specifying the interface type and number. Next, configure the IP address and subnet mask:

```
R1(config)#interface Serial0/0/0
R1(config-if)#ip address 192.168.2.1 255.255.255.0
```

It is good practice to configure a description on each interface to help document the network information:

```
R1(config-if)#description Ciruit#VBN32696-123 (help desk:1-800-555-1234)
```

Activate the interface:

```
R1(config-if)#no shutdown
```

In a lab environment, we add a clock rate on the DCE side. However, in production environments the service provider sets the clock:

```
R1(config-if)#clock rate 64000
```

Assuming the other side of the link is activated on R2, the serial interface will now be up. Finish R1 by configuring the FastEthernet 0/0 interface:

```
R1(config-if)#interface FastEthernet0/0
R1(config-if)#ip address 192.168.1.1 255.255.255.0
R1(config-if)#description R1 LAN
R1(config-if)#no shutdown
```

Assume R2 is fully configured and can route back to the 192.168.1.0/24 LAN attached to R1. We need to add a static route to R1 to ensure connectivity to R2's LAN. Static routing is reviewed in more detail on Day 14. For now, enter the following command:

```
R1(config)#ip route 192.168.3.0 255.255.255.0 192.168.2.2
```

To save the configuration, enter the **copy running-config startup-config** command or **copy run start**.

You can use the **show running-config** command to verify the full current configuration on the router; however, a few other basic commands can help you not only verify your configuration, but help you begin troubleshooting any potential problems.

First, make sure the networks for your interfaces are now in the routing table by using the **show ip route** command, as demonstrated in Example 16-1.

Example 16-1   The show ip route Command

```
R1#show ip route
Codes: C - connected, S - static, I - IGRP, R - RIP, M - mobile, B - BGP
       D - EIGRP, EX - EIGRP external, O - OSPF, IA - OSPF inter area
       N1 - OSPF NSSA external type 1, N2 - OSPF NSSA external type 2
       E1 - OSPF external type 1, E2 - OSPF external type 2, E - EGP
       i - IS-IS, L1 - IS-IS level-1, L2 - IS-IS level-2, ia - IS-IS inter area
       * - candidate default, U - per-user static route, o - ODR
       P - periodic downloaded static route

Gateway of last resort is not set

C    192.168.1.0/24 is directly connected, FastEthernet0/0
C    192.168.2.0/24 is directly connected, Serial0/0/0
S    192.168.3.0/24 [1/0] via 192.168.2.2
```

If a network is missing, check your interface status with the **show ip interface brief** command, as demonstrated in Example 16-2.

Example 16-2   The show ip interface brief Command

```
R1#show ip interface brief
Interface           IP-Address      OK? Method Status                Protocol
FastEthernet0/0     192.168.1.1     YES manual up                    up
FastEthernet0/1     unassigned      YES manual administratively down down
Serial0/0/0         192.168.2.1     YES manual up                    up
Serial0/0/1         unassigned      YES manual administratively down down
Vlan1               unassigned      YES manual administratively down down
```

The output from the **show ip interface brief** command provides you with three important pieces of information:

- IP address
- Line Status (column 5)
- Protocol Status (column 6)

The IP address should be correct, and the interface status should be "up" and "up". Table 16-2 summarizes the two status codes and their meanings.

Table 16-2   Interface Status Codes

Name	Location	General Meaning
Line status	First status code	Refers to the Layer 1 status—for example, is the cable installed, is it the right/wrong cable, is the device on the other end powered on?
Protocol status	Second status code	Refers generally to the Layer 2 status. It is always down if the line status is down. If the line status is up, a protocol status of down usually is caused by mismatched data link layer configuration.

Four combinations of settings exist for the status codes when troubleshooting a network. Table 16-3 lists the four combinations, along with an explanation of the typical reasons why an interface would be in that state.

Table 16-3   Combinations of Interface Status Codes

Line and Protocol Status	Typical Reasons
Administratively down, down	The interface has a shutdown command configured on it.
down, down	The interface has a no shutdown command configured, but the physical layer has a problem. For example, no cable has been attached to the interface, or with Ethernet, the switch interface on the other end of the cable is shut down, or the switch is powered off.
up, down	Almost always refers to data link layer problems, most often configuration problems. For example, serial links have this combination when one router was configured to use PPP, and the other defaults to use HDLC.
up, up	All is well, interface is functioning.

If necessary, use the more verbose **show interfaces** command if you need to track down a problem with an interface. Example 16-3 shows the output for FastEthernet 0/0.

Example 16-3   The show interfaces Command

```
R1#show interfaces fastethernet 0/0
FastEthernet0/0 is up, line protocol is up (connected)
  Hardware is Lance, address is 0007.eca7.1511 (bia 00e0.f7e4.e47e)
  Description: R1 LAN
  Internet address is 192.168.1.1/24
  MTU 1500 bytes, BW 100000 Kbit, DLY 100 usec, rely 255/255, load 1/255
  Encapsulation ARPA, loopback not set
  ARP type: ARPA, ARP Timeout 04:00:00,
  Last input 00:00:08, output 00:00:05, output hang never
  Last clearing of "show interface" counters never
  Queueing strategy: fifo
```

```
Output queue :0/40 (size/max)
5 minute input rate 0 bits/sec, 0 packets/sec
5 minute output rate 0 bits/sec, 0 packets/sec
    81833 packets input, 27556491 bytes, 0 no buffer
    Received 0 broadcasts, 0 runts, 0 giants, 0 throttles
    1 input errors, 0 CRC, 0 frame, 0 overrun, 1 ignored, 0 abort
    0 input packets with dribble condition detected
    55794 packets output, 3929696 bytes, 0 underruns
    0 output errors, 0 collisions, 1 interface resets
    0 babbles, 0 late collision, 4 deferred
    0 lost carrier, 0 no carrier
    0 output buffer failures, 0 output buffers swapped out
```

This command has a lot of output. However, sometimes this is the only way to find a problem. Therefore, Table 16-4 parses and explains each important part of the **show interfaces** output.

Table 16-4   show interfaces Output Explanation

Output	Description
FastEthernet…is {up	down	administratively down}	Indicates whether the interface hardware is currently active or down, or whether an administrator has taken it down.
line protocol is {up	down}	Indicates whether the software processes that handle the line protocol consider the interface usable (that is, whether keepalives are successful). If the interface misses three consecutive keepalives, the line protocol is marked as down.
Hardware	Hardware type (for example, MCI Ethernet, serial communications interface [SCI], cBus Ethernet) and address.
Description	Text string description configured for the interface (max 240 characters).
Internet address	IP address followed by the prefix length (subnet mask).
MTU	Maximum transmission unit (MTU) of the interface.
BW	Bandwidth of the interface, in kilobits per second. The bandwidth parameter is used to compute routing protocol metrics and other calculations.
DLY	Delay of the interface, in microseconds.
rely	Reliability of the interface as a fraction of 255 (255/255 is 100 percent reliability), calculated as an exponential average over 5 minutes.
load	Load on the interface as a fraction of 255 (255/255 is completely saturated), calculated as an exponential average over 5 minutes.
Encapsulation	Encapsulation method assigned to an interface.
loopback	Indicates whether loopback is set.
keepalive	Indicates whether keepalives are set.
ARP type:	Type of Address Resolution Protocol (ARP) assigned.
Last input	Number of hours, minutes, and seconds since the last packet was successfully received by an interface. Useful for knowing when a dead interface failed.

Output	Description
output	Number of hours, minutes, and seconds since the last packet was successfully transmitted by an interface. Useful for knowing when a dead interface failed.
output hang	Number of hours, minutes, and seconds (or never) since the interface was last reset because of a transmission that took too long. When the number of hours in any of the previous fields exceeds 24 hours, the number of days and hours is printed. If that field overflows, asterisks are printed.
Last clearing	Time at which the counters that measure cumulative statistics shown in this report (such as number of bytes transmitted and received) were last reset to 0. Note that variables that might affect routing (for example, load and reliability) are not cleared when the counters are cleared. Asterisks indicate elapsed time too large to be displayed. Reset the counters with the **clear interface** command.
Output queue, input queue, drops	Number of packets in output and input queues. Each number is followed by a slash (/), the maximum size of the queue, and the number of packets dropped because of a full queue.
Five minute input rate, Five minute output rate	Average number of bits and packets transmitted per second in the last 5 minutes. If the interface is not in promiscuous mode, it senses network traffic that it sends and receives (rather than all network traffic). The 5-minute input and output rates should be used only as an approximation of traffic per second during a given 5-minute period. These rates are exponentially weighted averages with a time constant of 5 minutes. A period of four time constants must pass before the average will be within 2 percent of the instantaneous rate of a uniform stream of traffic over that period.
packets input	Total number of error-free packets received by the system.
bytes input	Total number of bytes, including data and MAC encapsulation, in the error-free packets received by the system.
no buffers	Number of received packets discarded because there was no buffer space in the main system. Compare with "ignored count." Broadcast storms on Ethernet are often responsible for no input buffer events.
Received...broadcasts	Total number of broadcast or multicast packets received by the interface. The number of broadcasts should be kept as low as practicable. An approximate threshold is less than 20 percent of the total number of input packets.
runts	Number of Ethernet frames that are discarded because they are smaller than the minimum Ethernet frame size. Any Ethernet frame that is less than 64 bytes is considered a runt. Runts are usually caused by collisions. If there is more than 1 runt per million bytes received, it should be investigated.
giants	Number of Ethernet frames that are discarded because they exceed the maximum Ethernet frame size. Any Ethernet frame that is larger than 1518 bytes is considered a giant.
input error	Includes runts, giants, no buffer, cyclic redundancy check (CRC), frame, overrun, and ignored counts. Other input-related errors can also cause the input error count to be increased, and some datagrams can have more than one error. Therefore, this sum might not balance with the sum of enumerated input error counts.

continues

Table 16-4   show interfaces Output Explanation *continued*

Output	Description
CRC	CRC generated by the originating LAN station or far-end device does not match the checksum calculated from the data received. On a LAN, this usually indicates noise or transmission problems on the LAN interface or the LAN bus itself. A high number of CRCs is usually the result of collisions or a station transmitting bad data.
frame	Number of packets received incorrectly having a CRC error and a noninteger number of octets. On a LAN, this is usually the result of collisions or a malfunctioning Ethernet device.
overrun	Number of times the receiver hardware was unable to hand-receive data to a hardware buffer because the input rate exceeded the ability of the receiver to handle the data.
ignored	Number of received packets ignored by the interface because the interface hardware ran low on internal buffers. These buffers are different from the system buffers mentioned in the buffer description. Broadcast storms and bursts of noise can cause the ignored count to be increased.
input packets with dribble condition detected	Dribble bit error indicates that a frame is slightly too long. This frame error counter is incremented just for informational purposes; the router accepts the frame.
packets output	Total number of messages transmitted by the system.
bytes	Total number of bytes, including data and MAC encapsulation, transmitted by the system.
underruns	Number of times that the transmitter has been running faster than the router can handle. This might never be reported on some interfaces.
output errors	Sum of all errors that prevented the final transmission of datagrams out of the interface being examined. Note that this might not balance with the sum of the enumerated output errors, because some datagrams might have more than one error, and others might have errors that do not fall into any of the specifically tabulated categories.
collisions	Number of messages retransmitted because of an Ethernet collision. This is usually the result of an overextended LAN (Ethernet or transceiver cable too long, more than two repeaters between stations, or too many cascaded multiport transceivers). A packet that collides is counted only once in output packets.
interface resets	Number of times an interface has been completely reset. This can happen if packets queued for transmission were not sent within several seconds. On a serial line, this can be caused by a malfunctioning modem that is not supplying the transmit clock signal, or it can be caused by a cable problem. If the system notices that the carrier detect line of a serial interface is up, but the line protocol is down, it periodically resets the interface in an effort to restart it. Interface resets can also occur when an interface is looped back or shut down.

Verifying Network Connectivity

As reviewed on Day 20, "Host Addressing, DHCP, and DNS," **ping** and **traceroute** are helpful tools for verifying network connectivity. These tools work for routers as well. The only difference is the command output and the command syntax.

Example 16-4 demonstrates successful **ping** output on the router.

Example 16-4   Ping Output on a Router

```
R1#ping 192.168.3.10

Type escape sequence to abort.
Sending 5, 100-byte ICMP Echos to 192.168.3.10, timeout is 2 seconds:
!!!!!
Success rate is 100 percent (5/5), round-trip min/avg/max = 1/2/4 ms
R1#
```

Unsuccessful **ping** output shows periods (.) instead of exclamation points (!) as demonstrated in Example 16-5.

Example 16-5   Unsuccessful Ping Output on a Router

```
R1#ping 192.168.3.2

Type escape sequence to abort.
Sending 5, 100-byte ICMP Echos to 192.168.3.2, timeout is 2 seconds:
.....
Success rate is 0 percent (0/5)
```

When tracing the route to the destination, use the command **traceroute** on a router instead of the **tracert** command used on a Windows PC. Example 16-6 shows output from a successful **traceroute** command.

Example 16-6   Trace Route Output on a Router

```
R1#traceroute 192.168.3.10
Type escape sequence to abort.
Tracing the route to 192.168.3.10

  1    192.168.2.2     71 msec    70 msec    72 msec
  2    192.168.3.10    111 msec   133 msec   115 msec
R1#
```

Unsuccessful traces will show the last successful hop and the asterisks for each attempt until the user cancels. To cancel the **traceroute** command on a router, use the key combination **Ctrl+Shift+6**, and then the **x** key. Example 16-7 shows unsuccessful **traceroute** output.

Example 16-7   Unsuccessful Trace Route Output on a Router

```
R1#traceroute 192.168.3.2
Type escape sequence to abort.
Tracing the route to 192.168.3.2

  1   192.168.2.2     71 msec    70 msec    72 msec
  2   *       *       *
  3   *       *       *
  4   *       *       *
  5   *
R1#
```

Using Telnet or SSH to remotely access another device also tests connectivity. More importantly, these remote access methods will test whether a device has been correctly configured so that you can access it for management purposes. This can be very important when a device is truly remote (for example, across town or in another city). Day 8, "Mitigating Security Threats and Best Practices," reviews SSH configuration and verification in greater detail.

During our basic configuration tasks earlier, we entered the commands to properly configure the Telnet lines (vty 0 4) for remote access. Example 16-8 shows a success Telnet from R1 to R2.

Example 16-8   Successful Telnet to R2

```
R1#telnet 192.168.2.2
Trying 192.168.2.2 ...



User Access Verification

Password:
R2>
```

If R2 does not have a password configured, you might see the following output shown in Example 16-9.

Example 16-9   Unsuccessful Telnet to R2: Password Not Set

```
R1#192.168.2.2
Trying 192.168.2.2 ... Open

Password required, but none set

[Connection to 192.168.2.2 closed by foreign host]
R1#
```

Study Resources

For today's exam topics, refer to the following resources for more study.

Resource	Chapter	Topic	Where to Find It
Foundational Resources			
CCNA Exploration Online Curriculum: Network Fundamentals	Chapter 11, "Configuring and Testing Your Network"	All sections within the chapter	Sections 11.1–11.4
CCNA Exploration Online Curriculum: Routing Protocols and Concepts	Chapter 1, "Introduction to Routing and Packet Forwarding"	Basic Router Configuration	Section 1.2.2
	Chapter 2, "Static Routing"	Router Configuration Review Exploring Directly Connected Networks	Section 2.2 Section 2.3
CCNA Exploration Online Curriculum: Accessing the WAN	Chapter 4, "Network Security"	Using Cisco SDM	Section 4.4
CCNA Exploration Network Fundamentals Companion Guide	Chapter 11, "Configuring and Testing Your Network"	All topics within the chapter	pp. 410–463
CCNA Exploration Routing Protocols and Concepts Companion Guide	Chapter 1, "Introduction to Routing and Packet Forwarding"	Basic Router Configuration	pp. 25–34
	Chapter 2, "Static Routing"	Router Configuration Review	pp. 71–87
		Exploring Directly Connected Networks	pp. 87–104
CCNA Exploration Accessing the WAN Companion Guide	Chapter 4, "Network Security"	Using Cisco SDM	pp. 264–275
ICND1 Official Exam Certification Guide	Chapter 13, "Operating Cisco Routers"	Cisco Router IOS CLI	pp. 409–420
	Chapter 17, "WAN Configuration"	Configuring and Troubleshooting Internet Access Routers	pp. 546–559
ICND1 Authorized Self-Study Guide	Chapter 4, "LAN Connections"	Configuring a Cisco Router	pp. 283–295
		Understanding Cisco Router Security	pp. 305–309
		Using Cisco SDM Accessing Remote Devices	pp. 309–317 pp. 323–329
	Chapter 6, "Network Environment Management"	Managing Cisco Router Startup and Configuration	pp. 433–442
ICND2 Authorized Self-Study Guide	Chapter 1, "Review of Cisco IOS for Routers and Switches"	Review of Cisco IOS for Routers and Switches	pp. 3–8

Resource	Chapter	Topic	Where to Find It
Supplemental Resources			
CCNA Flash Cards and Exam Practice Pack	ICND1, Section 9	Configuring a Cisco Router	pp. 218–250
CCNA Video Mentor	ICND1, Lab1	Navigating a Router/ Switch Command-Line Interface	pp. 3–5 and DVD
	ICND1, Lab2	Router Configuration and Managing Configuration Files	pp. 7–10 and DVD

Managing Cisco IOS and Configuration Files

CCNA 640-802 Exam Topics

- Manage IOS configuration files (save, edit, upgrade, restore).
- Manage Cisco IOS.
- Verify router hardware and software operation using SHOW & DEBUG commands.

Key Topics

IOS images and configurations files can become corrupted through intentional attacks, unintentional user errors, and device failure. To prevent these problems, you have to be able to save, back up, and restore configuration and IOS images. Today we review file management operations.

The Cisco IOS File System

Cisco IOS devices provide a feature called the Cisco IOS Integrated File System (IFS). This system allows you to create, navigate, and manipulate directories on a Cisco device. The directories available depend on the platform.

IFS Commands

Example 15-1 shows output from the **show file systems** command.

Example 15-1   Default File System for an 1841 Router

```
Router#show file systems
File Systems:

        Size(b)       Free(b)       Type    Flags   Prefixes
              -             -      opaque      rw    archive:
              -             -      opaque      rw    system:
              -             -      opaque      rw    null:
              -             -     network      rw    tftp:
         196600        194101       nvram      rw    nvram:
*      63995904      31092736        disk      rw    flash:#
              -             -      opaque      wo    syslog:
              -             -      opaque      rw    xmodem:
              -             -      opaque      rw    ymodem:
```

```
              -            -    network      rw    rcp:
              -            -    network      rw    pram:
              -            -    network      rw    ftp:
              -            -    network      rw    http:
              -            -    network      rw    scp:
              -            -    network      rw    https:
              -            -    opaque       ro    cns:
Router#
```

The columns show the amount of available and free memory in bytes and the type of file system and its permissions. Permissions include read-only (ro), write-only (wo), and read and write (rw). Although several file systems are listed, of interest to us are the TFTP, flash, and NVRAM file systems.

Notice that the flash file system has an asterisk (*) preceding it, which indicates that this is the current default file system. Recall that the bootable IOS is located in flash. Therefore, the pound symbol (#) appended to the flash listing indicates that this is a bootable disk.

Example 15-2 lists the contents of the current default file system, which in this case is flash.

Example 15-2   Default File System Is Flash

```
Router#dir
Directory of flash:/

    1  -rw-      22063220   Mar 3 2007 08:29:52 +00:00   c1841-advipservicesk9-
              mz.124-10b.bin
    2  -rw-          1038   Apr 3 2008 15:02:46 +00:00   home.shtml
    3  -rw-          1821   Apr 3 2008 15:02:46 +00:00   sdmconfig-18xx.cfg
    4  -rw-        113152   Apr 3 2008 15:02:46 +00:00   home.tar
    5  -rw-       1164288   Apr 3 2008 15:02:50 +00:00   common.tar
    6  -rw-       6036480   Apr 3 2008 15:03:00 +00:00   sdm.tar
    7  -rw-        861696   Apr 3 2008 15:03:08 +00:00   es.tar
    8  -rw-        527849   Apr 3 2008 15:02:48 +00:00   128MB.sdf
    9  -rw-       1697952   Mar 3 2007 08:48:34 +00:00   securedesktop-ios-
              3.1.1.45-k9.pkg
   10  -rw-        415090   Mar 3 2007 08:49:02 +00:00   sslclient-win-
              1.1.2.169.pkg

63995904 bytes total (31092736 bytes free)
Router#
```

Of particular interest is the first listing, which is the filename for the IOS image.

Notice that the configuration files stored in NVRAM are not shown in the output. To see these, first change directories (**cd**) to the NVRAM directory (**nvram:**). Then list the contents with the **dir** command, as shown in Example 15-3.

Example 15-3   Listing Directory Contents for NVRAM

```
Router#cd nvram:
Router#dir
Directory of nvram:/

   189  -rw-           1399          <no date>  startup-config
   190  ----             24          <no date>  private-config
   191  -rw-           1399          <no date>  underlying-config
     1  -rw-              0          <no date>  ifIndex-table


196600 bytes total (194101 bytes free)
Router#
```

The file we are most interested in as CCNA exam candidates is the startup-config configuration file.

URL Prefixes for Specifying File Locations

File locations are specified in Cisco IFS using the URL convention as shown in the example in Figure 15-1.

Figure 15-1   Using a URL to Specify TFTP Location

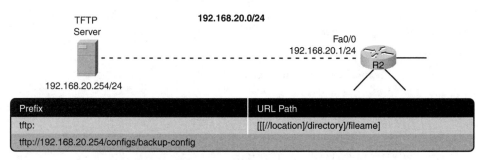

In Figure 15-1, the parts of the URL tftp://192.168.20.254/configs/backup-config can be dissected as follows:

- **tftp:** is the prefix specifying the protocol.
- Everything after the double slash (//) defines the file location.
- **192.168.20.254** is the location of the TFTP server.
- **configs** is the master directory on the TFTP server.
- **backup-config** is a sample filename.

The TFTP URL shown in Figure 15-1 is an example of a remote URL. Examples of URLs for accessing the local Cisco IFS include the following:

- flash:configs/backup-config
- system:running-config (this accesses RAM)
- nvram:startup-config

Commands for Managing Configuration Files

Knowing the URL structure is important because you use them when copying configuration files from one location to another. The Cisco IOS Software **copy** command is used to move configuration files from one component or device to another, such as RAM, NVRAM, or a TFTP server. Figure 15-2 shows the command syntax.

Figure 15-2   copy Command Syntax

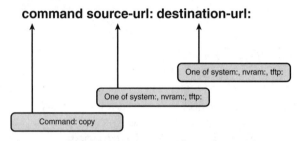

The source URL is where you are copying from. The destination URL is where you are copying to. For example, you are already familiar with the abbreviated command **copy run start**. However, in its most verbose form, this command specifies the file locations:

```
Router#copy system:running-config nvram:startup-config
```

The command states, "Copy the running configuration *from* the system's RAM *to* NVRAM and save it with the filename **startup-config**.

Other examples include copy *from* RAM *to* TFTP:

```
Router#copy system:running-config tftp:
```

Or simply,

```
Router#copy run tftp
```

Copying *from* TFTP *to* RAM:

```
Router#copy tftp: system:running-config
```

Or simply,

```
Router#copy tftp run
```

Copying *from* TFTP *to* the startup configuration file:

```
Router#copy tftp: nvram:startup-config
```

Or simply,

```
Router#copy tftp nvram
```

The **copy** commands using TFTP require more configurations (covered in the next section) after you enter them to carry out the instruction.

Cisco IOS File Naming Conventions

Because of the sheer number of platforms, feature sets, and possible versions of IOS, a file naming convention is used to provide some basic information about the IOS image. Figure 15-3 shows a sample IOS image filename and what each part means.

Figure 15-3   Sample IOS Image Filename

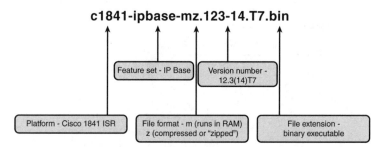

The following details each part of the IOS filename shown in Figure 15-3:

- **Platform:** The first part, **c1841**, identifies the platform on which the image runs. In this example, the platform is a Cisco 1841.

- **Features:** The second part, **ipbase**, specifies the feature set. In this case, **ipbase** refers to the basic IP internetworking image. Many feature sets are available:
  - **i:** Designates the IP feature set.
  - **j:** Designates the enterprise feature set (all protocols).
  - **s:** Designates a PLUS feature set (extra queuing, manipulation, or translations).
  - **56i:** Designates 56-bit IPsec DES encryption.
  - **3:** Designates the firewall/IDS.
  - **k2:** Designates 3DES IPsec encryption (168 bit).

- **Type:** The third part, **mz**, indicates where the image runs (m for RAM) and that the image is zip compressed (z). Other possible codes include the following:
  - **f:** The image runs from Flash memory.
  - **r:** The image runs from ROM.
  - **l:** The image is relocatable.
  - **x:** The image is mzip compressed.

- **Version:** The fourth part, **123-14.T7**, is the version number.

- **Extension:** The final part, **bin**, is the file extension. The *.bin* extension indicates that this is a binary executable file.

Manage IOS Images

As any network grows, storing Cisco IOS Software images and configuration files on the central TFTP server gives you control over the number and revision level of Cisco IOS images and configuration files that must be maintained. Figure 15-4 shows a sample topology with a TFTP server.

Figure 15-4   TFTP Topology

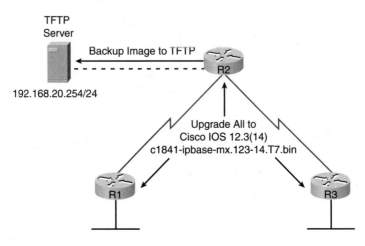

Backing Up an IOS image

Make sure a TFTP server is configured and running on the network. Then follow these steps to copy a Cisco IOS Software image from flash memory to the network TFTP server:

Step 1   Ping the TFTP server to make sure you have access to it:

```
R1#ping 192.168.20.254

Type escape sequence to abort.
Sending 5, 100-byte ICMP Echos to 192.168.20.254, timeout is 2 seconds:
!!!!!
Success rate is 100 percent (5/5), round-trip min/avg/max = 31/31/32 ms

R1#
```

Step 2   Copy the current system image file from the router to the network TFTP server, using the **copy flash: tftp:** command in privileged EXEC mode. You then are prompted. The command requires that you enter the IP address of the remote host and the name of the source and destination system image files:

```
R1#copy flash: tftp:
Source filename []? c1841-ipbase-mz.123-14.T7.bin
Address or name of remote host []? 192.168.20.254
Destination filename [c1841-ipbase-mz.123-14.T7.bin]? <CR>
!!!!!!!!!!!!!!!!!!!!!!!!!!!!!!!!!!!!!!!!!!!!!!!!!!!!!!!!!!!!
<Output omitted>
13832032 bytes copied in 113.061 secs (122341 bytes/sec)
R1#
```

During the copy process, exclamation points (!) indicate the progress. Each exclamation point signifies that one UDP segment has successfully transferred.

Restoring an IOS Image

Verify that the router has sufficient disk space to accommodate the new Cisco IOS Software image
with **show flash:** command, as shown in Example 15-4.

Example 15-4   Output from the show flash Command

```
R2#show flash

System flash directory:
File  Length    Name/status
  1   13832032 c1841-ipbase-mz.123-14.T7.bin
[13832032 bytes used, 18682016 available, 32514048 total]
32768K bytes of processor board System flash (Read/Write)

R2#
```

The **show flash** command helps you determine the following:

- The total amount of flash memory on the router

- The amount of flash memory available

- The names of all the files stored in the flash memory and the amount of flash occupied

Example 15-5 shows the commands necessary to copy an image stored on the TFTP server to flash.

Example 15-5   Upgrading the IOS Image from a TFTP Server

```
R1#copy tftp flash
Address or name of remote host []? 192.168.20.254
Source filename []? c1841-ipbasek9-mz.124-12.bin
Destination filename [c1841-ipbasek9-mz.124-12.bin]?

Loading c1841-ipbasek9-mz.124-12.bin from 192.168.20.254:
!!!!!!!!!!!!!!!!!!!!!!!!!!!!!!!!!!!!!!!!!!!!!!!!!!!!!!!!!!!!!!!!!!!!!!!!!!!!!!!!!!!!!
!!!!!!!!!!!!!!!!!!!!!!!!!!!!!!!!!!!!!!!!!!!!!!!!!!!!!!!!!!!!!!!!!!!!!!!!!!!!!!!!!!!!!!
!!!!!!!!!!!!!!!!!!!!!!!!!!!!!!!!!!!!!!!!!!!!!!!!!!!!!!!!!!!!!!!!!!!!!!!!!!!!!!!!!!!!!!
!!!!!!!!!!!!!!!!!!!!!!!!!!!!!!!!!!!!!!!!!!!!!!!!!!!!!!!!!!!!!!!!!!!!!!!!!!!!!!!!!!!!!!
!!!!!
[OK - 16599160 bytes]

16599160 bytes copied in 9.656 secs (384658 bytes/sec)
R1#
```

The command asks for the IP address of the TFTP server and then the IOS image filename stored
on the TFTP server that you want to copy over. When asked for the destination filename, you could
change it, but this is not recommended because the name has specific meanings as reviewed earlier.

In Example 15-5, there is plenty of room for the new image, so the older image is not erased. So
the next time the router boots, it will load the old image because the old image is listed first in the
flash directory, as shown in Example 15-6.

Example 15-6   Verify the IOS that Loads by Default

```
R1#show flash

System flash directory:
File   Length    Name/status
  2    13832032  c1841-ipbase-mz.123-14.T7.bin
  3    16599160  c1841-ipbasek9-mz.124-12.bin
[30431192 bytes used, 2082856 available, 32514048 total]
32768K bytes of processor board System flash (Read/Write)

R1#
```

In this case, to finalize the upgrade to the new image (listed as file 3 in Example 15-6), you could delete the first image listed in the flash directory. After all, you have a backup on the TFTP server. To do so, enter the **delete flash** command, making sure you specify the file you want to erase, as shown in Example 15-7:

Example 15-7   Using the delete Command to Erase an IOS Image

```
R1#delete flash:c1841-ipbase-mz.123-14.T7.bin
Delete filename [c1841-ipbase-mz.123-14.T7.bin]?<cr>
Delete flash:/c1841-ipbase-mz.123-14.T7.bin? [confirm]<cr>

R1#
```

A better solution might be to configure the router to boot the new image using **boot system** commands.

```
R2(config)#boot system flash c1841-ipbasek9-mz.124-12.bin
```

This form of the **boot system** command tells the router to use the specified IOS image stored in flash instead of the default image. Using this method allows you to have a local backup of an IOS image that you can use right away if something happens to the boot image.

Recovering an IOS Image Using a TFTP Server

If a router loses all the contents of flash intentionally or unintentionally, it automatically boots into ROMmon mode. Very few commands are available in ROMmon mode. You can view these commands by entering **?** at the **rommon>** command prompt, as demonstrated in Example 15-8.

Example 15-8   Available ROMmon Commands

```
rommon 1 > ?
boot              boot up an external process
confreg           configuration register utility
dir               list files in file system
help              monitor builtin command help
reset             system reset
set               display the monitor variables
tftpdnld          tftp image download
unset             unset a monitor variable
rommon 2 >
```

The pertinent command for recovering an IOS image is **tftpdnld** for TFTP download. To enable the router to use the **tftpdnld** command, first you must set specific ROMmon variables. These variables, shown in Example 15-9, are syntax- and case-sensitive.

Example 15-9   Using tftpdnld to Recover an IOS Image

```
rommon 2 > IP_ADDRESS=192.168.20.1
rommon 3 > IP_SUBNET_MASK=255.255.255.0
rommon 4 > DEFAULT_GATEWAY=192.168.20.254
rommon 5 > TFTP_SERVER=192.168.20.254
rommon 6 > TFTP_FILE=c1841-ipbase-mz.123-14.T7.bin
rommon 7 > tftpdnld

          IP_ADDRESS: 192.168.20.1
      IP_SUBNET_MASK: 255.255.255.0
     DEFAULT_GATEWAY: 192.168.20.254
         TFTP_SERVER: 192.168.20.254
           TFTP_FILE: c1841-ipbase-mz.123-14.T7.bin
Invoke this command for disaster recovery only.
WARNING: all existing data in all partitions on flash will be lost!

Do you wish to continue? y/n:  [n]:  y
Receiving c1841-ipbase-mz.123-14.T7.bin from 192.168.20.254 !!!!!!!!!!!!!!!!
<Output omitted>!!!!!!!
File reception completed.
Copying file c1841-ipbase-mz.123-14.T7.bin to flash.
Erasing flash at 0x607c0000
program flash location 0x605a0000
```

Recovering an IOS Image Using Xmodem

If for some reason you are not able to use the Fast Ethernet interfaces on a router, you can recover an IOS image by transferring it over a console cable by using Xmodem. The method is much slower than using **tftpdnld** because you are transferring at 9600 bps instead of 100 Mbps.

To use Xmodem, connect a console cable and open up a terminal session with the router. Then use the **xmodem** command as demonstrated in Example 15-10.

Example 15-10   Using xmodem to Recover an IOS Image

```
rommon1>xmodem -c c1841-ipbase-mz.123-14.T7.bin

Do not start the sending program yet...
device does not contain a valid magic number
dir: cannot open device "flash:"

WARNING: All existing data in bootflash will be lost!
Invoke this application only for disaster recovery.
Do you wish to continue? y/n [n]: y
Ready to receive file c1841-ipbase-mz.123-14.T7.bin
```

Now use the "Send File" command for your terminal software to start the IOS transfer. For HyperTerminal, "Send File" is in the Transfer menu. Browse to the location of the file and send it. The terminal software then provides feedback on the file transfer status as it occurs. When the transfer is complete, the router automatically reloads with the new Cisco IOS image.

Recovering a Lost Password

Password recovery procedures for any Cisco router or switch are readily available online. For example, search for "1841 password recovery" and you will quickly find the procedures you need to follow to reset the password. This is why physical security is a must for all networking devices. Routers and switches should be behind locked doors.

Step 1   Use the power switch to turn off the router, and then turn the router back on.

Step 2   Press the break key specified by your terminal software within 60 seconds of powerup to access the ROMmon prompt. For HyperTerminal, use the **Break** key. For Tera Term, use the key combination **Alt+b**.

Step 3   Enter **confreg 0x2142** at the ROMmon prompt. This causes the router to bypass the startup configuration where the forgotten password is stored.

Step 4   Enter **reset** at the prompt. The router reboots, but it ignores the saved configuration. However, the file still exists in NVRAM.

Step 5   Press **Ctrl-C** to skip the initial setup procedure.

Step 6   Enter **enable** at the **Router>** prompt. This puts you into privileged EXEC mode, where you should be able to see the Router# prompt.

Step 7   Enter **copy startup-config running-config** to copy the backup NVRAM config file into memory.

Step 8   Enter configure terminal.

Step 9   Enter **enable secret** *password* command to change the enable secret password.

Step 10   Issue the **no shutdown** command on every interface that you want to activate.

Step 11   From global configuration mode, enter **config-register 0x2102** to restore the original configuration registry setting.

Step 12   Press **Ctrl-Z** or enter **end** to leave configuration mode.

Step 13   Enter **copy running-config startup-config** to commit the changes. You can issue the **show ip interface brief** command to confirm that your interface configuration is correct. Every interface that you want to use should display "up" and "up".

You have now completed password recovery. Entering the **show version** command confirms that the router will use the configured config register setting on the next reboot.

Study Resources

For today's exam topics, refer to the following resources for more study.

Resource	Chapter	Topic	Where to Find It
Foundational Resources			
CCNA Exploration Online Curriculum: Accessing the WAN	Chapter 4, "Network Security"	Secure Router Management	Section 4.5
CCNA Exploration Accessing the WAN Companion Guide	Chapter 4, "Network Security"	Secure Router Management	pp. 275–300
ICND1 Official Exam Certification Guide	Chapter 13, "Operating Cisco Routers"	Upgrading a Cisco IOS Software Image into Flash Memory	pp. 420–423
ICND1 Authorized Self-Study Guide	Chapter 6, "Network Environment Management"	Managing Cisco Devices	pp. 442–455
Supplemental Resources			
CCNA Flash Cards and Exam Practice Pack	ICND1, Section 12	Managing Your Network Environment	pp. 314–342
CCNA Video Mentor	ICND1, Lab2	Router Configuration and Managing Configuration Files	pp. 7–10 and DVD

Static, Default, and RIP Routing

CCNA 640-802 Exam Topics

- Perform and verify routing configuration tasks for a static or default route given specific routing requirements.
- Configure, verify, and troubleshoot RIPv2.

Key Topics

Today we focus on static, default, and RIP routing for IPv4. Static routes are a common part of an enterprise's routing policy. Static routes can be used to force traffic to use a specific path or to establish a default route out of the enterprise. Static routes are hard-coded into the routing table by the network administrator. Thus, a network administrator must monitor and maintain static routes to ensure connectivity.

Dynamic routing, on the other hand, automatically maintains routing information without a network administrator's intervention. The first routing protocol, Routing Information Protocol (RIP), comes in two versions for IPv4 and another version for IPv6.

Static Route Configuration

One of the common uses for a static route is routing to a stub network. A stub network is a network accessed by a single route. To configure a static route, use the **ip route** command with the following relevant syntax:

```
Router(config)#ip route network-address subnet-mask {ip-address ¦
  exit-interface}
```

Explanation for each parameter is as follows:

- *network-address*: Destination network address of the remote network to be added to the routing table.
- *subnet-mask*: Subnet mask of the remote network to be added to the routing table. The subnet mask can be modified to summarize a group of networks.

One or both of the following parameters are used:

- *ip-address*: Commonly referred to as the next-hop router's IP address.
- *exit-interface*: Outgoing interface that would be used in forwarding packets to the destination network.

Figure 14-1 and Table 14-1 show the topology and addressing scheme we are using today to review static and default routing.

Figure 14-1   Static and Default Routing Topology

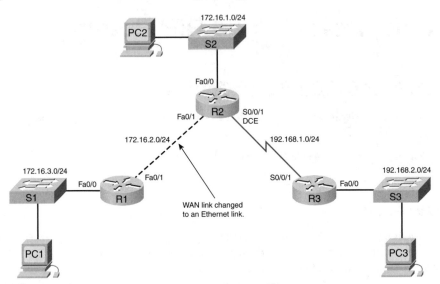

Table 14-1   Chapter Topology Addressing Scheme

Device	Interface	IP Address	Subnet Mask	Default Gateway
R1	Fa0/0	172.16.3.1	255.255.255.0	N/A
	S0/0/0	172.16.2.1	255.255.255.0	N/A
R2	Fa0/0	172.16.1.1	255.255.255.0	N/A
	S0/0/0	172.16.2.2	255.255.255.0	N/A
	S0/0/1	192.168.1.2	255.255.255.0	N/A
R3	Fa0/0	192.168.2.1	255.255.255.0	N/A
	S0/0/0	192.168.1.1	255.255.255.0	N/A
PC1	NIC	172.16.3.10	255.255.255.0	172.16.3.1
PC2	NIC	172.16.1.10	255.255.255.0	172.16.1.1
PC3	NIC	192.168.2.10	255.255.255.0	192.168.2.1

Assume R1 is configured and knows about its own directly connected networks. Example 14-1 shows the routing table for R1 before any static routing is configured.

Example 14-1   R1 Routing Table Before Static Routes Are Configured

```
R1#show ip route
<output omitted>

Gateway of last resort is not set

     172.16.0.0/24 is subnetted, 2 subnets
C       172.16.2.0 is directly connected, Serial0/0/0
C       172.16.3.0 is directly connected, FastEthernet0/0
R1#
```

The remote networks that R1 does not know about are as follows:

- **172.16.1.0/24**: The LAN on R2

- **192.168.1.0/24**: The serial network between R2 and R3

- **192.168.2.0/24**: The LAN on R3

Static Routes Using the "Next Hop" Parameter

Using the "next hop" parameter, R1 can be configured with three static routes—one for each of the networks R1 does not yet know about. Example 14-2 shows the command syntax.

Example 14-2   Static Route Configuration with "Next Hop" Parameter

```
R1(config)#ip route 172.16.1.0 255.255.255.0 172.16.2.2
R1(config)#ip route 192.168.1.0 255.255.255.0 172.16.2.2
R1(config)#ip route 192.168.2.0 255.255.255.0 172.16.2.2
```

The interface that routes to the next hop must be "up" and "up" before the static routes can be entered in the routing table. Example 14-3 verifies that the static routes are now in the routing table.

Example 14-3   R1 Routing Table After Static Routes Are Configured

```
R1#show ip route
<output omitted>

Gateway of last resort is not set

     172.16.0.0/24 is subnetted, 3 subnets
S       172.16.1.0 [1/0] via 172.16.2.2
C       172.16.2.0 is directly connected, Serial0/0/0
C       172.16.3.0 is directly connected, FastEthernet0/0
S     192.168.1.0/24 [1/0] via 172.16.2.2
S     192.168.2.0/24 [1/0] via 172.16.2.2
R1#
```

Notice that a route exists to the 172.16.2.0/24 network, which the "next hop" 172.16.2.2 belongs to. After performing a recursive lookup to find the exit interface, R1 will send packets for each of the three static routes out the Serial 0/0/0 interface.

Static Routes Using the Exit Interface Parameter

To avoid a recursive lookup and have a router immediately send packets to the exit interface, configure the static route using the *exit-interface* parameter instead of the "next hop" (*ip-address*) parameter.

For example, on R2 we can configure a static route to the 172.16.3.0/24 network and specify the Serial 0/0/0 interface as the exit interface:

```
R2(config)#ip route 172.16.3.0 255.255.255.0 serial 0/0/0
```

Any previous static routes to this network using a next-hop IP address should be removed. R2 now has a static route in its routing table, as shown in Example 14-4, that it can use immediately to route to the 172.16.3.0/24 network without having to do a recursive route lookup.

Example 14-4 R2 Routing Table After Static Route Is Configured

```
R2#show ip route
<output omitted>

Gateway of last resort is not set

     172.16.0.0/24 is subnetted, 3 subnets
C       172.16.1.0 is directly connected, FastEthernet0/0
C       172.16.2.0 is directly connected, Serial0/0/0
S       172.16.3.0 is directly connected, Serial0/0/0
C     192.168.1.0/24 is directly connected, Serial0/0/1
R2#
```

Default Static Routes

A default route is a special kind of static route used to represent all routes with zero or no bits matching. In other words, when there are no routes that have a more specific match in the routing table, the default route will be a match.

The destination IP address of a packet can match multiple routes in the routing table. For example, consider having the following two static routes in the routing table:

```
     172.16.0.0/24 is subnetted, 3 subnets
S       172.16.1.0 is directly connected, Serial0/0/0
S       172.16.0.0/16 is directly connected, Serial0/0/1
```

A packet destined for 172.16.1.10, the packet's destination IP address, matches both routes. However, the 172.16.1.0 route is the more specific route because the destination matches the first 24 bits, whereas the destination matches only the first 16 bits of the 172.16.0.0 route. Therefore, the router will use the route with the most specific match.

A default static route is a route that will match all packets. Commonly called a *quad-zero route*, a default static route uses 0.0.0.0 (thus, the term "quad-zero") for both the *network-address* and *subnet-mask* parameter, as shown in this syntax:

```
Router(config)#ip route 0.0.0.0 0.0.0.0 {ip-address ¦ exit-interface}
```

Referring to the topology shown in Figure 14-1, assume that R3 has a connection to the Internet. From the perspective of R2, all default traffic can be sent to R3 for routing outside the domain known to R2.

The following command configures R2 with a default static route pointing to R3 using the "next hop" parameter:

```
R2(config)#ip route 0.0.0.0 0.0.0.0 192.168.1.1
```

R2 now has a "gateway of last resort" listed in the routing table—a candidate default route indicated by the asterisk (*) next to the S code, as shown in Example 14-5.

Example 14-5   R2 Routing Table After Default Route is Configured

```
R2#show ip route
<some codes omitted>
        * - candidate default, U - per-user static route, o - ODR
        P - periodic downloaded static route

Gateway of last resort is 192.168.1.1 to network 0.0.0.0

     172.16.0.0/24 is subnetted, 3 subnets
C       172.16.1.0 is directly connected, FastEthernet0/0
C       172.16.2.0 is directly connected, Serial0/0/0
S       172.16.3.0 is directly connected, Serial0/0/0
C    192.168.1.0/24 is directly connected, Serial0/0/1
S*   0.0.0.0/0 [1/0] via 192.168.1.1
R2#
```

From R1's perspective, R2 is the default route. The following command configures R1 with a default static route pointing to R2 using the *exit-interface* parameter:

    R1(config)#ip route 0.0.0.0 0.0.0.0 serial 0/0/0

Again, we can verify that the default route is now in the routing table for R1, as shown in Example 14-6.

Example 14-6   R1 Routing Table After Default Route Is Configured

```
R1#show ip route
<some codes omitted>
        * - candidate default, U - per-user static route, o - ODR
        P - periodic downloaded static route

Gateway of last resort is 0.0.0.0 to network 0.0.0.0

     172.16.0.0/24 is subnetted, 3 subnets
S       172.16.1.0 [1/0] via 172.16.2.2
C       172.16.2.0 is directly connected, Serial0/0/0
C       172.16.3.0 is directly connected, FastEthernet0/0
S    192.168.1.0/24 [1/0] via 172.16.2.2
S    192.168.2.0/24 [1/0] via 172.16.2.2
S*   0.0.0.0/0 is directly connected, Serial0/0/0
R1#
```

After additional static routes are configured, the routing tables for R1 and R2 are complete. However, R3 does not have routes back to any of the 172.16.0.0 networks. So any traffic from PC1 to the PC3 will reach PC3, but return traffic from PC3 will be dropped by R3 because R3 does not have a route back to any of R1's directly connected networks. We can see that the problem is with R3 from the traceroute output in Example 14-7.

Example 14-7   traceroute from PC1 to PC3 Fails at R3

```
C:\>tracert 192.168.2.10


Tracing route to 192.168.2.10 over a maximum of 30 hops:

  1    92 ms     74 ms     75 ms     172.16.3.1
  2   114 ms    110 ms    126 ms     172.16.2.2
  3    *          *          *        Request timed out.
  4   ^C
C:\>
```

From the output, you can see that R2 (172.16.2.2) responded to PC1. R2 then routes the next trace to R3. We know this because R2 has a default route pointing to R3. However, when the trace arrives at R3, it does not have a route back to PC1, so it drops the packet. R3 needs a route back to the 172.16.3.0/24 network.

Before configuring three separate static routes for each of the 172.16.0.0 networks, notice that the three routes can be summarized into one route. We reviewed summary routes on Day 21, so we will not detail the process here. Example 14-8 shows the three routes in binary with the bits in common highlighted.

Example 14-8   Summary Route Calculation for R3

```
10101100.00010000.00000001.00000000
10101100.00010000.00000010.00000000
10101100.00010000.00000011.00000000
```

Therefore, the summary route would be 172.16.0.0/22. Although not part of the current addressing scheme, this summary static route would also include the route 172.16.0.0/24.

You can now configure R3 with one static route:

```
R3(config)#ip route 172.16.0.0 255.255.252.0 serial 0/0/1
```

Now PC1 can successfully trace a route to PC3 as shown in Example 14-9.

Example 14-9   traceroute from PC1 to PC3 Succeeds

```
C:\>tracert 192.168.2.10


Tracing route to 192.168.2.10 over a maximum of 30 hops:

  1    70 ms     82 ms     78 ms     172.16.3.1
  2    99 ms    103 ms     87 ms     172.16.2.2
  3   156 ms    161 ms    151 ms     192.168.1.1
  4   246 ms    242 ms    242 ms     192.168.2.10

Trace complete.

C:\>
```

The trace is successful because R3 now has a route back to PC1's network, as shown in Example 14-10.

Example 14-10 R3 Routing Table with Summary Static Route

```
R3#show ip route
<output omitted>


Gateway of last resort is not set


     172.16.0.0/22 is subnetted, 1 subnets
S       172.16.0.0 is directly connected, Serial0/0/1
C     192.168.1.0/24 is directly connected, Serial0/0/1
C     192.168.2.0/24 is directly connected, FastEthernet0/0
R3#
```

RIP Concepts

Because RIPv2 is actually an enhancement of RIPv1, you should be able to compare and contrast the two version's concepts and configurations. First, let's look briefly at RIPv1.

RIPv1 Message Format

RIPv1 is a classful, distance vector routing protocol for IPv4. It uses hop count as its only metric for path selection with a hop count greater than 15 considered unreachable. RIPv1 routing messages are encapsulated in a UDP segment using port number 520 and are broadcast every 30 seconds. Figure 14-2 shows the RIPv1 message encapsulation from the data link layer up to and including the RIPv1 message.

Figure 14-2   RIPv1 Message Encapsulation

Data Link Frame Header	IP Packet Header	UDP Segment Header	RIP Message (512 Bytes: Up to 25 Routes)

Data Link Frame
MAC Source Address = Address of Sending Interface
MAC Destination Address = Broadcast: FF-FF-FF-FF-FF-FF

IP Packet
IP Source Address = Address of Sending Interface
IP Destination Address = Broadcast: 255.255.255.255
Protocol Field = 17 for UDP

UDP Segment
Source Port = 520
Destination Port = 520

RIP Message
Command: Request (1); Response (2)
Version = 1
Address Family ID = 2 for IP
Routes: Network IP Address
Metric: Hop Count

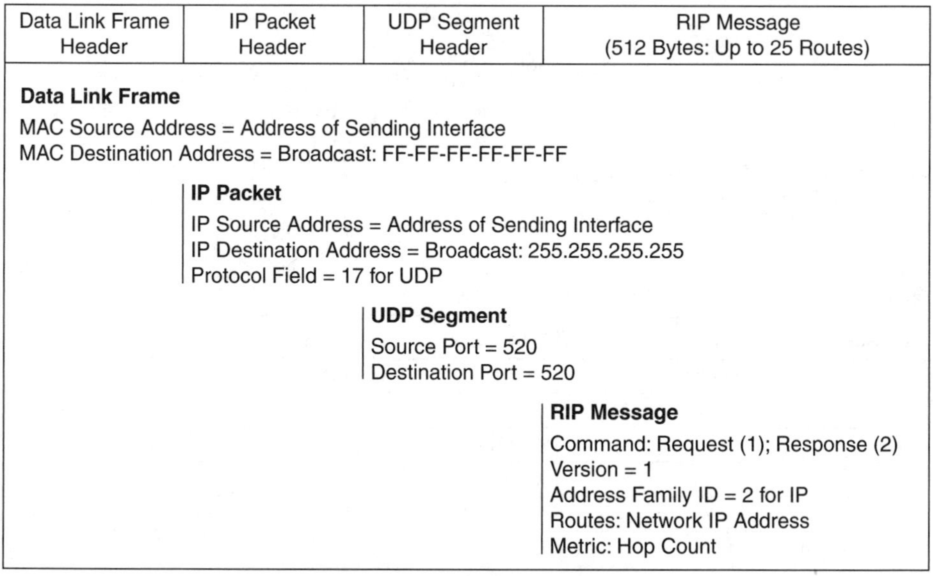

RIPv1 Operation

Notice in the RIP message that RIP uses two message types specified in the Command field. Command 1 is a Request message and Command 2 is a Response message.

Each RIP-configured interface sends out a Request message on startup, requesting that all RIP neighbors send their complete routing tables. A Response message is sent back by RIP-enabled neighbors. When the requesting router receives the responses, it evaluates each route entry. If a route entry is new, the receiving router installs the route in the routing table. If the route is already in the table, the existing entry is replaced if the new entry has a better hop count. The startup router then sends a triggered update out all RIP-enabled interfaces containing its own routing table so that RIP neighbors can be informed of any new routes.

RIPv1 does not send subnet mask information in the update. Therefore, a router either uses the subnet mask configured on a local interface or applies the default subnet mask based on the address class. Because of this limitation, RIPv1 networks cannot be discontiguous, nor can they implement VLSM or supernetting.

RIP has a default administrative distance of 120. When compared to other interior gateway protocols, RIP is the least-preferred routing protocol.

RIPv1 Configuration

Figure 14-3 and Table 14-2 show the RIPv1 topology for our first scenario and the addressing scheme we will use to review RIPv1 configuration and verification.

Figure 14-3   RIPv1 Topology: Scenario A

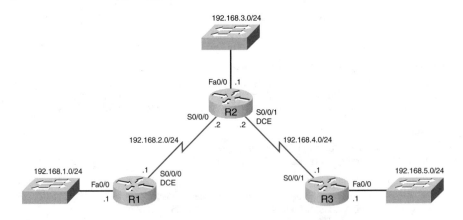

Table 14-2   Scenario A Addressing Scheme

Device	Interface	IP Address	Subnet Mask
R1	Fa0/0	192.168.1.1	255.255.255.0
	S0/0/0	192.168.2.1	255.255.255.0
R2	Fa0/0	192.168.3.1	255.255.255.0
	S0/0/0	192.168.2.2	255.255.255.0
	S0/0/1	192.168.4.2	255.255.255.0
R3	Fa0/0	192.168.5.1	255.255.255.0
	S0/0/1	192.168.4.1	255.255.255.0

In Figure 14-3, we are using six separate classful networks, so each network must be configured individually. Assuming the interfaces on R1, R2, and R3 are configured and active, Example 14-11 shows the RIPv1 configuration for the routers.

Example 14-11 RIPv1 Standard Configuration: Scenario A

```
R1(config)#router rip
R1(config-router)#network 192.168.1.0
R1(config-router)#network 192.168.2.0

R2(config)#router rip
R2(config-router)#network 192.168.2.0
R2(config-router)#network 192.168.3.0
R2(config-router)#network 192.168.4.0

R3(config)#router rip
R3(config-router)#network 192.168.4.0
R3(config-router)#network 192.168.5.0
```

RIPv1 Verification and Troubleshooting

The following verification commands, used in order, will quickly verify if routing is operational as intended.

- **show ip route**

- **show ip protocols**

- **debug ip rip**

If routing is not functioning correctly, these commands will help you track down the problem in the most efficient manner.

To verify that routing is operational, start with the **show ip route** command. For the topology in Figure 14-3, all routes should be in the routing table for each router. Example 14-12 shows the routing table for R2.

Example 14-12 R2 Routing Table with RIP Routes Installed

```
R2#show ip route
Codes: C - connected, S - static, I - IGRP, R - RIP, M - mobile, B - BGP
<some codes omitted>

Gateway of last resort is not set

R    192.168.1.0/24 [120/1] via 192.168.2.1, 00:00:17, Serial0/0/0
C    192.168.2.0/24 is directly connected, Serial0/0/0
C    192.168.3.0/24 is directly connected, FastEthernet0/0
C    192.168.4.0/24 is directly connected, Serial0/0/1
R    192.168.5.0/24 [120/1] via 192.168.4.1, 00:00:23, Serial0/0/1
R2#
```

To better understand the output from the **show ip route** command, let's focus on one RIP route learned by R2 and interpret the output shown in the routing table:

```
R      192.168.5.0/24 [120/1] via 192.168.4.1, 00:00:23, Serial0/0/1
```

Table 14-3 lists and describes each part of the output.

Table 14-3   Interpreting a RIP Route

Output	Description
R	Identifies the source of the route as RIP.
192.168.5.0	Indicates the address of the remote network.
/24	Indicates the subnet mask used for this network.
[120/1]	Shows the administrative distance (120) and the metric (1 hop).
via 192.168.4.1,	Specifies the address of the next-hop router (R2) to send traffic to for the remote network.
00:00:23,	Specifies the amount of time since the route was updated (here, 23 seconds). Another update is due in 7 seconds.
Serial0/0/1	Specifies the local interface through which the remote network can be reached.

If the routing table is missing one or more expected routes, use the **show ip protocols** command on the local router first to make sure RIP is configured and operating correctly. This command displays the routing protocol that is currently configured on the router. The output can be used to verify most RIP parameters to confirm the following:

- RIP routing is configured.
- The correct interfaces send and receive RIP updates.
- The router advertises the correct networks.
- RIP neighbors are sending updates.

Figure 14-4 shows the output from the **show ip protocols** command, with numbers by each portion of the output. The descriptions that follow the figure correspond to the numbers in the figure.

Figure 14-4   Interpreting show ip protocols Output

```
     R2#show ip protocols
①—Routing Protocol is "rip"
②{  Sending updates every 30 seconds, next due in 23 seconds
    Invalid after 180 seconds, hold down 180, flushed after 240
   ⎧ Outgoing update filter list for all interfaces is not set
③⎨ Incoming update filter list for all interfaces is not set
   ⎩ Redistributing: rip
   ⎧ Default version control: send version 1, receive any version
   ⎪   Interface           Send  Recv  Triggered RIP  Key-chain
④⎨   FastEthernet0/0       1     1 2
   ⎪   Serial0/0/0          1     1 2
   ⎩   Serial0/0/1          1     1 2
⑤{  Automatic network summarization is in effect
    Maximum path: 4
   ⎧ Routing for Networks:
⑥⎨    192.168.2.0
   ⎪    192.168.3.0
   ⎩    192.168.4.0
   ⎧ Routing Information Sources:
   ⎪   Gateway         Distance      Last Update
⑦⎨   192.168.2.1          120       00:00:18
   ⎪   192.168.4.1          120       00:00:22
   ⎩ Distance: (default is 120)
```

1. The first line of output verifies that RIP routing is configured and running on R2.

2. These are the timers that show when the next round of updates will be sent out from this router—23 seconds from now, in the example.

3. Filtering and redistribution information shown here are both CCNP-level topics.

4. This block of output contains information about which RIP version is currently configured and which interfaces are participating in RIP updates.

5. This part of the output shows that R2 is currently summarizing at the classful network boundary and, by default, will use up to four equal-cost routes to load-balance traffic.

6. The classful networks configured with the network command are listed next. These are the networks that R2 will include in its RIP updates.

7. Here the RIP neighbors are listed as Routing Information Sources. Gateway is the next-hop IP address of the neighbor that is sending R2 updates. Distance is the AD that R2 uses for updates sent by this neighbor. Last Update is the seconds since the last update was received from this neighbor.

Most RIP configuration errors involve an incorrect **network** statement configuration, a missing **network** statement configuration, or the configuration of discontiguous subnets in a classful environment. As shown in Figure 14-5, **debug ip rip** can be used to find issues with RIP updates.

Figure 14-5   Interpreting debug ip rip Output

```
R2#debug ip rip
RIP protocol debugging is on
① { RIP: received v1 update from 192.168.2.1 on Serial0/0/0
        192.168.1.0 in 1 hops
② { RIP: received v1 update from 192.168.4.1 on Serial0/0/1
        192.168.5.0 in 1 hops
   ⌈ RIP: sending  v1 update to 255.255.255.255 via FastEthernet0/0
   |     (192.168.3.1)
   | RIP: build update entries
③ ⟨       network 192.168.1.0 metric 2
   |       network 192.168.2.0 metric 1
   |       network 192.168.4.0 metric 1
   ⌊       network 192.168.5.0 metric 2
   ⌈ RIP: sending  v1 update to 255.255.255.255 via Serial0/0/1
   |     (192.168.4.2)
④ ⟨ RIP: build update entries
   |       network 192.168.1.0 metric 2
   |       network 192.168.2.0 metric 1
   ⌊       network 192.168.3.0 metric 1
   ⌈ RIP: sending  v1 update to 255.255.255.255 via Serial0/0/0
   |     (192.168.2.2)
⑤ ⟨ RIP: build update entries
   |       network 192.168.3.0 metric 1
   |       network 192.168.4.0 metric 1
   ⌊       network 192.168.5.0 metric 2
⑥ { R2#undebug all
    All possible debugging has been turned off
```

This command displays RIP routing updates as they are sent and received, which allows you the opportunity to track down potential sources of a routing problem. The list that follows corresponds to the numbers in Figure 14-5.

1. You see an update coming in from R1 on interface Serial 0/0/0. Notice that R1 sends only one route to the 192.168.1.0 network. No other routes are sent, because doing so would violate the split horizon rule. R1 is not allowed to advertise networks back to R2 that R2 previously sent to R1.

2. The next update that is received is from R3. Again, because of the split horizon rule, R3 sends only one route: the 192.168.5.0 network.

3. R2 sends out its own updates. First, R2 builds an update to send out the FastEthernet 0/0 interface. The update includes the entire routing table except for network 192.168.3.0, which is attached to FastEthernet 0/0.

4. Next, R2 builds an update to send to R3. Three routes are included. R2 does not advertise the network R2 and R3 share, nor does it advertise the 192.168.5.0 network because of split horizon.

5. Finally, R2 builds an update to send to R1. Three routes are included. R2 does not advertise the network that R2 and R1 share, nor does it advertise the 192.168.1.0 network because of split horizon.

6. To stop monitoring RIP updates on R2, enter the **no debug ip rip** command or **undebug all**, as shown in the figure.

Passive Interfaces

In the topology shown in Figure 14-3, notice that there is no reason to send updates out the Fast Ethernet interfaces on any of the routers. Therefore, you should configure these as passive interfaces for two reasons:

- Enhance security by preventing someone attached to one of the LANs from intercepting, inspecting, and possibly modifying the RIP updates.

- Improve the efficiency of the routers' processing.

Use the **passive-interface** *interface-type interface-number* command to stop sending RIP updates out the Fast Ethernet interfaces, as shown in Example 14-13 for R2. The **show ip protocols** command is then used to verify the passive interface configuration.

Example 14-13 Disabling Updates with the passive-interface Command

```
R2(config)#router rip
R2(config-router)#passive-interface FastEthernet 0/0
R2(config-router)#end
R2#show ip protocols
Routing Protocol is "rip"
Sending updates every 30 seconds, next due in 26 seconds
Invalid after 180 seconds, hold down 180, flushed after 240
Outgoing update filter list for all interfaces is not set
Incoming update filter list for all interfaces is not set
Redistributing: rip
Default version control: send version 1, receive any version
  Interface           Send  Recv  Triggered RIP  Key-chain
  Serial0/0/0          1     2 1
  Serial0/0/1          1     2 1
Automatic network summarization is in effect
Maximum path: 4
Routing for Networks:
    192.168.2.0
    192.168.3.0
    192.168.4.0
Passive Interface(s):
    FastEthernet0/0
Routing Information Sources:
    Gateway         Distance      Last Update
    192.168.2.1          120      00:00:12
    192.168.4.1          120      00:00:00
Distance: (default is 120)
R2#
```

Notice that the interface is no longer listed under **Interface** but under a new section called **Passive Interface(s)**. Also notice that the network 192.168.3.0 is still listed under **Routing for Networks:**, which means that this network is still included as a route entry in RIP updates that are sent to R1 and R3. All routing protocols support the **passive-interface** command.

Automatic Summarization

RIP automatically summarizes at the classful network boundary. Figure 14-6 and Table 14-4 shows the RIPv1 topology for Scenario B and the addressing scheme we will use for the remainder of our RIPv1 review.

Figure 14-6   RIPv1 Topology: Scenario B

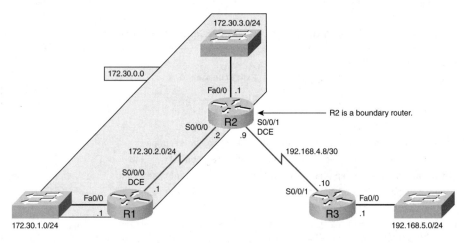

Table 14-4   RIPv1 Scenario B Addressing Scheme

Device	Interface	IP Address	Subnet Mask
R1	Fa0/0	172.30.1.1	255.255.255.0
	S0/0/0	172.30.2.1	255.255.255.0
R2	Fa0/0	172.30.3.1	255.255.255.0
	S0/0/0	172.30.2.2	255.255.255.0
	S0/0/1	192.168.4.9	255.255.255.252
R3	Fa0/0	192.168.5.1	255.255.255.0
	S0/0/1	192.168.4.10	255.255.255.252

Assuming all interfaces are configured and activated, Example 14-14 shows the RIP configuration for R1, R2, and R3.

Example 14-14 RIPv1 Standard Configuration: Scenario B

```
R1(config)#router rip
R1(config-router)#network 172.30.0.0

R2(config)#router rip
R2(config-router)#network 172.30.0.0
R2(config-router)#network 192.168.4.0

R3(config)#router ip
R3(config-router)#network 192.168.4.0
R3(config-router)#network 192.168.5.0
```

Notice in the RIP configuration for all routers, the classful network address was entered instead of each subnet. If we had entered the subnets instead, Cisco IOS would have summarized them to the classful network address. This is because a RIP router either uses the subnet mask configured on a local interface or applies the default subnet mask based on the address class. Therefore, RIPv1 cannot support discontiguous subnets, supernets, or VLSM addressing schemes. Example 14-15 shows what R2 sends in its updates to R1 and R3.

Example 14-15 R2 RIPv1 Updates

```
R2#debug ip rip
RIP protocol debugging is on
RIP: sending  v1 update to 255.255.255.255 via Serial0/0/0 (172.30.2.2)
RIP: build update entries
      network 172.30.3.0 metric 1
      network 192.168.4.0 metric 1
      network 192.168.5.0 metric 2
RIP: sending  v1 update to 255.255.255.255 via Serial0/0/1 (192.168.4.9)
RIP: build update entries
      network 172.30.0.0 metric 1
```

When R2 sends updates to R1, it sends the 172.30.3.0 network because the Serial 0/0/0 interface is using a /24 mask for the 172.30.2.0 network. However, it summarizes the 192.168.4.8 subnet to 192.168.4.0 before sending the update to R1 because R1 will apply the default classful mask to the routing update. R2 is a boundary router for the 192.168.4.0 network. For its update to R3, R2 summarizes subnets 172.30.1.0, 172.30.2.0, and 172.30.3.0 to the classful network 172.30.0.0 because R2 is the boundary router for the 172.30.0.0 network and assumes R3 does not have any other way to get to the 172.30.0.0 network.

Default Routing and RIPv1

Using the same addressing scheme from Table 14-4, let's modify the topology as shown in Figure 14-7 so that R2 and R3 are using static and default routing.

Figure 14-7   RIPv1 Topology: Scenario B (Modified)

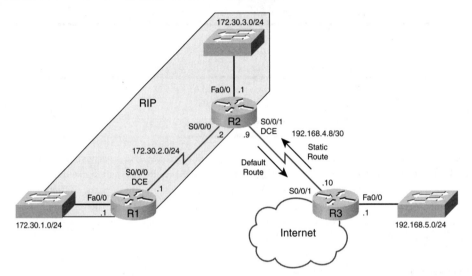

Example 14-16 shows the configuration changes made to R2 and R3. R3 is providing service to the Internet. So R2 will use a default route to send all traffic for unknown destination to R3. R3 will use a summary route to send all traffic to the 172.30.0.0 subnets.

Example 14-16   Configuration Changes to R2 and R3

```
R2(config)#router rip
R2(config-router)#no network 192.168.4.0
R2(config-router)#exit
R2(config)#ip route 0.0.0.0 0.0.0.0 serial 0/0/1

R3(config)#no router rip
R3(config)#ip route 172.30.0.0 255.255.252.0 serial 0/0/1
```

We could configure R1 with a default route pointing to R2. But a better and more scalable solution is to use the **default-information originate** command to have R2 propagate its default route to R1 in its RIP routing updates.

```
R2(config)#router rip
R2(config-router)#default-information originate
```

As shown in Example 14-17, R1 now has a RIP route tagged with the asterisk (*) code indicating that this route is a default gateway.

Example 14-17 Verifying Default Route Propagation

```
R1#show ip route
<output omitted>
Gateway of last resort is 172.30.2.2 to network 0.0.0.0

     172.30.0.0/24 is subnetted, 3 subnets
C       172.30.1.0 is directly connected, FastEthernet0/0
C       172.30.2.0 is directly connected, Serial0/0/0
R       172.30.3.0 [120/1] via 172.30.2.2, 00:00:02, Serial0/0/0
R*   0.0.0.0/0 [120/1] via 172.30.2.2, 00:00:02, Serial0/0/0
R1#
```

RIPv2 Configuration

Like Version 1, RIPv2 is encapsulated in a UDP segment using port 520 and can carry up to 25 routes. Figure 14-8 shows the RIPv1 and RIPv2 message formats.

For review purposes, the most important extension RIPv2 provides in the addition of the subnet mask field, which allows a 32-bit mask to be included in the RIP route entry. As a result, the receiving router no longer depends on the subnet mask of the inbound interface or the classful mask when determining the subnet mask for a route. This means that RIPv1's three main limitations—lack of discontiguous network designs, supernetting, and VLSM support—are no longer an issue.

By default, the RIP process on Cisco routers sends RIPv1 messages but can receive both RIPv1 and RIPv2. You can see this in the **show ip protocols** output shown previously in Example 14-13. To enable the sending of RIPv2 messages in our topology, enter the command **version 2** in router configuration mode, as demonstrated in Example 14-18.

Example 14-18 Configuring RIPv2

```
R2(config)#router rip
R2(config-router)#version 2
R2(config-router)#end
R2#show ip protocols
Routing Protocol is "rip"
Sending updates every 30 seconds, next due in 11 seconds
Invalid after 180 seconds, hold down 180, flushed after 240
Outgoing update filter list for all interfaces is not set
Incoming update filter list for all interfaces is not set
Redistributing: rip
Default version control: send version 2, receive 2
  Interface           Send  Recv  Triggered RIP  Key-chain
  FastEthernet0/0      2     2
  Serial0/0/0          2     2
Automatic network summarization is in effect
```

Figure 14-8   RIPv1 and RIPv2 Message Formats

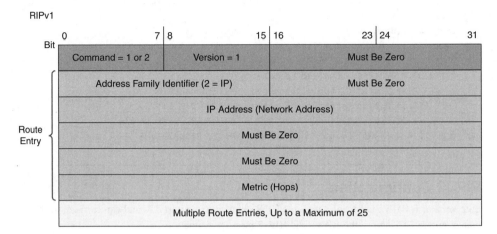

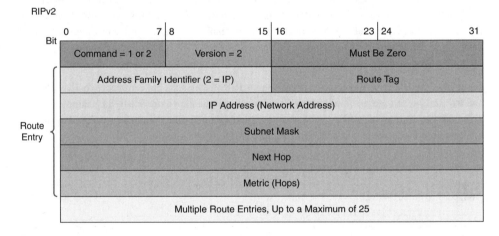

With this configuration, R2 will now send and receive only RIPv2 messages. That means we must con-figure R1 with the **version 2** command as well because R2 will ignore the RIPv1 messages sent by R1.

Disabling Autosummarization

Notice the line in the **show ip protocols** output from Example 14-18 that states:

```
Automatic network summarization is in effect
```

By default, RIPv2 automatically summarizes networks to the classful boundary just like RIPv1. So, to support discontiguous subnets and VLSM, you must first disable automatic summarization with the **no auto-summary** command on all RIPv2 routers to ensure that individual subnets are sent in routing updates—not the classful network address.

RIPv2 Verification and Troubleshooting

There are several ways to verify and troubleshoot RIPv2. You can use many of the same commands for RIPv2 to verify and troubleshoot other routing protocols. It is always best to begin with the basics:

- Make sure that all the links (interfaces) are up and operational.

- Check the cabling.

- Make sure that you have the correct IP address and subnet mask on each interface.

- Remove any configuration commands that are no longer necessary or have been replaced by other commands.

Commands to use are the same as for RIPv1 as well as your standard use of **show ip interface brief**, **show run**, and **ping**. But also consider the following RIPv2 specific issues:

- **Version:** A good place to begin troubleshooting a network that is running RIP is to verify that the **version 2** command is configured on all routers. RIPv1 does not support discontiguous subnets, VLSM, or CIDR supernet routes.

- **Network statements:** Another source of problems might be incorrectly configured or missing network statements configured with the **network** command. Remember, the **network** command does two things:

  — It enables the routing protocol to send and receive updates on any local interfaces that belong to that network.

  — It includes the configured network in its routing updates to its neighboring routers.

  A missing or incorrect network statement will result in missed routing updates and routing updates not being sent or received on an interface.

- **Automatic summarization:** If there is a need or expectation for sending specific subnets and not just summarized routes, make sure that automatic summarization has been disabled with the **no auto-summary** command.

Study Resources

For today's exam topics, refer to the following resources for more study.

Resource	Chapter	Topic	Where to Find It
Foundational Resources			
CCNA Exploration Online Curriculum: Routing Protocols and Concepts	Chapter 2, "Static Routing"	Static Routes with "Next-Hop" Addresses	Section 2.4
		Static Routes with Exit Interfaces	Section 2.5
		Summary and Default Static Routes	Section 2.6
		Managing and Troubleshooting Static Routes	Section 2.7
	Chapter 5, "RIP version 1"	RIPv1: Distance Vector, Classful Routing Protocol	Section 5.1
		Basic RIPv1 Configuration	Section 5.2
		Automatic Summarization	Section 5.4
		Default Route and RIPv1	Section 5.5
	Chapter 7, "RIPv2"	RIPv1 Limitations	Section 7.1
		Configuring RIPv2	Section 7.2

Resource	Chapter	Topic	Where to Find It
CCNA Exploration Routing Protocols and Concepts Companion Guide	Chapter 2, "Static Routing"	Static Routes with "Next-Hop" Addresses	pp. 104–115
		Static Routes with Exit Interfaces	pp. 115–123
		Summary and Default Static Routes	pp. 123–130
		Managing and Troubleshooting Static Routes	pp. 130–134
	Chapter 5, "RIP version 1"	RIPv1: Distance Vector, Classful Routing Protocol	pp. 220–227
		Basic RIPv1 Configuration	pp. 227–231
		Automatic Summarization	pp. 238–250
		Default Route and RIPv1	pp. 250–254
	Chapter 7, "RIPv2"	RIPv1 Limitations	pp. 291–309
		Configuring RIPv2	pp. 309–320
ICND1 Official Exam Certification Guide	Chapter 14, "Routing Protocol Concepts and Configuration"	All topics in this chapter	pp. 439–466
ICND2 Official Exam Certification Guide	Chapter 4, "IP Routing"	Static Routes	pp. 180–193
ICND1 Authorized Self-Study Guide	Chapter 5, "WAN Connections"	Enabling Static Routing	pp. 374–380
		Enabling RIP	pp. 394–408
Supplemental Resources			
CCNA Flash Cards and Exam Practice Pack	ICND1, Section 8	Exploring the Functions of Routing	pp. 192–216
	ICND1, Section 11	RIP Routing	pp. 294–312
CCNA Video Mentor	ICND1, Lab 8	Static and Connected Routes	pp. 33–36
	ICND1, Lab 9	RIP Configuration	pp. 37–42

EIGRP Routing

CCNA 640-802 Exam Topics

- Configure, verify, and troubleshoot EIGRP.

Key Topics

Enhanced Interior Gateway Routing Protocol (EIGRP) is a distance vector, classless routing protocol that was released in 1992 with Cisco IOS Software Release 9.21. As its name suggests, EIGRP is an enhancement of the Interior Gateway Routing Protocol (IGRP). Both are Cisco proprietary protocols and operate only on Cisco routers. Today we review the operation, configuration, verification, and troubleshooting of EIGRP.

EIGRP Operation

EIGRP includes several features that are not commonly found in other distance vector routing protocols such as Routing Information Protocol (RIPv1 and RIPv2) and IGRP. These features include the following:

- Reliable Transport Protocol (RTP)

- Bounded updates

- Diffusing Update Algorithm (DUAL)

- Establishing adjacencies

- Neighbor and topology tables

Although EIGRP might act like a link-state routing protocol, it is still a distance vector routing protocol. Table 13-1 summarizes the main differences between a traditional distance vector routing protocol, such as RIP, and the enhanced distance vector routing protocol EIGRP.

Table 13-1   Comparing Traditional Distance Vector and EIGRP

Traditional Distance Vector Routing Protocols	Enhanced Distance Vector Routing Protocol: EIGRP
Uses the Bellman-Ford or Ford-Fulkerson algorithm.	Uses DUAL.
Ages out routing entries and uses periodic updates.	Does not age out routing entries or use periodic updates.
Keeps track of only the best routes; the best path to a destination network.	Maintains a topology table separate from the routing table, which includes the best path and any loop-free backup paths.
When a route becomes unavailable, the router must wait for a new routing update.	When a route becomes unavailable, DUAL uses a backup path if one exists in the topology table.
Slower convergence because of hold-down timers.	Faster convergence because of the absence of hold-down timers and a system of coordinated route calculations.

EIGRP Message Format

Figure 13-1 shows an example of an encapsulated EIGRP message.

Figure 13-1   Encapsulated EIGRP Message

Data Link Frame Header	IP Packet Header	EIGRP Packet Header	Type/Length/Values Types
Data Link Frame MAC Source Address = Address of Sending Interface MAC Destination Address = Multicast: 01-00-5E-00-00-0A			
	IP Packet IP Source Address = Address of Sending Interface IP Destination Address = Multicast: 224.0.0.10 Protocol Field = 88 for EIGRP		
		EIGRP Packet Header Opcode for EIGRP Packet Type AS Number	
			TLV Types **Some Types Include:** 0x0001 EIGRP Parameters 0x0102 IP Internal Routes 0x0103 IP External Routes

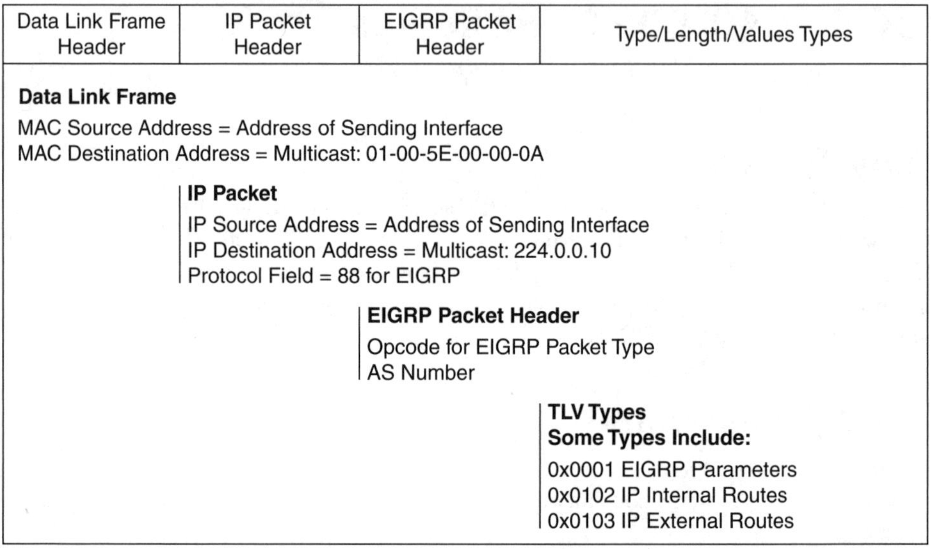

Beginning from the right side of Figure 13-1, notice that the data field is called Type/Length/Value, or TLV. The types of TLVs relevant to the CCNA are EIGRP Parameters, IP Internal Routes, and IP External Routes.

The EIGRP packet header, shown in Figure 13-2, is included with every EIGRP packet, regardless of its TLV. The EIGRP packet header and TLV are then encapsulated in an IP packet. In the IP packet header, the protocol field is set to 88 to indicate EIGRP, and the destination address is set to the multicast address of 224.0.0.10. If the EIGRP packet is encapsulated in an Ethernet frame, the destination MAC address is also a multicast address: 01-00-5E-00-00-0A.

Important fields for our discussion include the Opcode field and the Autonomous System Number field. Opcode specifies the EIGRP packet type. The autonomous system number specifies the EIGRP routing process. Unlike RIP, Cisco routers can run multiple instances of EIGRP. The autonomous system number is used to track multiple instances of EIGRP.

RTP and EIGRP Packet Types

Reliable Transport Protocol (RTP) is the protocol used by EIGRP for the delivery and reception of EIGRP packets. EIGRP was designed as a network layer–independent routing protocol; therefore, it cannot use the services of UDP or TCP because IPX and AppleTalk do not use protocols from the TCP/IP protocol suite.

Although reliable is part of its name, RTP includes both reliable delivery and unreliable delivery of EIGRP packets. Reliable RTP requires an acknowledgment to be returned, whereas an unreliable RTP packet does not require an acknowledgment.

Figure 13-2   EIGRP Packet Header

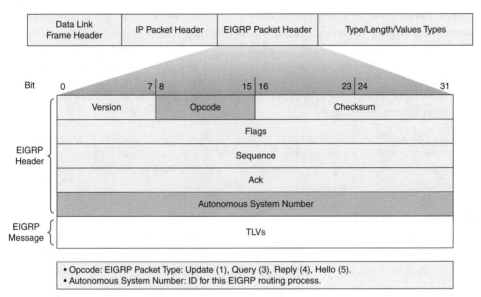

RTP can send packets either as a unicast or a multicast. Multicast EIGRP packets use the reserved multicast address of 224.0.0.10. EIGRP uses five packet types:

- **Hello:** Hello packets are used by EIGRP to discover neighbors and to form adjacencies with those neighbors. EIGRP hello packets are multicasts and use unreliable delivery, so no response is required from the recipient. On most networks, EIGRP hello packets are sent every 5 seconds. On multipoint nonbroadcast multiaccess (NBMA) networks such as X.25, Frame Relay, and ATM interfaces with access links of T1 (1.544 Mbps) or slower, hellos are unicast every 60 seconds. By default, the hold time is 3 times the hello interval, or 15 seconds on most networks and 180 seconds on low-speed NBMA networks. If the hold time expires, EIGRP declares the route as down, and DUAL searches for a new path in the topology table or by sending out queries.

- **Update:** EIGRP does not send periodic updates. Update packets are sent only when necessary, contain only the routing information needed, and are sent only to those routers that require it. EIGRP update packets use reliable delivery. Update packets are sent as a multicast when required by multiple routers, or as a unicast when required by only a single router.

- **Acknowledgement:** Acknowledgment (ACK) packets are sent by EIGRP when reliable delivery is used. RTP uses reliable delivery for EIGRP update, query, and reply packets. EIGRP acknowledgment packets are always sent as an unreliable unicast.

- **Query:** A query packet is used by DUAL when searching for networks. Queries use reliable delivery and can use multicast or unicast.

- **Reply:** A reply packet is sent in response to a query packet regardless of whether the replying router has information about the queried route. Replies use reliable delivery and unlike queries, replies are always sent as unicast (never as multicast).

DUAL

Distance vector routing protocols such as RIP prevent routing loops with hold-down timers. The primary way that EIGRP prevents routing loops is with the DUAL algorithm. DUAL is used to obtain loop-freedom at every instant throughout a route computation. This allows all routers involved in a topology change to synchronize at the same time. Routers that are not affected by the topology changes are not involved in the recomputation because queries and replies are bounded to only those routers that need or have the route-specific information. This method provides EIGRP with faster convergence times than other distance vector routing protocols.

Because recomputation of DUAL can be processor intensive, it is advantageous to avoid recompu-tation whenever possible. Therefore, DUAL maintains a list of backup routes it has already deter-mined to be loop-free. If the primary route in the routing table fails, the best backup route is immediately added to the routing table.

Administrative Distance

EIGRP has a default AD of 90 for internal routes and 170 for routes imported from an external source, such as default routes. When compared to other interior gateway protocols, EIGRP is the most preferred by Cisco IOS Software because it has the lowest AD.

Notice in Table 13-2 that EIGRP has a third AD value, of 5, for summary routes. Later in this chapter, you learn how to configure EIGRP summary routes.

Table 13-2   Default Administrative Distance

Route Source	AD
Connected	0
Static	1
EIGRP summary route	5
External BGP	20
Internal EIGRP	90
IGRP	100
OSPF	110
IS-IS	115
RIP	120
External EIGRP	170
Internal BGP	200

EIGRP Configuration

To review the EIGRP configuration commands, we will use the topology in Figure 13-3 and the addressing scheme in Table 13-3.

Figure 13-3   EIGRP Configuration Topology

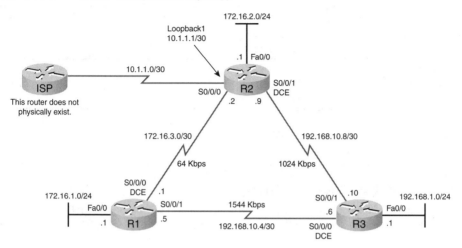

Table 13-3   Addressing Scheme for EIGRP

Device	Interface	IP Address	Subnet Mask
R1	Fa0/0	172.16.1.1	255.255.255.0
	S0/0/0	172.16.3.1	255.255.255.252
	S0/0/1	192.168.10.5	255.255.255.252
R2	Fa0/0	172.16.2.1	255.255.255.0
	S0/0/0	172.16.3.2	255.255.255.252
	S0/0/1	192.168.10.9	255.255.255.252
	Lo1	10.1.1.1	255.255.255.252
R3	Fa0/0	192.168.1.1	255.255.255.0
	S0/0/0	192.168.10.6	255.255.255.252
	S0/0/1	192.168.10.10	255.255.255.252

Notice in Figure 13-3 that the ISP router does not actually exist. For our review of default routing in EIGRP, we will use a simulated, loopback interface.

The network Command

Assuming the interfaces of all the routers are configured and activated according to the IP addresses in Table 13-3, Example 13-1 shows the EIGRP configuration using the **network** command.

Example 13-1   EIGRP Configuration

```
R1(config)#router eigrp 1
R1(config-router)#network 172.16.0.0
R1(config-router)#network 192.168.10.0

R2(config)#router eigrp 1
R2(config-router)#network 172.16.0.0
R2(config-router)#network 192.168.10.0

R3(config)#router eigrp 1
R3(config-router)#network 192.168.1.0
R3(config-router)#network 192.168.10.0
```

Automatic Summarization

Like RIP, EIGRP automatically summarizes networks to the classful boundary. In Example 13-2, we see that R1 and R2 are both sending the classful network 172.16.0.0/16 to R3.

Example 13-2   R3's Routing Table: Automatic Summarization

```
R3#show ip route
<output omitted>

Gateway of last resort is not set

D    172.16.0.0/16 [90/2172416] via 192.168.10.9, 00:00:57, Serial0/0/1
                   [90/2172416] via 192.168.10.5, 00:00:54, Serial0/0/0
C    192.168.1.0/24 is directly connected, FastEthernet0/0
     192.168.10.0/24 is variably subnetted, 3 subnets, 2 masks
D       192.168.10.0/24 is a summary, 00:00:54, Null0
C       192.168.10.4/30 is directly connected, Serial0/0/0
C       192.168.10.8/30 is directly connected, Serial0/0/1
R3#
```

R3 does not have the more specific subnet information. Because both paths are equal cost, R3 will load balance traffic to subnets for the 172.16.0.0/16 network. This will result in less than optimum routing at least half of the time. For example, to send traffic to a destination belonging to the 172.16.1.0/24 subnet, R3 will send traffic to both R1 and R2. Clearly, from the topology shown in Figure 13-3, R1 is the optimum path.

To ensure EIGRP routers are getting full subnet information, disable automatic summarization with the **no auto-summary** command, as shown in Example 13-3.

Example 13-3   Disable Automatic Summarization

```
R1(config)#router eigrp 1
R1(config-router)#no auto-summary

R2(config)#router eigrp 1
R2(config-router)#no auto-summary

R3(config)#router eigrp 1
R3(config-router)#no auto-summary
```

Now R3 will send traffic for the R1 LAN to R1 and the R2 LAN to R2. Example 13-4 shows the new routing table for R3 after automatic summarization is disabled.

Example 13-4   R3's Routing Table: Automatic Summarization Disabled

```
R3#show ip route
<output omitted>


Gateway of last resort is not set


     172.16.0.0/16 is variably subnetted, 3 subnets, 2 masks
D       172.16.1.0/24 [90/2172416] via 192.168.10.5, 00:01:28, Serial0/0/0
D       172.16.2.0/24 [90/2172416] via 192.168.10.9, 00:01:28, Serial0/0/1
D       172.16.3.0/30 [90/2681856] via 192.168.10.9, 00:01:28, Serial0/0/1
                      [90/2681856] via 192.168.10.5, 00:01:28, Serial0/0/0
C    192.168.1.0/24 is directly connected, FastEthernet0/0
     192.168.10.0/30 is subnetted, 2 subnets
C       192.168.10.4 is directly connected, Serial0/0/0
C       192.168.10.8 is directly connected, Serial0/0/1
```

Manual Summarization

With automatic summarization disabled, EIGRP no longer benefits from the smaller routing tables that can result from summarized classful network routes. To control the size of routing tables, you can use manual summarization to specify that a specific interface sends a summary route instead of the individual subnets. This also works for sending supernets.

For example, assume that R3 also has routes to the 192.168.0.0/24, 192.168.2.0/24, and 192.168.3.0/24 networks in addition to the 192.168.1.0/24 LAN. We can simulate these three routes by configuring loopbacks on R3 and then add these networks to the EIGRP configuration on R3, as shown in Example 13-5.

Example 13-5   Simulated LANs on R3

```
R3(config)#interface loopback 0
R3(config-if)#ip address 192.168.0.1 255.255.255.0
R3(config-if)#interface loopback 2
R3(config-if)#ip address 192.168.2.1 255.255.255.0
R3(config-if)#interface loopback 3
R3(config-if)#ip address 192.168.3.1 255.255.255.0
R3(config-if)#router eigrp 1
R3(config-router)#network 192.168.0.0
R3(config-router)#network 192.168.2.0
R3(config-router)#network 192.168.3.0
```

R1 and R2 will now have larger routing tables, as shown for R2 in Example 13-6.

Example 13-6   Larger Routing Table on R2

```
R2#sh ip route
<output limited to 192.168 routes>


Gateway of last resort is not set

D    192.168.0.0/24 [90/2297856] via 192.168.10.10, 00:01:20, Serial0/0/1
D    192.168.1.0/24 [90/2172416] via 192.168.10.10, 00:04:45, Serial0/0/1
D    192.168.2.0/24 [90/2297856] via 192.168.10.10, 00:01:18, Serial0/0/1
D    192.168.3.0/24 [90/2297856] via 192.168.10.10, 00:01:16, Serial0/0/1
```

The routes in Example 13-6 can be summarized into one supernet route advertised by R3 to both R1 and R2. A supernet is a collection of contiguous classful network addresses aggregated into one route. Instead of sending four /24 routes for the classful networks 192.168.0.0, 192.168.1.0, 192.168.2.0, and 192.168.3.0, we can configure a manual summary route as 192.168.0.0/22.

Manual summary routes must be configured on the interface that you want the summary route to be sent out of. The syntax for manual summary routes with EIGRP is as follows:

```
Router(config-if)#ip summary-address eigrp as-number network-address subnet-mask
```

Because R3 has two EIGRP neighbors, the EIGRP manual summarization in configured on both Serial 0/0/0 and Serial 0/0/1, as shown in Example 13-7.

Example 13-7   Configuring Manual Summary Routes for EIGRP

```
R3(config)#interface serial 0/0/0
R3(config-if)#ip summary-address eigrp 1 192.168.0.0 255.255.252.0
R3(config-if)#interface serial 0/0/1
R3(config-if)#ip summary-address eigrp 1 192.168.0.0 255.255.252.0
```

R1 and R2 now have smaller routing tables because the four networks are summarized into one route, as highlighted in Example 13-8 for R2.

Example 13-8   Smaller Routing Table for R2

```
R2#show ip route
<output omitted>


Gateway of last resort is not set

     192.168.10.0/30 is subnetted, 2 subnets
D       192.168.10.4 [90/2681856] via 192.168.10.10, 00:01:11, Serial0/0/1
                     [90/2681856] via 172.16.3.1, 00:00:06, Serial0/0/0
C       192.168.10.8 is directly connected, Serial0/0/1
     172.16.0.0/16 is variably subnetted, 3 subnets, 2 masks
D       172.16.1.0/24 [90/2172416] via 172.16.3.1, 00:00:06, Serial0/0/0
C       172.16.2.0/24 is directly connected, FastEthernet0/0
C       172.16.3.0/30 is directly connected, Serial0/0/0
     10.0.0.0/30 is subnetted, 1 subnets
C       10.1.1.0 is directly connected, Loopback1
D       192.168.0.0 [90/2681856] via 192.168.10.10, 00:01:11, Serial0/0/1
```

EIGRP Default Route

The "quad zero" default static route can be used with any currently supported routing protocols. In our example, we configure the static default route on R2 because it is simulating a connection to ISP. Example 13-9 shows the default static route configuration on R2.

Example 13-9   Configuring and Redistributing a Default Route in EIGRP

```
R2(config)#ip route 0.0.0.0 0.0.0.0 loopback 1
R2(config)#router eigrp 1
R2(config-router)#redistribute static
```

The **redistribute static** command tells EIGRP to include this static route in its EIGRP updates to other routers. Example 13-10 shows the routing table for R1 with the default route highlighted.

Example 13-10 R1 Routing Table with Default Route Installed

```
R1#show ip route
Codes: C - connected, S - static, I - IGRP, R - RIP, M - mobile, B - BGP
       D - EIGRP, EX - EIGRP external, O - OSPF, IA - OSPF inter area
<some codes omitted>


Gateway of last resort is 172.16.3.2 to network 0.0.0.0

     192.168.10.0/30 is subnetted, 2 subnets
C       192.168.10.4 is directly connected, Serial0/0/1
D       192.168.10.8 [90/2681856] via 192.168.10.6, 00:07:03, Serial0/0/1
                     [90/2681856] via 172.16.3.2, 00:05:58, Serial0/0/0
     172.16.0.0/16 is variably subnetted, 3 subnets, 2 masks
C       172.16.1.0/24 is directly connected, FastEthernet0/0
D       172.16.2.0/24 [90/2172416] via 172.16.3.2, 00:05:58, Serial0/0/0
C       172.16.3.0/30 is directly connected, Serial0/0/0
D EX*   0.0.0.0 [170/2297856] via 172.16.3.2, 00:00:00, Serial0/0/0
D       192.168.0.0 [90/2681856] via 192.168.10.6, 00:07:03, Serial0/0/1
```

Modifying the EIGRP Metric

EIGRP uses the values bandwidth, delay, reliability, and load in its composite metric to calculate the preferred path to a network. By default, EIGRP uses only bandwidth and delay in its metric calculation, as shown in Figure 13-4.

The bandwidth metric is a static value assigned by Cisco IOS to interface types. For example, most serial interfaces are assigned the default value 1544 kbps, the bandwidth of a T1 connection. This value might or might not reflect the actual bandwidth of the interface.

Delay is the measure of time it takes for a packet to traverse a route. The delay metric is a static value based on the type of link to which the interface is connected and is measured in microseconds.

Figure 13-4   Calculating the EIGRP Default Metric

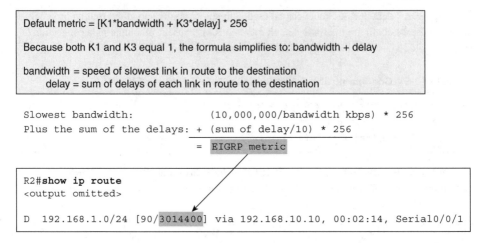

Because the bandwidth might default to a value that does not reflect the actual value, you can use the interface command **bandwidth** to modify the bandwidth metric:

```
Router(config-if)#bandwidth kilobits
```

In the topology shown in Figure 13-3, notice that the link between R1 and R2 has a bandwidth of 64 kbps, and the link between R2 and R3 has a bandwidth of 1024 kbps. Example 13-11 shows the configurations used on all three routers to modify the bandwidth.

Example 13-11 Modifying the Bandwidth

```
R1(config)#interface serial 0/0/0
R1(config-if)#bandwidth 64

R2(config)#interface serial 0/0/0
R2(config-if)#bandwidth 64
R2(config-if)#interface serial 0/0/1
R2(config-if)#bandwidth 1024

R3(config)#interface serial 0/0/1
R3(config-if)#bandwidth 1024
```

Modifying Hello Intervals and Hold Times

Hello intervals and hold times are configurable on a per-interface basis and do not have to match with other EIGRP routers to establish adjacencies. The syntax for the command to modify the hello interval is as follows:

```
Router(config-if)#ip hello-interval eigrp as-number seconds
```

If you change the hello interval, make sure that you also change the hold time to a value equal to or greater than the hello interval. Otherwise, neighbor adjacency will go down after the hold time expires and before the next hello interval. The command to configure a different hold time is as follows:

```
Router(config-if)#ip hold-time eigrp as-number seconds
```

The *seconds* value for both hello and holdtime intervals can range from 1 to 65,535. In Example 13-12, R1 and R2 are configured to use a 60-second hello interval and 180-second hold time.

Example 13-12 Modifying the Hello Intervals and Hold Times

```
R1(config)#interface s0/0/0
R1(config-if)#ip hello-interval eigrp 1 60
R1(config-if)#ip hold-time eigrp 1 180

R2(config)#interface s0/0/0
R2(config-if)#ip hello-interval eigrp 1 60
R2(config-if)#ip hold-time eigrp 1 180
```

EIGRP Verification and Troubleshooting

To verify any routing configuration, you will most likely depend on the **show ip route**, **show ip interface brief**, and **show ip protocols** commands. The routing table should have all the expected routes. If not, check the status of the interfaces to make sure that no interfaces are down or mis-configured. Use the **show ip protocols** command to verify that EIGRP and that most of your EIGRP configurations are operational, as shown in Example 13-13.

Example 13-13 Verify EIGRP Configuration with the show ip protocols Command

```
R2#show ip protocols
Routing Protocol is "eigrp 1"
  Outgoing update filter list for all interfaces is not set
  Incoming update filter list for all interfaces is not set
  Default networks flagged in outgoing updates
  Default networks accepted from incoming updates
  EIGRP metric weight K1=1, K2=0, K3=1, K4=0, K5=0
  EIGRP maximum hopcount 100
  EIGRP maximum metric variance 1
  Redistributing: static, eigrp 1
  EIGRP NSF-aware route hold timer is 240s
  Automatic network summarization is not in effect
  Maximum path: 4
  Routing for Networks:
    172.16.0.0
    192.168.10.0
  Routing Information Sources:
    Gateway         Distance      Last Update
    192.168.10.10         90      00:02:53
    172.16.3.1           90      00:02:53
  Distance: internal 90 external 170
```

For EIGRP, you can use two tables in addition to the routing table to verify and troubleshoot the configuration—the neighbor table and the topology table.

First, verify that the expected neighbors have established adjacency with the **show ip eigrp neighbors** command. Figure 13-5 shows the output for R2 with a brief explanation of each part.

Figure 13-5   The EIGRP Neighbor Table

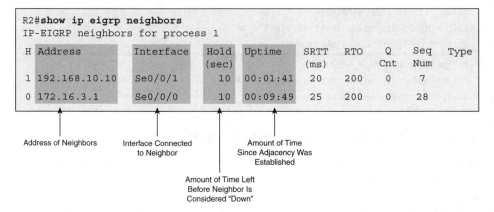

If EIGRP is not routing as you expect, you can use the **show ip eigrp topology** command to view all the routes that are currently part of the EIGRP database, including routes that are installed in the routing table and potential backup routes as shown in Example 13-14 for R2.

Example 13-14 The EIGRP Topology Table

```
R2#show ip eigrp topology
IP-EIGRP Topology Table for AS(1)/ID(10.1.1.1)


Codes: P - Passive, A - Active, U - Update, Q - Query, R - Reply,
       r - reply Status, s - sia Status


P 0.0.0.0/0, 1 successors, FD is 128256
        via Rstatic (128256/0)
P 192.168.10.4/30, 1 successors, FD is 3523840
        via 192.168.10.10 (3523840/2169856), Serial0/1/1
P 192.168.0.0/22, 1 successors, FD is 3014400
        via 192.168.10.10 (3014400/28160), Serial0/1/1
P 192.168.10.8/30, 1 successors, FD is 3011840
        via Connected, Serial0/1/1
P 172.16.1.0/24, 1 successors, FD is 3526400
        via 192.168.10.10 (3526400/2172416), Serial0/1/1
        via 172.16.3.1 (40514560/28160), Serial0/1/0
P 172.16.2.0/24, 1 successors, FD is 28160
        via Connected, FastEthernet0/0
P 172.16.3.0/30, 1 successors, FD is 40512000
        via Connected, Serial0/1/0
```

EIGRP-specific terms you should know so you can interpret the output in Example 13-14 include the following:

- **Successor:** A neighboring router that is used for packet forwarding and is the least-cost route to the destination network.

- **Feasible Distance (FD):** Lowest calculated metric to reach the destination network.

- **Feasible Successor (FS):** A neighbor who has a loop-free backup path to the same network as the successor by satisfying the feasibility condition.

- **Feasibility Condition (FC):** The FC is met when a neighbor's reported distance (RD) to a network is less than the local router's FD to the same destination network.

To review the concepts of successor, feasible distance, and feasible successor, let's look at a detailed description of the highlighted entry in Example 13-13.

The first line displays the following:

- **P:** This route is in the passive state, which means the route is stable and not actively seeking a replacement. All routes in the topology table should be in the passive state for a stable routing domain.

- **172.16.1.0/24:** This is the destination network that is also found in the routing table.

- **1 successors:** This shows the number of successors for this network. If multiple equal-cost paths exist to this network, there will be multiple successors.

- **FD is 3526400:** This is the FD, the EIGRP metric to reach the destination network.

The first entry shows the successor:

- **via 192.168.10.10:** This is the next-hop address of the successor, R3. This address is shown in the routing table.

- **3526400:** This is the FD to 172.16.1.0/24. It is the metric shown in the routing table.

- **2172416:** This is the RD of the successor and is R3's cost to reach this network.

- **Serial0/1/1:** This is the outbound interface used to reach this network, also shown in the routing table.

The second entry shows the feasible successor, R1. (If no second entry exists, there are no FSs.)

- **via 172.16.3.1:** This is the next-hop address of the FS, R1.

- **40514560:** This would be R2's new FD to 192.168.1.0/24 if R1 became the new successor.

- **28160:** This is the RD of the FS or R1's metric to reach this network. This value, RD, must be less than the current FD of 3526400 to meet the FC.

- **Serial0/1/0:** This is the outbound interface used to reach the FC, if this router becomes the successor.

To see all the possible routes in the EIGRP topology database, including routes that do not meet the feasibility condition, use the **all-links** option, as shown in Example 13-15.

Example 13-15 The EIGRP Topology Table with All Links

```
R2#show ip eigrp topology all-links
IP-EIGRP Topology Table for AS(1)/ID(10.1.1.1)


Codes: P - Passive, A - Active, U - Update, Q - Query, R - Reply,
       r - reply Status, s - sia Status


P 0.0.0.0/0, 1 successors, FD is 128256, serno 3
        via Rstatic (128256/0)
P 192.168.10.4/30, 1 successors, FD is 3523840, serno 8
        via 192.168.10.10 (3523840/2169856), Serial0/1/1
        via 172.16.3.1 (41024000/20512000), Serial0/1/0
P 192.168.0.0/22, 1 successors, FD is 3014400, serno 9
        via 192.168.10.10 (3014400/28160), Serial0/1/1
        via 172.16.3.1 (41026560/20514560), Serial0/1/0
P 192.168.10.8/30, 1 successors, FD is 3011840, serno 6
        via Connected, Serial0/1/1
        via 172.16.3.1 (41536000/21024000), Serial0/1/0
P 172.16.1.0/24, 1 successors, FD is 3526400, serno 10
        via 192.168.10.10 (3526400/2172416), Serial0/1/1
        via 172.16.3.1 (40514560/28160), Serial0/1/0
P 172.16.2.0/24, 1 successors, FD is 28160, serno 1
        via Connected, FastEthernet0/0
        via 172.16.3.1 (41538560/21026560), Serial0/1/0
P 172.16.3.0/30, 1 successors, FD is 40512000, serno 2
```

By comparing the output from Example 13-14 with the output from Example 13-15, you can see that EIGRP has more routes in the routing table than shown initially. But these additional routes do not meet the feasibility condition. Therefore, DUAL must first query neighbors to make sure there is not a better route out there before installing a route that does not meet the feasibility condition. This is the essence of how DUAL avoids loops.

DUAL's finite state machine—how the algorithm comes to a final decision—is graphically represented in the flow chart in Figure 13-6.

To monitor DUAL's FSM in action, use the **debug eigrp fsm** command. Then shut down an interface on the router to see how DUAL reacts to the change in the topology.

Figure 13-6   DUAL Finite State Machine

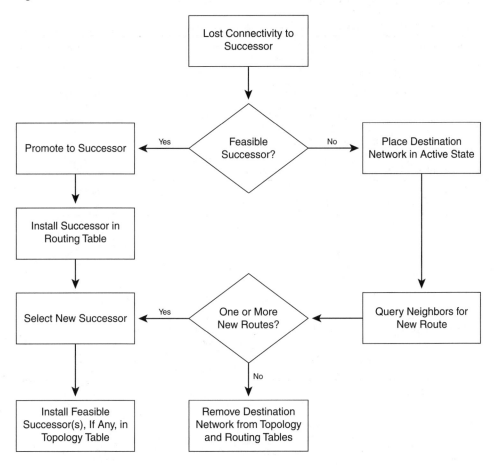

Study Resources

For today's exam topics, refer to the following resources for more study.

Resource	Chapter	Topic	Where to Find It
Foundational Resources			
CCNA Exploration Online Curriculum: Routing Protocols and Concepts	Chapter 9, "EIGRP"	All sections within this chapter	Sections 9.1–9.5
CCNA Exploration Routing Protocols and Concepts Companion Guide	Chapter 9, "EIGRP"	All topics within this chapter	pp. 393–461
ICND2 Official Exam Certification Guide	Chapter 10, "EIGRP"	All topics within this chapter	pp. 380–402
ICND2 Authorized Self-Study Guide	Chapter 5, "Implementing EIGRP"	Implementing EIGRP	pp. 171–191
Supplemental Resources			
CCNA Flash Cards and Exam Practice Pack	ICND2, Section 6	Implementing EIGRP	pp. 492–510
CCNA Video Mentor	ICND2, Lab 5	EIGRP Configuration and Operation	pp. 68–71
	ICND2, Lab 6	Understanding EIGRP Metric Calculations	pp. 73–78

OSPF Routing

CCNA 640-802 Exam Topics

- Configure, verify, and troubleshoot OSPF.

Key Topics

Open Shortest Path First (OSPF) is a link-state routing protocol that was developed as a replacement for Routing Information Protocol (RIP). OSPF's major advantages over RIP are its fast convergence and its scalability to much larger network implementations. Today we review the operation, configuration, verification, and troubleshooting of basic OSPF.

OSPF Operation

IETF chose OSPF over Intermediate System-to-Intermediate System (IS-IS) as its recommended Interior Gateway Protocol (IGP). In 1998, the OSPFv2 specification was updated in RFC 2328 and is the current RFC for OSPF. RFC 2328, OSPF Version 2, is on the IETF website at http://www.ietf.org/rfc/rfc2328. Cisco IOS Software will choose OSPF routes over RIP routes because OSPF has an administrative distance of 110 versus RIP's AD of 120.

OSPF Message Format

The data portion of an OSPF message is encapsulated in a packet. This data field can include one of five OSPF packet types. Figure 12-1 shows an encapsulated OSPF message in an Ethernet frame.

Figure 12-1   Encapsulated OSPF Message

Data Link Frame Header	IP Packet Header	OSPF Packet Header	OSPF Packet Type-Specific Data

Data Link Frame (Ethernet Fields Shown Here)
MAC Source Address = Address of Sending Interface
MAC Destination Address = Multicast: 01-00-5E-00-00-05 or 01-00-5E-00-00-06

IP Packet
IP Source Address = Address of Sending Interface
IP Destination Address = Multicast: 224.0.0.5 or 224.0.0.6
Protocol Field = 89 for OSPF

OSPF Packet Header
Type Code for OSPF Packet Type
Router ID and Area ID

OSPF Packet Types
0x01 Hello
0x02 Database Description
0x03 Link State Request
0x04 Link State Update
0x05 Link State Acknowledgment

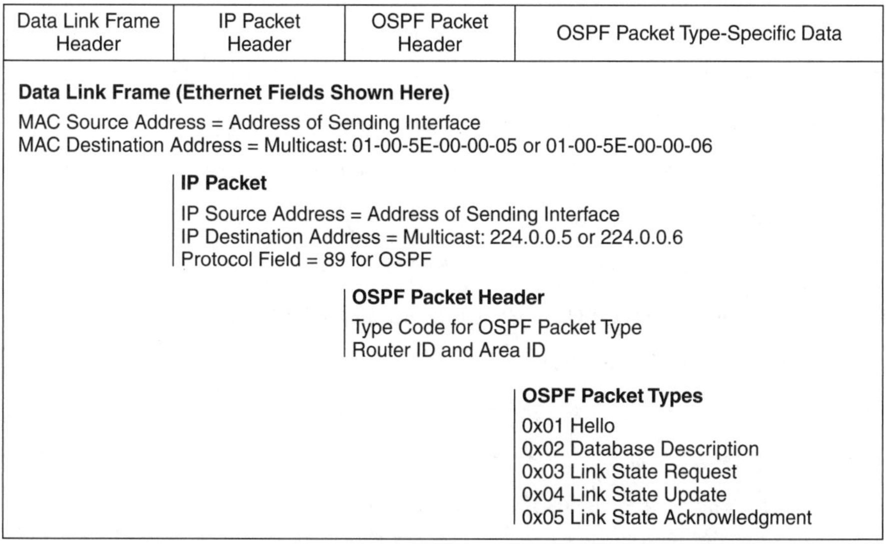

The OSPF packet header is included with every OSPF packet, regardless of its type. The OSPF packet header and packet type-specific data are then encapsulated in an IP packet. In the IP packet header, the protocol field is set to 89 to indicate OSPF, and the destination address is typically set to one of two multicast addresses: 224.0.0.5 or 224.0.0.6. If the OSPF packet is encapsulated in an Ethernet frame, the destination MAC address is also a multicast address: 01-00-5E-00-00-05 or 01-00-5E-00-00-06.

OSPF Packet Types

These five OSPF packet types each serve a specific purpose in the routing process:

- **Hello:** Hello packets are used to establish and maintain adjacency with other OSPF routers.

- **DBD:** The database description (DBD) packet contains an abbreviated list of the sending router's link-state database and is used by receiving routers to check against the local link-state database.

- **LSR:** Receiving routers can then request more information about any entry in the DBD by sending a link-state request (LSR).

- **LSU:** Link-state update (LSU) packets are used to reply to LSRs and to announce new information. LSUs contain 11 types of link-state advertisements (LSA).

- **LSAck:** When an LSU is received, the router sends a link-state acknowledgment (LSAck) to confirm receipt of the LSU.

Neighbor Establishment

Hello packets are exchanged between OSPF neighbors to establish adjacency. Figure 12-2 shows the OSPF header and Hello packet.

Important fields shown in the figure include the following:

- **Type:** OSPF packet type: Hello (Type 1), DBD (Type 2), LS Request (Type 3), LS Update (Type 4), LS ACK (Type 5)

- **Router ID:** ID of the originating router

- **Area ID:** Area from which the packet originated

- **Network Mask:** Subnet mask associated with the sending interface

- **Hello Interval:** Number of seconds between the sending router's Hellos

- **Router Priority:** Used in DR/BDR election (discussed later in the section "DR/BDR Election")

- **Designated Router (DR):** Router ID of the DR, if any

- **Backup Designated Router (BDR):** Router ID of the BDR, if any

- **List of Neighbors:** Lists the OSPF Router ID of the neighboring router(s)

Hello packets are used to do the following:

- Discover OSPF neighbors and establish neighbor adjacencies

- Advertise parameters on which two routers must agree to become neighbors

- Elect the DR and BDR on multiaccess networks such as Ethernet and Frame Relay

Figure 12-2   OSPF Packet Header and Hello Packet

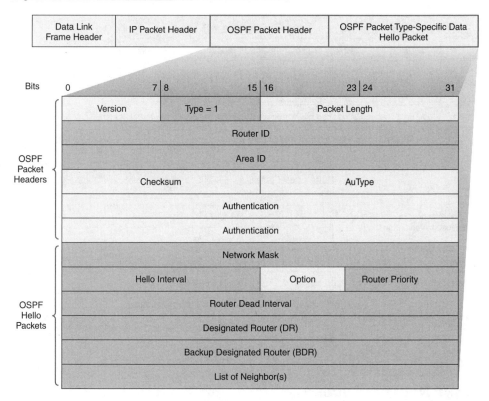

Receiving an OSPF Hello packet on an interface confirms for a router that another OSPF router exists on this link. OSPF then establishes adjacency with the neighbor. To establish adjacency, two OSPF routers must have the following matching interface values:

- Hello Interval

- Dead Interval

- Network Type

Before both routers can establish adjacency, both interfaces must be part of the same network, including the same subnet mask. Then full adjacency will happen after both routers have exchanged any necessary LSUs and have identical link-state databases. By default, OSPF Hello packets are sent to the multicast address 224.0.0.5 (*ALLSPFRouters*) every 10 seconds on multiaccess and point-to-point segments and every 30 seconds on nonbroadcast multiaccess (NBMA) segments (Frame Relay, X.25, ATM). The default dead interval is four times the Hello interval.

Link-State Advertisements

Link-state updates (LSUs) are the packets used for OSPF routing updates. An LSU packet can contain 11 types of link-state advertisements (LSAs), as shown in Figure 12-3.

Figure 12-3   LSUs Contain LSAs

Type	Packet Name	Description
1	Hello	Discovers neighbors and builds adjacencies between them.
2	DBD	Checks for database synchronization between routers.
3	LSR	Requests specific link-state records from router to router.
4	LSU	Sends specifically requested link-state records.
5	LSAck	Acknowledges the other packet types.

The acronyms LSA and LSU are often used interchangeably.

An LSU contains one or more LSAs.

LSAs contain route information for destination networks.

LSA specifics are discussed in CCNP.

LSA Type	Description
1	Router LSAs
2	Network LSAs
3 or 4	Summary LSAs
5	Autonomous System External LSAs
6	Multicast OSPF LSAs
7	Defined for Not-So-Stubby Areas
8	External Attributes LSA for Border Gateway Protocol (BGP)
9, 10, 11	Opaque LSAs

OSPF Network Types

OSPF defines five network types:

- Point-to-point

- Broadcast multiaccess

- Nonbroadcast multiaccess

- Point-to-multipoint

- Virtual links

Multiaccess networks create two challenges for OSPF regarding the flooding of LSAs:

- Creation of multiple adjacencies, one adjacency for every pair of routers

- Extensive flooding of LSAs

DR/BDR Election

The solution to managing the number of adjacencies and the flooding of LSAs on a multiaccess network is the designated router (DR). To reduce the amount of OSPF traffic on multiaccess networks, OSPF elects a DR and backup DR (BDR). The DR is responsible for updating all other OSPF routers when a change occurs in the multiaccess network. The BDR monitors the DR and takes over as DR if the current DR fails.

The following criteria is used to elect the DR and BDR:

1. DR: Router with the highest OSPF interface priority.

2. BDR: Router with the second highest OSPF interface priority.

3. If OSPF interface priorities are equal, the highest router ID is used to break the tie.

When the DR is elected, it remains the DR until one of the following conditions occurs:

- The DR fails.

- The OSPF process on the DR fails.

- The multiaccess interface on the DR fails.

If the DR fails, the BDR assumes the role of DR, and an election is held to choose a new BDR. If a new router enters the network after the DR and BDR have been elected, it will not become the DR or the BDR even if it has a higher OSPF interface priority or router ID than the current DR or BDR. The new router can be elected the BDR if the current DR or BDR fails. If the current DR fails, the BDR will become the DR, and the new router can be elected the new BDR.

Without additional configuration, you can control the routers that win the DR and BDR elections by doing either of the following:

- Boot the DR first, followed by the BDR, and then boot all other routers.

- Shut down the interface on all routers, followed by a **no shutdown** on the DR, then the BDR, and then all other routers.

However, the recommended way to control DR/BDR elections is to change the interface priority, which we review in the "OSPF Configuration" section.

OSPF Algorithm

Each OSPF router maintains a link-state database containing the LSAs received from all other routers. When a router has received all the LSAs and built its local link-state database, OSPF uses Dijkstra's shortest path first (SPF) algorithm to create an SPF tree. This algorithm accumulates costs along each path, from source to destination. The SPF tree is then used to populate the IP routing table with the best paths to each network.

For example, in Figure 12-4 each path is labeled with an arbitrary value for cost. The cost of the shortest path for R2 to send packets to the LAN attached to R3 is 27 (20 + 5 + 2 = 27). Notice that this cost is not 27 for all routers to reach the LAN attached to R3. Each router determines its own cost to each destination in the topology. In other words, each router uses the SPF algorithm to calculate the cost of each path to a network and determines the best path to that network from its own perspective.

Figure 12-4   Dijkstra's Shortest Path First Algorithm

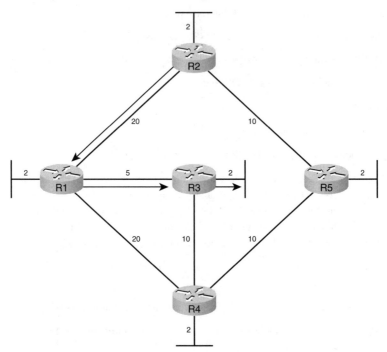

Shortest Path for Host on R2 LAN to Reach Host on R3 LAN:
R2 to R1 (20) + R1 to R3 (5) + R3 to LAN (2) = 27

Table 12-1 lists, for R1, the shortest path to each LAN, along with the cost.

Table 12-1   SPF Tree for R1

Destination	Shortest Path	Cost
R2 LAN	R1 to R2	22
R3 LAN	R1 to R3	7
R4 LAN	R1 to R3 to R4	17
R5 LAN	R1 to R3 to R4 to R5	27

You should be able to create a similar table for each of the other routers in Figure 12-4.

Link-State Routing Process

The following list summarizes the link-state routing process used by OSPF. All OSPF routers complete the following generic link-state routing process to reach a state of convergence:

1. Each router learns about its own links, and its own directly connected networks. This is done by detecting that an interface is in the up state, including a Layer 3 address.

2. Each router is responsible for establishing adjacency with its neighbors on directly connected networks by exchanging Hello packets.

3. Each router builds a link-state packet (LSP) containing the state of each directly connected link. This is done by recording all the pertinent information about each neighbor, including neighbor ID, link type, and bandwidth.

4. Each router floods the LSP to all neighbors, who then store all LSPs received in a database. Neighbors then flood the LSPs to their neighbors until all routers in the area have received the LSPs. Each router stores a copy of each LSP received from its neighbors in a local database.

5. Each router uses the database to construct a complete map of the topology and computes the best path to each destination network. The SPF algorithm is used to construct the map of the topology and to determine the best path to each network. All routers will have a common map or tree of the topology, but each router independently determines the best path to each network within that topology.

OSPF Configuration

To review the OSPF configuration commands, we will use the topology in Figure 12-5 and the addressing scheme in Table 12-2.

Figure 12-5   OSPF Configuration Topology

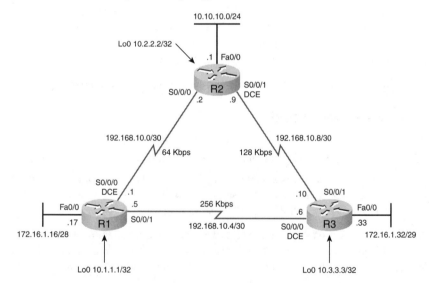

Table 12-2   Addressing Scheme for OSPF

Device	Interface	IP Address	Subnet Mask
R1	Fa0/0	172.16.1.17	255.255.255.240
	S0/0/0	192.168.10.1	255.255.255.252
	S0/0/1	192.168.10.5	255.255.255.252
	Lo0	10.1.1.1	255.255.255.255

continues

Table 12-2   Addressing Scheme for OSPF   *continued*

Device	Interface	IP Address	Subnet Mask
R2	Fa0/0	10.10.10.1	255.255.255.0
	S0/0/0	192.168.10.2	255.255.255.252
	S0/0/1	192.168.10.9	255.255.255.252
	Lo0	10.2.2.2	255.255.255.255
R3	Fa0/0	172.16.1.33	255.255.255.248
	S0/0/0	192.168.10.6	255.255.255.252
	S0/0/1	192.168.10.10	255.255.255.252
	Lo0	10.3.3.3	255.255.255.255

The router ospf Command

OSPF is enabled with the **router ospf** *process-id* global configuration command:

```
R1(config)#router ospf 1
```

The *process-id* is a number between 1 and 65,535 and is chosen by the network administrator. The process ID is locally significant. It does not have to match other OSPF routers to establish adjacencies with those neighbors. This differs from EIGRP. The EIGRP process ID or autonomous system number must match before two EIGRP neighbors will become adjacent.

For our review, we will enable OSPF on all three routers using the same process ID of 1.

The network Command

The **network** command is used in router configuration mode:

```
Router(config-router)#network network-address wildcard-mask area area-id
```

The OSPF **network** command uses a combination of *network-address* and *wildcard-mask*. The network address, along with the wildcard mask, is used to specify the interface or range of interfaces that will be enabled for OSPF using this **network** command.

The wildcard mask is customarily configured as the inverse of a subnet mask. For example, R1's FastEthernet 0/0 interface is on the 172.16.1.16/28 network. The subnet mask for this interface is /28 or 255.255.255.240. The inverse of the subnet mask results in the wildcard mask 0.0.0.15.

The **area** *area-id* refers to the OSPF area. An OSPF area is a group of routers that share link-state information. All OSPF routers in the same area must have the same link-state information in their link-state databases. Therefore, all the routers within the same OSPF area must be configured with the same area ID on all routers. By convention, the area ID is 0.

Example 12-1 shows the **network** commands for all three routers, enabling OSPF on all interfaces.

Example 12-1   Configuring OSPF Networks

```
R1(config)#router ospf 1
R1(config-router)#network 172.16.1.16 0.0.0.15 area 0
R1(config-router)#network 192.168.10.0 0.0.0.3 area 0
R1(config-router)#network 192.168.10.4 0.0.0.3 area 0

R2(config)#router ospf 1
R2(config-router)#network 10.10.10.0 0.0.0.255 area 0
R2(config-router)#network 192.168.10.0 0.0.0.3 area 0
R2(config-router)#network 192.168.10.8 0.0.0.3 area 0

R3(config)#router ospf 1
R3(config-router)#network 172.16.1.32 0.0.0.7 area 0
R3(config-router)#network 192.168.10.4 0.0.0.3 area 0
R3(config-router)#network 192.168.10.8 0.0.0.3 area 0
```

Router ID

The router ID plays an important role in OSPF. It is used to uniquely identify each router in the OSPF routing domain. Cisco routers derive the router ID based on three criteria in the following order:

1. Use the IP address configured with the OSPF **router-id** command.

2. If the router ID is not configured, the router chooses the highest IP address of any of its loopback interfaces.

3. If no loopback interfaces are configured, the router chooses the highest active IP address of any of its physical interfaces.

The router ID can be viewed with several commands including **show ip ospf interfaces**, **show ip protocols**, and **show ip ospf**.

Two ways to influence the router ID are to configure a loopback address or configure the router ID. The advantage of using a loopback interface is that, unlike physical interfaces, it cannot fail. Therefore, using a loopback address for the router ID provides stability to the OSPF process.

Because the OSPF **router-id** command is a fairly recent addition to Cisco IOS Software (Release 12.0[1]T), it is more common to find loopback addresses used for configuring OSPF router IDs.

Example 12-2 shows the loopback configurations for the routers in our topology.

Example 12-2   Loopback Configurations

```
R1(config)#interface loopback 0
R1(config-if)#ip address 10.1.1.1 255.255.255.255

R2(config)#interface loopback 0
R2(config-if)#ip address 10.2.2.2 255.255.255.255

R3(config)#interface loopback 0
R3(config-if)#ip address 10.3.3.3 255.255.255.255
```

To configure the router ID, use the following command syntax:

```
Router(config)#router ospf process-id
Router(config-router)#router-id ip-address
```

The router ID is selected when OSPF is configured with its first OSPF **network** command. So the loopback or router ID command should already be configured. However, you can force OSPF to release its current ID and use the loopback or configured router ID by either reloading the router or using the following command:

```
Router#clear ip ospf process
```

Modifying the OSPF Metric

Cisco IOS Software uses the cumulative bandwidths of the outgoing interfaces from the router to the destination network as the cost value. At each router, the cost for an interface is calculated using the following formula:

Cisco IOS Cost for OSPF = 10^8/bandwidth in bps

In this calculation, the value 10^8 is known as the *reference bandwidth*. The reference bandwidth can be modified to accommodate networks with links faster than 100,000,000 bps (100 Mbps) using the OSPF command **auto-cost reference-bandwidth** interface command. When used, this command should be entered on all routers so that the OSPF routing metric remains consistent. Table 12-3 shows the default OSPF costs using the default reference bandwidth for several types of interfaces.

Table 12-3   Cisco IOS OSPF Cost Values

Interface Type	10^8/bps = Cost
Fast Ethernet and faster	10^8/100,000,000 bps = 1
Ethernet	10^8/10,000,000 bps = 10
E1	10^8/2,048,000 bps = 48
T1	10^8/1,544,000 bps = 64
128 kbps	10^8/128,000 bps = 781
64 kbps	10^8/64,000 bps = 1562
56 kbps	10^8/56,000 bps = 1785

You can modify the OSPF metric in two ways:

- Use the **bandwidth** command to modify the bandwidth value used by the Cisco IOS Software in calculating the OSPF cost metric.

- Use the **ip ospf cost** command, which allows you to directly specify the cost of an interface.

Table 12-4 shows the two alternatives that can be used in modifying the costs of the serial links in the topology. The right side shows the **ip ospf cost** command equivalents of the **bandwidth** commands on the left.

Table 12-4   Equivalent bandwidth and ip ospf cost Commands

bandwidth Commands		ip ospf cost Commands
Router R1		**Router R1**
R1(config)#interface serial 0/0/0	=	R1(config)#interface serial 0/0/0
R1(config-if)#bandwidth 64		R1(config-if)#ip ospf cost 1562
R1(config)#interface serial 0/0/1	=	R1(config)#interface serial 0/0/1
R1(config-if)#bandwidth 256		R1(config-if)#ip ospf cost 390
Router R2		**Router R2**
R2(config)#interface serial 0/0/0	=	R2(config)#interface serial 0/0/0
R2(config-if)#bandwidth 64		R2(config-if)#ip ospf cost 1562
R2(config)#interface serial 0/0/1	=	R2(config)#interface serial 0/0/1
R2(config-if)#bandwidth 128		R2(config-if)#ip ospf cost 781
Router R3		**Router R3**
R3(config)#interface serial 0/0/0	=	R3(config)#interface serial 0/0/0
R3(config-if)#bandwidth 256		R3(config-if)#ip ospf cost 390
R3(config)#interface serial 0/0/1	=	R3(config)#interface serial 0/0/0
R3(config-if)#bandwidth 128		R3(config-if)#ip ospf cost 781

Controlling the DR/BDR Election

Because the DR becomes the focal point for the collection and distribution of LSAs in a multiaccess network, it is important for this router to have sufficient CPU and memory capacity to handle the responsibility. Instead of relying on the router ID to decide which routers are elected the DR and BDR, it is better to control the election of these routers with the **ip ospf priority** interface command:

```
Router(config-if)#ip ospf priority {0 - 255}
```

The priority value defaults to 1 for all router interfaces, which means the router ID determines the DR and BDR. If you change the default value from 1 to a higher value, however, the router with the highest priority becomes the DR, and the router with the next highest priority becomes the BDR. A value of 0 makes the router ineligible to become a DR or BDR.

All the routers in Figure 12-6 booted at the same time with a complete OSPF configuration. In such a situation, RouterC is elected the DR, and RouterB is elected the BDR based on the highest router IDs.

Let's assume RouterA is the better candidate to be DR and RouterB should be BDR. However, you do not want to change the addressing scheme. Example 12-3 shows a way to control the DR/BDR election in the topology shown in Figure 12-6.

Figure 12-6   Multiaccess Topology

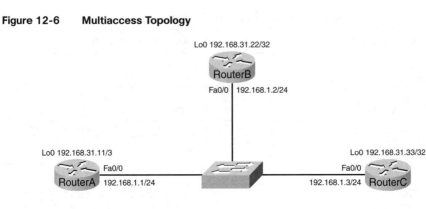

Example 12-3   Modifying the OSPF Interface Priority

```
RouterA(config)#interface fastethernet 0/0
RouterA(config-if)#ip ospf priority 200

RouterB(config)#interface fastethernet 0/0
RouterB(config-if)#ip ospf priority 100
```

Notice we changed both routers. Although RouterB was the BDR without doing anything, it would lose this role to RouterC if we did not configure RouterB's priority to be higher than the default.

Redistributing a Default Route

Returning to the first topology shown in Figure 12-5, we can simulate a connection to the Internet on R1 by configuring a loopback interface. R1 is now called an Autonomous System Boundary Router (ASBR). Then we can redistribute the default static route to R2 and R3 with the **default-information originate** command, as demonstrated in Example 12-4.

Example 12-4   ASBR Static Default Route Configuration

```
R1(config)#interface loopback 1
R1(config-if)#ip add 172.30.1.1 255.255.255.252
R1(config-if)#exit
R1(config)#ip route 0.0.0.0 0.0.0.0 loopback 1
R1(config)#router ospf 1
R1(config-router)#default-information originate
```

Modifying Hello Intervals and Hold Times

It might be desirable to change the OSPF timers so that routers will detect network failures in less time. Doing this will increase traffic, but sometimes there is a need for quick convergence that outweighs the extra traffic.

OSPF Hello and Dead intervals can be modified manually using the following interface commands:

```
Router(config-if)#ip ospf hello-interval seconds
Router(config-if)#ip ospf dead-interval seconds
```

Example 12-5 shows the Hello and Dead intervals modified to 5 seconds and 20 seconds, respectively, on the Serial 0/0/0 interface for R1.

Example 12-5   Modifying Hello and Dead Intervals on R1

```
R1(config)#interface serial 0/0/0
R1(config-if)#ip ospf hello-interval 5
R1(config-if)#ip ospf dead-interval 20
R1(config-if)#end
```

Remember, unlike EIGRP, OSPF Hello and Dead intervals must be equivalent between neighbors. So R2 should be configured with the same intervals.

Verifying and Troubleshooting OSPF

To verify any routing configuration, you will most likely depend on the **show ip route**, **show ip interface brief**, and **show ip protocols** commands. The routing table should have all the expected routes. If not, check the status of all interfaces to ensure that an interface is not down or misconfigured. For our example, the routing tables for OSPF will have an **O*E2** route on R2 and R3 as shown in R2's routing table in Example 12-6.

Example 12-6   R2's Routing Table

```
R2#show ip route
Codes: C - connected, S - static, R - RIP, M - mobile, B - BGP
       D - EIGRP, EX - EIGRP external, O - OSPF, IA - OSPF inter area
       N1 - OSPF NSSA external type 1, N2 - OSPF NSSA external type 2
       E1 - OSPF external type 1, E2 - OSPF external type 2
       i - IS-IS, su - IS-IS summary, L1 - IS-IS level-1, L2 - IS-IS level-2
       ia - IS-IS inter area, * - candidate default, U - per-user static route
       o - ODR, P - periodic downloaded static route

Gateway of last resort is 192.168.10.10 to network 0.0.0.0

     192.168.10.0/30 is subnetted, 3 subnets
C       192.168.10.0 is directly connected, Serial0/0/0
O       192.168.10.4 [110/1171] via 192.168.10.10, 00:02:24, Serial0/0/1
C       192.168.10.8 is directly connected, Serial0/0/1
     172.16.0.0/16 is variably subnetted, 2 subnets, 2 masks
O       172.16.1.32/29 [110/782] via 192.168.10.10, 00:02:24, Serial0/0/1
O       172.16.1.16/28 [110/1172] via 192.168.10.10, 00:02:24, Serial0/0/1
     10.0.0.0/8 is variably subnetted, 2 subnets, 2 masks
C       10.2.2.2/32 is directly connected, Loopback0
C       10.10.10.0/24 is directly connected, FastEthernet0/0
O*E2 0.0.0.0/0 [110/1] via 192.168.10.10, 00:02:24, Serial0/0/1
```

OSPF external routes fall into one of two categories:

- **External Type 1 (E1):** OSPF accumulates cost for an E1 route as the route is being propagated throughout the OSPF area.

- **External Type 2 (E2):** The cost of an E2 route is always the external cost, irrespective of the interior cost to reach that route.

In this topology, because the default route has an external cost of 1 on the R1 router, R2 and R3 also show a cost of 1 for the default E2 route. E2 routes at a cost of 1 are the default OSPF configuration.

You can verify that expected neighbors have established adjacency with the **show ip ospf neighbor** command. Example 12-7 shows the neighbor tables for all three routers.

Example 12-7   Verifying Neighbor Adjacency with the show ip ospf neighbor Command

```
R1#show ip ospf neighbor

Neighbor ID     Pri   State        Dead Time   Address        Interface
10.3.3.3        0     FULL/  -     00:00:19    192.168.10.6   Serial0/0/1
10.2.2.2        0     FULL/  -     00:00:18    192.168.10.2   Serial0/0/0
R2#show ip ospf neighbor

Neighbor ID     Pri   State        Dead Time   Address        Interface
10.3.3.3        0     FULL/  -     00:00:16    192.168.10.10  Serial0/0/1
172.30.1.1      0     FULL/  -     00:00:15    192.168.10.1   Serial0/0/0
R3#show ip ospf neighbor

Neighbor ID     Pri   State        Dead Time   Address        Interface
172.30.1.1      0     FULL/  -     00:00:19    192.168.10.5   Serial0/0/0
10.2.2.2        0     FULL/  -     00:00:19    192.168.10.9   Serial0/0/1
```

For each neighbor, this command displays the following output:

- **Neighbor ID:** The router ID of the neighboring router.

- **Pri:** The OSPF priority of the interface. These all show 0 because point-to-point links do not elect a DR or BDR.

- **State:** The OSPF state of the interface. FULL state means that the router's interface is fully adjacent with its neighbor and they have identical OSPF link-state databases.

- **Dead Time:** The amount of time remaining that the router will wait to receive an OSPF Hello packet from the neighbor before declaring the neighbor down. This value is reset when the interface receives a Hello packet.

- **Address:** The IP address of the neighbor's interface to which this router is directly connected.

- **Interface:** The interface on which this router has formed adjacency with the neighbor.

As shown in Example 12-8, you can use the **show ip protocols** command as a quick way to verify vital OSPF configuration information, including the OSPF process ID, the router ID, networks the router is advertising, the neighbors from which the router is receiving updates, and the default AD, which is 110 for OSPF.

Example 12-8   Verify OSPF Configuration with the show ip protocols Command

```
R2#show ip protocols
Routing Protocol is "ospf 1"
  Outgoing update filter list for all interfaces is not set
  Incoming update filter list for all interfaces is not set
  Router ID 10.2.2.2
  Number of areas in this router is 1. 1 normal 0 stub 0 nssa
  Maximum path: 4
  Routing for Networks:
    10.10.10.0 0.0.0.255 area 0
    192.168.10.0 0.0.0.3 area 0
    192.168.10.8 0.0.0.3 area 0
  Reference bandwidth unit is 100 mbps
  Routing Information Sources:
    Gateway         Distance      Last Update
    10.3.3.3            110       00:07:17
    172.30.1.1          110       00:07:17
  Distance: (default is 110)
```

The **show ip ospf** command shown in Example 12-9 for R2 can also be used to examine the OSPF process ID and router ID. In addition, this command displays the OSPF area information and the last time the SPF algorithm was calculated.

Example 12-9   The show ip ospf Command

```
R2#show ip ospf
 Routing Process "ospf 1" with ID 10.2.2.2
 Supports only single TOS(TOS0) routes
 Supports opaque LSA
 Supports Link-local Signaling (LLS)
 Supports area transit capability
 Initial SPF schedule delay 5000 msecs
 Minimum hold time between two consecutive SPFs 10000 msecs
 Maximum wait time between two consecutive SPFs 10000 msecs
 Incremental-SPF disabled
 Minimum LSA interval 5 secs
 Minimum LSA arrival 1000 msecs
 LSA group pacing timer 240 secs
 Interface flood pacing timer 33 msecs
 Retransmission pacing timer 66 msecs
 Number of external LSA 1. Checksum Sum 0x0025BD
 Number of opaque AS LSA 0. Checksum Sum 0x000000
```

```
Number of DCbitless external and opaque AS LSA 0
Number of DoNotAge external and opaque AS LSA 0
Number of areas in this router is 1. 1 normal 0 stub 0 nssa
Number of areas transit capable is 0
External flood list length 0
IETF NSF helper support enabled
Cisco NSF helper support enabled
    Area BACKBONE(0)
        Number of interfaces in this area is 3
        Area has no authentication
        SPF algorithm last executed 02:09:55.060 ago
        SPF algorithm executed 4 times
        Area ranges are
        Number of LSA 3. Checksum Sum 0x013AB0
        Number of opaque link LSA 0. Checksum Sum 0x000000
        Number of DCbitless LSA 0
        Number of indication LSA 0
        Number of DoNotAge LSA 0
        Flood list length 0
```

The quickest way to verify Hello and Dead intervals is to use the **show ip ospf interface** command. As shown in Example 12-10 for R2, adding the interface name and number to the command displays output for a specific interface.

Example 12-10 The show ip ospf interface Command

```
R2#show ip ospf interface serial 0/0/0
Serial0/0/0 is up, line protocol is up
  Internet Address 192.168.10.2/30, Area 0
  Process ID 1, Router ID 10.2.2.2, Network Type POINT_TO_POINT, Cost: 1562
  Transmit Delay is 1 sec, State POINT_TO_POINT
  Timer intervals configured, Hello 5, Dead 20, Wait 20, Retransmit 5
    oob-resync timeout 40
    Hello due in 00:00:03
  Supports Link-local Signaling (LLS)
  Cisco NSF helper support enabled
  IETF NSF helper support enabled
  Index 1/1, flood queue length 0
  Next 0x0(0)/0x0(0)
  Last flood scan length is 1, maximum is 1
  Last flood scan time is 0 msec, maximum is 0 msec
  Neighbor Count is 1, Adjacent neighbor count is 1
    Adjacent with neighbor 172.30.1.1
  Suppress hello for 0 neighbor(s)
```

As highlighted in Example 12-10, the **show ip ospf interface** command also shows you the router ID, network type, and the cost for the link, as well as the neighbor to which this interface is adjacent.

Study Resources

For today's exam topics, refer to the following resources for more study.

Resource	Chapter	Topic	Where to Find It
Foundational Resources			
CCNA Exploration Online Curriculum: Routing Protocols and Concepts	Chapter 11, "OSPF"	All sections within the chapter	Section 11.1-11.5
CCNA Exploration Routing Protocols and Concepts Companion Guide	Chapter 11, "OSPF"	All topics within the chapter	pp. 500–553
ICND2 Official Exam Certification Guide	Chapter 9, "OSPF"	All topics within the chapter	pp. 347–373
ICND2 Authorized Self-Study Guide	Chapter 4, "Single-Area OSPF Implementation"	Implementing OSPF	pp. 139–160
Supplemental Resources			
CCNA Flash Cards and Exam Practice Pack	ICND2, Section 5	Implementing OSPF in a Single Area	pp. 452–490
CCNA Video Mentor	ICND2, Lab4	Single Area and Multi-Area OSPF Configuration	pp. 59–66

Troubleshooting Routing

CCNA 640-802 Exam Topics

- Troubleshoot routing issues.

Key Topics

During the past three days, we have reviewed both static and dynamic routing, including static routes, default routes, RIPv1, RIPv2, EIGRP, and OSPF. These reviews by their very nature included some brief discussion on troubleshooting routing issues related to each of the routing methods. Today we finish our review of routing concepts and configuration with a focus on troubleshooting routing issues.

The Basic Commands

Troubleshooting routing issues may begin with basic **ping** and **traceroute** commands to discover where connectivity is lacking. In the case of a large network, however, these two commands are probably not the most efficient way to find a problem. In addition, if these commands do track down a problem, you still have to discover the cause.

A better method might be to start with your core devices. These devices should be a collection point for all routes in the enterprise. To check for missing routes and track down the reason, the following method can be used for issues related to dynamic routing:

1. Check the routing tables for convergence with the **show ip route** command. All expected routes should be in the routing table. Barring a security policy that prevents some routes, the device should be able to route to any other location in the enterprise.

2. If you find a missing route or routes, use the **show ip protocols** command to investigate the routing protocol operation on the local router. The **show ip protocols** command summarizes just about every detail of a routing protocol's operation. Helpful information for all protocols includes the following:

   — **Enable routing protocol:** If the expected routing protocol is not enabled, configure it.

   — **Routing for networks:** If a network that should be advertised is missing, it could be that the **network** command is missing for that route. However, it might also be that the interface or interfaces that belong to that network are not functioning. If so, use **show ip interface brief** to isolate problems with interfaces.

   — **Routing information sources:** This is a list of neighbors from which the local router is receiving updates. A missing neighbor could be a problem with the local router (missing **network** command or down interface). Or the problem could be with the neighbor. For EIGRP and OSPF, you can use the display of neighbor relationships as a first step in discovering why a neighbor is not advertising routes to the local router (via the **show ip eigrp neighbors** and **show ip ospf neighbor** commands). If neighbor relationships are operating as expected, log in to the neighbor router to discover why the neighbor is not advertising routes.

3. If a static route is missing from the routing table, verify that it is configured using the **show running-config** command. If configured, either the local exit interface is down or the interface with the next-hop address is down.

VLSM Troubleshooting

The following list summarizes the key troubleshooting points to consider when you're troubleshooting potential variable-length subnet masking (VLSM) problems on the exam:

- Pay close attention to whether the design really uses VLSM. If it does, note whether a classless routing protocol is used.

- Be aware that overlapping subnets can indeed be configured.

- The outward problem symptoms might be that some hosts in a subnet work well, but others cannot send packets outside the local subnet.

- Use the **traceroute** command to look for routes that direct packets to the wrong part of the network. This could be a result of the overlapped subnets.

- On the exam, you might see a question you think is related to VLSM and IP addresses. In that case, the best plan of attack might well be to analyze the math for each subnet and ensure that no overlaps exist, rather than troubleshooting using **ping** and **traceroute**.

Discontiguous Networks

Automatic summarization does not cause any problems as long as the summarized network is contiguous rather than discontiguous. For RIPv2 and EIGRP, you must disable automatic summarization in a discontiguous network or you will have a less-than-full convergence situation.

Even a contiguous network design can become discontiguous if one or more link failures divide a classful network into two or more parts. Figure 11-1 shows an internetwork with two contiguous classful networks: 10.0.0.0 and 172.16.0.0.

Figure 11-1   Contiguous Network Topology

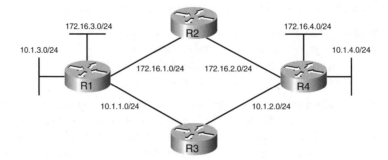

In this figure, with all links up and working and automatic summarization in effect, all hosts can ping all other hosts. In this design, packets for network 172.16.0.0 flow over the high route, and packets for network 10.0.0.0 flow over the low route.

However, if any link between the routers fails, one of the two classful networks becomes discontiguous. For example, if the link between R3 and R4 fails, the route from R1 to R4 passes through subnets of network 172.16.0.0, so network 10.0.0.0 is discontiguous. The solution, as always, is to use a classless routing protocol with automatic summarization disabled.

Troubleshooting RIP

Most RIP configuration errors involve an incorrect **network** statement configuration, a missing **network** statement configuration, or the configuration of discontiguous subnets in a classful environment. As shown in Figure 11-2, using **debug ip rip** can be an effective way to find issues with RIP updates. This output is from the topology we used on Day 14, "Static, Default, and RIP Routing," shown in Figure 14-3.

Figure 11-2   Interpreting debug ip rip Output

```
R2#debug ip rip
RIP protocol debugging is on
① { RIP: received v1 update from 192.168.2.1 on Serial0/0/0
         192.168.1.0 in 1 hops
② { RIP: received v1 update from 192.168.4.1 on Serial0/0/1
         192.168.5.0 in 1 hops
    RIP: sending  v1 update to 255.255.255.255 via FastEthernet0/0
         (192.168.3.1)
    RIP: build update entries
③       network 192.168.1.0 metric 2
        network 192.168.2.0 metric 1
        network 192.168.4.0 metric 1
        network 192.168.5.0 metric 2
    RIP: sending  v1 update to 255.255.255.255 via Serial0/0/1
         (192.168.4.2)
④   RIP: build update entries
        network 192.168.1.0 metric 2
        network 192.168.2.0 metric 1
        network 192.168.3.0 metric 1
    RIP: sending  v1 update to 255.255.255.255 via Serial0/0/0
         (192.168.2.2)
⑤   RIP: build update entries
        network 192.168.3.0 metric 1
        network 192.168.4.0 metric 1
        network 192.168.5.0 metric 2
⑥ { R2#undebug all
    All possible debugging has been turned off
```

This command displays RIPv1 routing updates as they are sent and received. Because it's RIPv1, the subnet masks are not included. Because updates are periodic, you need to wait for the next round of updates before seeing any output. The list that follows corresponds to the numbers in Figure 11-2.

1. You see an update coming in from R1 on interface Serial 0/0/0. Notice that R1 sends only one route to the 192.168.1.0 network. No other routes are sent because doing so would violate the split horizon rule. R1 is not allowed to advertise networks back to R2 that R2 previously sent to R1.

2. The next update that is received is from R3. Again, because of the split horizon rule, R3 sends only one route: the 192.168.5.0 network.

3. R2 sends out its own updates. First, R2 builds an update to send out the FastEthernet 0/0 interface. The update includes the entire routing table except for network 192.168.3.0, which is attached to FastEthernet 0/0.

4. Next, R2 builds an update to send to R3. Three routes are included. R2 does not advertise the network R2 and R3 share, nor does it advertise the 192.168.5.0 network because of split horizon.

5. Finally, R2 builds an update to send to R1. Three routes are included. R2 does not advertise the network that R2 and R1 share, nor does it advertise the 192.168.1.0 network because of split horizon.

6. Don't forget to disable debugging with either **no debug ip rip** or, as shown in the figure, **undebug all**.

Troubleshooting EIGRP and OSPF Interface Issues

This section reviews how to verify the interfaces on which the routing protocol has been enabled. Both EIGRP and OSPF configuration enables the routing protocol on an interface by using the **network** router subcommand. For any interfaces matched by the **network** commands, the routing protocol tries the following two actions:

- Attempts to find potential neighbors on the subnet connected to the interface

- Advertises the subnet connected to that interface

At the same time, the **passive-interface** router subcommand can be configured so that the router does not attempt to find neighbors on the interface (the first action listed) but still advertises the connected subnet (the second action listed).

Table 11-1 summarizes the three **show** commands you need in order to know exactly which interfaces have been enabled with EIGRP and OSPF and which interfaces are passive.

Table 11-1   Key Commands to Find Routing Protocol Enabled Interfaces

Command	Key Information
show ip eigrp interfaces	Lists the interfaces on which the routing protocol is enabled (based on the network commands), except passive interfaces.
show ip ospf interface brief	Lists the interfaces on which the OSPF is enabled (based on the network commands), including passive interfaces.
show ip protocols	Lists the contents of the network configuration commands for each routing process, and lists enabled but passive interfaces.

Troubleshooting Neighbor Adjacency Issues

When a routing protocol has been enabled on an interface, and the interface is not configured as a passive interface, the routing protocol attempts to discover neighbors and form a neighbor relationship with each neighbor that shares the common subnet.

OSPF and EIGRP both use Hello messages to learn about new neighbors and to exchange information used to perform some basic verification checks. After an EIGRP or OSPF router hears a Hello from a new neighbor, the routing protocol examines the information in the Hello, along with some local settings, to decide if the two neighbors should even attempt to become neighbors. Table 11-2 lists the neighbor requirements for both EIGRP and OSPF.

Table 11-2   Neighbor Requirements for EIGRP and OSPF

Requirement	EIGRP	OSPF
Interfaces must be in an up/up state	Yes	Yes
Interfaces must be in the same subnet	Yes	Yes
Must pass neighbor authentication (if configured)	Yes	Yes
Must use the same ASN/process-ID on the router configuration command	Yes	No
Hello and hold/dead timers must match	No	Yes
IP MTU must match	No	Yes
Router IDs must be unique	No[1]	Yes
K-values must match	Yes	N/A
Must be in the same area	N/A	Yes

[1]Having duplicate EIGRP RIDs does not prevent routers from becoming neighbors, but it can cause problems when external EIGRP routes are added to the routing table. Determining the EIGRP router ID is not discussed at the CCNA level.

Any two EIGRP routers that connect to the same data link, and whose interfaces have been enabled for EIGRP and are not passive, will at least consider becoming neighbors. To quickly and definitively know which potential neighbors have passed all the neighbor requirements for EIGRP, look at the output of the **show ip eigrp neighbors** command. If one or more expected neighbors are not listed, and the two routers can ping each other's IP address on their common subnet, the problem is probably related to one of the neighbor requirements listed in Table 11-2. Table 11-3 summarizes the EIGRP neighbor requirements and notes the best commands with which to determine which requirement is the root cause of the problem.

Table 11-3   EIGRP Neighbor Requirements and the Best show/debug Commands

Requirement	Best Command(s) to Isolate the Problem
Must be in the same subnet	**show interfaces**
Must pass any neighbor authentication	**debug eigrp packets**
Must use the same ASN on the router configuration command	**show ip eigrp interfaces**, **show protocols**
K-values must match	**show protocols**

Similar to EIGRP, the **show ip ospf neighbor** command lists all the neighboring routers that have met all the requirements to become an OSPF neighbor as listed in Table 11-2.

If one or more expected neighbors exist, before moving on to look at OSPF neighbor requirements, you should confirm that the two routers can ping each other on the local subnet. As soon as the two neighboring routers can ping each other, if the two routers still do not become OSPF neighbors, the next step is to examine each of the OSPF neighbor requirements. Table 11-4 summarizes the requirements, listing the most useful commands with which to find the answers.

Table 11-4   OSPF Neighbor Requirements and the Best show/debug Commands

Requirement	Best Command(s) to Isolate the Problem
Must be in the same subnet	**show interfaces, debug ip ospf hello**
Must pass any neighbor authentication	**debug ip ospf adj**
Hello and hold/dead timers must match	**show ip ospf interface, debug ip ospf hello**
Must be in the same area	**debug ip ospf adj, show ip ospf interface brief**
Router IDs must be unique	**Show ip ospf**

Study Resources

For today's exam topics, refer to the following resources for more study.

Resource	Chapter	Topic	Where to Find It
Foundational Resources			
CCNA Exploration Online Curriculum: Routing Protocols and Concepts	Chapter 2, "Static Routing" Chapter 5, "RIP version 1" Chapter 7, "RIPv2"	Managing and Troubleshooting Static Routes Verification and Troubleshooting Verifying and Troubleshooting RIPv2	Section 2.7 Section 5.3 Section 7.4
CCNA Exploration Routing Protocols and Concepts Companion Guide	Chapter 2, "Static Routing" Chapter 5, "RIP version 1" Chapter 7, "RIPv2"	Managing and Troubleshooting Static Routes Verification and Troubleshooting Verifying and Troubleshooting RIPv2	pp. 130–134 pp. 231–238 pp. 323–329
ICND1 Official Exam Certification Guide	Chapter 15, "Troubleshooting IP Routing"	All topics within the chapter	pp. 475–504
ICND2 Official Exam Certification Guide	Chapter 7, "Troubleshooting IP Routing" Chapter 11, "Troubleshooting Routing Protocols"	All topics within the chapter All topics within the chapter	pp. 270–300 pp. 408–427
ICND2 Authorized Self-Study Guide	Chapter 4, "Single-Area OSPF Implementation" Chapter 5, "Implementing EIGRP"	Troubleshooting OSPF Troubleshooting EIGRP	pp. 160–167 pp. 192–200

Part V

Wireless Concepts and Configuration

Day 10:   Wireless Standards, Components, and Security

Day 9:   Configuring and Troubleshooting Wireless Networks

Day 10

Wireless Standards, Components, and Security

CCNA 640-802 Exam Topics

- Describe standards associated with wireless media (IEEE, Wi-Fi Alliance, ITU/FCC).
- Identify and describe the purpose of the components in a small wireless network (SSID, BSS, ESS).
- Compare and contrast wireless security features and capabilities of WPA security (open, WEP, WPA-1/2).

Key Topics

For the next two days, we will review wireless concepts and configurations. Today we look at the basic wireless concepts, components, and security features.

Wireless Standards

Four organizations have a great deal of impact on the standards used for wireless LANs today. Table 10-1 lists these organizations and describes their roles.

Table 10-1   Organizations That Set or Influence WLAN Standards

Organization	Standardization Role
ITU-R	Worldwide standardization of communications that use radiated energy, particularly managing the assignment of frequencies
IEEE	Standardization of wireless LANs (802.11)
Wi-Fi Alliance	An industry consortium that encourages interoperability of products that implement WLAN standards through their Wi-Fi certified program
Federal Communications Commission (FCC)	The U.S. government agency that regulates the usage of various communications frequencies in the United States

The IEEE introduced wireless LAN (WLAN) standards with the creation of the 1997 ratification of the 802.11 standard, which has been replaced by more advanced standards. In order of ratification, the standards are 802.11b, 802.11a, and 802.11g. Of note, the 802.11n standard is in draft form. Final ratification is not expected until December 2009. However, draft standard products are already available.

Table 10-2 lists some key points about the currently ratified standards.

Table 10-2   WLAN Standards

Feature	802.11a	802.11b	802.11g
Year ratified	1999	1999	2003
Maximum speed using DSSS	—	11 Mbps	11 Mbps
Maximum speed using OFDM	54 Mbps	—	54 Mbps
Frequency band	5 GHz	2.4 GHz	2.4 GHz
Channels (nonoverlapped)	23 (12)	11 (3)	11 (3)
Speeds required by standard (Mbps)	6, 12, 24	1, 2, 5.5, 11	6, 12, 24

Wireless Modes of Operation

WLANs can use one of two modes:

- **Ad hoc mode:** With ad hoc mode, a wireless device wants to communicate with only one or a few other devices directly, usually for a short period of time. In these cases, the devices send WLAN frames directly to each other.

- **Infrastructure mode:** In infrastructure mode, each device communicates with a wireless access point (AP), with the AP connecting via wired Ethernet to the rest of the network infrastructure. Infrastructure mode allows the WLAN devices to communicate with servers and the Internet in an existing wired network.

  Infrastructure mode supports two sets of services, called service sets. The first, called a Basic Service Set (BSS), uses a single AP to create the wireless LAN. The other, called Extended Service Set (ESS), uses more than one AP, often with overlapping cells to allow roaming in a larger area.

Table 10-3 summarizes the wireless modes.

Table 10-3   Different WLAN Modes and Names

Mode	Service Set Name	Description
Ad hoc	Independent Basic Service Set (IBSS)	Allows two devices to communicate directly. No AP is needed.
Infrastructure (one AP)	Basic Service Set (BSS)	A single wireless LAN created with an AP and all devices that associate with that AP.
Infrastructure (more than one AP)	Extended Service Set (ESS)	Multiple APs create one wireless LAN, allowing roaming and a larger coverage area.

Wireless Frequencies

The FCC defines three unlicensed frequency bands. The bands are referenced by a particular frequency in the band, although by definition, a frequency band is a range of frequencies. Table 10-4 lists the frequency bands that matter to some degree for WLAN communications.

Table 10-4   FCC Unlicensed Frequency Bands of Interest

Frequency Range	Name	Sample Devices
900 KHz	Industrial, Scientific, Mechanical (ISM)	Older cordless telephones
2.4 GHz	ISM	Newer cordless phones and 802.11, 802.11b, 802.11g WLANs
5 GHz	Unlicensed National Information Infrastructure (U-NII)	Newer cordless phones and 802.11a, 802.11n WLANs

Wireless Encoding and Channels

You should know the names of three general classes of encoding, in part because the type of encoding requires some planning and forethought for some WLANs:

- **Frequency Hopping Spread Spectrum (FHSS):** FHSS uses all frequencies in the band, hopping to different ones. By using slightly different frequencies for consecutive transmissions, a device can hopefully avoid interference from other devices that use the same unlicensed band. The original 802.11 WLAN standards used FHSS, but the current standards do not.

- **Direct Sequence Spread Spectrum (DSSS):** DSSS was designed for use in the 2.4 GHz unlicensed band and is used by 802.11b. As regulated by the FCC, this band can have 11 overlapping DSSS channels. Three of the channels (channels 1, 6, and 11) do not overlap enough to impact each other. So when designing an ESS WLAN, APs with overlapping areas should be set to use different nonoverlapping channels, as shown in Figure 10-1.

Figure 10-1   Using Nonoverlapping DSSS 2.4-GHz Channels in an ESS WLAN

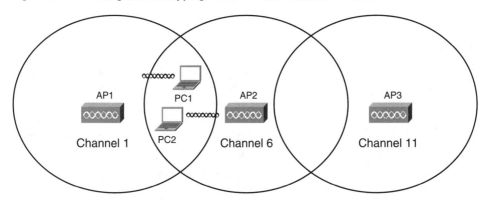

- **Orthogonal Frequency Division Multiplexing (OFDM):** Like DSSS, WLANs that use OFDM can use multiple nonoverlapping channels. OFDM is used by 802.11a.

Note: 802.11g uses Extended Rate Physical (ERP), which borrows OFDM techniques from 802.11a.

Wireless Coverage Area

The actual size of a WLAN's coverage area depends on a large number of factors, including the following:

- The frequency band used by the WLAN standard

- The obstructions between and near the WLAN devices

- The interference from other sources of radio frequency (RF) energy

- The antennas used on both the clients and APs

- The options used by DSSS and OFDM when encoding data over the air.

Generally speaking, WLAN standards that use higher frequencies can send data faster, but with the price of smaller coverage areas. To cover all the required space, an ESS that uses higher frequencies would then require more APs, driving up the cost of the WLAN deployment.

Table 10-5 lists the main IEEE WLAN ratified standards, the maximum speed, and the number of nonoverlapping channels.

Table 10-5   WLAN Speed and Frequency Reference

IEEE Standard	Maximum Speed (Mbps)	Other Speeds (Mbps)	Frequency	Nonoverlapping Channels
802.11b	11 Mbps	1, 2, 5.5	2.4 GHz	3
802.11a	54 Mbps	6, 9, 12, 18, 24, 36, 48	5 GHz	12
802.11g	54 Mbps	Same as 802.11a	2.4 GHz	3

CSMA/CA

Unlike Ethernet switching technologies, you cannot isolate the wireless signals from hosts sharing the same AP from interfering with each other. So if two or more WLAN devices send at the same time, using the same or overlapping frequency ranges, a collision occurs, and none of the transmitted signals can be understood by those receiving the signal. In addition, the device that is transmitting data cannot concurrently listen for received data. This means that the sending devices do not know that the collision occurred.

The solution is to use the carrier sense multiple access with collision avoidance (CSMA/CA) algorithm to minimize the statistical chance that collisions could occur. However, CSMA/CA does not prevent collisions, so the WLAN standards must have a process to deal with collisions when they do occur. The following list summarizes the key points about the CSMA/CA algorithm:

1. Listen to ensure that the medium (space) is not busy (no radio waves currently are being received at the frequencies to be used).
2. Set a random wait timer before sending a frame to statistically reduce the chance of devices all trying to send at the same time.
3. When the random timer has passed, listen again to ensure that the medium is not busy. If it isn't, send the frame.

4. After the entire frame has been sent, wait for an acknowledgment.

5. If no acknowledgment is received, resend the frame, using CSMA/CA logic to wait for the appropriate time to send again.

Wireless Security Risks

WLANs introduce a number of vulnerabilities that do not exist for wired Ethernet LANs. Threats to WLAN security include the following:

- **War drivers:** A person who drives around, trying to find APs that have no security or weak security.

- **Hackers:** The motivation for hackers is to either find information or deny services. Interestingly, the end goal might be to compromise the hosts inside the wired network, using the wireless network as a way to access the enterprise network without having to go through Internet connections that have firewalls.

- **Employees:** An employee could install an access point (AP) in his office, using default settings of no security, and create a small wireless LAN. This would allow a hacker easy access to the rest of the enterprise.

- **Rogue AP:** The attacker captures packets in the existing wireless LAN, finding the service set identifier (SSID) and cracking any used security keys. Then the attacker can set up an AP, which the enterprise's clients unwittingly associate with.

To reduce the risk of such attacks, three main types of tools can be used on a WLAN:

- **Mutual authentication:** A process that uses a secret password, called a key, on both the client and the AP. By using some sophisticated mathematical algorithms, the AP can confirm that the client does indeed know the right key value.

- **Encryption:** Uses a secret key and a mathematical formula to scramble the contents of the WLAN frame. The receiving device then uses another formula to decrypt the data.

- **Intrusion tools:** Includes intrusion detection systems (IDS) and intrusion prevention systems (IPS), as well as WLAN-specific tools. Cisco defines the Structured Wireless-Aware Network (SWAN) architecture. It includes many tools, some of which specifically address the issue of detecting and identifying rogue APs, and whether they represent threats.

Table 10-6 lists the key vulnerabilities, along with the general solution.

Table 10-6   WLAN Vulnerabilities and Solutions

Vulnerability	Solution
War drivers	Strong authentication
Hackers stealing information in a WLAN	Strong encryption
Hackers gaining access to the rest of the network	Strong authentication
Employee AP installation	Intrusion DETECTION SYSTEMS (IDS), including Cisco SWAN
Rogue AP	Strong authentication, IDS/SWAN

Wireless Security Standards

The initial security standard for WLANs, called Wired Equivalent Privacy (WEP), had many problems. The next three standards represent a progression whose goal in part was to fix the problems
created by WEP. In chronological order, Cisco first addressed the problem with some proprietary
solutions. Then the Wi-Fi Alliance helped fix the problem by defining an industrywide standard.
Finally, the IEEE completed work on an official public standard, 802.11i.

The following is a brief review of these four security standards:

- **WEP:** In 1997, the original security standard provided authentication and encryption, which
  can be easily cracked. Main issues included:

  — Static preshared keys (PSKs) that required manual configuration, thus people simply left
    the defaults.

  — PSK values were short with only 40 unique bits, making them easy to crack.

- **Cisco Interim Solution:** Cisco's proprietary answer to the problems with WEP came out in
  2001 to provide a solution quicker than the Wi-Fi Alliance or IEEE promised solutions. The
  Cisco answer included some proprietary improvements for encryption, along with the IEEE
  802.1x standard for end user authentication. The main features of Cisco enhancements included the following:

  — Dynamic key exchange so that if a key is discovered, it is short-lived

  — A new encryption key for each packet

  — User authentication using 802.1x instead of device authentication

- **Wi-Fi Protected Access (WPA):** WPA came out in 2003 and essentially does the same thing
  as the Cisco interim solution. WPA includes the option to use dynamic key exchange, using
  the Temporal Key Integrity Protocol (TKIP). Cisco used a proprietary version of TKIP. WPA
  allows for the use of either IEEE 802.1X user authentication or simple device authentication
  using preshared keys. The encryption algorithm uses the Message Integrity Check (MIC)
  algorithm, again similar to the process used in the Cisco-proprietary solution. WPA improved
  security and, through the Wi-Fi Alliance certification program, gave vendors an incentive to
  have their products carry the Wi-Fi certification label.

- **802.11i (WPA2):** In 2005, IEEE ratified 802.11i, which includes dynamic key exchange,
  much stronger encryption using the Advanced Encryption Standard (AES), and user authentication. 802.11i is not backward compatible with either Cisco's solution or WPA. Because the
  Wi-Fi Alliance certification is so popular and well known, 802.11i products are certified with
  the WPA2 label.

Table 10-7 summarizes the key features of the various WLAN security standards.

Table 10-7   Comparisons of WLAN Security Features

Standard	Key Distribution	Device Authentication	User Authentication	Encryption
WEP	Static	Yes (weak)	None	Yes (weak)
Cisco	Dynamic	Yes	Yes (802.1x)	Yes (TKIP)
WPA	Both	Yes	Yes (802.1x)	Yes (TKIP)
802.11i (WPA2)	Both	Yes	Yes (802.1x)	Yes (AES)

Study Resources

For today's exam topics, refer to the following resources for more study.

Resource	Chapter	Topic	Where to Find It
Foundational Resources			
CCNA Exploration Online Curriculum: LAN Switching and Wireless	Chapter 7, "Basic Wireless Concepts and Configuration"	The Wireless LAN Wireless LAN Security	Section 7.1 Section 7.2
CCNA Exploration LAN Switching and Wireless Companion Guide	Chapter 7, "Basic Wireless Concepts and Configuration"	The Wireless LAN Wireless LAN Security	pp. 379–402 pp. 402–410
ICND1 Official Exam Certification Guide	Chapter 11, "Wireless LANs"	Wireless LAN Concepts Wireless LAN Security	pp. 302–315 pp. 320–326
ICND1 Authorized Self-Study Guide	Chapter 3, "Wireless LANs"	Exploring Wireless Networking Understanding WLAN Security	pp. 207–215 pp. 215–221
Supplemental Resources			
CCNA Flash Cards and Exam Practice Pack	ICND1, Section 7	Extending the LAN	pp. 174–188

Configuring and Troubleshooting Wireless Networks

CCNA 640-802 Exam Topics

- Identify the basic parameters to configure on a wireless network to ensure that devices connect to the correct access point.

- Identify common issues with implementing wireless networks (interface, misconfigurations).

Key Topics

Wireless access points can be configured through a command-line interface (CLI), or more commonly through a browser graphical user interface (GUI). *Cisco Networking Academy* students use a Linksys WRT300N multifunction device in a lab environment to practice configuring basic parameters. However, the CCNA 640-802 exam topics do not include the ability to *configure* wireless devices. Instead, you must be able to *identify* the basic configuration parameters as well as common issues with wireless implementations.

Therefore, our review today will not include specific configuration tasks with screenshots of a GUI, but will be a general overview of wireless implementations that are applicable to any wireless device. However, I strongly recommend that you at least practice implementing some of the technologies we reviewed on Day 10, "Wireless Standards, Components, and Security." If you are a *Cisco Networking Academy* student, you also have access to Packet Tracer, which includes a simulation of a Linksys WRT300N. However, you might also have your own home router that includes a wireless access point (AP). You can practice configuring your own home wireless router with customized settings such as the service set identifier (SSID), security, and encryption.

Implementing a WLAN

Basic wireless access point parameters include SSID, radio frequency (RF) channel with optional power, and authentication (security), whereas basic wireless client parameters include only authentication. Wireless clients need fewer parameters because a wireless network interface card (NIC) scans all the available radio frequencies it can to locate the RF channel (meaning an IEEE 802.11b/g card scans the 2.4 GHz range and does not scan 5 GHz) and usually initiates the connection with a default configuration to discover the available APs. Therefore, by 802.11 design, if you are using open authentication, the result is "plug-and-play." When security is configured with preshared keys (PSKs) for older Wired Equivalent Privacy (WEP) or current Wi-Fi Protected Access (WPA), remember that the key must be an exact match to allow connectivity.

Wireless LAN Implementation Checklist

The following basic checklist can help guide the installation of a WLAN:

Step 1   Verify the existing wired network.

The existing wired network should be operational, including virtual LANs (VLANs), Dynamic Host Configuration Protocol (DHCP) services, and Internet connectivity. Basic practices suggest connecting all APs in the same Extended Service Set (ESS) to the same VLAN. For example, in Figure 9-1 each of the APs is connected to a switch port that belongs to VLAN 2.

Figure 9-1   **ESS WLAN with All APs in Same VLAN**

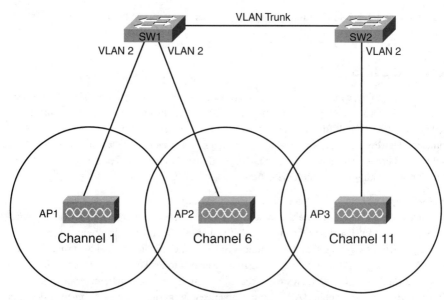

A quick way to test the wired network is to connect a PC to the switch port that the AP will use. If the device acquires IP addressing automatically through DHCP services, the wired network is ready for the AP.

Step 2   Install and configure the AP's wired and IP details.

The next step is to attach the AP to the switch port with a straight-through cable and then configure or verify its connectivity to the wired network, including the AP's IP address, mask, and default gateway. Just like a switch, the IP addressing will allow remote management of an AP, which is a Layer 2 device.

Step 3   Configure the AP's WLAN details.

Most APs have a plug-and-play capability; however, both consumer-grade and enterprise-grade APs can be configured with a variety of parameters, including the following list (security parameters are covered in Step 6):

— IEEE standard (a, b, g, or multiple)

— Wireless channel

— SSID, which is a 32-character text identifier for the WLAN

— Transmit power

Many APs today support multiple WLAN standards. In some cases, they can support multiple standards on the same AP at the same time. However, these mixed-mode implementations, particularly with 802.11b/g in this same AP, tend to slow down the WLAN. Also note that when you configure an ESS WLAN, each of the APs should be configured with the same SSID, which allows for roaming between APs, but inside the same WLAN.

Step 4   Install and configure one wireless client.

To be a WLAN client, the device needs a WLAN NIC that supports the same WLAN standard as the AP. Typically, clients by default do not have any security enabled. When the client starts working, it tries to discover all APs by listening on all frequency channels for the WLAN standards it supports by default. For example, if a client were using the WLAN shown in Figure 9-1, with three APs, each using a different channel, the client might discover all three APs. The client would then use the AP from which the client receives the strongest signal. Also, the client learns the SSID from the AP, again removing the need for any client configuration.

Step 5   Verify that the WLAN works from the client.

The wireless client should be able to access the same resources as the wired client that was attached to the same switch port as the AP earlier in Step 1. If not, the problem might be the location of the AP or APs. During the planning stages, a site survey should have been conducted to determine the best locations for APs to ensure full coverage of the WLAN area. If the client cannot communicate, check the following in regard to the site survey:

— Is the AP at the center of the area in which the clients reside?

— Is the AP or client right next to a lot of metal?

— Is the AP or client near a source of interference?

— Is the AP's coverage area wide enough to reach the client?

In addition to the site survey, the following list notes a few other common problems with a new installation:

— Check to make sure that the NIC's and AP's radios are enabled. In particular, check the physical switch as well as the software setting to enable or disable the radio.

— Check the AP to ensure that it has the latest firmware.

— Check the AP configuration—in particular, the channel configuration—to ensure that it does not use a channel that overlaps with other APs in the same location.

Step 6   Configure wireless security.

After you have verified that that the wireless client can access resources without security enabled, it's time to implement wireless security. Configure wireless security with WPA/WPA2. Use WEP only if the AP or wireless client does not support WPA/WPA2.

Step 7   Verify the secure WLAN.

Now that security is enabled, verify that the WLAN works again in the presence of the security features by testing to make sure the wireless client can still access all the resources it could access without the security enabled.

Wireless Troubleshooting

If you follow the recommended steps for implementing a wireless network, the divide-and-conquer troubleshooting methodology will most likely isolate the problem in the most efficient manner. The following are the most common causes of configuration problems:

- Configuring a defined SSID on the client that does not match the access point
- Configuring incompatible security methods

Both the wireless client and access point must match for authentication method, Extensible Authentication Protocol (EAP) or PSK, and encryption method (Temporal Key Integrity Protocol [TKIP] or Advanced Encryption Standard [AES]). Other common problems resulting from initial RF installation can sometimes be identified by answering the following questions:

- Is the radio enabled on both the access point and client for the correct RF (2.4 GHz ISM or 5 GHz UNII)?
- Is an external antenna connected and facing the correct direction (straight upward for dipole)?
- Is the antenna location too high or too low relative to wireless clients (within 20 vertical feet)?
- Are there metal objects in the room reflecting RF and causing poor performance?
- Is the AP the client is attempting to reach at too great of a distance?

Study Resources

For today's exam topics, refer to the following resources for more study.

Resource	Chapter	Topic	Where to Find It
Foundational Resources			
CCNA Exploration Online Curriculum: LAN Switching and Wireless	Chapter 7, "Basic Wireless Concepts and Configuration"	Configure Wireless LAN Access Troubleshooting Simple WLAN Problems	Section 7.3 Section 7.4
CCNA Exploration LAN Switching and Wireless Companion Guide	Chapter 7, "Basic Wireless Concepts and Configuration"	Configure Wireless LAN Access Troubleshooting Simple WLAN Problems	pp. 410–424 pp. 424–435
ICND1 Official Exam Certification Guide	Chapter 11, "Wireless LANs"	Deploying WLANs	pp. 315–320
ICND1 Authorized Self-Study Guide	Chapter 3, "Wireless LANs"	Implementing a WLAN	pp. 221–230
Supplemental Resources			
CCNA Flash Cards and Exam Practice Pack	ICND1, Section 7	Extending the LAN	pp. 174–188

Part VI

Basic Security Concepts and Configuration

Day 8:   Mitigating Security Threats and Best Practices

Mitigating Security Threats and Best Practices

CCNA 640-802 Exam Topics

- Describe today's increasing network security threats and explain the need to implement a comprehensive security policy to mitigate the threats.

- Explain general methods to mitigate common security threats to network devices, hosts, and applications.

- Describe the functions of common security appliances and applications.

- Describe security recommended practices including initial steps to secure network devices.

Key Topics

Security is a fundamental component of every network design. Attacks that previously required an advanced knowledge in computing can now be done with easily downloaded and freely available tools that any average computer-literate person can figure out how to use. Security is clearly a big issue, and one that requires serious attention. For the purposes of the exam topics for today, the goal is to review some of the basic terminology, types of security issues, and some of the common tools used to mitigate security risks.

The Importance of Security

Attacks can be launched from various locations both inside and outside the organization, as shown in Figure 8-1.

As e-business and Internet applications continue to grow, finding the balance between being isolated and being open is critical. In addition, the rise of mobile commerce and wireless networks demands that security solutions become seamlessly integrated, more transparent, and more flexible. Network administrators must carefully balance accessibility to network resources with security.

Attacker Terminology

Over the years, network attack tools and methods have evolved, as well as the terminology to describe the individuals involved. Some of the most common terms are the following:

- **White hat:** An individual who looks for vulnerabilities in systems or networks and then reports these vulnerabilities to the system's owners so that they can be fixed.

- **Hacker:** A general term that has historically been used to describe a computer programming expert. More recently, this term is often used in a negative way to describe an individual with malicious intent who attempts to gain unauthorized access to network resources.

Figure 8-1   Security Is Important at All Entry Points into the Network

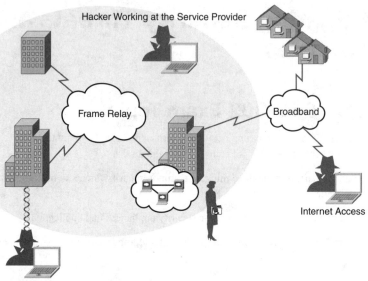

Today's networks must balance accessibility to network resources with the protection of sensitive data from theft.

- **Black hat:** Another term for individuals who use their knowledge of computer systems to break into systems or networks that they are not authorized to use.

- **Cracker:** Someone with malicious intent who tries to gain unauthorized access to network resources.

- **Phreaker:** An individual who manipulates the phone network to cause it to perform a function that is not allowed, such as to make free long-distance calls.

- **Spammer:** An individual who sends large quantities of unsolicited email messages.

- **Phisher:** Uses email or other means to masquerade as a trusted party so that victims are enticed into providing sensitive information, such as credit card numbers or passwords.

Thinking Like an Attacker

Many attackers use this seven-step process to gain information and start an attack:

Step 1   Perform footprint analysis (reconnaissance).

A company web page can lead to information, such as the IP addresses of servers. From there, an attacker can create a picture of the company's security profile or "footprint."

Step 2   Enumerate information.

An attacker can expand on the footprint by monitoring network traffic with a packet sniffer such as Wireshark, finding useful information such as version numbers of FTP servers and mail servers.

Step 3   Manipulate users to gain access.

Sometimes employees choose passwords that are easily crackable. In other instances, employees can be duped by talented attackers into giving up sensitive access-related information (social engineering).

Step 4   Escalate privileges.

After attackers gain basic access, they use their skills to increase their network privileges.

Step 5   Gather additional passwords and secrets.

With improved access privileges, attackers use their talents to gain access to well-guarded, sensitive information.

Step 6   Install back doors.

Back doors give the attacker a way to enter the system without being detected. The most common back door is an open listening TCP or UDP port.

Step 7   Leverage the compromised system.

After a system is compromised, an attacker uses it to stage attacks on other hosts in the network.

Balancing Security and Availability

Organizations must find a balance between two important needs:

- Keeping networks open to support evolving business requirements

- Protecting private, personal, and strategic business information

To address these needs, network security models follow a progressive scale. On one end is "open," which means that any service is permitted unless it is expressly denied. Although the security risks are self-evident, there are some advantages to an open network:

- Easy to configure and administer.

- Easy for end users to access network resources.

- Security costs are much less.

On the other end is the most restrictive network system, which means that services are denied by default unless deemed necessary. Although the benefits of implementing a completely restrictive network system are evident, it does present some drawbacks:

- More difficult to configure and administer.

- More difficult for end users to access resources.

- Security costs are greater than those for an open network.

Developing a Security Policy

The first step any organization should take to protect its data and itself from a liability challenge is to develop a security policy. A security policy is a set of principles that guides decision-making processes and enables leaders in an organization to distribute authority confidently. A security policy can be as simple as a brief "Acceptable Use Policy" for network resources, or it can be several hundred pages long and detail every element of connectivity and associated policies.

A security policy meets the following goals:

- Informs users, staff, and managers of their obligations for protecting technology and information assets.

- Specifies the mechanisms through which these requirements can be met.

- Provides a baseline from which to acquire, configure, and audit computer systems and networks for compliance with the policy.

Common Security Threats

When discussing network security, three common factors are vulnerabilities, threats, and attacks, as described in the sections that follow.

Vulnerabilities

Vulnerability is the degree of weakness that is inherent in every network and device. Threats are people who are interested in and capable of taking advantage of each security weakness.

Following are the three primary categories of vulnerabilities:

- Technological weaknesses, including the following:
  - The TCP/IP protocol suite
  - Operating system security issues
  - Network equipment weaknesses
- Configuration weaknesses, including the following:
  - Unsecured user accounts
  - System accounts with easily guessed passwords
  - Misconfigured Internet services
  - Unsecured default settings
  - Misconfigured network equipment
- Security policy weaknesses, including the following:
  - Lack of written security policy
  - Corporate politics making it difficult to implement a consistent policy
  - Lack of continuity
  - Inadequate monitoring and auditing of security
  - Software and hardware installations and upgrades that do not follow policy
  - Nonexistent disaster recovery plan

Threats to Physical Infrastructure

An attacker can deny the use of network resources if those resources can be physically compromised. The four classes of physical threats are as follows:

- **Hardware threats:** Theft or vandalism causing physical damage to servers, routers, switches, cabling plants, and workstations

- **Environmental threats:** Temperature extremes or humidity extremes

- **Electrical threats:** Voltage spikes, insufficient supply voltage, unconditioned power, and total power loss

- **Maintenance threats:** Poor handling of key electrical components, lack of critical spare parts, poor cabling, and poor labeling

Threats to Networks

Crimes that have implications for network security can be grouped into two primary classes of threats to networks:

- **Unstructured threats:** Consist of mostly inexperienced individuals using easily available hacking tools, such as shell scripts and password crackers.

- **Structured threats:** Structured threats come from individuals or groups who are more highly motivated and technically competent. These people know system vulnerabilities and use sophisticated hacking techniques to penetrate unsuspecting businesses.

These two primary classes of threats can further be categorized as follows:

- **External threats:** External threats can arise from individuals or organizations working outside of a company who do not have authorized access to the computer systems or network.

- **Internal threats:** Internal threats occur when someone has authorized access to the network with either an account or physical access.

Types of Network Attacks

Various types of attacks can be launched against an organization. There are four primary classes of attacks:

- **Reconnaissance attacks:** The unauthorized discovery and mapping of systems, services, or vulnerabilities using readily available tools to launch the following attacks:

  — **Internet information queries:** Use of tools such as **nslookup** and **whois** utilities to easily determine the IP address space assigned to the target organization.

  — **Ping sweeps:** After IP address space is discovered, the attacker uses a ping utility to send pings to every IP address in the address space to determine which addresses are open.

  — **Port scans:** The attacker then scans the active IP addresses to see which ports are open.

  — **Packet capturing sniffers:** Internal attackers may attempt to "eavesdrop" on network traffic to gather or steal information.

- **Access attacks:** Entering or accessing systems by running a hack, script, or tool that exploits a known vulnerability of the system or application being attacked. Common access attacks include the following:

  — **Password attacks:** Password attacks usually refer to repeated attempts to log in to a shared resource, such as a server or router, to identify a user account, password, or both. These repeated attempts are called dictionary attacks or brute-force attacks.

  — **Trust exploitation:** The process of compromising a trusted host and then using it to stage attacks on other hosts in a network.

  — **Port redirection:** A type of trust exploitation attack that uses a compromised host to pass traffic through a firewall that would otherwise be blocked.

  — **Man-in-the-Middle attacks:** An attack carried out by persons who manage to position themselves between two legitimate hosts. If attackers manage to get into a strategic position, they can steal information, hijack an ongoing session to gain access to private network resources, conduct denial-of-service attacks, corrupt transmitted data, or introduce new information into network sessions.

- **Denial-of-service (DoS) attacks:** DoS attacks involve rendering a system unavailable by physically disconnecting a system, crashing the system, or slowing it down to the point that it is unusable. Some examples of DoS attacks include the following:

  — **Ping-of-Death attacks:** Sending ping packets that are much larger than expected, which may crash older network systems.

  — **SYN Flood attacks:** Sending thousands of requests for a TCP connection (SYN bit is set) to a targeted server. The server leaves the connection open, waiting for an acknowledgement from the attacker, which never comes.

  — **Distributed DoS (DDoS) attacks:** Similar to DoS, but with hundreds or thousands of attack points that attempt to overwhelm a target.

- **Malicious code attacks:** Malicious software can be inserted onto a host to damage or corrupt a system; replicate itself; or deny access to networks, systems, or services. Common names for this type of software are worms, viruses, and Trojan horses.

  — **Worm:** A worm executes code and installs copies of itself in the memory of the infected computer, which can, in turn, infect other hosts.

  — **Virus:** A virus is malicious software that is attached to another program to execute a particular unwanted function on a workstation. A virus normally requires a deliver mechanism, such as a zip file or some other executable file attached to an email. The key element that distinguishes a computer worm from a computer virus is that human interaction is required to facilitate the spread of a virus.

  — **Trojan horse:** Differs from a worm or virus only in that the entire application is written to look like something else, when in fact it is an attack tool.

General Mitigation Techniques

Each type of network attack reviewed has mitigation techniques that you should implement, including end user systems, servers, and network devices. The sections that follow describe these mitigation techniques in more detail.

Host and Server Security

Host- and server-based security must be applied to all network systems. Mitigation techniques for these devices include the following:

- **Device hardening:** New systems usually arrive with default values that are rarely secure enough to adhere to the security policy. Most new systems require the following out-of-the-box security configuration:

  - Default usernames and passwords should be changed.

  - Administrator-level resources should be restricted to those authorized access.

  - Unnecessary services should be disabled or uninstalled.

  - System logging and tracking should be configured.

- **Antivirus software:** Install host antivirus software to protect against known attacks, and make sure it is updated regularly.

- **Personal firewalls:** Personal firewalls are meant for PCs that connect directly to the Internet without the benefit of corporate firewalls.

- **Operating system patches:** The most effective way to mitigate a worm and its variants is to download security updates and patch all vulnerable systems.

Intrusion Detection and Prevention

Intrusion detection systems (IDS) detect attacks against a network and send logs to a management console. Intrusion prevention systems (IPS) prevent attacks against the network. Either technology can be implemented at the network level or host level, or both for maximum protection.

Host-based intrusion prevention (HIPS) stops an attack, prevents damage, and blocks the propagation of worms and viruses. Active detection can be set to shut down the network connection or stop impacted services automatically. Corrective action can be taken immediately.

The advantage of HIPS is that it can monitor operating system processes and protect critical system resources, including files that may exist only on that specific host. This means it can notify network managers when some external process tries to modify a system file in a way that might include a hidden back-door program.

Security Appliances and Applications

Figure 8-2 shows a common network topology with a firewall. The firewall's role is to stop packets that the network administrator has deemed unsafe. The firewall mainly looks at the transport layer port numbers and the application layer headers to prevent certain ports and applications from getting packets into the enterprise.

Figure 8-2   Typical Enterprise Internet Connection with a Firewall

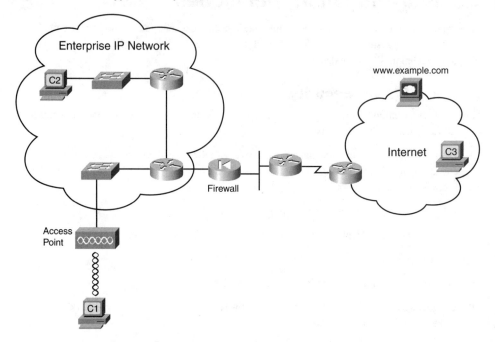

However, a firewall by itself is no longer adequate for securing a network. An integrated approach involving a firewall, intrusion prevention, and a virtual private network (VPN) might be necessary.

An integrated approach to security and the devices necessary to make it happen follow these building blocks:

- **Threat control:** Regulates network access, isolates infected systems, prevents intrusions, and protects assets by counteracting malicious traffic. Cisco devices and applications that provide threat control solutions include the following:

  — Cisco ASA 5500 series Adaptive Security Appliances (ASA)

  — Integrated Services Routers (ISR)

  — Network admission control (NAC)

  — Cisco Security Agent for Desktops

  — Cisco intrusion prevention systems

- **Secure communications:** Secures network endpoints with a VPN. The devices that allow an organization to deploy a VPN are Cisco ISR routers with a Cisco IOS VPN solution, and the Cisco 5500 ASA and Cisco Catalyst 6500 switches.

- **Network admission control:** Provides a roles-based method of preventing unauthorized access to a network. Cisco offers a NAC appliance.

Maintaining Security

The network security wheel shown in Figure 8-3 can assist with the compliance of the security policy as well as provide a way to improve security as new threats are revealed.

Figure 8-3   **The Network Security Wheel**

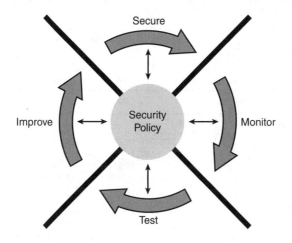

The security policy is the hub upon which the four steps of the security wheel are based:

Step 1   **Secure:** Secure the network by applying the security policy and implementing the following security solutions:

— Threat defense using device-hardening techniques, antivirus, and spyware tools.

— Intrusion prevention systems to actively stop malicious traffic.

— Vulnerability patching to stop the exploitation of known vulnerabilities.

— Disable unnecessary services.

— Stateful inspection and packet filtering.

— VPNs to encrypt network traffic when traversing the public Internet.

— Trust and identity constraints.

— Authentication.

— Policy enforcement.

Step 2   **Monitor:** Monitoring security involves both active and passive methods of detecting security violations. System administrators must ensure that all sensitive and vital hosts on the network are being audited. They must also take the time to check and interpret the log file entries.

An added benefit of network monitoring is verifying that the security measures implemented in Step 1 are working properly.

Step 3   **Test:** Security measures are proactively tested. Specifically, the functionality of the security solutions implemented in Step 1 and the system auditing and intrusion detection methods implemented in Step 2 are verified.

Step 4   **Improve:** Analyze the data collected during the monitoring and testing phases in order to develop and implement improvement mechanisms that augment the security policy and results in adding items to Step 1. The cycle now repeats with Step 1.

Study Resources

For today's exam topics, refer to the following resources for more study.

Resource	Chapter	Topic	Where to Find It
Foundational Resources			
CCNA Exploration Online Curriculum: Accessing the WAN	Chapter 4, "Network Security"	Introduction to Network Security Securing Cisco Routers Securing Router Network Services	Section 4.1 Section 4.2 Section 4.3
CCNA Exploration Accessing the WAN Companion Guide	Chapter 4, "Network Security"	Introduction to Network Security Securing Cisco Routers Securing Router Network Services	pp. 190–232 pp. 232–250 pp. 250–264
ICND1 Official Exam Certification Guide	Chapter 6, "Fundamentals of TCP/IP Transport, Applications, and Security"	Network Security	pp. 153–162
ICND1 Authorized Self-Study Guide	Chapter 1, "Building a Simple Network"	Securing the Network	pp. 21–31
Supplemental Resources			
CCNA Flash Cards and Exam Practice Pack	ICND1, "Chapter 1"	Building a Simple Network	pp. 4–36

Part VII

ACL and NAT Concepts and Configuration

Day 7:   ACL Concepts and Configurations

Day 6:   Verifying and Troubleshooting ACL Implementations

Day 5:   NAT Concepts, Configuration, and Troubleshooting

ACL Concepts and Configurations

CCNA 640-802 Exam Topics

- Describe the purpose and types of ACLs.
- Configure and apply ACLs based on network filtering requirements.
- Configure and apply an ACL to limit Telnet and SSH access to the router using CLI and SDM.

Key Topics

One of the most important skills a network administrator needs is mastery of access control lists (ACLs). Administrators use ACLs to stop traffic or permit only specified traffic while stopping all other traffic on their networks. Standard and extended ACLs can be used to apply a number of security features, including policy-based routing, quality of service (QoS), Network Address Translation (NAT), and Port Address Translation (PAT).

You can also configure standard and extended ACLs on router interfaces to control the type of traffic that is permitted through a given router. Today, we review the purpose and types of ACLs as well as configuration and application of ACLs to filter traffic.

ACL Concepts

A router's default operation is to forward all packets as long as a route exists for the packet and the link is up. ACLs can be used to implement a basic level of security. They are not, however, the only security solution a large organization would want to implement. In fact, ACLs increase the latency of routers. So if the organization is very large with routers managing the traffic of hundreds or thousands of users, you more than likely will use a combination of other security implementations, such as a Cisco PIX firewall and authentication services.

Defining an ACL

An ACL is a router configuration script (a list of statements) that controls whether a router permits or denies packets to pass based on criteria found in the packet header. To determine whether a packet is to be permitted or denied, it is tested against the ACL statements in sequential order. When a statement matches, no more statements are evaluated. The packet is either permitted or denied. There is an implicit **deny any** statement at the end of the ACL. If a packet does not match any of the statements in the ACL, it is dropped.

Processing Interface ACLs

ACLs can be applied to an interface for inbound and outbound traffic. However, you need a separate ACL for each direction.

Figure 7-1   ACL Interface Processing for Inbound and Outbound Traffic

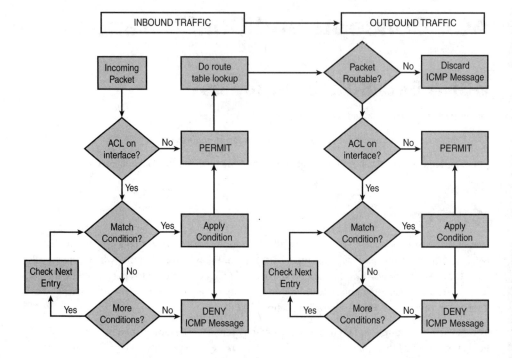

For inbound traffic, the router checks for an inbound ACL applied to the interface *before* doing a route table lookup. Then, for outbound traffic, the router makes sure that a route exists to the destination before checking for ACLs. Finally, if an ACL statement results in a dropped packet, the router sends an ICMP destination unreachable message.

Types of ACLs

ACLs can be configured to filter any type of protocol traffic including other network layer protocols such as AppleTalk and IPX. For the CCNA exam, we focus on IPv4 ACLs, which come in the following types:

- **Standard ACLs:** Filters traffic based on source address only

- **Extended ACLs:** Can filter traffic based on source and destination address, specific protocols, as well as source and destination TCP and UDP ports

You can use two methods to identify both standard and extended ACLs:

- Numbered ACLs use a number for identification.

- Named ACLs use a descriptive name or number for identification.

Although named ACLs must be used with some types of IOS configurations that are beyond the scope of the CCNA exam topics, they do provide two basic benefits:

- By using a descriptive name (such as BLOCK-HTTP), a network administrator can more quickly determine the purpose of an ACL. This is particularly helpful in larger networks where a router can have many ACLs with hundreds of statements.

- Reduce the amount of typing you must do to configure each statement in a named ACL, as you will see in the section "Configuring Named ACLs."

Both numbered and named ACLs can be configured for both standard and extended ACL implementations.

ACL Identification

Table 7-1 lists the different ACL number ranges for the IPv4 protocol as well as a few other protocols. The table is not exhaustive.

Table 7-1   Protocol ACL Numbers

Protocol	Range
IP	1–99
Extended IP	100–199
AppleTalk	600–699
Ethernet address	700–799
IPX	800–899
Extended IPX	900–999
Standard IP (expanded)	1300–1999
Extended IP (expanded)	2000–2699

Named IP ACLs give you more flexibility in working with the ACL entries. In addition to using more memorable names, the other major advantage of named ACLs over numbered ACLs is that you can delete individual statements in a named IP access list.

With Cisco IOS Software Release 12.3, IP access list entry sequence numbering was introduced for both numbered and named ACLs. IP access list entry sequence numbering provides the following benefits:

- You can edit the order of ACL statements.

- You can remove individual statements from an ACL.

- You can use the sequence number to insert new statements into the middle of the ACL.

Sequence numbers are automatically added to the ACL if not entered explicitly at the time the ACL is created. No support exists for sequence numbering in software versions earlier than Cisco IOS Software Release 12.3; therefore, all the ACL additions for earlier software versions are placed at the end of the ACL.

ACL Design Guidelines

Well-designed and well-implemented ACLs add an important security component to your network. Follow these general principles to ensure that the ACLs you create have the intended results:

- Based on the test conditions, choose a standard or extended, numbered, or named ACL.

- Only one ACL per protocol, per direction, and per interface is allowed.

- Organize the ACL to enable processing from the top down. Organize your ACL so that the more specific references to a network or subnet appear before ones that are more general. Place conditions that occur more frequently before conditions that occur less frequently.

- All ACLs contain an implicit **deny any** statement at the end.

- Create the ACL before applying it to an interface.

- Depending on how you apply the ACL, the ACL filters traffic either going through the router or going to and from the router, such as traffic to or from the vty lines.

- You should typically place extended ACLs as close as possible to the source of the traffic that you want to deny. Because standard ACLs do not specify destination addresses, you must put the standard ACL as close as possible to the destination of the traffic you want to deny so the source can reach intermediary networks.

Configuring Standard Numbered ACLs

Standard IPv4 ACLs, which are numbered ACLs in the range of 1 to 99 and 1300 to 1999 or are named ACLs, filter packets based on a source address and mask, and they permit or deny the entire TCP/IP protocol suite. Configuring an ACL requires two steps:

Step 1   Create the ACL.

Step 2   Apply the ACL.

Let's use the simple topology shown in Figure 7-2 to demonstrate how to configure both standard and extended ACLs.

Figure 7-2   ACL Configuration Topology

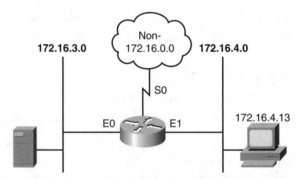

Standard Numbered ACL: Permit Specific Network

Create an ACL to prevent traffic that is not part of the internal networks (172.16.0.0/16) from traveling out either of the Ethernet interfaces.

Step 1   Create the ACL.

Use the **access-list** global configuration command to create an entry in a standard IPv4 ACL:

```
RouterX(config)#access-list 1 permit 172.16.0.0 0.0.255.255
```

The sample statement matches any address that starts with 172.16.x.x. You can use the **remark** option to add a description to your ACL.

Step 2   Apply the ACL.

Use the interface configuration command to select an interface to which to apply the ACL. Then use the **ip access-group** interface configuration command to activate the existing ACL on an interface for a specific direction (**in** or **out**).

```
RouterX(config)#interface ethernet 0
RouterX(config-if)#ip access-group 1 out
RouterX(config)#interface ethernet 1
RouterX(config-if)#ip access-group 1 out
```

This step activates the standard IPv4 ACL 1 on both the interfaces as an outbound filter.

This ACL allows only traffic from source network 172.16.0.0 to be forwarded out on E0 and E1. Traffic from networks other than 172.16.0.0 is blocked with the implied "deny any".

Standard Numbered ACL: Deny a Specific Host

Create an ACL to prevent traffic that originates from host 172.16.4.13 from traveling out Ethernet interface E0. Create and apply the ACL with the commands shown in Example 7-1.

Example 7-1   ACL Preventing Traffic Originating from a Specific Host

```
RouterX(config)#access-list 1 deny 172.16.4.13 0.0.0.0
RouterX(config)#access-list 1 permit 0.0.0.0 255.255.255.255
RouterX(config)#interface ethernet 0
RouterX(config-if)#ip access-group 1 out
```

This ACL is designed to block traffic from a specific address, 172.16.4.13, and to allow all other traffic to be forwarded on interface Ethernet 0. The first statement can also be written with the keyword **host** replacing the **0.0.0.0** wildcard mask as follows:

```
RouterX(config)#access-list 1 deny host 172.16.4.13
```

In fact, starting with Cisco IOS Software Release 12.3, you can enter the following:

```
RouterX(config)#access-list 1 deny 172.16.4.13
```

The second statement can be written with the keyword **any** replacing the source address **0.0.0.0** and wildcard mask **255.255.255.255** as follows:

```
RouterX(config)#access-list 1 permit any
```

Standard Numbered ACL: Deny a Specific Subnet

Create an ACL to prevent traffic that originates from the subnet 172.16.4.0/24 from traveling out Ethernet interface E0. Create and apply the ACL with the commands shown in Example 7-2.

Example 7-2   ACL Preventing Traffic Originating from a Specific Subnet

```
RouterX(config)#access-list 1 deny 172.16.4.0 0.0.0.255
RouterX(config)#access-list 1 permit any
RouterX(config)#interface ethernet 0
RouterX(config-if)#ip access-group 1 out
```

This ACL is designed to block traffic from a specific subnet, 172.16.4.0, and to allow all other traffic to be forwarded out E0.

Standard Numbered ACL: Deny Telnet Access to the Router

To control traffic into and out of the router (not through the router), deny Telnet access to the router by applying an ACL to the vty ports. Restricting vty access is primarily a technique for increasing network security and defining which addresses are allowed Telnet access to the router EXEC process. Create and apply the ACL with the commands shown in Example 7-3.

Example 7-3   Access List Preventing Telnet Activity

```
RouterX(config)#access-list 12 permit host 172.16.4.13
RouterX(config)#line vty 0 4
RouterX(config-line)#access-class 12 in
```

In this example, only host 172.16.4.13 is allowed to Telnet into RouterX. All other IP addresses are denied implicitly.

Configuring Extended Numbered ACLs

For more precise traffic-filtering control, use extended IP ACLs, which are numbered ACLs in the range of 100 to 199 and 2000 to 2699 or are named ACLs, which check for the source and destination IP address. In addition, at the end of the extended ACL statement, you can specify the protocol and optional TCP or UDP application to filter more precisely. To configure numbered extended IPv4 ACLs on a Cisco router, create an extended IP ACL and activate that ACL on an interface. For CCNA exam purposes, the extended ACL command syntax is as follows:

```
Router(config)#access-list access-list-number {permit | deny} protocol source
   source-wildcard [operator port] destination destination-wildcard [operator
   port] [established] [log]
```

Table 7-2 explains the syntax of the command.

Table 7-2   Command Parameters for a Numbered Extended ACL

Command Parameter	Description
access-list-number	Identifies the list using a number in the ranges of 100–199 or 2000–2699.
**permit	deny**	Indicates whether this entry allows or blocks the specified address.
protocol	If **ip** is specified, the entire TCP/IP protocol suite is filtered. Other protocols you can filter include TCP, UDP, ICMP, EIGRP, and OSPF. Use the **?** after the **permit	deny** argument to see all the available protocols.

Command Parameter	Description
source and *destination*	Identifies source and destination IP addresses.
source-wildcard and *destination-wildcard*	Wildcard mask; 0s indicate positions that must match, and 1s indicate "don't care" positions.
operator [*port* |*app_name*]	The operator can be **lt** (less than), **gt** (greater than), **eq** (equal to), or **neq** (not equal to). The port number referenced can be either the source port or the destination port, depending on where in the ACL the port number is configured. As an alternative to the port number, well-known application names can be used, such as Telnet, FTP, and SMTP.
established	For inbound TCP only. Allows TCP traffic to pass if the packet is a response to an outbound-initiated session. This type of traffic has the acknowledgement (ACK) bits set. (See the Extended ACL with the Established Parameter example.)
log	Sends a logging message to the console.

Extended Numbered ACL: Deny FTP from Subnets

For the network in Figure 7-2, create an ACL to prevent FTP traffic originating from the subnet 172.16.4.0/24 and going to the 172.16.3.0/24 subnet from traveling out Ethernet interface E0. Create and apply the ACL with the commands shown in Example 7-4.

Example 7-4   Access List Preventing FTP Traffic from Specific Subnets

```
RouterX(config)#access-list 101 deny tcp 172.16.4.0 0.0.0.255 172.16.3.0
  0.0.0.255 eq 21
RouterX(config)#access-list 101 deny tcp 172.16.4.0 0.0.0.255 172.16.3.0
  0.0.0.255 eq 20
RouterX(config)#access-list 101 permit ip any any
RouterX(config)#interface ethernet 0
RouterX(config-if)#ip access-group 101 out
```

The **deny** statements deny FTP traffic from subnet 172.16.4.0 to subnet 172.16.3.0. The **permit** statement allows all other IP traffic out interface E0. Two statements must be entered for the FTP application because port 20 is used to establish, maintain, and terminate an FTP session while port 21 is used for the actual file transfer task.

Extended Numbered ACL: Deny Only Telnet from Subnet

Create an ACL to prevent Telnet traffic that originates from the subnet 172.16.4.0/24 from traveling out Ethernet interface E0. Create and apply the ACL with the commands shown in Example 7-5.

Example 7-5   Access List Preventing Telnet Traffic from a Specific Subnet

```
RouterX(config)#access-list 101 deny tcp 172.16.4.0 0.0.0.255 any eq 23
RouterX(config)#access-list 101 permit ip any any
RouterX(config)#interface ethernet 0
RouterX(config-if)#ip access-group 101 out
```

This example denies Telnet traffic from 172.16.4.0 that is being sent out interface E0. All other IP traffic from any other source to any destination is permitted out E0.

Configuring Named ACLs

The named ACL feature allows you to identify standard and extended ACLs with an alphanumeric string (name) instead of the current numeric representations.

Because you can delete individual entries with named ACLs, you can modify your ACL without having to delete and then reconfigure the entire ACL. With Cisco IOS Software Release 12.3 and later, you can insert individual entries using an appropriate sequence number.

Standard Named ACL Steps and Syntax

The following are the steps and syntax used to create a standard named ACL:

Step 1   Name the ACL.

Starting from global configuration mode, use the **ip access-list standard** *name* command to name the standard ACL. ACL names are alphanumeric and must be unique:

```
Router(config)ip access-list standard name
```

Step 2   Create the ACL.

From standard named ACL configuration mode, use the **permit** or **deny** statements to specify one or more conditions for determining whether a packet is forwarded or dropped. If you do not specify a sequence number, IOS will increment the sequence number by 10 for every statement you enter:

```
Router(config-std-nacl)#[sequence-number] {permit ¦ deny} source source-
    wildcard [log]
```

Step 3   Apply the ACL.

Activate the named ACL on an interface with the **ip access-group** *name* command:

```
Router(config-if)#ip access-group name [in ¦ out]
```

Standard Named ACL: Deny a Single Host from a Given Subnet

For the network shown previously in Figure 7-2, create a standard ACL named "troublemaker" to prevent traffic that originates from the host 172.16.4.13 from traveling out Ethernet interface E0. Create and apply the ACL with the commands shown in Example 7-6.

Example 7-6   Named ACL Preventing Traffic from a Specific Host

```
RouterX(config)#ip access-list standard troublemaker
RouterX(config-std-nacl)#deny host 172.16.4.13
RouterX(config-std-nacl)#permit 172.16.4.0 0.0.0.255
RouterX(config-std-nacl)#interface e0
RouterX(config-if)#ip access-group troublemaker out
```

Extended Named ACL Steps and Syntax

The following are the steps and syntax used to create an extended named ACL:

Step 1 Name the ACL.

Starting from global configuration mode, use the **ip access-list extended** *name* command to name the extended ACL:

```
Router(config)ipaccess-list extended name
```

Step 2 Create the ACL.

From extended named ACL configuration mode, use the **permit** or **deny** statements to specify one or more conditions for determining whether a packet is forwarded or dropped:

```
Router(config-ext-nacl)#[sequence-number] {deny ¦ permit} protocol source
source-wildcard [operator port] destination destination-wildcard [operator port]
    [established] [log]
```

Step 3 Apply the ACL.

Activate the named ACL on an interface with the **ip access-group** *name* command:

```
Router(config-if)#ip access-group name [in ¦ out]
```

Extended Named ACL: Deny a Telnet from a Subnet

Using Figure 7-2 again, create an extended ACL named "badgroup" to prevent Telnet traffic that originates from the subnet 172.16.4.0/24 from traveling out Ethernet interface E0. Create and apply the ACL with the commands shown in Example 7-7.

Example 7-7   Access List Preventing Telnet Traffic from a Specific Subnet

```
RouterX(config)#ip access-list extended badgroup
RouterX(config-ext-nacl)#deny tcp 172.16.4.0 0.0.0.255 any eq 23
RouterX(config-ext-nacl)#permit ip any any
RouterX(config-ext-nacl)#interface e0
RouterX(config-if)#ip access-group badgroup out
```

Adding Comments to Named or Numbered ACLs

You can add comments to ACLs using the **remark** argument in place of the **permit** or **deny**. Remarks are descriptive statements you can use to better understand and troubleshoot either named or numbered ACLs.

Example 7-8 shows how to add a comment to a numbered ACL.

Example 7-8   Adding Comments to a Numbered ACL

```
RouterX(config)#access-list 101 remark Permitting_John to Telnet to Server
RouterX(config)#access-list 101 permit tcp host 172.16.4.13 host 172.16.3.10 eq
    telnet
```

Example 7-9 shows how to add a comment to a named ACL.

Example 7-9   Adding Comments to a Named ACL

```
RouterX(config)#ip access-list standard PREVENTION
RouterX(config-std-nacl)#remark Do not allow Jones subnet through
RouterX(config-std-nacl)#deny 172.16.4.0 0.0.0.255
```

Complex ACLs

Standard and extended ACLs can become the basis for other types of ACLs that provide additional functionality. These other types of ACLs include the following:

- Dynamic ACLs (lock-and-key)

- Reflexive ACLs

- Time-based ACLs

Configuration of these ACL types is beyond the scope of the CCNA exam, but you should at least be familiar with the concepts behind them. You can review the concepts and configurations in your Study Resources.

Study Resources

For today's exam topics, refer to the following resources for more study.

Resource	Chapter	Topic	Where to Find It
Foundational Resources			
CCNA Exploration Online Curriculum: Accessing the WAN	Chapter 5, "ACLs"	All sections within the chapter	Section 5.1–5.4
CCNA Exploration Accessing the WAN Companion Guide	Chapter 5, "ACLs"	All topics within the chapter	pp. 310–367
ICND2 Official Exam Certification Guide	Chapter 6, "IP Access Control Lists"	All topics within the chapter	pp. 231–264
ICND2 Authorized Self-Study Guide	Chapter 6, "Managing Traffic with Access Control Lists"	Access Control List Operation Configuring ACLs	pp. 205–222 pp. 222–239
Supplemental Resources			
CCNA Flash Cards and Exam Practice Pack	ICND2, Section 7	Managing Traffic with ACLs	pp. 514–536
CCNA Video Mentor	ICND2, Lab10 ICND2, Lab11	Access Lists Access Lists II	pp. 91–93 pp. 95–98

Verifying and Troubleshooting ACL Implementations

CCNA 640-802 Exam Topics

- Verify and monitor ACLs in a network environment.
- Troubleshoot ACL issues.

Key Topics

Today's review topics are rather brief compared to yesterday's. This is so you can take the opportunity to fully review ACL implementations, including their configuration, verification, and troubleshooting. Today we review the verification commands and look at some possible troubleshooting scenarios.

Verifying ACLs

When you finish configuring an ACL, use the **show** commands to verify the configuration. Use the **show access-lists** command to display the contents of all ACLs, as demonstrated in Example 6-1. By entering the ACL name or number as an option for this command, you can display a specific ACL. To display only the contents of all IP ACLs, use the **show ip access-list** command.

Example 6-1   Verifying Access List Configuration

```
RouterX#show access-lists
Standard IP access list SALES
    10 permit 10.3.3.1
    20 permit 10.4.4.1
    30 permit 10.5.5.1
    40 deny   10.1.1.0, wildcard bits 0.0.0.255
    50 permit any
Extended IP access list ENG
    10 permit tcp host 10.22.22.1 any eq telnet (25 matches)
    20 permit tcp host 10.33.33.1 any eq ftp
    30 permit tcp host 10.33.33.1 any eq ftp-data
```

Notice in the output from the **show access-lists** command in Example 6-1 that sequence numbers are incremented by 10—most likely because the administrator did not enter a sequence number. Also notice that this command tells you how many times IOS has matched a packet to a statement—25 times in the case of the first statement in the named ACL **ENG**.

The **show ip interface** command displays IP interface information and indicates whether any IP ACLs are set on the interface. In the **show ip interface e0** command output shown in Example 6-2, IP ACL 1 has been configured on the E0 interface as an inbound ACL. No outbound IP ACL has been configured on the E0 interface.

Example 6-2   Verifying Access List Configuration on a Specific Interface

```
RouterX#show ip interface e0
Ethernet0 is up, line protocol is up
  Internet address is 10.1.1.11/24
  Broadcast address is 255.255.255.255
  Address determined by setup command
  MTU is 1500 bytes
  Helper address is not set
  Directed broadcast forwarding is disabled
  Outgoing access list is not set
  Inbound access list is 1
  Proxy ARP is enabled
  <output omitted>
```

Finally, you can also verify your ACL creation and application with the **show running-config** command (shown in Example 6-3) or **show startup-config**.

Example 6-3   Verifying ACL Creation and Application in the Running Configuration

```
RouterX# show running-config
Building configuration...
!
<output omitted>
!
interface Ethernet0
 ip address 10.44.44.1 255.255.255.0
 ip access-group ENG out
!
interface Serial0
ip address 172.16.2.1 255.255.255.252
 ip access-group SALES in
!
<output omitted>
ip access-list standard SALES
 permit 10.3.3.1
 permit 10.4.4.1
 permit 10.5.5.1
 deny   10.1.1.0 0.0.0.255
 permit any
!
ip access-list extended ENG
```

```
permit tcp host 10.22.22.1 any eq telnet
permit tcp host 10.33.33.1 any eq ftp
permit tcp host 10.33.33.1 any eq ftp-data
!
<output omitted>
```

Troubleshooting ACLs

Using the **show** commands described in the previous section reveals most of the more common ACL errors before they cause problems in your network. When you troubleshoot an ACL, check it against the rules you learned about how to design ACLs correctly. Most errors occur because these basic rules are ignored. In fact, the most common errors are entering ACL statements in the wrong order and not applying adequate criteria to your rules. Let's look at a series of common problems and their solutions using the topology shown in Figure 6-1.

Figure 6-1   Topology for Troubleshooting ACLs

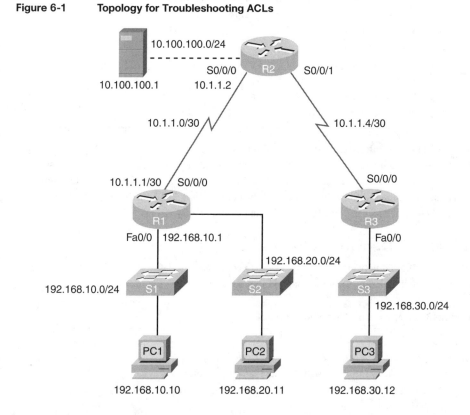

Problem 1: Host Has No Connectivity

Host 192.168.10.10 has no connectivity with 192.168.30.12. The access list shown in Example 6-4 is applied inbound to R3's s0/0/0 interface.

Example 6-4   Problem 1: Host Has No Connectivity

```
R3#show access-lists 100
Extended IP access list 100
    10 deny tcp 192.168.10.0 0.0.0.255 any
    20 permit tcp host 192.168.10.10 any
    30 permit ip any any
```

Because ACLs are processed sequentially until a match is made, traffic from host 192.168.10.10 is denied by the first statement. Statement 20, which permits host 192.168.10.10, never gets processed. The solution is to change the position of statement 20 so that it comes before statement 10. You can do this with the commands shown in Example 6-5.

Example 6-5   Solution 1: Correcting the "Host Has No Connectivity" Problem

```
R3(config)#ip access-list extended 100
R3(config-ext-nacl)#no 20 permit tcp host 192.168.10.10 any
R3(config-ext-nacl)#5 permit tcp host 192.168.10.10 any
R3(config-ext-nacl)#end
R3#show access-lists 100
Extended IP access list 100
    5 permit tcp host 192.168.10.10 any
    10 deny tcp 192.168.10.0 0.0.0.255 any
    30 permit ip any any
```

First, notice that we entered named ACL configuration mode in order to edit the sequence numbers for the extended numbered ACL. Second, we removed statement 20. Finally, we reapplied statement 20 with a new sequence number lower than 10—5 in the example. Notice from the **show access-lists** output that the statement order is now correct. Host 192.168.10.10 will be permitted, and all other traffic from the 192.168.10.0/24 subnet will be denied.

Problem 2: Denied Protocols

The 192.168.10.0/24 network cannot use TFTP to connect to the 192.168.30.0/24 network. The access list shown in Example 6-6 is applied inbound to R1's Fa0/0 interface.

Example 6-6   Problem 2: Denied Protocols

```
R1#show access-lists 120
Extended IP access list 120
    10 deny tcp 192.168.10.0 0.0.0.255 any eq telnet
    20 deny tcp 192.168.10.0 0.0.0.255 host 10.100.100.1 eq smtp
    30 permit tcp any any
```

The 192.168.10.0/24 network cannot use TFTP to connect to the 192.168.30.0/24 network because TFTP uses the transport protocol UDP. Statement 30 in access list 120 allows all other TCP traffic. Because TFTP uses UDP, it is implicitly denied. The solution is to replace the **permit tcp any any** statement with **permit ip any any** as shown in Example 6-7.

Example 6-7   Solution 2: Correcting the "Denied Protocols" Problem

```
R1(config)#ip access-list extended 120
R1(config-ext-nacl)#no 30 permit tcp any any
R1(config-ext-nacl)#permit ip any any
R1(config-ext-nacl)#end
R1#show access-lists 120
Extended IP access list 120
    10 deny tcp 192.168.10.0 0.0.0.255 any eq telnet
    20 deny tcp 192.168.10.0 0.0.0.255 host 10.100.100.1 eq smtp
    30 permit ip any any
```

Notice that we did not have to include a sequence number for the new **permit ip any any** statement because this statement comes at the end of the list. IOS will automatically increment it by 10.

Problem 3: Telnet is Allowed #1

The 192.168.10.0/24 network can use Telnet to connect to 192.168.30.0/24, but this connection should not be allowed. The access list is shown in Example 6-8.

Example 6-8   Problem 3: Telnet Is Allowed #1

```
R1#show access-lists 130
Extended IP access list 130
    10 deny tcp any eq telnet any
    20 deny tcp 192.168.10.0 0.0.0.255 host 10.100.100.1 eq smtp
    30 permit ip any any
```

The 192.168.10.0/24 network can use Telnet to connect to the 192.168.30.0/24 network because Telnet in statement 10 of access list 130 is listed in the wrong position. The source port would not be Telnet's port 23, but some randomly chosen port numbered above 1024. The destination port number (or application) must be set to Telnet as shown in the solution to this problem in Example 6-9.

Example 6-9   Solution 3: Correcting the "Telnet Is Allowed #1" Problem

```
R1(config)#ip access-list extended 130
R1(config-ext-nacl)#no 10 deny tcp any eq telnet any
R1(config-ext-nacl)#10 deny tcp any any eq telnet
R1(config-ext-nacl)#end
R1#show access-lists 130
Extended IP access list 130
    10 deny tcp any any eq telnet
    20 deny tcp 192.168.10.0 0.0.0.255 host 10.100.100.1 eq smtp
    30 permit ip any any
```

Problem 4: Telnet Is Allowed #2

Host 192.168.10.10 can use Telnet to connect to 192.168.30.12, but this connection should not be allowed. The access list is shown in Example 6-10.

Example 6-10 Problem 4: Telnet Is Allowed #2

```
R1#show access-lists 140
Extended IP access list 140
    10 deny tcp host 192.168.10.1 any eq telnet
    20 deny tcp 192.168.10.0 0.0.0.255 host 10.100.100.1 eq smtp
    30 permit ip any any
```

Host 192.168.10.10 can use Telnet to connect to 192.168.30.12 because no rules deny host 192.168.10.10 or its network as the source. Statement 10 denies the router interface from which traffic would be departing. However, as Telnet packets depart the router, they have the source address of 192.168.10.10, not the address of the router interface. Example 6-11 shows the solution to this problem.

Example 6-11 Solution 4: Correcting the "Telnet Is Allowed #2" Problem

```
R1(config)#ip access-list extended 140
R1(config-ext-nacl)#no 10 deny tcp host 192.168.10.1 any eq telnet
R1(config-ext-nacl)#10 deny tcp host 192.168.10.10 any eq telnet
R1(config-ext-nacl)#end
R1#show access-lists 140
Extended IP access list 140
    10 deny tcp host 192.168.10.10 any eq telnet
    20 deny tcp 192.168.10.0 0.0.0.255 host 10.100.100.1 eq smtp
    30 permit ip any any
```

Problem 5: Telnet Is Allowed #3

Host 192.168.30.12 can use Telnet to connect to 192.168.10.10, but this connection should not be allowed. The access list shown in Example 6-12 is applied inbound to R3's s0/0/0 interface.

Example 6-12 Problem 5: Telnet Is Allowed #3

```
R3#show access-lists 150
Extended IP access list 150
    10 deny tcp host 192.168.30.12 any eq telnet
    20 permit ip any any
```

Host 192.168.30.12 can use Telnet to connect to 192.168.10.10 because of the direction in which access list 150 is applied to the S0/0/0 interface. Statement 10 denies the source address of 192.168.30.12, but that address would be the source only if the traffic were outbound on S0/0/0, not inbound. Example 6-13 shows the solution to this problem.

Example 6-13   Solution 5: Correcting the "Telnet Is Allowed #3" Problem

```
R3(config)# interface serial 0/0/0
R3(config-if)# no ip access-group 150 in
R3(config-if)# ip access-group 150 out
```

Notice that this solution does not block Telnet traffic from 192.168.30.12 to the Fa0/0 interface on R3. A better solution might be to apply the ACL to the Fa0/0 interface for inbound traffic.

Study Resources

For today's exam topics, refer to the following resources for more study.

Resource	Chapter	Topic	Where to Find It
Foundational Resources			
CCNA Exploration Online Curriculum: Accessing the WAN	Chapter 5, "ACLs"	All sections within the chapter	Sections 5.1–5.4
CCNA Exploration Accessing the WAN Companion Guide	Chapter 5, "ACLs"	All topics within the chapter	pp. 310–367
ICND2 Official Exam Certification Guide	Chapter 6, "IP Access Control Lists"	All topics within the chapter	pp. 231–264
ICND2 Authorized Self-Study Guide	Chapter 6, "Managing Traffic with Access Control Lists"	Configuring ACLs Troubleshooting ACLs	pp. 222–239 pp. 239–244
Supplemental Resources			
CCNA Flash Cards and Exam Practice Pack	ICND2, Section 7	Managing Traffic with ACLs	pp. 514–536

NAT Concepts, Configuration, and Troubleshooting

CCNA 640-802 Exam Topics

- Explain the basic operation of NAT.
- Configure NAT for given network requirements using (CLI/SDM).
- Troubleshoot NAT issues.

Key Topics

To cope with the depletion of IPv4 addresses, several short-term solutions were developed. One short-term solution is to use private addresses and Network Address Translation (NAT). NAT enables inside network hosts to borrow a legitimate Internet IP address while accessing Internet resources. When the requested traffic returns, the legitimate IP address is repurposed and available for the next Internet request by an inside host. Using NAT, network administrators need only one or a few IP addresses for the router to provide to the hosts, instead of one unique IP address for every client joining the network. Today, we review the concepts, configuration, and troubleshooting of NAT.

NAT Concepts

NAT, defined in RFC 3022, has many uses. But its key use is to conserve IP addresses by allowing networks to use private IP addresses. NAT translates nonroutable, private, internal addresses into routable, public addresses. NAT is also a natural firewall. It hides internal IP addresses from outside networks.

A NAT-enabled device typically operates at the border of a stub network. In Figure 5-1, R2 is the border router.

In NAT terminology, the inside network is the set of networks that are subject to translation (every network in the shaded region in Figure 5-1). The outside network refers to all other addresses. Figure 5-2 shows how to refer to the addresses when configuring NAT.

- **Inside local address:** Most likely a private address. In the figure, the IP address 192.168.10.10 assigned to PC1 is an inside local address.
- **Inside global address:** A valid public address that the inside host is given when it exits the NAT router. When traffic from PC1 is destined for the web server at 209.165.201.1, R2 must translate the inside local address to an inside global address, which is 209.165.200.226 in this case.
- **Outside global address:** A reachable IP address assigned to a host on the Internet. For example, the web server can be reached at IP address 209.165.201.1.
- **Outside local address:** The local IP address assigned to a host on the outside network. In most situations, this address is identical to the outside global address of that outside device. (Outside local addresses are beyond the scope of the CCNA.)

Figure 5-1   NAT Topology

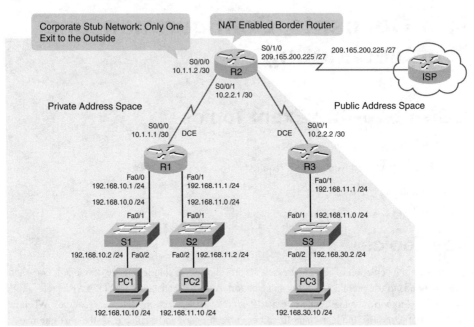

Figure 5-2   NAT Terminology

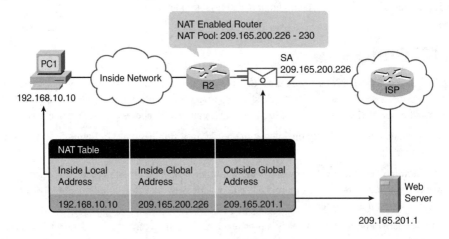

A NAT Example

The following steps illustrate the NAT process when PC1 sends traffic to the Internet:

1. PC1 sends a packet destined for the Internet to R1, the default gateway.

2. R1 forwards the packet to R2, as directed by its routing table.

3. R2 refers to its routing table and identifies the next hop as the ISP router. It then checks to see if the packet matches the criteria specified for translation. R2 has an ACL that identifies the inside network as a valid host for translation. Therefore, it translates an inside local IP address to an inside global IP address, which in this case is 209.165.200.226. It stores this mapping of the local to global address in the NAT table.

4. R2 modifies the packet with the new source IP address (the inside global address) and sends it to the ISP router.

5. The packet eventually reaches its destination, which then sends its reply to the inside global address 209.165.200.226.

6. When replies from the destination arrive back at R2, it consults the NAT table to match the inside global address to the correct inside local address. R2 then modifies the packet with the inside local address (192.168.10.10) and sends it to R1.

7. R1 receives the packet and forwards it to PC1.

Dynamic and Static NAT

The two types of NAT translation are as follows:

- **Dynamic NAT:** Uses a pool of public addresses and assigns them on a first-come, first-served basis. When a host with a private IP address requests access to the Internet, dynamic NAT chooses an IP address from the pool that is not already in use by another host.

- **Static NAT:** Uses a one-to-one mapping of local and global addresses, and these mappings remain constant. Static NAT is particularly useful for web servers or hosts that must have a consistent address that is accessible from the Internet.

NAT Overload

NAT overloading (sometimes called Port Address Translation [PAT]) maps multiple private IP addresses to a single public IP address or a few addresses. To do this, each private address is also tracked by a port number. When a response comes back from outside, port numbers determine to which client the NAT router translates the packets.

Figure 5-3 and the following steps illustrate the NAT overload process.

Figure 5-3   NAT Overload Example

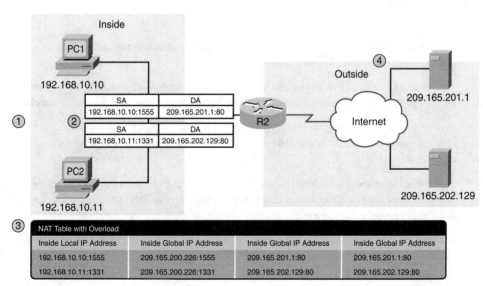

1. PC1 and PC2 send packets destined for the Internet.

2. When the packets arrive at R2, NAT overload changes the source address to the inside global IP address and keeps the assigned port numbers (1555 and 1331 in this example) to identify the client from which the packet originated.

3. R2 updates its NAT table. Notice the assigned ports. R2 then routes the packets to the Internet.

4. When the web server replies, R2 uses the destination source port to translate the packet to the correct client.

NAT overload attempts to preserve the original source port. However, if this source port is already used, NAT overload assigns the first available port number starting from the beginning of the appropriate port group 0 to 511, 512 to 1023, or 1024 to 65535.

NAT Benefits

The benefits of using NAT include the following:

- NAT conserves registered IP address space because, with NAT overload, internal hosts can share a single public IP address for all external communications.

- NAT increases the flexibility of connections to the public network. Multiple pools, backup pools, and load-balancing pools can be implemented to ensure reliable public network connections.

- NAT allows the existing scheme to remain while supporting a new public addressing scheme. This means an organization could change ISPs and not need to change any of its inside clients.

- NAT provides a layer of network security because private networks do not advertise their inside local addresses outside the organization.

NAT Limitations

The limitations of using NAT include the following:

- **Performance is degraded:** NAT increases switching delays because translating each IP address within the packet headers takes time.

- **End-to-end functionality is degraded:** Many Internet protocols and applications depend on end-to-end functionality, with unmodified packets forwarded from the source to the destination.

- **End-to-end IP traceability is lost:** It becomes much more difficult to trace packets that undergo numerous packet address changes over multiple NAT hops, making troubleshooting challenging.

- **Tunneling is more complicated:** Using NAT also complicates tunneling protocols, such as IPsec, because NAT modifies values in the headers that interfere with the integrity checks done by IPsec and other tunneling protocols.

- **Services may be disrupted:** Services that require the initiation of TCP connections from the outside network, or stateless protocols such as those using UDP, can be disrupted.

Configuring Static NAT

Static NAT is a one-to-one mapping between an inside address and an outside address. Static NAT allows connections initiated by external devices to inside devices. For instance, you might want to map an inside global address to a specific inside local address that is assigned to your web server. The steps and syntax to configure static NAT are as follows:

Step 1   Configure the static translation of an inside local address to an inside global address:

```
Router(config)#ip nat inside source static local-ip global-ip
```

Step 2   Specify the inside interface:

```
Router(config)#interface type number
Router(config-if)#ip nat inside
```

Step 3   Specify the outside interface:

```
Router(config)#interface type number
Router(config-if)#ip nat outside
```

Figure 5-4 shows a sample static NAT topology.

Figure 5-4   Static NAT Topology

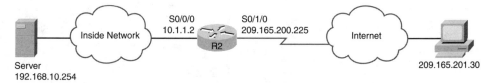

Server
192.168.10.254

Example 5-1 shows the static NAT configuration.

Example 5-1   Static NAT Configuration

```
R2(config)#ip nat inside source static 192.168.10.254 209.165.200.254
R2(config)#interface serial0/0/0
R2(config-if)#ip nat inside
R2(config-if)#interface serial 0/1/0
R2(config-if)#ip nat outside
```

This configuration statically maps the inside IP address of 192.168.10.254 to the outside address of 209.165.10.254. This allows outside hosts to access the internal web server using the public IP address 209.165.10.254.

Configuring Dynamic NAT

Dynamic NAT maps private IP addresses to public addresses drawn from a NAT pool. The steps and syntax to configure dynamic NAT are as follows:

Step 1   Define a pool of global addresses to be allocated:

```
Router(config)#ip nat pool name start-ip end-ip {netmask netmask ¦
prefix-length prefix-length}
```

Step 2   Define a standard access list permitting those addresses that are to be translated:

```
Router(config)#access-list access-list-number source source-wildcard
```

Step 3   Bind the pool of addresses to the access list:

```
Router(config)#ip nat inside source list access-list-number pool name
```

Step 4   Specify the inside interface:

```
Router(config)#interface type number
Router(config-if)#ip nat inside
```

Step 5   Specify the outside interface:

```
Router(config)#interface type number
Router(config-if)#ip nat outside
```

Figure 5-5 shows a sample dynamic NAT topology.

Figure 5-5   Dynamic NAT Topology

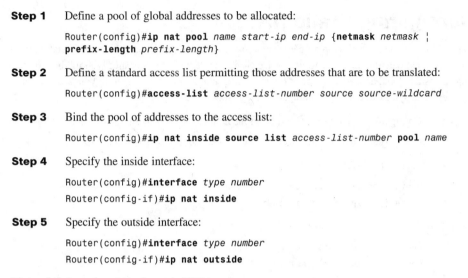

192.168.10.10

192.168.11.10

Example 5-2 shows the dynamic NAT configuration.

Example 5-2   Dynamic NAT Configuration

```
R2(config)#ip nat pool NAT-POOL1 209.165.200.226 209.165.200.240 netmask
255.255.255.224
R2(config)#access-list 1 permit 192.168.0.0 0.0.255.255
R2(config)#ip nat inside source list 1 pool NAT-POOL1
R2(config)#interface serial 0/0/0
R2(config-if)#ip nat inside
R2(config-if)#interface serial s0/1/0
R2(config-if)#ip nat outside
```

Configuring NAT Overload

Commonly with home networks and small to medium-sized businesses, the ISP assigns only one registered IP address to your router. Therefore, it is necessary to overload that one IP address so that multiple inside clients can use it simultaneously.

The configuration is similar to dynamic NAT, except that instead of a pool of addresses, the **interface** keyword is used to identify the outside IP address. Therefore, no NAT pool is defined. The **overload** keyword enables the addition of the port number to the translation.

Example 5-3 shows how R2 in Figure 5-5 would be configured to overload its registered IP address on the serial interface.

Example 5-3   Configuring NAT to Overload an Interface Address

```
R2(config)#access-list 1 permit 192.168.0.0 0.0.255.255
R2(config)#ip nat inside source list 1 interface serial 0/1/0 overload
R2(config)#interface serial 0/0/0
R2(config-if)#ip nat inside
R2(config-if)#interface serial s0/1/0
R2(config-if)#ip nat outside
```

You can also overload a NAT pool of addresses, which might be necessary in organizations that potentially have many clients simultaneously needing translations. In our previous Example 5-2, NAT is configured with a pool of 15 addresses (209.165.200.226 to 209.165.200.240). If, at any given moment, R2 is translating all 15 addresses, packets for the 16th client will be queued for processing and possibly timeout. To avoid this problem, add the keyword **overload** to the command that binds the access list to the NAT pool as follows:

```
R2(config)#ip nat inside source list 1 pool NAT-POOL1 overload
```

Interestingly, IOS will use the first IP address in the pool until it runs out of available port numbers. Then it will move to the next IP address in the pool.

Verifying NAT

Assume that both the static and dynamic NAT topologies shown in Figures 5-4 and 5-5 are configured on R2 with the inside server statically translated to 209.165.200.254 and the **NAT-POOL1** configured with the **overload** keyword. Further assume that two inside clients have connected to an outside host. You can use the **show ip nat translations** command to verify the current translations in the R2 NAT table, as shown in Example 5-4.

Example 5-4   Verifying NAT Operations with show ip nat translations

```
R2#show ip nat translations
Pro  Inside global         Inside local         Outside local        Outside global
---   209.165.200.254      192.168.20.254       ---                  ---
tcp 209.165.200.226:1025  192.168.10.10:1025   209.165.201.30:80    209.165.201.30:80
tcp 209.165.200.226:1024  192.168.11.10:1025   209.165.201.30:80    209.165.201.30:80
```

The static entry is always in the table. Currently, there are two dynamic entries. Notice that both inside clients received the same inside global address, but the port numbers are different.

The **show ip nat statistics** command shown in Example 5-5 displays information about the total number of active translations, NAT configuration parameters, how many addresses are in the pool, and how many have been allocated.

Example 5-5   Verifying NAT Operations with show ip nat statistics

```
R2#show ip nat statistics
Total translations: 3 (1 static, 2 dynamic, 2 extended)
Outside Interfaces: Serial0/1/0
Inside Interfaces: FastEthernet0/0 , Serial0/0/0 , Serial0/0/1
Hits: 29  Misses: 7
Expired translations: 5
Dynamic mappings:
-- Inside Source
access-list 1 pool NAT-POOL1 refCount 2
 pool NAT-POOL1: netmask 255.255.255.224
        start 209.165.200.226 end 209.165.200.240
        type generic, total addresses 3 , allocated 1 (7%), misses 0
```

Alternatively, use the **show run** command and look for NAT, access command list, interface, or pool-related commands with the required values. Examine the output from these commands carefully to discover any errors.

It is sometimes useful to clear the dynamic entries sooner than the default. This is especially true when testing the NAT configuration. To clear dynamic entries before the timeout has expired, use the **clear ip nat translation *** privileged EXEC command.

Troubleshooting NAT

When you have IP connectivity problems in a NAT environment, it is often difficult to determine the cause of the problem. The first step in solving your problem is to rule out NAT as the cause. Follow these steps to verify that NAT is operating as expected:

Step 1   Based on the configuration, clearly define what NAT is supposed to achieve. This might reveal a problem with the configuration.

Step 2   Verify that correct translations exist in the translation table using the **show ip nat translations** command.

Step 3   Use the **clear** and **debug** commands to verify that NAT is operating as expected. Check to see if dynamic entries are re-created after they are cleared.

Step 4   Review in detail what is happening to the packet, and verify that routers have the correct routing information to forward the packet.

Use the **debug ip nat** command to verify the operation of the NAT feature by displaying information about every packet that the router translates, as shown in Example 5-6.

Example 5-6   Troubleshooting NAT with debug ip nat

```
R2#debug ip nat
IP NAT debugging is on
R2#
NAT: s=192.168.10.10->209.165.200.226, d=209.165.201.30[8]
NAT*: s=209.165.201.30, d=209.165.200.226->192.168.10.10[8]
NAT: s=192.168.10.10->209.165.200.226, d=209.165.201.30[8]
NAT: s=192.168.10.10->209.165.200.226, d=209.165.201.30[8]
NAT*: s=209.165.201.30, d=209.165.200.226->192.168.10.10[8]
NAT*: s=209.165.201.30, d=209.165.200.226->192.168.10.10[8]
NAT: s=192.168.10.10->209.165.200.226, d=209.165.201.30[8]
NAT: s=192.168.10.10->209.165.200.226, d=209.165.201.30[8]
NAT*: s=209.165.201.30, d=209.165.200.226->192.168.10.10[8]
NAT*: s=209.165.201.30, d=209.165.200.226->192.168.10.10[8]
NAT: s=192.168.10.10->209.165.200.226, d=209.165.201.30[8]
R2#
```

You can see that inside host 192.168.10.10 initiated traffic to outside host 209.165.201.30 and has been translated into address 209.165.200.226.

When decoding the debug output, note what the following symbols and values indicate:

- ***:** The asterisk next to NAT indicates that the translation is occurring in the fast-switched path. The first packet in a conversation is always process-switched, which is slower. The remaining packets go through the fast-switched path if a cache entry exists.

- **s=:** Refers to the source IP address.

- **a.b.c.d->w.x.y.z:** Indicates that source address a.b.c.d is translated into w.x.y.z.

- **d=:** Refers to the destination IP address.

- **[xxxx]:** The value in brackets is the IP identification number. This information may be useful for debugging because it enables correlation with other packet traces from protocol analyzers.

Study Resources

For today's exam topics, refer to the following resources for more study.

Resource	Chapter	Topic	Where to Find It
Foundational Resources			
CCNA Exploration Online Curriculum: Accessing the WAN	Chapter 7, "IP Addressing Services"	Scaling Networks with NAT	Section 7.2
CCNA Exploration Accessing the WAN Companion Guide	Chapter 7, "IP Addressing Services"	Scaling Networks with NAT	pp. 460–485
ICND2 Official Exam Certification Guide	Chapter 16, "Network Address Translation" Lab 7	All topics within the chapter NAT Overload (PAT)	pp. 549–572 Video Training CD
ICND2 Authorized Self-Study Guide	Chapter 7, "Managing Address Space with NAT and IPv6"	Scaling the Network with NAT and PAT	pp. 249–270
Supplemental Resources			
CCNA Flash Cards and Exam Practice Pack	ICND1, Section 10 ICND2, Section 8	Understanding WAN Technologies Managing Address Space with NAT and IPv6	pp. 254–292 pp. 538–568
CCNA Video Mentor	ICND2, Lab 7	NAT Overload (PAT)	pp. 79–82

Part VIII

WAN Concepts and Configuration

Day 4:   WAN and VPN Technologies

Day 3:   PPP Configuration and Troubleshooting

Day 2:   Frame Relay Configuration and Troubleshooting

Day 1:   CCNA Skills Review and Practice

WAN and VPN Technologies

CCNA 640-802 Exam Topics

- Describe different methods for connecting to a WAN.
- Describe VPN technology (importance, benefits, role, impact, components).

Key Topics

Today is a whirlwind review of WAN technologies, WAN connection options, and VPN. Because these exam topics are conceptual in nature, requiring no configuration skills, read this review several times. If necessary, refer to your study resources for more in-depth review.

WAN Technology Concepts

WAN access standards typically describe both physical layer delivery methods and data link layer requirements, including physical addressing, flow control, and encapsulation. The physical layer protocols describe how to provide electrical, mechanical, operational, and functional connections to a service provider. The data link layer protocols define how data is encapsulated and the mechanisms for transferring the resulting frames. A variety of technologies are used, such as Frame Relay and Asynchronous Transfer Mode (ATM). Some of these protocols use the same basic framing mechanism as High-Level Data Link Control (HDLC), an ISO standard, or one of its subsets or variants.

WAN Components and Devices

Figure 4-1 illustrates the terminology commonly used to describe physical WAN connections.

The WAN components shown in Figure 4-1 are described in further detail in the following list:

- **Customer Premises Equipment (CPE):** The devices located at the premises of the WAN subscriber. The subscriber either owns or leases the CPE.
- **Data Communications Equipment (DCE):** Consists of devices that put data on the local loop. The DCE primarily provides an interface to connect subscribers to the WAN cloud.
- **Data Terminal Equipment (DTE):** The customer devices that pass the data from a customer network to the DCE for transmission over the WAN.
- **Local loop:** The copper or fiber cable that connects the CPE the central office (CO) of the service provider. The local loop is sometimes called the "last mile."
- **Demarcation point:** A point where customer equipment is separated from service provider equipment. It is the place where the responsibility for the connection changes from the customer to the service provider.
- **Central office (CO):** A local service provider facility or building where local cables link to long-haul, all-digital, fiber-optic communications lines through a system of switches and other equipment.

Figure 4-1   WAN Physical Layer Terminology

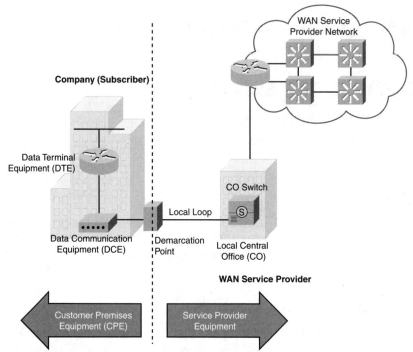

WANs use numerous types of devices that are specific to WAN environments:

- **Modem:** Modulates and demodulates between analog and digital signals.

- **CSU/DSU:** A channel service unit (CSU) and a data service unit (DSU) often combined into a single piece of equipment to provide the termination for the digital signal and ensure connection integrity through error correction and line monitoring. It interprets frames from the carrier into frames that LAN devices can interpret and vice versa.

- **Access server:** Concentrates dial-in and dial-out user communications. An access server might have a mixture of analog and digital interfaces and support hundreds of simultaneous users.

- **WAN switch:** A multiport internetworking device used in carrier networks. These devices typically switch traffic such as Frame Relay, ATM, or X.25 and operate at the data link layer of the OSI reference model. Public switched telephone network (PSTN) switches might also be used within the cloud for circuit-switched connections such as (ISDN) or analog dialup.

- **Router:** Provides internetworking and WAN access interface ports that are used to connect to the service provider network.

- **Core router:** A service provider router that resides within the middle or backbone of the WAN rather than at its periphery. To fulfill this role, a router must be able to support multiple telecommunications interfaces of the highest speed in use in the WAN core, and it must be able to forward IP packets at full speed on all those interfaces. The router must also support the routing protocols being used in the core.

Figure 4-2 shows the name and typical location of various WAN devices.

Figure 4-2   WAN Devices

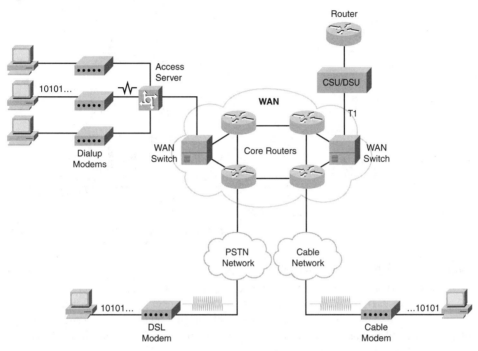

WAN Physical Layer Standards

The WAN physical layer also describes the interface between the DTE and DCE. A Cisco router's serial interface is capable of connecting to a CSU/DSU that uses any of the following standards:

- **EIA/TIA-232:** This protocol allows signal speeds of up to 64 kbps on a 25-pin D-connector over short distances. It was formerly known as RS-232. The ITU-T V.24 specification is effectively the same.

- **EIA/TIA-449/530:** This protocol is a faster (up to 2 Mbps) version of EIA/TIA-232. It uses a 36-pin D-connector and is capable of longer cable runs. Several versions exist. This standard is also known as RS-422 and RS-423.

- **V.35:** This is the ITU-T standard for synchronous communications between a network access device and a packet network. Originally specified to support data rates of 48 kbps, it now supports speeds of up to 2.048 Mbps using a 34-pin rectangular connector.

- **X.21:** This protocol is an ITU-T standard for synchronous digital communications. It uses a 15-pin D-connector.

- **EIA/TIA-612/613:** (not shown in Figure 4-3) This standard describes the High-Speed Serial Interface (HSSI) protocol, which provides access to services up to 52 Mbps on a 60-pin D-connector.

Notice in Figure 4-3 that the router connection at the top is the same regardless of the connection used by CSU/DSU. The network administrator simply chooses the correct cable for the CSU/DSU connection.

Figure 4-3   WAN Cable Connectors

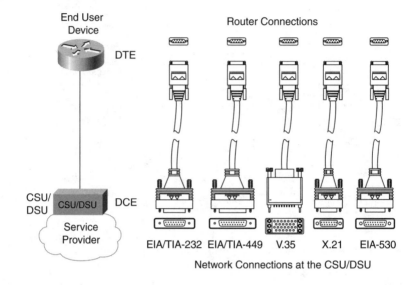

Network Connections at the CSU/DSU

WAN Data Link Protocols

Each WAN connection type uses a Layer 2 protocol to encapsulate a packet while it is crossing the WAN link. To ensure that the correct encapsulation protocol is used, the Layer 2 encapsulation type used for each router serial interface must be configured, if different than the default. The choice of encapsulation protocols depends on the WAN technology and the equipment. The most common WAN data link protocols are as follows:

- HDLC (Cisco default)

- Point-to-Point Protocol (PPP)

- Frame Relay

- Asynchronous Transfer Mode (ATM)

WAN Switching

WAN switched networks are categorized as either circuit-switched or packet-switched. A circuit-switched network is one that establishes a dedicated circuit (or channel) between nodes and terminals before the users can communicate. Although the circuit is dedicated for the duration of the call, the physical link is share by multiple end users through a process called time-division multiplexing (TDM). TDM gives each conversation a share of the connection in turn and ensures that a fixed-capacity connection is made available to the subscriber. PSTN and ISDN are two types of circuit-switching technology that can be used to implement a WAN in an enterprise setting.

In contrast to circuit switching, packet switching splits traffic data into packets that are routed over a shared network. Packet-switching networks do not require a circuit to be established, and they allow many pairs of end users to communicate over the same channel. The switches in a packet-switched network use one of the following methods to determine which link the packet must be sent on next from the addressing information in each packet:

- **Connectionless systems**, such as the Internet, carry full addressing information in each packet. Each packet switch or router must evaluate the destination IP address to determine where to send the packet.

- **Connection-oriented systems** predetermine a packet's route, and each packet only has to carry an identifier, such as Data Link Connection Identifiers (DLCIs) in Frame Relay.

Packet-switched networks can establish routes through the switches for particular end-to-end connections. These routes are called virtual circuits (VCs). A VC is a logical circuit between two network devices to help ensure reliable communications. Two types of VCs exist:

- **Permanent virtual circuit (PVC):** A permanently established virtual circuit that consists of one mode—data transfer. PVCs are used in situations in which data transfer between devices is constant.

- **Switched virtual circuit (SVC):** A VC that is dynamically established on demand and terminated when transmission is complete. Communication over an SVC consists of three phases: circuit establishment, data transfer, and circuit termination. SVCs are used in situations in which data transmission between devices is intermittent, largely to save costs.

WAN Connection Options

Many options for implementing WAN solutions are currently available. They differ in technology, speed, and cost. Figure 4-4 provides a high-level view of the various WAN link connection options, and the sections that follow describe these options in more detail.

Figure 4-4   WAN Link Connection Options

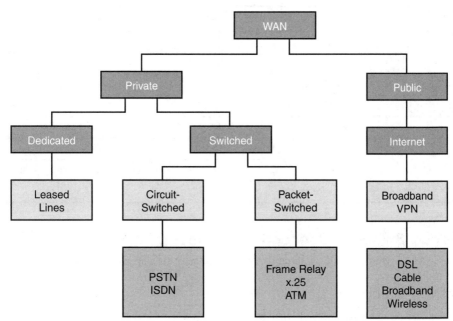

Dedicated Connection Options

Also called leased lines, dedicated connections are preestablished point-to-point WAN connections from the customer premises through the provider network to a remote destination, as shown in Figure 4-5.

Figure 4-5   Leased Lines

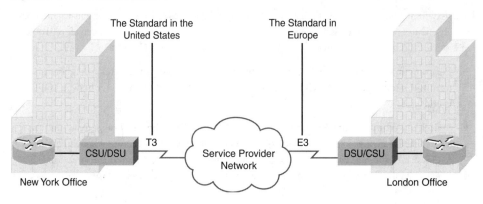

Leased lines are usually more expensive than switched services because of the dedicated, "always on" cost of providing WAN service to the customer. The dedicated capacity removes latency and jitter and provides a layer of security because only the customer's traffic is allowed on the link. Table 4-1 lists the available leased-line types and their bit-rate capacities.

Table 4-1   Leased Line Types and Capacities

Line Type	Bit Rate Capacity	Line Type	Bit-Rate Capacity
56k	56 kbps	OC-9	466.56 Mbps
64k	64 kbps	OC-12	622.08 Mbps
T1	1.544 Mbps	OC-18	933.12 Mbps
E1	2.048 Mbps	OC-24	1244.16 Mbps
J1	2.048 Mbps	OC-36	1866.24 Mbps
E3	34.064 Mbps	OC-48	2488.32 Mbps
T3	44.736 Mbps	OC-96	4976.64 Mbps
OC-1	51.84 Mbps	OC-192	9953.28 Mbps
OC-3	155.54 Mbps	OC-768	39,813.12 Mbps

Circuit-Switched Connection Options

The two main types of circuit-switched connections are analog dialup and ISDN.

Analog Dialup

Analog dialup using modems and telephone lines is an ideal WAN connection solution when intermittent, low-volume data transfers are needed. Figure 4-6 shows a typical analog dialup connection.

Figure 4-6   Analog Dialup

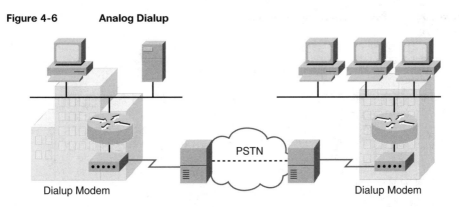

Dialup Modem   Dialup Modem

These relatively low-speed dialup connections are adequate for the exchange of sales figures, prices, routine reports, and email. Using automatic dialup at night or on weekends for large file transfers and data backup can take advantage of lower off-peak tariffs (line charges). The advantages of modem and analog lines are simplicity, availability, and low implementation cost. The disadvantages are the low data rates and a relatively long connection time.

ISDN

ISDN turns the local loop into a TDM digital connection, which enables it to carry digital signals that result in higher-capacity switched connections. The connection uses 64-kbps bearer (B) channels to carry voice or data and a signaling, delta (D) channel for call setup and other purposes. There are two types of ISDN interfaces:

- **Basic Rate Interface (BRI):** Provides two 64-kbps B channels for voice or data transfer and a 16-kbps D channel used for control signaling.

- **Primary Rate Interface (PRI):** Provides 23 B channels with 64 kbps and one D channel with 64 kbps in North America, for a total bit rate of up to 1.544 Mbps. Europe uses 30 B channels and one D channel, for a total bit rate of up to 2.048 Mbps.

Figure 4-7 illustrates the various differences between ISDN BRI and PRI lines.

Packet-Switched Connection Options

The most common packet-switching technologies used in today's enterprise WANs include legacy X.25, Frame Relay, and ATM.

X.25

X.25 is a legacy network-layer protocol. SVCs are established through the network for intermittent use of applications such as point-of-sale card readers. X.25 networks vary from 2400 bps up to 2 Mbps and are now in dramatic decline, being replaced by newer technologies such as Frame Relay, ATM, and DSL.

Frame Relay

Figure 4-8 shows a simplified Frame Relay network.

Figure 4-7   ISDN Network Infrastructure and PRI/BRI Line Capacity

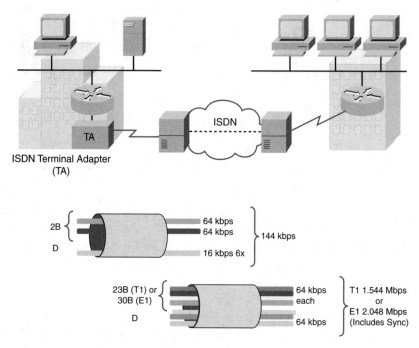

Figure 4-8   Frame Relay Network

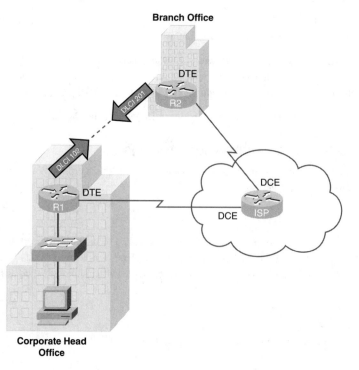

Frame Relay differs from X.25 in several ways. Most importantly, it is a much simpler protocol, operating strictly at Layer 2, whereas X.25 additionally provides Layer 3 services. Unlike X.25, Frame Relay implements no error or flow control. The simplified handling of frames leads to reduced latency, and measures taken to avoid frame buildup at intermediate switches help reduce jitter. Frame Relay offers data rates up to 4 Mbps, with some providers offering even higher rates. Frame Relay VCs are uniquely identified by a DLCI, which ensures bidirectional communication from one DTE device to another. Most Frame Relay connections are PVCs rather than SVCs.

ATM

Figure 4-9 shows an ATM network.

Figure 4-9   ATM Network

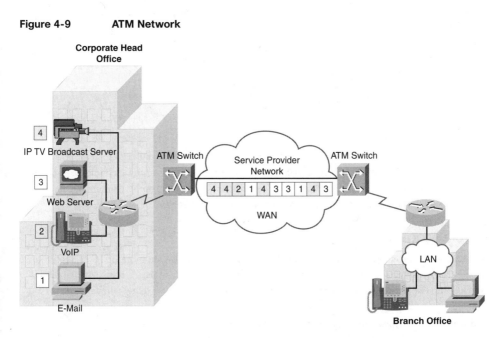

ATM is built on a cell-based architecture rather than on a frame-based architecture. ATM cells are always a fixed length of 53 bytes. The ATM cell contains a 5-byte ATM header followed by 48 bytes of ATM payload. Small, fixed-length cells are well suited for carrying voice and video traffic, because this traffic is intolerant of delay. Video and voice traffic do not have to wait for a larger data packet to be transmitted. Although ATM is less efficient than Frame Relay because of its 5 byte per cell overhead, it offers link speeds of T1/E1 to OC-12 (622 Mbps) and higher.

Internet Connection Options

Broadband connection options typically are used to connect telecommuting employees to a corporate site over the Internet. These options include DSL, cable, wireless, and Metro Ethernet.

DSL

DSL technology, shown in Figure 4-10, is an always-on connection technology that uses existing twisted-pair telephone lines to transport high-bandwidth data and provides IP services to subscribers.

Figure 4-10   Teleworker DSL Connection

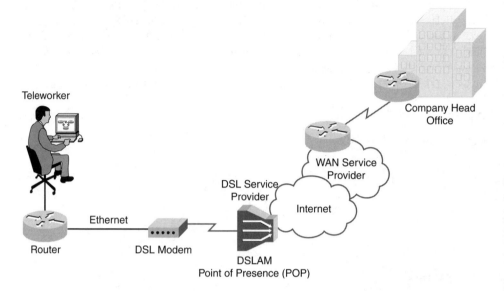

Current DSL technologies use sophisticated coding and modulation techniques to achieve data rates of up to 8.192 Mbps. A variety of DSL types, standards, and emerging technologies exist. DSL is now a popular choice for enterprise IT departments to support home workers. Generally, a subscriber cannot choose to connect to an enterprise network directly.

Cable Modem

Cable modems provide an always-on connection and a simple installation. Figure 4-11 shows how a subscriber connects a computer or LAN router to the cable modem, which translates the digital signals into the broadband frequencies used for transmitting on a cable television network.

Figure 4-11   Teleworker Cable Modem Connection

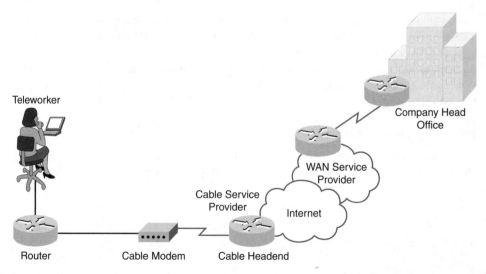

Broadband Wireless

Until recently, the main limitation of wireless access has been the need to be within range of a wireless router or a wireless modem that has a wired connection to the Internet. The following new developments in broadband wireless technology are changing this situation:

- **Municipal Wi-Fi:** Many cities have begun setting up municipal wireless networks. Some of these networks provide high-speed Internet access for free or for substantially less than the price of other broadband services.

- **WiMAX:** Worldwide Interoperability for Microwave Access (WiMAX) is a new IEEE 802.16 technology that is just beginning to come into use. It provides high-speed broadband service with wireless access and provides broad coverage like a cell phone network rather than through small Wi-Fi hotspots.

- **Satellite Internet:** Typically used by rural users where cable and DSL are unavailable.

Metro Ethernet

Metro Ethernet uses IP-aware Ethernet switches in the service provider's network cloud to offer enterprises converged voice, data, and video services at Ethernet speeds. Some benefits of Metro Ethernet include the following:

- **Reduced expenses and administration:** Enables businesses to inexpensively connect numerous sites in a metropolitan area to each other and to the Internet without the need for expensive conversions to ATM or Frame Relay.

- **Easy integration with existing networks:** Connects easily to existing Ethernet LANs.

- **Enhanced business productivity:** Metro Ethernet enables businesses to take advantage of productivity-enhancing IP applications that are difficult to implement on TDM or Frame Relay networks, such as hosted IP communications, VoIP, and streaming and broadcast video.

Choosing a WAN Link Option

Table 4-2 compares the advantages and disadvantages of the various WAN connection options reviewed.

Table 4-2   Choosing a WAN Link Connection

Option	Description	Advantages	Disadvantages	Sample Protocols
Leased line	Point-to-point connection between two computers' LANs.	Most secure	Expensive	PPP, HDLC, SDLC
Circuit switching	A dedicated circuit path is created between endpoints. Best example is dialup connections.	Less expensive	Call setup	PPP, ISDN
Packet switching	Devices transport packets via a shared single point-to-point or point-to-multipoint link across a carrier inter network. Variable-length packets are transmitted over PVCs or SVCs.	Highly efficient use of bandwidth	Shared media across link	X.25, Frame Relay

continues

Table 4-2   Choosing a WAN Link Connection   *continued*

Option	Description	Advantages	Disadvantages	Sample Protocols
Cell relay	Similar to packet switching, but uses fixed-length cells instead of variable-length packets. Data is divided into fixed-length cells and then transported across virtual circuits.	Best for simultaneous use of voice and data	Overhead can be considerable	ATM
Internet	Connectionless packet switching using the Internet as the WAN infrastructure. Uses network addressing to deliver packets. Because of security issues, VPN technology must be used.	Least expensive, globally available	Least secure	DSL, cable modem, wireless

VPN Technology

A virtual private network (VPN) is an encrypted connection between private networks over a public network such as the Internet. Instead of using a dedicated Layer 2 connection such as a leased line, a VPN uses virtual connections called VPN tunnels, which are routed through the Internet from the company's private network to the remote site or employee host.

VPN Benefits

Benefits of VPN include the following:

- **Cost savings:** Eliminates the need for expensive dedicated WAN links and modem banks.

- **Security:** Uses advanced encryption and authentication protocols that protect data from unauthorized access.

- **Scalability:** Can add large amounts of capacity without adding significant infrastructure.

- **Compatibility with broadband technology:** Supported by broadband service providers so mobile workers and telecommuters can take advantage of their home high-speed Internet service to access their corporate networks.

Types of VPN Access

Two types of VPN access exist:

- **Site-to-site VPNs:** Connect entire networks to each other. For example, they can connect a branch office network to a company headquarters network, as shown in Figure 4-12. Each site is equipped with a VPN gateway, such as a router, firewall, VPN concentrator, or security appliance. In the figure, a remote branch office uses a site-to-site VPN to connect with the corporate head office.

Figure 4-12   Site-to-Site VPNs

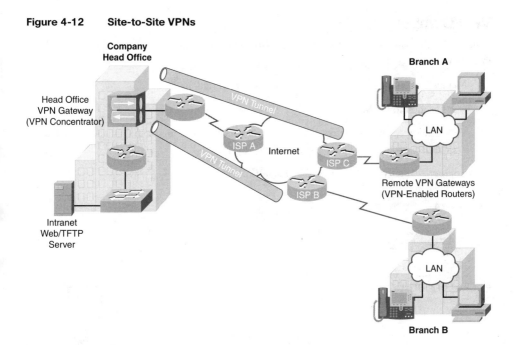

- **Remote-access VPNs:** Remote-access VPNs enable individual hosts, such as telecommuters, mobile users, and extranet consumers, to access a company network securely over the Internet, as shown in Figure 4-13. Each host typically has VPN client software loaded or uses a web-based client.

Figure 4-13   Remote-Access VPNs

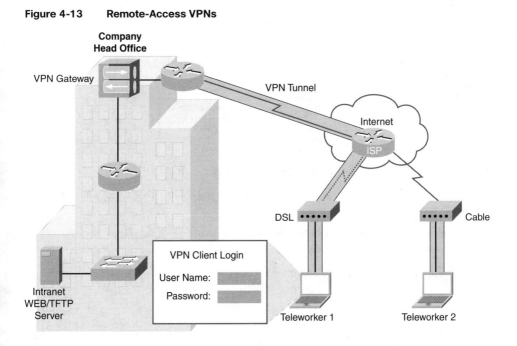

VPN Components

Figure 4-14 illustrates a typical VPN topology. Components required to establish this VPN include the following:

- An existing enterprise network with servers and workstations

- A connection to the Internet

- VPN gateways, such as routers, firewalls, VPN concentrators, and ASAs, that act as endpoints to establish, manage, and control VPN connections

- Appropriate software to create and manage VPN tunnels

Figure 4-14   VPN Components

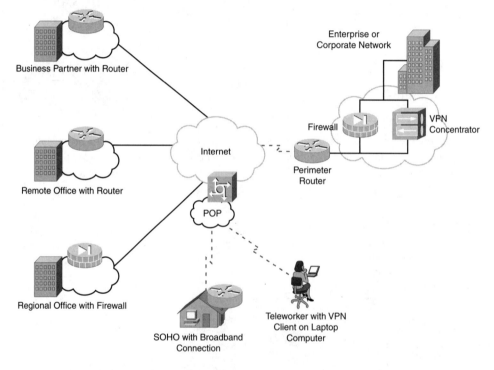

Establishing Secure VPN Connections

VPNs secure data by encapsulating and encrypting it. With regard to VPNs, encapsulation and encryption are defined as follows:

- Encapsulation is also called tunneling, because encapsulation transmits data transparently from source network to destination network through a shared network infrastructure.

- Encryption codes data into a different format using a secret key, which is then used on the other side on the connection to decrypt.

VPN Tunneling

Tunneling uses three classes of protocols:

- **Carrier protocol:** The protocol over which information travels (Frame Relay, ATM, MPLS).

- **Encapsulating protocol:** The protocol that is wrapped around the original data (GRE, IPsec, L2F, PPTP, L2TP).

- **Passenger protocol:** The protocol over which the original data was carried (IPX, AppleTalk, IPv4, IPv6).

Figure 4-15 illustrates an email message traveling through the Internet over a VPN connection.

Figure 4-15   Packet Encapsulation in a VPN Tunnel

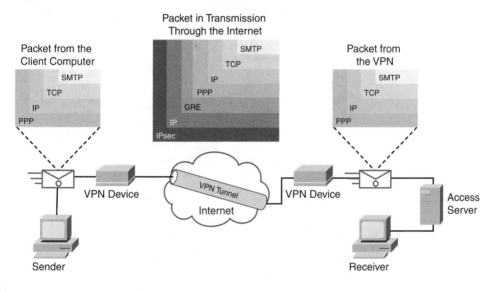

VPN Encryption Algorithms

The degree of security provided by any encryption algorithm depends on the key's length. Some of the more common encryption algorithms and the length of the keys they use are as follows:

- **Data Encryption Standard (DES) algorithm:** Uses a 56-bit key, ensuring high-performance encryption. DES is a symmetric key cryptosystem.

- **Triple DES (3DES) algorithm:** A newer variant of DES that encrypts with one key, decrypts with a different key, and then encrypts a final time with another key.

- **Advanced Encryption Standard (AES):** AES provides stronger security than DES and is computationally more efficient than 3DES. AES offers three key lengths: 128-, 192-, and 256-bit keys.

- **Rivest, Shamir, and Adleman (RSA):** An asymmetric key cryptosystem. The keys use a bit length of 512, 768, 1024, or larger.

Symmetric encryption is when the encryption key and decryption key are the same. With asymmetric encryption, they are different.

Hashes

VPNs use a keyed hashed message authentication code (HMAC) data-integrity algorithm to guarantee a message's integrity and authenticity without using any additional mechanisms.

The cryptographic strength of the HMAC depends on the cryptographic strength of the underlying hash function, on the key's size and quality, and the size of the hash output length in bits. The two common HMAC algorithms are

- **Message Digest 5 (MD5):** Uses a 128-bit shared secret key.

- **Secure Hash Algorithm 1 (SHA-1):** Uses a 160-bit secret key.

Figure 4-16 shows an example using MD5 as the HMAC algorithm.

Figure 4-16   Creating and Verifying a Message Digest

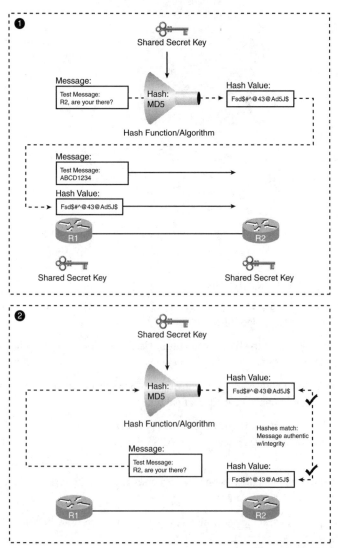

An HMAC has two parameters: a message input and a shared secret key known only to the message originator and intended receivers. In Figure 4-16, both R1 and R2 know the shared secret key. The process in Figure 4-16 uses the following steps:

1. R1 uses MD5 to perform the hashing function, which outputs a hash value. This hash value is then appended to the original message and sent to R2.

2. R2 the removes the hash value from the original message, runs the same hash operation, and then compares its hash value with the hash value sent by R1. If the two hashes match, the data integrity has not been compromised.

VPN Authentication

The device on the other end of the VPN tunnel must be authenticated before the communication path is considered secure. The two peer authentication methods are as follows:

- **Preshared key (PSK):** A secret key is shared between the two parties using a secure channel before it needs to be used.

- **RSA signature:** Uses the exchange of digital certificates to authenticate the peers.

IPsec Security Protocols

IPsec spells out the messaging necessary to secure VPN communications but relies on existing algorithms. The two main IPsec framework protocols are as follows:

- **Authentication Header (AH):** Used when confidentiality is not required or permitted. AH provides data authentication and integrity for IP packets passed between two systems. It verifies the originators of any messages and that any message passed has not been modified during transit. AH does not provide data confidentiality (encryption) of packets. Used alone, the AH protocol provides weak protection. Consequently, it is used with the ESP protocol to provide data encryption and tamper-aware security features.

- **Encapsulating Security Payload (ESP):** Provides confidentiality and authentication by encrypting the IP packet. Although both encryption and authentication are optional in ESP, at a minimum, one of them must be selected.

IPsec relies on existing algorithms to implement encryption, authentication, and key exchange. Figure 4-17 shows how IPsec is structured.

IPsec provides the framework, and the administrator chooses the algorithms used to implement the security services within that framework. As Figure 4-17 illustrates, the administrator must fill the four IPsec framework squares:

- Choose an IPsec protocol.

- Choose the encryption algorithm that is appropriate for the desired level of security.

- Choose an authentication algorithm to provide data integrity.

- The last square is the Diffie-Hellman (DH) algorithm group, which establishes the sharing of key information between peers. Choose which group to use—DH1, DH2, or DH5.

Figure 4-17   IPsec Framework

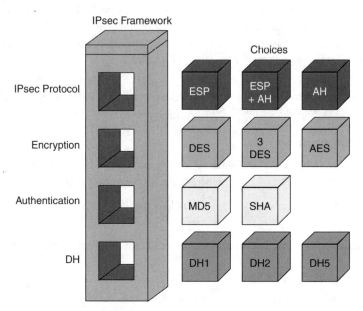

Study Resources

For today's exam topics, refer to the following resources for more study.

Resource	Chapter	Topic	Where to Find It
Foundational Resources			
CCNA Exploration Online Curriculum: Network Fundamentals	Chapter 10, "Planning and Cabling Networks"	Making WAN Connections	Section 10.2.3
CCNA Exploration Online Curriculum: Accessing the WAN	Chapter 1, "Introduction to WANs"	WAN Technology Concepts	Section 1.3
		WAN Connections Options	Section 1.4
	Chapter 6, "Teleworker Services"	Broadband Services	Section 6.2
		VPN Technology	Section 6.3
CCNA Exploration Network Fundamentals Companion Guide	Chapter 10, "Planning and Cabling Networks"	Making WAN Connections	pp. 384–388
CCNA Exploration Accessing the WAN Companion Guide	Chapter 1, "Introduction to WANs"	WAN Technology Concepts	pp. 17–29
		WAN Connections Options	pp. 29–47
	Chapter 6, "Teleworker Services"	Broadband Services	pp. 384–401
		VPN Technology	pp. 401–418

Resource	Chapter	Topic	Where to Find It
ICND1 Official Exam Certification Guide	Chapter 4, "Fundamentals of WANs"	All topics within the chapter	pp. 71–90
	Chapter, 16, "WAN Concepts"	All topics within the chapter	pp. 514–535
ICND2 Official Exam Certification Guide	Chapter 15, "Virtual Private Networks"	All topics within the chapter	pp. 528–539
ICND1 Authorized Self-Study Guide	Chapter 5, "WAN Connections"	Understanding WAN Technologies	pp. 346–356
		Enabling the Internet Connection	pp. 356–374
ICND2 Authorized Self-Study Guide	Chapter 8, "Extending the Network into the WAN"	Introducing VPN Solutions	pp. 298–315
Supplemental Resources			
CCNA Flash Cards and Exam Practice Pack	ICND1, Section 10	Understanding WAN Technologies	pp. 254–292
	ICND2, Section 9	Establishing Serial Point-to-Point Connections	pp. 572–592
	ICND2, Section 11	Introducing VPN Solutions	pp. 618–632

PPP Configuration and Troubleshooting

CCNA 640-802 Exam Topics

- Configure and verify a basic WAN serial connection.
- Configure and verify a PPP connection between Cisco routers.

Key Topics

Today we review basic WAN serial configuration and verification with both High-Level Data Link Control (HDLC) and Point-to-Point Protocol (PPP). HDLC is important for two reasons:

- It is the fundamental basis of most every other WAN protocol, including PPP and Frame Relay.
- The Cisco version of HDLC is the default encapsulation for synchronous serial interfaces on Cisco routers.

PPP is supported on just about any hardware you choose to connect to. In addition, PPP offers a bundle of additional benefits that might entice you to use it instead of HDLC, even in an environment with all Cisco routers.

HDLC

High-Level Data Link Control (HDLC) uses synchronous serial transmission to provide error-free communication between two points. HDLC defines a Layer 2 framing structure that allows for flow control and error control through the use of acknowledgments. Each frame has the same format, whether it is a data frame or a control frame. HDLC is the default setting on Cisco synchronous serial interfaces.

HDLC Encapsulation

Although Cisco HDLC (also called cHDLC) is proprietary, Cisco has allowed many other network equipment vendors to implement it. Cisco HDLC frames contain a field for identifying the network protocol being encapsulated. Figure 3-1 compares standard HDLC to Cisco HDLC.

Figure 3-1   Standard and Cisco HDLC Frame Formats

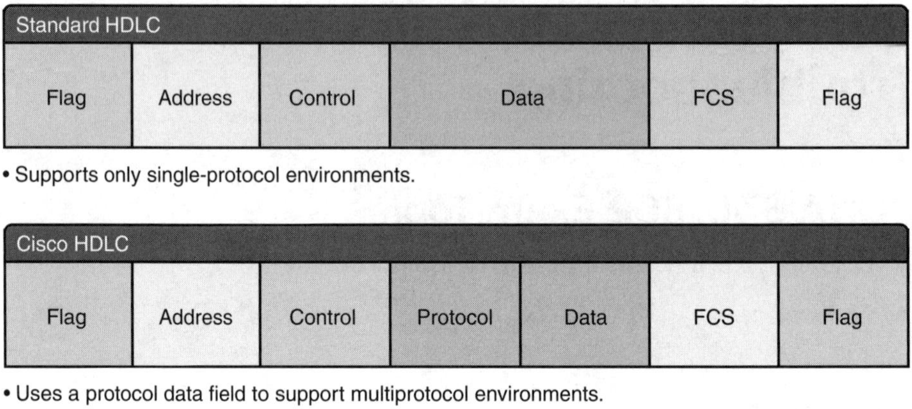

Standard HDLC					
Flag	Address	Control	Data	FCS	Flag

• Supports only single-protocol environments.

Cisco HDLC						
Flag	Address	Control	Protocol	Data	FCS	Flag

• Uses a protocol data field to support multiprotocol environments.

The following descriptions summarize the fields illustrated in the figure:

■ **Flag:** The frame always starts and ends with an 8-bit flag with the pattern 01111110. When frames are transmitted consecutively, the end flag of the first frame is used as the start flag of the next frame.

■ **Address**: In point-to-point HDLC connections, this field is empty.

■ **Control:** The Control field uses three formats, depending on the type of HDLC frame used:

— **Information (I) frame:** I-frames carry upper-layer information and some control information.

— **Supervisory (S) frame:** S-frames provide control information and are sequenced.

— **Unnumbered (U) frame:** U-frames support control purposes and are not sequenced.

■ **Protocol (used only in Cisco HDLC):** This field specifies the protocol type encapsulated within the frame (such as 0x0800 for IP).

■ **Data:** A variable-length field that contains Layer 3 packets.

■ **Frame check sequence (FCS):** Usually a cyclic redundancy check (CRC) used by the receiver to check for errors.

Configuring HDLC

By default, you use Cisco HDLC as a point-to-point protocol on leased lines between two Cisco devices. If you are connecting to a non-Cisco device that does not support Cisco HDLC, use synchronous PPP.

If the default encapsulation method has been changed, use the **encapsulation hdlc** command to reenable HDLC as shown in the following configuration:

```
R1(config)#interface serial 0/0/0
R1(config-router)#encapsulation hdlc
```

Verifying HDLC

When configured or at the default setting, "Encapsulation HDLC" should be reflected in the command output of the **show interfaces** command, as shown in Example 3-1.

Example 3-1   Verifying HDLC with show interfaces

```
R1#show interface serial 0/0/0
Serial0/0/0 is up, line protocol is up (connected)
  Hardware is HD64570
  Description: Link to R2
  Internet address is 10.1.1.1/30
  MTU 1500 bytes, BW 1544 Kbit, DLY 20000 usec, rely 255/255, load 1/255
  Encapsulation HDLC, loopback not set, keepalive set (10 sec)
  Last input never, output never, output hang never
  Last clearing of "show interface" counters never
<output omitted>
```

PPP Concepts

PPP provides several basic but important functions that are useful on a leased line that connects two devices, as reviewed in the following list:

- Definition of a header and trailer that allows delivery of a data frame over the link

- Support for both synchronous and asynchronous links

- A protocol type field in the header, allowing multiple Layer 3 protocols to pass over the same link

- Built-in authentication tools: Password Authentication Protocol (PAP) and Challenge Handshake Authentication Protocol (CHAP)

- Control protocols for each higher-layer protocol that rides over PPP, allowing easier integration and support of those protocols

The PPP Frame Format

One of the more important features included in the PPP standard is the standardized protocol field, which identifies the type of packet inside the frame. Notice in Figure 3-2 that PPP was built upon the HDLC frame. The HDLC frame shown is the Cisco format.

PPP defines a set of Layer 2 control messages that perform various link control functions. These control functions fall into two main categories:

- Those needed regardless of the Layer 3 protocol sent across the link

- Those specific to each Layer 3 protocol

The PPP Link Control Protocol (LCP) implements the control functions that work the same, regardless of the Layer 3 protocol.

Figure 3-2   Comparing the Cisco HDLC and PPP Frames

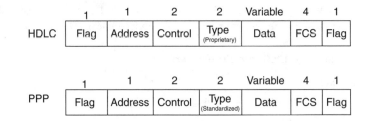

For features related to any higher-layer protocols, typically Layer 3 protocols, PPP uses a series of PPP control protocols (CP), such as IP Control Protocol (IPCP). PPP uses one instance of LCP per link, and one CP for each Layer 3 protocol defined on the link. For example, on a PPP link using IPv4, IPv6, and Cisco Discovery Protocol (CDP), the link uses one instance of LCP, plus IPCP (for IPv4), IPv6CP (for IPv6), and CDPCP (for CDP). Commonly in the literature, you will see these referred to collectively as Network Control Protocols (NCP).

PPP Link Control Protocol (LCP)

LCP provides four notable features summarized in Table 3-1.

Table 3-1   LCP Features

Function	LCP Feature	Description
Looped link detection	Magic number	Detects if the link is looped, and disables the interface, allowing rerouting over a working route.
Error detection	Link Quality Monitoring (LQM)	Disables an interface that exceeds an error percentage threshold, allowing rerouting over better routes.
Multilink support	Multilink PPP	Load-balances traffic over multiple parallel links.
Authentication	PAP and CHAP	Exchanges names and passwords so that each device can verify the identity of the device on the other end of the link.

Looped Link Detection

LCP notices looped links quickly using a feature called magic numbers. PPP LCP messages include a magic number, which is different on each router. If a line is looped (such as during testing by a Telco technician), the router receives an LCP message with its own magic number instead of getting a message with the other router's magic number. PPP helps the router recognize a looped link quickly so that it can bring down the interface and possibly use an alternative route. If the router can immediately notice that the link is looped, it can put the interface in a "down and down" status, and the routing protocols can change their routing updates based on the fact that the link is down.

Enhanced Error Detection

When a network has redundant links, you can use PPP to monitor the frequency with which frames are received in error. After the configured error rate has been exceeded, PPP can take down the interface, allowing routing protocols install a better backup route. PPP LCP analyzes the error rates on a link using a PPP feature called Link Quality Monitoring (LQM).

PPP Multilink

In a redundant configuration between two routers, the routers use Layer 3 load balancing alternating traffic between the two links, which does not always result in truly balanced sharing of the traffic. Multilink PPP load-balances the traffic equally over the links while allowing the Layer 3 logic in each router to treat the parallel links as a single link. When encapsulating a packet, PPP fragments the packet into smaller frames, sending one fragment over each link. Multilink PPP allows the Layer 3 routing tables to use a single route that refers to the combined links, keeping the routing table smaller.

PPP Authentication

PAP and CHAP authenticate the endpoints on either end of a point-to-point serial link. CHAP is the preferred method today because the identification process uses values hidden with a Message Digest 5 (MD5) one-way hash, which is more secure than the clear-text passwords sent by PAP.

Figure 3-3 shows the different processes used by PAP and CHAP. With PAP, the username and password are sent in the first message. With CHAP, the protocol begins with a message called a challenge, which asks the other router to send its username and password.

Figure 3-3   PPP Authentication Protocols

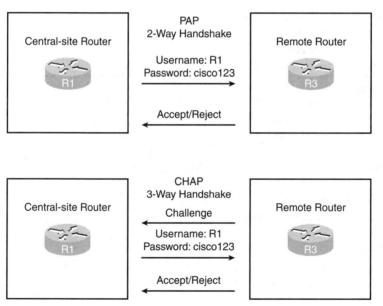

PAP is much less secure than CHAP because PAP sends the hostname and password in clear text in the message. CHAP instead uses a one-way hash algorithm, with input to the algorithm being a password that never crosses the link, plus a shared random number. The CHAP challenge states the random number; both routers are preconfigured with the password. The challenged router runs the hash algorithm using the just-learned random number and the secret password and sends the results back to the router that sent the challenge. The router that sent the challenge runs the same algorithm using the random number (sent across the link) and the password (not sent across the link). If the results match, the passwords must match. With the random number, the hash value is different every time.

PPP Configuration and Verification

For this section, we will use the topology shown in Figure 3-4.

Figure 3-4   PPP Topology

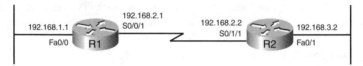

Basic PPP

Configuring PPP requires only the **encapsulation ppp** command on both ends of the link. Example 3-2 shows a simple configuration using the two routers shown in Figure 3-4.

Example 3-2   Basic PPP Configuration and Verification

```
R1(config)#interface serial 0/0/1
R1(config-if)#ip address 192.168.2.1 255.255.255.0
R1(config-if)#encapsulation ppp
R1(config-if)#clock rate 64000
R1(config-if)#no shutdown
%LINK-5-CHANGED: Interface Serial0/0/1, changed state to down

R2(config)#interface serial 0/1/1
R2(config-if)#ip address 192.168.2.2 255.255.255.0
R2(config-if)#encapsulation ppp
R2(config-if)#no shutdown
%LINK-5-CHANGED: Interface Serial0/1/1, changed state to up
%LINEPROTO-5-UPDOWN: Line protocol on Interface Serial0/1/1, changed state to up
R2(config-if)#end
R2#show interfaces serial 0/1/1
Serial0/1/1 is up, line protocol is up (connected)
  Hardware is HD64570
  Internet address is 192.168.2.2/24
  MTU 1500 bytes, BW 1544 Kbit, DLY 20000 usec, rely 255/255, load 1/255
  Encapsulation PPP, loopback not set, keepalive set (10 sec)
  LCP Open
  Open: IPCP, CDPCP
<output omitted>
```

The **show interfaces** command at the bottom of the example shows the normal output when the link is up and working. A few lines into the output, the highlighted phrases show that PPP is indeed configured, and that LCP has completed its work successfully, as noted with the "LCP Open" phrase. Additionally, the output lists the fact that two CPs, CDPCP and IPCP, have also successfully been enabled—all good indications that PPP is working properly.

CHAP

Although CHAP is optional, it should be configured to provide a secure point-to-point link. The simplest version of CHAP configuration requires only a few commands. The configuration uses a password configured on each router. As an alternative, the password could be configured on an external authentication, authorization, and accounting (AAA) server outside the router. The configuration steps are as follows:

Step 1   Configure the routers' hostnames using the **hostname** *name* global configuration command.

Step 2   Configure the name of the other router, and the shared secret password, using the **username** *name* **password** *password* global configuration command.

Step 3   Enable CHAP on the interface on each router using the **ppp authentication chap** interface subcommand.

Example 3-3 shows a sample configuration using the routers in Figure 3-4. Because the hostnames are already configured, that step is not shown.

Example 3-3   CHAP Configuration

```
R1(config)#username R2 password itsasecret
R1(config)#interface serial 0/0/1
R1(config-if)#ppp authentication chap
%LINEPROTO-5-UPDOWN: Line protocol on Interface Serial0/0/1, changed state to down

R2(config)#username R1 password itsasecret
%LINEPROTO-5-UPDOWN: Line protocol on Interface Serial0/1/1, changed state to up
R2(config)#interface serial 0/1/1
R2(config-if)#ppp authentication chap
%LINEPROTO-5-UPDOWN: Line protocol on Interface Serial0/1/1, changed state to down
%LINEPROTO-5-UPDOWN: Line protocol on Interface Serial0/1/1, changed state to up
```

Notice that as soon as CHAP is configured on R1, the interface goes down. Then, on R2, after the password is configured correctly, the interface comes back up. Finally, it goes down briefly before coming back up when CHAP is configured on R2.

The commands themselves are not complicated, but it is easy to misconfigure the hostnames and passwords. Notice that each router refers to the other router's hostname in the **username** command, but both routers must configure the same password value. Also, not only are the passwords (itsasecret in this case) case sensitive, but the hostnames, as referenced in the **username** command, also are also case sensitive.

Because CHAP is a function of LCP, if the authentication process fails, LCP does not complete, and the interface falls to an "up and down" interface state.

PAP

Like CHAP, PAP is optional. You would only use it if one of the devices does not support CHAP. PAP uses the same configuration commands as CHAP, except that the **ppp authentication pap** command is used instead of **ppp authentication chap**. The rest of the verification commands work the same, regardless of which of the two types of authentication are used. For example, if PAP authentication fails, LCP fails, and the link settles into an "up and down" state.

Cisco IOS Software also supports the capability to configure the router to first try one authentication method and, if the other side does not respond, try the other option. The full command syntax for the **ppp authentication** command is as follows:

```
Router(config-if)#ppp authentication {pap | chap | pap chap | chap pap}
```

For example, the **ppp authentication chap pap** interface subcommand tells the router to send CHAP messages, and if no reply is received, to try PAP. Note that the second option is not tried if the CHAP messages flow between the two devices, and the result is that authentication failed. It uses the other option only if the other device does not send back any messages.

Study Resources

For today's exam topics, refer to the following resources for more study.

Resource	Chapter	Topic	Where to Find It
Foundational Resources			
CCNA Exploration Online Curriculum: Accessing the WAN	Chapter 2, "PPP"	All sections within the chapter	Sections 2.1–2.2
CCNA Exploration Accessing the WAN Companion Guide	Chapter 2, "PPP"	All topics within the chapter	pp. 56–119
ICND1 Official Exam Certification Guide	Chapter 17, "WAN Configuration"	Configuring Point-to-Point WANs	pp. 542–546
ICND2 Official Exam Certification Guide	Chapter 12, "Point-to-Point WANs"	PPP Concepts PPP Configuration	pp. 436–442 pp. 442–444
ICND1 Authorized Self-Study Guide	Chapter 5, "WAN Connections"	Configuring Serial Encapsulation	pp. 380–394
ICND2 Authorized Self-Study Guide	Chapter 8, "Extending the Network into the WAN"	Establishing a Point-to-Point WAN Connection with PPP	pp. 315–325
Supplemental Resources			
CCNA Flash Cards and Exam Practice Pack	ICND1, Section 10 ICND2, Section 9	Understanding WAN Technologies Establishing Serial Point-to-Point Connections	pp. 254–292 pp. 572–592
CCNA Video Mentor	ICND2, Lab9	PPP and CHAP Configuration	pp. 87–90

Frame Relay Configuration and Troubleshooting

CCNA 640-802 Exam Topics

- Configure and verify Frame Relay on Cisco routers.
- Troubleshoot WAN implementation issues.

Key Topics

Today we finish our review of CCNA exam topics with a look at Frame Relay and basic WAN troubleshooting. Frame Relay is currently the most popular choice for WAN implementations. Therefore, you must have a basic understanding of Frame Relay, including its conceptual framework, configuration, and verification. As a final topic, we review various WAN errors and their potential causes.

Frame Relay Concepts

Frame Relay is a connection-oriented data-link technology that is streamlined to provide high performance and efficiency. For error protection, it relies on upper-layer protocols and dependable fiber and digital networks.

Frame Relay defines the interconnection process between the router and the local Frame Relay of the service provider, as shown in Figure 2-1.

Figure 2-1   Frame Relay

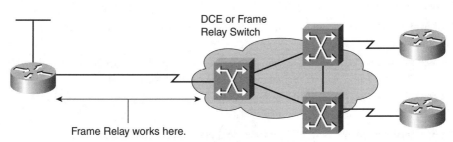

Devices attached to a Frame Relay WAN fall into the following two categories:

- **Data terminal equipment (DTE):** Examples of DTE devices are Frame Relay Access Devices (FRAD), routers, and bridges.
- **Data communications equipment (DCE):** In most cases, the switches in a WAN are Frame Relay switches.

Frame Relay Components

Frame Relay provides a means for statistically multiplexing many logical data conversations, referred to as virtual circuits (VC), over a single physical transmission link by assigning connection identifiers to each pair of DTE devices. The service provider switching equipment constructs a switching table that maps the connection identifier to outbound ports. When a frame is received, the switching device analyzes the connection identifier and delivers the frame to the associated outbound port. The complete path to the destination is established prior to the transmission of the first frame. Figure 2-2 illustrates a Frame Relay connection and identifies the many components within Frame Relay.

Figure 2-2   **Frame Relay Components**

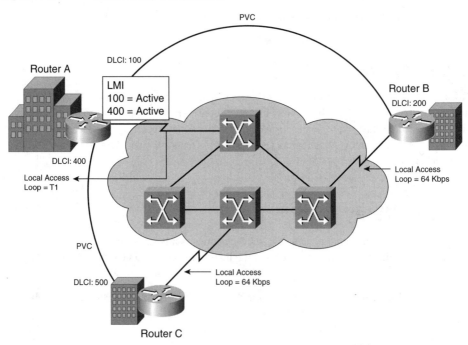

The following terms are used frequently in Frame Relay discussions:

- **Local access rate:** The rate at which data travels into or out of the network, regardless of other settings.

- **Virtual circuit (VC):** Logical circuit, uniquely identified by a data-link connection identifier (DLCI), that is created to ensure bidirectional communication from one DTE device to another.

- **Permanent virtual circuit (PVC):** Provides permanently established connections that are used for frequent and consistent data transfers.

- **Switched virtual circuit (SVC):** Provides temporary connections that are used in situations that require only sporadic data transfer between DTE devices across the Frame Relay network.

- **Data-link connection identifier (DLCI):** Contains a 10-bit number in the address field of the Frame Relay frame header that identifies the VC. DLCIs have local significance because the identifier references the point between the local router and the local Frame Relay switch to which the DLCI is connected. Therefore, devices at opposite ends of a connection can use different DLCI values to refer to the same virtual connection.

As shown in Figure 2-2, Router A has two virtual circuits that are configured on one physical interface. A DLCI of 100 identifies the VC that connects to Router B. A DLCI of 400 identifies the VC that connects to Router C. At the other end, a different DLCI number can be used to identify the VC.

- **Committed information rate (CIR):** When subscribing to a Frame Relay service, you specify the CIR, which is the local access rate—for example, 56 kbps or T1. Typically, you are also asked to specify a CIR for each DLCI. If you send information faster than the CIR on a given DLCI, the network flags some frames with a discard eligible (DE) bit.

- **Inverse Address Resolution Protocol (ARP):** A method of dynamically associating the network layer address of the remote router with a local DLCI.

- **Local Management Interface (LMI):** A signaling standard between the router (DTE device) and the local Frame Relay switch (DCE device) that is responsible for managing the connection and maintaining status between the router and the Frame Relay switch.

- **Forward explicit congestion notification (FECN):** A bit in the address field of the Frame Relay frame header. If the network is congested, DCE devices (Frame Relay switches) set the FECN bit value of the frames to 1 to signal downstream DTE devices that flow control might be warranted.

- **Backward explicit congestion notification (BECN):** A bit in the address field of the Frame Relay frame header. Operates like the FECN bit but travels in the opposite direction, informing upstream DTE devices that congestion is occurring and that flow control might be warranted.

Frame Relay Topologies

Frame Relay allows you to interconnect your remote sites in a variety of topologies.

Figure 2-3 illustrates these topologies, which are described in the list that follows.

Figure 2-3   Frame Relay Topologies

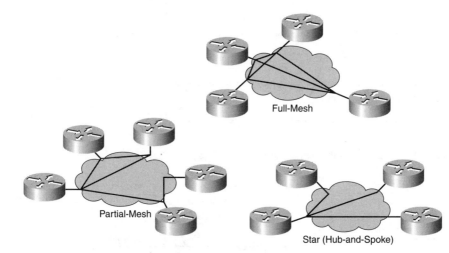

Full-Mesh

Partial-Mesh

Star (Hub-and-Spoke)

- **Partial-mesh topology:** Not all sites have direct access to all other sites.

- **Full-mesh topology:** All routers have VCs to all other destinations. Use the **n (n − 1) / 2** formula to calculate the total number of links that are required to implement a full-mesh topology, where **n** is the number of end points (nodes).

- **Star topology:** The star topology, also known as a hub-and-spoke configuration, is the least expensive topology because it requires the least number of PVCs.

NBMA Limitations and Solutions

By default, a Frame Relay network provides nonbroadcast multiaccess (NBMA) connectivity between remote sites. An NBMA environment is treated like other broadcast media environments, such as Ethernet, where all the routers are on the same subnet.

However, to reduce cost, NBMA clouds are usually built in a hub-and-spoke topology. With a hub-and-spoke topology, the physical topology does not provide the multiaccess capabilities that Ethernet does, so each router might not have separate PVCs to reach the other remote routers on the same subnet. Split horizon is one of the main issues you encounter when Frame Relay is running multiple PVCs over a single interface.

In any Frame Relay topology, when a single interface must be used to interconnect multiple sites, you can have reachability issues because of the NBMA nature of Frame Relay. The Frame Relay NBMA topology can cause the following two problems:

- **Routing update reachability:** Split horizon prevents a routing update that is received on an interface from being forwarded out the same interface. So a hub router will not send updates from one spoke router to another spoke router if the update must go out the same interface (Split horizon applies only to distance vector routing protocols).

- **Broadcast replication:** With routers that support multipoint connections over a single interface that terminate many PVCs, the router must replicate broadcast packets, such as routing update broadcasts, on each PVC to the remote routers. These replicated broadcast packets consume bandwidth and cause significant latency variations in user traffic.

The following methods exist to solve the routing update reachability issue:

- Turn off split horizon; however, disabling split horizon increases the chances of routing loops in your network. (Split horizon is not an issue if you use a link-state routing protocol.)

- Use a fully meshed topology; however, this topology increases the cost.

- Use subinterfaces. When you use a Frame Relay point-to-point subinterface, each subinterface is on its own subnet.

Figure 2-4 shows how to resolve the issues using subinterfaces.

Figure 2-4   Using Subinterfaces with Frame Relay

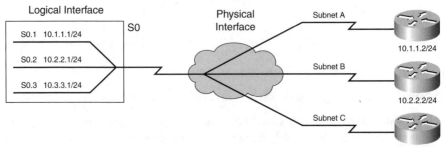

Inverse ARP and LMI Concepts

Routers can automatically discover their local DLCI from the local Frame Relay switch using the LMI protocol. Then the local DLCI can be dynamically mapped to the remote router network layer addresses with Inverse ARP.

As shown in Figure 2-5, using Inverse ARP, the router on the left can automatically discover the remote router IP address and then map it to the local DLCI. In this case, the local DLCI of 500 is mapped to the 10.1.1.1 IP address.

Figure 2-5   Frame Relay Address Mapping

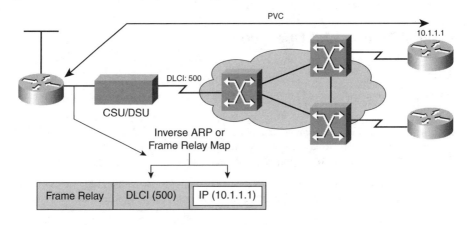

Frame Relay signaling is required between the router and the Frame Relay switch. Figure 2-6 shows how the signaling is used to get information about the different DLCIs.

Figure 2-6   Frame Relay Signaling

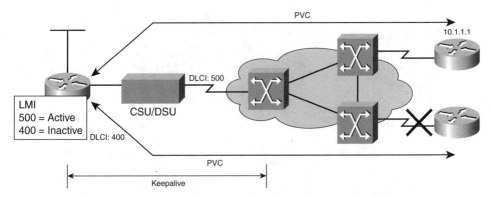

The LMI is a signaling standard between the router and the Frame Relay switch. The LMI is responsible for managing the connection and maintaining the status between the devices.

Although the LMI is configurable, beginning in Cisco IOS Release 11.2, the Cisco router tries to autosense which LMI type the Frame Relay switch is using. The router sends one or more full LMI status requests to the Frame Relay switch. The Frame Relay switch responds with one or more LMI types, and the router configures itself with the last LMI type received. Cisco routers support the following three LMI types: Cisco, ANSI, and Q 933A.

When the router receives LMI information, it updates its VC status to one of the following three states:

- **Active:** Indicates that the VC connection is active and that routers can exchange data over the Frame Relay network.

- **Inactive:** Indicates that the local connection to the Frame Relay switch is working, but the remote router connection to the remote Frame Relay switch is not working.

- **Deleted:** Indicates that either no LMI is being received from the Frame Relay switch or no service exists between the router and local Frame Relay switch.

Inverse ARP and LMI Operation

The following is a summary of how Inverse ARP and LMI signaling work with a Frame Relay connection:

1. Each router connects to the Frame Relay switch through a channel service unit/data service unit (CSU/DSU).

2. When Frame Relay is configured on an interface, the router sends an LMI status inquiry message to the Frame Relay switch. The message notifies the switch of the router status and asks the switch for the connection status of the router VCs.

3. When the Frame Relay switch receives the request, it responds with an LMI status message that includes the local DLCIs of the PVCs to the remote routers to which the local router can send data.

4. For each active DLCI, each router sends an Inverse ARP packet to introduce itself.

    Figure 2-7 illustrates the first four steps of this process.

Figure 2-7   Stages of Inverse ARP and LMI Operation

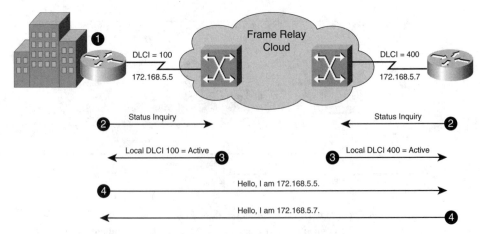

5. When a router receives an Inverse ARP message, it creates a map entry in its Frame Relay map table that includes the local DLCI and the remote router network layer address.

6. Every 60 seconds, routers send Inverse ARP messages on all active DLCIs. Every 10 seconds, the router exchanges LMI information with the switch (keepalives).

7. The router changes the status of each DLCI to active, inactive, or deleted, based on the LMI response from the Frame Relay switch.

Figure 2-8 illustrates Steps 5–7 of this process.

Figure 2-8   Stages of Inverse ARP and LMI Operation Continued

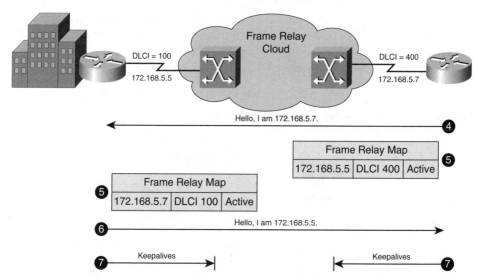

Configuring and Verifying Frame Relay

The following list summarizes the Frame Relay configuration steps.

Step 1   Configure the physical interface to use Frame Relay encapsulation (**encapsulation frame-relay** interface subcommand).

Step 2   Configure an IP address on the interface or subinterface (**ip address** subcommand).

Step 3   (Optional) Manually set the LMI type on each physical serial interface (**frame-relay lmi-type** interface subcommand).

Step 4   (Optional) Change from the default encapsulation of **cisco** to **ietf** by doing the following:

    a. For all VCs on the interface, add the **ietf** keyword to the **encapsulation frame-relay** interface subcommand.

    b. For a single VC, add the **ietf** keyword to the **frame-relay interface dlci** interface subcommand (point-to-point subinterfaces only) or to the **frame-relay map** command.

Step 5   (Optional) If you aren't using the (default) Inverse ARP to map the DLCI to the next-hop router's IP address, define static mapping using the **frame-relay map ip** *dlci ip-address* **broadcast** subinterface subcommand.

Step 6   On subinterfaces, associate one (point-to-point) or more (multipoint) DLCIs with the subinterface in one of two ways:

    a. Using the **frame-relay interface-dlci** *dlci* subinterface subcommand

    b. As a side effect of static mapping using the **frame-relay map ip** *dlci ip-address* **broadcast** subinterface subcommand

Full Mesh with One Subnet

The first example shows the briefest possible Frame Relay configuration—one that uses just the first two steps of the configuration checklist in this chapter. For the topology shown in Figure 2-9, configure a full mesh Frame Relay network using subnet 10.1.1.0/24. Use default settings for LMI, Inverse ARP, and encapsulation. Examples 2-1, 2-2, and 2-3 show the full configuration using EIGRP as the routing protocol.

Figure 2-9   **Full Mesh Topology with One Subnet**

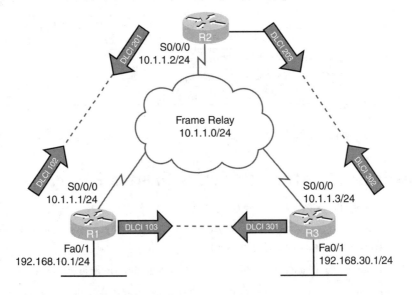

Example 2-1   **Frame Relay Full Mesh with One Subnet: R1**

```
R1(config)#interface serial 0/0/0
R1(config-if)#encapsulation frame-relay
R1(config-if)#ip address 10.1.1.1 255.255.255.0
R1(config-if)#no shutdown
R1(config-if)#interface fastethernet 0/0
R1(config-if)#ip address 192.168.10.1 255.255.255.0
R1(config-if)#no shutdown
R1(config-if)#router eigrp 1
R1(config-router)#network 10.0.0.0
R1(config-router)#network 192.168.10.0
```

Example 2-2   Frame Relay Full Mesh with One Subnet: R2

```
R2(config)#interface serial 0/0/0
R2(config-if)#encapsulation frame-relay
R2(config-if)#ip address 10.1.1.2 255.255.255.0
R2(config-if)#no shutdown
R2(config-if)#router eigrp 1
R2(config-router)#network 10.0.0.0
```

Example 2-3   Frame Relay Full Mesh with One Subnet: R2

```
R3(config)#interface serial 0/0/0
R3(config-if)#encapsulation frame-relay
R3(config-if)#ip address 10.1.1.3 255.255.255.0
R3(config-if)#no shutdown
R3(config-if)#interface fastethernet 0/0
R3(config-if)#ip address 192.168.30.1 255.255.255.0
R3(config-if)#no shutdown
R3(config-if)#router eigrp 1
R3(config-router)#network 10.0.0.0
R3(config-router)#network 192.168.30.0
```

This simple configuration takes advantage of the following IOS default settings:

- The LMI type is automatically sensed.
- The (default) encapsulation is Cisco instead of IETF.
- PVC DLCIs are learned via LMI status messages.
- Inverse ARP is enabled (by default) and is triggered when the status message declaring that the VCs are up is received.

Configuring the Encapsulation

If one of the routers in a full mesh, one subnet configuration does not support the Cisco Frame Relay encapsulation, change the encapsulation to IETF on the Cisco routers with the following command:

```
Router(config-if)#encapsulation frame-relay ietf
```

Configuring the LMI Type

LMI operates between the local router and the local Frame Relay switch. The LMI message type used by the local Frame Relay switch might need to be hard-coded on the local router, either because the IOS version does not support autosensing or network administration policy requires that the LMI type be documented on the interface for verification and troubleshooting purposes. Assume the Frame Relay switch used by R2 is an ANSI switch. The following command would change the LMI type on R2 to use the ANSI LMI type:

```
R2(config)#interface serial 0/0/0
R2(config-if)#frame-relay lmi-type ansi
```

The LMI setting is a per-physical-interface setting, even if subinterfaces are used, so the **frame-relay lmi-type** command is always a subcommand under the physical interface.

Configuring Static Frame Relay Maps

Although the DLCIs for each PVC are shown in Figure 2-9, they were not needed for our basic Frame Relay configuration. Inverse ARP automatically mapped the remote IP address with the necessary local DLCI to reach the remote network. This dynamic process can be verified with the **show frame-relay pvc** and **show frame-relay map** as shown in Example 2-4 for R2.

Example 2-4   Verifying Inverse ARP with show frame-relay Commands

```
R2#show frame-relay pvc


PVC Statistics for interface Serial0/0/0 (Frame Relay DTE)
DLCI = 201, DLCI USAGE = LOCAL, PVC STATUS = ACTIVE, INTERFACE = Serial0/0/0

input pkts 14055        output pkts 32795       in bytes 1096228
out bytes 6216155       dropped pkts 0          in FECN pkts 0
in BECN pkts 0          out FECN pkts 0         out BECN pkts 0
in DE pkts 0            out DE pkts 0
out bcast pkts 32795    out bcast bytes 6216155


DLCI = 203, DLCI USAGE = LOCAL, PVC STATUS = ACTIVE, INTERFACE = Serial0/0/0

input pkts 14055        output pkts 32795       in bytes 1096228
out bytes 6216155       dropped pkts 0          in FECN pkts 0
in BECN pkts 0          out FECN pkts 0         out BECN pkts 0
in DE pkts 0            out DE pkts 0
out bcast pkts 32795    out bcast bytes 6216155


R2#show frame-relay map
Serial0/0/0 (up): ip 10.1.1.1 dlci 201, dynamic,
                  broadcast, CISCO, status defined, active
Serial0/0/0 (up): ip 10.1.1.3 dlci 203, dynamic,
                  broadcast, CISCO, status defined, active
```

Although in a production network you would probably use Inverse ARP, for the exam, you need to know how to configure the static map command statements. Example 2-5 lists the static Frame Relay map for the three routers shown in Figure 2-9, along with the configuration used to disable Inverse ARP.

Example 2-5   Manually Configuring Frame Relay Mapping

```
R1(config)#interface s0/0/0
R1(config-if)#frame-relay map ip 10.1.1.2 102 broadcast
R1(config-if)#frame-relay map ip 10.1.1.3 103 broadcast

R2(config)#interface serial 0/0/0
R2(config-if)#frame-relay map ip 10.1.1.1 201 broadcast
R2(config-if)#frame-relay map ip 10.1.1.3 203 broadcast

R3(config)#interface serial 0/0/0
R3(config-if)#frame-relay map ip 10.1.1.1 301 broadcast
R3(config-if)#frame-relay map ip 10.1.1.2 302 broadcast
```

Note   The **broadcast** keyword is required when the router needs to send broadcasts or multicasts to the neighboring router—for example, to support routing protocol messages such as Hellos.

Partial Mesh with One Subnet per PVC

The network in Figure 2-10 is a modification of Figure 2-9. R2 is now serving as the hub router for the spoke routers R1 and R2. This reduces the cost of the Frame Relay implementation from three PVCs to two PVCs. This configuration uses one subnet per PVC and point-to-point subinterfaces. Examples 2-6 through 2-8 show the configuration for this network.

Figure 2-10   Partial Mesh Topology with One Subnet per PVC

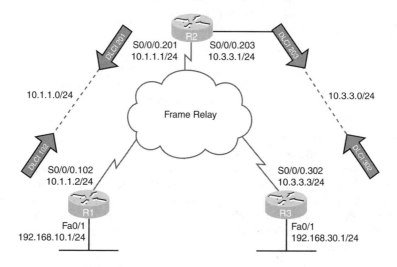

Example 2-6   Frame Relay Partial Mesh with One Subnet per PVC: R2

```
R2(config)#interface serial 0/0/0
R2(config-if)#encapsulation frame-relay
R2(config-if)#interface serial 0/0/0.201
R2(config-if)#interface serial 0/0/0.201 point-to-point
R2(config-subif)#ip address 10.1.1.1 255.255.255.0
R2(config-subif)#frame-relay interface-dlci 201
R2(config-subif)#interface serial 0/0/0.203 point-to-point
R2(config-subif)#ip address 10.3.3.1 255.255.255.0
R2(config-subif)#frame-relay interface-dlci 203
```

Example 2-7   Frame Relay Partial Mesh with One Subnet per PVC: R1

```
R1(config-if)#encapsulation frame-relay
R1(config)#interface serial0/0/0.102 point-to-point
R1(config-subif)#ip address 10.1.1.2 255.255.255.0
R1(config-subif)#frame-relay interface-dlci 102
```

Example 2-8   Frame Relay Partial Mesh with One Subnet per PVC: R3

```
R3(config)#interface serial 0/0/0
R3(config-if)#encapsulation frame-relay
R3(config-if)#interface serial 0/0/0.302 point-to-point
R3(config-subif)#ip address 10.3.3.2 255.255.255.0
R3(config-subif)#frame-relay interface-dlci 302
```

Two new commands create the configuration required with point-to-point subinterfaces. First, the **interface serial 0/0/0.201 point-to-point** command creates logical subinterface number 201 under physical interface Serial 0/0/0 on R2. The **frame-relay interface-dlci 201** subinterface subcommand then tells the router which single DLCI is associated with that subinterface. In the example, subinterface numbers and DLCIs match, but this is not a requirement—only a convenient method to help identify which DLCI the subinterface belongs to.

To understand why we need the **frame-relay interface-dlci** command, consider R2. R2 receives LMI messages on Serial0/0/0 stating that two PVCs, with DLCIs 201 and 203, are up. Which PVC goes with which subinterface? Cisco IOS Software needs to associate the correct PVC with the correct subinterface. This is accomplished with the **frame-relay interface-dlci** command.

Frame Relay Verification

Examples of the **show frame-relay pvc** and **show frame-relay map** commands were shown previously in Example 2-4. The **show frame-relay pvc** command lists useful management information. For instance, the packet counters for each VC, plus the counters for FECN and BECN, can be particularly useful. Likewise, comparing the packets/bytes sent on one router versus the counters of what is received on the router on the other end of the VC is also quite useful. This reflects the number of packets/bytes lost inside the Frame Relay cloud. Also, the PVC status is a great place to start when troubleshooting.

The **show frame-relay map** command lists mapping information. In a fully meshed network, in which the configuration does not use any subinterfaces, a Layer 3 address is listed with each DLCI. For a point-to-point subinterface configuration, a DLCI is listed in each entry, but no mention of corresponding Layer 3 addresses is made. The reason is that the information is stored somewhere else. Subinterfaces require the use of the **frame-relay interface-dlci** configuration command.

The **debug frame-relay lmi** command shown in Example 2-9 can be used to verify that the physical interface is sending and receiving LMI messages from the local Frame Relay switch.

Example 2-9   Frame Relay debug Output

```
R2#debug frame-relay lmi
Serial0/0/0(out): StEnq, myseq 1, yourseen 0, DTE up
datagramstart = 0xE7829994, datagramsize = 13
FR encap = 0x00010308
00 75 51 01 00 53 02 01 00
Serial0/0/0(in): Status, myseq 1, pak size 21
RT IE 1, length 1, type 0
KA IE 3, length 2, yourseq 1 , myseq 1
PVC IE 0x7 , length 0x6 , dlci 201, status 0x0 , bw 0
```

Troubleshooting WAN Implementations

Troubleshooting your overall WAN implementation—not just Frame Relay aspects—often starts with investigating the state of the local router's serial interface. The **show interfaces serial** command in Example 2-10 has the default HDLC encapsulation.

Example 2-10   Output from the show interfaces Command

```
R1#show interface serial 0/0/0
Serial0/0/0 is up, line protocol is up (connected)
  Hardware is HD64570
  Description: Link to R2
  Internet address is 10.1.1.1/30
  MTU 1500 bytes, BW 1544 Kbit, DLY 20000 usec, rely 255/255, load 1/255
  Encapsulation HDLC, loopback not set, keepalive set (10 sec)
  Last input never, output never, output hang never
  Last clearing of "show interface" counters never
  Input queue: 0/75/0 (size/max/drops); Total output drops: 0
  Queueing strategy: weighted fair
  Output queue: 0/1000/64/0 (size/max total/threshold/drops)
     Conversations  0/0/256 (active/max active/max total)
     Reserved Conversations 0/0 (allocated/max allocated)
  5 minute input rate 3 bits/sec, 0 packets/sec
  5 minute output rate 2 bits/sec, 0 packets/sec
     3 packets input, 210 bytes, 0 no buffer
     Received 0 broadcasts, 0 runts, 0 giants, 0 throttles
     0 input errors, 0 CRC, 0 frame, 0 overrun, 0 ignored, 0 abort
     2 packets output, 140 bytes, 0 underruns
     0 output errors, 0 collisions, 0 interface resets
     0 output buffer failures, 0 output buffers swapped out
     0 carrier transitions
     DCD=up  DSR=up  DTR=up  RTS=up  CTS=up
```

Highlighted in the output are the three main areas to look first for possible errors.

- The interface must be "up" and "up" before it can forward traffic.

- The IP address and subnet mask must be configured correctly.

- The encapsulation must be correct: HDLC, PPP, or Frame Relay.

Potential errors two and three and their solutions are relatively straightforward: correct the IP addressing or correct the encapsulation. The **show interfaces serial** command returns one of six possible states. You can see any of the following possible states in the interface status line:

- Serial x is up, line protocol is up

- Serial x is down, line protocol is down

- Serial x is up, line protocol is down

- Serial x is up, line protocol is up (looped)

- Serial x is up, line protocol is down (disabled)

- Serial x is administratively down, line protocol is down

Troubleshooting Layer 1 Problems

A down line status on the serial link typically points to a Layer 1 problem. The following list describes the most likely reasons:

- The leased line is down (a telco problem).

- The line from the telco is not plugged in to either or both CSU/DSUs.

- A CSU/DSU has failed or is misconfigured.

- A serial cable from a router to its CSU/DSU is disconnected or faulty.

The details of how to further isolate these four problems is beyond the scope of the CCNA exam.

One other common physical layer problem can occur that results in both routers' interfaces being in an up/down state. On a back-to-back serial link, if the required **clock rate** command is missing on the router with a DCE cable installed, both routers' serial interfaces will fail and end up with a line status of up but a line protocol status of down.

To check for this error, use the **show controllers** command on the side that should be DCE. You might be surprised to find that a DTE cable is attached. Or you might discover that no clock is set, as shown in Example 2-11.

Example 2-11   Problem: No clock rate Command on the DCE End

```
R1#show controllers serial 0/0/0
Interface Serial0/0/0
Hardware is PowerQUICC MPC860
DCE V.35, no clock
idb at 0x81081AC4, driver data structure at 0x81084AC0
SCC Registers:
<output omitted>
```

Troubleshooting Layer 2 Problems

Table 2-1 lists three common data-link layer problems.

Table 2-1   Likely Reasons for Data-Link Problems on Serial Links

Line Status	Protocol Status	Likely Reason
Up	Down (stable) on both ends or Down (stable) on one end, flapping between up and down on the other	Mismatched encapsulation commands.
Up	Down on one end, up on the other	Keepalive is disabled on the end in an up state.
Up	Down (stable) on both ends	PAP/CHAP authentication failure.

The first problem is easy to identify and fix. As we have seen, the **show interfaces** command will tell you the encapsulation type currently used on the interface.

The second problem in Table 2-1 relates to keepalives sent by Cisco routers by default every 10 seconds. This feature helps a router recognize when a link is no longer functioning so that the router can bring down the interface, hoping to then use an alternative IP route. If one end of the link is configured with the **no keepalives** command, it will remain in the "up" and "up" state. However, the other side of the link will continually flap up and down because it is not receiving keepalives. You can see whether keepalives are being sent with the show interfaces command, as highlighted in the partial output in Example 2-12.

Example 2-12   Verifying Keepalives with the show interfaces Command

```
R1#show interface serial 0/0/0
Serial0/0/0 is up, line protocol is up (connected)
  Hardware is HD64570
  Description: Link to R2
  Internet address is 10.1.1.1/30
  MTU 1500 bytes, BW 1544 Kbit, DLY 20000 usec, rely 255/255, load 1/255
  Encapsulation HDLC, loopback not set, keepalive set (10 sec)
  Last input never, output never, output hang never
```

The third problem in Table 2-1 is the result of an authentication failure between the two routers on each side of the link. Use the **debug ppp authentication** command to discover the root cause why authentication is failing.

In Example 2-13, we know that either the username or password is misconfigured on one or both sides of the link.

Example 2-13   PPP CHAP Authentication Failure in debug ppp authentication Output

```
R1#debug ppp authentication
PPP authentication debugging is on
Se0/0/0 PPP: Authorization required
Se0/0/0 CHAP: O CHALLENGE id 57 len 23 from "R1"
Se0/0/0 CHAP: I CHALLENGE id 66 len 23 from "R2"
Se0/0/0 CHAP: Using hostname from unknown source
Se0/0/0 CHAP: Using password from AAA
Se0/0/0 CHAP: O RESPONSE id 66 len 23 from "R1"
Se0/0/0 CHAP: I RESPONSE id 57 len 23 from "R2"
Se0/0/0 PPP: Sent CHAP LOGIN Request
Se0/0/0 PPP: Received LOGIN Response FAIL
Se0/0/0 CHAP: O FAILURE id 57 len 25 msg is "Authentication failed"
```

Troubleshooting Layer 3 Problems

A serial interface can be in the "up" and "up" state on both sides of the router, yet connectivity between the two routers fails because of a Layer 3 misconfiguration.

For default HDLC interfaces, if the IP addresses configured on the serial interfaces on the two routers are in different subnets, a ping to the IP address on the other end of the link will fail because the routers do not have a matching route.

Be careful with PPP in this same situation. With misconfigured IP addresses, both routers' interfaces are in the "up" and "up" state, but the ping to the other router's IP address actually works. PPP advertises its serial interface IP address to the other router, with a /32 prefix, which is a route to reach just that one host. So, both routers have a route with which to route packets to the other end of the link, even though two routers on opposite ends of a serial link have mismatched their IP addresses.

Although the **ping** to the other end of the link works, the routing protocols still do not advertise routes because of the IP subnet mismatch on the opposite ends of the link. So, when troubleshooting a network problem, do not assume that a serial interface in an "up" and "up" state is fully working, or even that a serial interface over which a **ping** works is fully working. Also make sure the routing protocol is exchanging routes and that the IP addresses are in the same subnet.

Study Resources

For today's exam topics, refer to the following resources for more study.

Resource	Chapter	Topic	Where to Find It
Foundational Resources			
CCNA Exploration Online Curriculum: Accessing the WAN	Chapter 3, "Frame Relay"	All sections within the chapter	Sections 3.1–3.4
	Chapter 8, "Network Troubleshooting"	Review of WAN Communications	Section 8.3
		Network Troubleshooting	Section 8.4
CCNA Exploration Accessing the WAN Companion Guide	Chapter 3, "Frame Relay"	All topics within the chapter	pp. 128–179
	Chapter 8, "Network Troubleshooting"	Review of WAN Communications	pp. 560–571
		Network Troubleshooting	pp. 571–594
ICND2 Official Exam Certification Guide	Chapter 12, "Point-to-Point WANs"	Troubleshooting Serial Links	pp. 444–452
	Chapter 13, "Frame Relay Concepts"	All topics within the chapter	pp. 461–480
	Chapter 14, "Frame Relay Configuration and Troubleshooting"	All topics within the chapter	pp. 487–519
ICND2 Authorized Self-Study Guide	Chapter 8, "Extending the Network into the WAN"	Establishing a WAN Connection with Frame Relay	pp. 325–347
		Troubleshooting Frame Relay WANs	pp. 347–354
Supplemental Resources			
CCNA Flash Cards and Exam Practice Pack	ICND1, Section 10	Understanding WAN Technologies	pp. 254–292
	ICND2, Section 10	Establishing Frame Relay Connections	pp. 594–616

CCNA Skills Review and Practice

Key Topics

Tomorrow you take the CCNA exam. Therefore, today you should take the time to do some relaxed skimming of all the previous days' topics focusing on areas where you are still weak. If you have access to a timed practice test like the ones available in the *CCNA Official Exam Certification Library, Third Edition*, use these to help isolate areas in which you may need a little further study.

As part of this book, I have included a CCNA Skills Practice that includes most of the CCNA configuration skills in one topology. This scenario should help you quickly review many of the commands covered by the CCNA.

CCNA Skills Practice

Note to Cisco Networking Academy Students: Although there are some slight differences, this scenario is based on the online version of the CCNA Skills Integration Challenge Packet Tracer Activity you can find at the end of Chapter 8, "Network Troubleshooting" in the online version of the course *CCNA Exploration: Accessing the WAN*.

Introduction

In this comprehensive CCNA skills activity, the XYZ Corporation uses a combination of Frame Relay and PPP for WAN connections. The HQ router provides access to the server farm and the Internet through NAT. HQ also uses a basic firewall ACL to filter inbound traffic. B1 is configured for inter-VLAN routing and DHCP. The switches attached to B1 are configured with port security, VLANs, VTP, and STP. Routing is achieved through EIGRP as well as static and default routes. Your job is to successfully implement all these technologies, leveraging what you have learned during your CCNA studies.

You are responsible for configuring HQ and the Branch routers, B1, B2, and B3. Assume routers and switches under your administration have no configuration.

Topology Diagram

Figure 1-1 shows the topology for this CCNA Skills Review.

Figure 1-1   CCNA Skills Review Topology

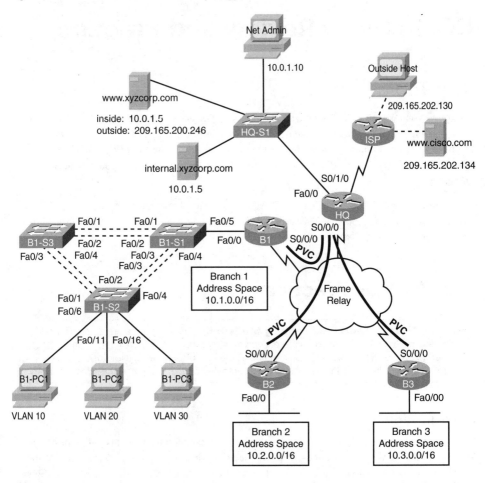

Addressing Table

Table 1-1 shows the addressing scheme for the network shown in Figure 1-1.

Table 1-1   CCNA Skills Review Addressing Scheme

Device	Interface	IP Address	Subnet Mask	DLCI Mappings
HQ	Fa0/0	10.0.1.1	255.255.255.0	N/A
	S0/0/0.41	10.255.255.1	255.255.255.252	DLCI 41 to B1
	S0/0/0.42	10.255.255.5	255.255.255.252	DLCI 42 to B2
	S0/0/0.43	10.255.255.9	255.255.255.252	DLCI 43 to B3
	S0/1/0	209.165.201.1	255.255.255.252	N/A
B1	Fa0/0.1	10.1.1.1	255.255.255.0	N/A
	Fa0/0.10	10.1.10.1	255.255.255.0	N/A

Device	Interface	IP Address	Subnet Mask	DLCI Mappings
	Fa0/0.20	10.1.20.1	255.255.255.0	N/A
	Fa0/0.30	10.1.30.1	255.255.255.0	N/A
	S0/0/0	10.255.255.2	255.255.255.252	N/A
B1-S1	VLAN 1	10.1.1.21	255.255.255.0	N/A
B1-S2	VLAN 1	10.1.1.22	255.255.255.0	N/A
B1-S3	VLAN 1	10.1.1.23	255.255.255.0	N/A
B2	Fa0/0	10.2.0.1	255.255.0.0	N/A
	S0/0/0	10.255.255.6	255.255.255.252	N/A
B3	Fa0/0	10.3.0.1	255.255.0.0	N/A
	S0/0/0	10.255.255.10	255.255.255.252	N/A

VLAN Configuration and Port Mappings

Table 1-2 shows the VLAN configuration information for the B1 switches, including names, subnets, and port mappings.

Table 1-2   VLAN Configuration and Port Mappings

VLAN Number	Network Address	VLAN Name	Port Mappings
10	10.1.10.0/24	Admin	B1-S1, Fa0/6–Fa0/10
20	10.1.20.0/24	Sales	B1-S2, Fa0/11–Fa0/15
30	10.1.30.0/24	Production	B1-S3, Fa0/16–Fa0/20

ISP Configuration

If you choose to configure this network on real equipment or a network simulator, use the script in Example 1-1 to configure ISP.

Example 1-1   ISP Configuration

```
hostname ISP
!
username HQ password ciscochap
!
interface FastEthernet0/0
 description Link to Outside Host
 ip address 209.165.202.129 255.255.255.252
 no shutdown
!
interface FastEthernet0/1
 description Link to Cisco web server
```

```
 ip address 209.165.202.133 255.255.255.252
 no shutdown
!
interface Serial0/0/0
 ip address 209.165.201.2 255.255.255.252
 encapsulation ppp
 ppp authentication chap
 clock rate 64000
 no shutdown
!
ip route 209.165.200.240 255.255.255.248 Serial0/0/0
!
end
copy run start
```

Task 1: Configure Frame Relay in a Hub-and-Spoke Topology

Step 1   Configure the Frame Relay core.

Use Table 1-1 and the following requirements:

- HQ is the hub router. B1, B2, and B3 are the spokes.

— HQ uses a point-to-point subinterface for each of the Branch routers.

— B3 must be manually configured to use IETF encapsulation.

— The LMI type must be manually configured as q933a for HQ, B1, and B2. B3 uses ANSI.

Step 2   Configure the LAN interface on HQ.

Step 3   Verify that HQ can ping each of the Branch routers.

Task 2: Configure PPP with CHAP

Step 1   Configure the WAN link from HQ to ISP using PPP encapsulation and CHAP authentication.

The CHAP password is **ciscochap**.

Step 2   Verify that HQ can ping ISP.

Task 3: Configure Static and Dynamic NAT on HQ

Step 1   Configure NAT.

Use the following requirements:

— Allow all addresses for the 10.0.0.0/8 address space to be translated.

— XYZ Corporation owns the 209.165.200.240/29 address space. The pool, XYZCORP, uses addresses .241 through .245 with a /29 mask.

— The www.xyzcorp.com website at 10.0.1.2 is registered with the public DNS system at IP address 209.165.200.246.

Step 2   Verify that NAT is operating by using extended ping.

From HQ, ping the serial 0/0/0 interface on ISP using the HQ LAN interface as the source address. This ping should succeed.

Verify that NAT translated the ping with the **show ip nat translations** command.

Task 4: Configure Default Routing

Step 1   Configure HQ with a default route to ISP.

Use the exit interface as an argument.

Step 2   Verify connectivity beyond ISP.

The NetAdmin PC should be able to ping the www.cisco.com web server.

Task 5: Configure Inter-VLAN Routing

Step 1   Configure B1 for inter-VLAN routing.

Using the addressing table B1, configure and activate the LAN interface for inter-VLAN routing.

Step 2   Verify routing tables.

B1 should now have six directly connected networks and one static default route.

Task 6: Configure and Optimize EIGRP Routing

Step 1   Configure HQ, B1, B2, and B3 with EIGRP.

— Use AS 100.

— HQ should redistribute its default route to the branch routers.

— Manually summarize EIGRP routes so that B1 advertises the 10.1.0.0/16 address space only to HQ.

Step 2   Verify routing tables and connectivity.

HQ and the Branch routers should now have complete routing tables.

The NetAdmin PC should now be able to ping each LAN interface and the VLAN subinterfaces on B1.

Task 7: Configure VTP, Trunking, the VLAN Interface, and VLANs

Step 1   Configure the B1 switches with VTP.

— B1-S1 is the VTP server. B1-S2 and B1-S3 are VTP clients.

— The domain name is **XYZCORP**.

— The password is **xyzvtp**.

Step 2   Configure trunking.

Configure the appropriate interfaces in trunking mode.

Step 3   Configure the VLAN interface and default gateway on B1-S1, B1-S2, and B1-S3.

Step 4   Create the VLANs on B1-S1.

Create and name the VLANs listed in Table 1-2 on B1-S1 only. VTP advertises the new VLANs to B1-S2 and B1-S3.

Step 5   Verify that VLANs have been sent to B1-S2 and B1-S3.

Task 8: Assign VLANs and Configure Port Security

Step 1   Assign VLANs to the access ports on B1-S2.

Use Table 1-2 to complete the following requirements:

— Configure access ports.

— Assign VLANs to the access ports.

Step 2   Configure port security.

Use the following policy to establish port security on the B1-S2 access ports:

— Allow only one MAC address.

— Configure the first learned MAC address to "stick" to the configuration.

— Set the port to shut down if a security violation occurs.

Step 3   Verify VLAN assignments and port security.

Use the appropriate commands to verify that access VLANs are correctly assigned and that the port security policy has been enabled.

Task 9: Configure STP

Step 1   Configure B1-S1 as the root bridge.

Set the priority level to 4096 on B1-S1 so that this switch is always the root bridge for all VLANs.

Step 2   Configure B1-S3 as the backup root bridge.

Set the priority level to 8192 on B1-S3 so that this switch is always the backup root bridge for all VLANs.

Step 3   Verify that B1-S1 is the root bridge.

Task 10: Configure DHCP

Step 1 Configure DHCP pools for each VLAN.

On B1, configure DHCP pools for each VLAN using the following requirements:

— Exclude the first 10 IP addresses in each pool for the LANs.

— The pool name is **B1_VLAN##** where ## is the VLAN number.

— Include the DNS server attached to the HQ server farm as part of the DHCP configuration.

Step 2 Verify that the PCs have an IP address.

Step 3 Verify connectivity.

All PCs physically attached to the network should be able to ping the www.cisco.com web server.

Task 11: Configure a Firewall ACL

Step 1 Verify connectivity from Outside Host.

The Outside Host PC should be able to ping the server at www.xyzcorp.com.

Step 2 Implement a basic firewall ACL.

Because ISP represents connectivity to the Internet, configure a named ACL called **FIREWALL** in the following order:

1. Allow inbound HTTP requests to the www.xyzcorp.com server.

2. Allow only established TCP sessions from ISP and any source beyond ISP.

3. Allow only inbound ping replies from ISP and any source beyond ISP.

4. Explicitly block all other inbound access from ISP and any source beyond ISP.

Step 3 Verify connectivity from Outside Host.

The Outside Host PC should not be able to ping the server at www.xyzcorp.com. However, the Outside Host PC should be able to request a web page.

CCNA Skills Practice (Answers)

The following are the scripts and verification commands you would enter for each of the tasks.

Task 1: Configure Frame Relay in a Hub-and-Spoke Topology

Step 1   Configure the Frame Relay core.

```
!-----------
!HQ
!-----------
enable
configure terminal
host HQ
!
interface Serial0/0/0
 no ip address
 encapsulation frame-relay
 frame-relay lmi-type q933a
 no shutdown
!
interface Serial0/0/0.41 point-to-point
 ip address 10.255.255.1 255.255.255.252
 frame-relay interface-dlci 41
!
interface Serial0/0/0.42 point-to-point
 ip address 10.255.255.5 255.255.255.252
 frame-relay interface-dlci 42
!
interface Serial0/0/0.43 point-to-point
 ip address 10.255.255.9 255.255.255.252
 frame-relay interface-dlci 43
end
copy run start

!-----------
!B1
!-----------
enable
configure terminal
host B1
!
interface Serial0/0/0
 ip address 10.255.255.2 255.255.255.252
 encapsulation frame-relay
 frame-relay lmi-type q933a
 no shutdown
end
```

```
copy run start

!-----------
!B2
!-----------
enable
configure terminal
host B2
!
interface Serial0/0/0
 ip address 10.255.255.6 255.255.255.252
 encapsulation frame-relay
 frame-relay lmi-type q933a
 no shutdown
end
copy run start

!-----------
!B3
!-----------
enable
configure terminal
host B3
!
interface Serial0/0/0
 ip address 10.255.255.10 255.255.255.252
 encapsulation frame-relay ietf
 frame-relay lmi-type ansi
 no shutdown
end
copy run start
```

Step 2   Configure the LAN interface on HQ.

```
!
interface FastEthernet0/0
 description Server Farm
 ip address 10.0.1.1 255.255.255.0
 no shutdown
!
```

Step 3   Verify that HQ can ping each of the Branch routers.

HQ#**ping 10.255.255.2**

```
Type escape sequence to abort.
Sending 5, 100-byte ICMP Echos to 10.255.255.2, timeout is 2 seconds:
!!!!!
Success rate is 100 percent (5/5), round-trip min/avg/max = 40/71/89 ms
```

```
HQ#ping 10.255.255.6

Type escape sequence to abort.
Sending 5, 100-byte ICMP Echos to 10.255.255.6, timeout is 2 seconds:
!!!!!
Success rate is 100 percent (5/5), round-trip min/avg/max = 35/60/69 ms


HQ#ping 10.255.255.10

Type escape sequence to abort.
Sending 5, 100-byte ICMP Echos to 10.255.255.10, timeout is 2 seconds:
!!!!!
Success rate is 100 percent (5/5), round-trip min/avg/max = 23/58/87 ms
```

Task 2: Configure PPP with CHAP

Step 1   Configure the WAN link from HQ to ISP using PPP encapsulation and CHAP authentication.

The CHAP password is **ciscochap**.

```
username ISP password ciscochap
interface Serial0/1/0
 description Link to ISP
 ip address 209.165.201.1 255.255.255.252
 encapsulation ppp
 ppp authentication chap
 no shutdown
```

Step 2   Verify that HQ can ping ISP.

```
HQ#ping 209.165.201.2

Type escape sequence to abort.
Sending 5, 100-byte ICMP Echos to 209.165.201.2, timeout is 2 seconds:
!!!!!
Success rate is 100 percent (5/5), round-trip min/avg/max = 17/30/38 ms
```

Task 3: Configure Static and Dynamic NAT on HQ

Step 1   Configure NAT.

Use the following requirements:

```
ip access-list standard NAT_LIST
 permit 10.0.0.0 0.255.255.255
!
ip nat pool XYZCORP 209.165.200.241 209.165.200.245 netmask
   255.255.255.248
ip nat inside source list NAT_LIST pool XYZCORP overload
ip nat inside source static 10.0.1.2 209.165.200.246
!
```

```
interface fa0/0
 ip nat inside
interface s0/0/0.41 point-to-point
 ip nat inside
interface s0/0/0.42 point-to-point
 ip nat inside
interface s0/0/0.43 point-to-point
 ip nat inside
interface s0/1/0
 ip nat outside
```

Step 2   Verify that NAT is operating by using extended ping.

```
HQ#ping
Protocol [ip]:
Target IP address: 209.165.201.2
Repeat count [5]:
Datagram size [100]:
Timeout in seconds [2]:
Extended commands [n]: y
Source address or interface: 10.0.1.1
Type of service [0]:
Set DF bit in IP header? [no]:
Validate reply data? [no]:
Data pattern [0xABCD]:
Loose, Strict, Record, Timestamp, Verbose[none]:
Sweep range of sizes [n]:
Type escape sequence to abort.
Sending 5, 100-byte ICMP Echos to 209.165.201.2, timeout is 2 seconds:
Packet sent with a source address of 10.0.1.1
!!!!!
Success rate is 100 percent (5/5), round-trip min/avg/max = 18/34/42 ms
```

Verify that NAT translated the ping with the **show ip nat translations** command.

```
HQ#show ip nat translations
Pro  Inside global      Inside local      Outside local      Outside global
icmp 209.165.200.241:3510.0.1.1:35      209.165.201.2:35      209.165.201.2:35
icmp 209.165.200.241:3610.0.1.1:36      209.165.201.2:36      209.165.201.2:36
icmp 209.165.200.241:3710.0.1.1:37      209.165.201.2:37      209.165.201.2:37
icmp 209.165.200.241:3810.0.1.1:38      209.165.201.2:38      209.165.201.2:38
icmp 209.165.200.241:3910.0.1.1:39      209.165.201.2:39      209.165.201.2:39
---  209.165.200.246    10.0.1.2          ---                ---
```

Task 4: Configure Default Routing

Step 1   Configure HQ with a default route to ISP.

```
ip route 0.0.0.0 0.0.0.0 Serial0/1/0
```

Step 2   Verify connectivity beyond ISP.

```
!From NetAdmin
C:\>ping 209.165.202.134

Pinging 209.165.202.134 with 32 bytes of data:

Reply from 209.165.202.134: bytes=32 time=12ms TTL=126
Reply from 209.165.202.134: bytes=32 time=188ms TTL=126
Reply from 209.165.202.134: bytes=32 time=8ms TTL=126
Reply from 209.165.202.134: bytes=32 time=8ms TTL=126

Ping statistics for 209.165.202.134:
    Packets: Sent = 4, Received = 4, Lost = 0 (0% loss),
Approximate round trip times in milli-seconds:
    Minimum = 8ms, Maximum = 188ms, Average = 54ms
```

Task 5: Configure Inter-VLAN Routing

Step 1   Configure B1 for inter-VLAN routing.

```
!
interface FastEthernet0/0
 no shutdown
!
interface FastEthernet0/0.1
 description Mgmt&Native VLAN 1
 encapsulation dot1Q 1 native
 ip address 10.1.1.1 255.255.255.0
!
interface FastEthernet0/0.10
 description Admin VLAN 10
 encapsulation dot1Q 10
 ip address 10.1.10.1 255.255.255.0
!
interface FastEthernet0/0.20
 description Sales VLAN 20
 encapsulation dot1Q 20
 ip address 10.1.20.1 255.255.255.0
!
interface FastEthernet0/0.30
 description Production VLAN 30
 encapsulation dot1Q 30
 ip address 10.1.30.1 255.255.255.0
!
```

Step 2   Verify routing tables.

```
B1#show ip route
<output omitted>


Gateway of last resort is not set

     10.0.0.0/8 is variably subnetted, 5 subnets, 2 masks
C       10.1.1.0/24 is directly connected, FastEthernet0/0.1
C       10.1.10.0/24 is directly connected, FastEthernet0/0.10
C       10.1.20.0/24 is directly connected, FastEthernet0/0.20
C       10.1.30.0/24 is directly connected, FastEthernet0/0.30
C       10.255.255.0/30 is directly connected, Serial0/0/0
```

Task 6: Configure and Optimize EIGRP Routing

Step 1   Configure HQ, B1, B2, and B3 with EIGRP.

```
!-----------------
!All Routers
!-----------------
router eigrp 100
network 10.0.0.0
 no auto-summary
!
!On HQ...
 redistribute static
!
!On B1...
interface serial 0/0/0
 ip summary-address eigrp 10.1.0.0 255.255.0.0
```

Step 2   Verify routing tables and connectivity.

```
!
HQ#show ip route
<output omitted>


Gateway of last resort is 0.0.0.0 to network 0.0.0.0

     10.0.0.0/8 is variably subnetted, 7 subnets, 3 masks
C       10.0.1.0/24 is directly connected, FastEthernet0/0
D       10.1.0.0/16 [90/2681856] via 10.255.255.2, 00:29:42,
     Serial0/0/0.41
D       10.2.0.0/16 [90/2172416] via 10.255.255.6, 00:29:40,
     Serial0/0/0.42
D       10.3.0.0/16 [90/2172416] via 10.255.255.10, 00:29:40,
     Serial0/0/0.43
C       10.255.255.0/30 is directly connected, Serial0/0/0.41
C       10.255.255.4/30 is directly connected, Serial0/0/0.42
C       10.255.255.8/30 is directly connected, Serial0/0/0.43
```

```
      209.165.201.0/30 is subnetted, 1 subnets
C        209.165.201.0 is directly connected, Serial0/1/0
S*   0.0.0.0/0 is directly connected, Serial0/1/0
HQ#
!Pings are shown for one LAN interface per branch router
!From NetAdmin PC


C:\>ping 10.1.10.1

Pinging 10.1.10.1 with 32 bytes of data:

Reply from 10.1.10.1: bytes=32 time=104ms TTL=254
Reply from 10.1.10.1: bytes=32 time=104ms TTL=254
Reply from 10.1.10.1: bytes=32 time=100ms TTL=254
Reply from 10.1.10.1: bytes=32 time=132ms TTL=254

Ping statistics for 10.1.10.1:
    Packets: Sent = 4, Received = 4, Lost = 0 (0% loss),
Approximate round trip times in milli-seconds:
    Minimum = 100ms, Maximum = 132ms, Average = 110ms

C:\>ping 10.2.0.1

Pinging 10.2.0.1 with 32 bytes of data:

Reply from 10.2.0.1: bytes=32 time=83ms TTL=254
Reply from 10.2.0.1: bytes=32 time=152ms TTL=254
Reply from 10.2.0.1: bytes=32 time=118ms TTL=254
Reply from 10.2.0.1: bytes=32 time=103ms TTL=254

Ping statistics for 10.2.0.1:
    Packets: Sent = 4, Received = 4, Lost = 0 (0% loss),
Approximate round trip times in milli-seconds:
    Minimum = 83ms, Maximum = 152ms, Average = 114ms

C:\>ping 10.3.0.1

Pinging 10.3.0.1 with 32 bytes of data:

Reply from 10.3.0.1: bytes=32 time=114ms TTL=254
Reply from 10.3.0.1: bytes=32 time=99ms TTL=254
Reply from 10.3.0.1: bytes=32 time=108ms TTL=254
Reply from 10.3.0.1: bytes=32 time=153ms TTL=254

Ping statistics for 10.3.0.1:
    Packets: Sent = 4, Received = 4, Lost = 0 (0% loss),
Approximate round trip times in milli-seconds:
    Minimum = 99ms, Maximum = 153ms, Average = 118ms
```

Task 7: Configure VTP, Trunking, the VLAN Interface, and VLANs

Step 1   Configure the B1 switches with VTP.

Step 2   Configure trunking.

Configure the appropriate interfaces in trunking mode.

Step 3   Configure the VLAN interface and default gateway on B1-S1, B1-S2, and B1-S3.

Step 4   Create the VLANs on B1-S1.

```
!
!----------
!S1
!----------
enable
configure terminal
host B1-S1
!
vtp mode server
vtp domain XYZCORP
vtp password xyzvtp
!
interface range Fa0/1 - Fa0/5
 switchport mode trunk
!
interface vlan 1
 ip address 10.1.1.21 255.255.255.0
 no shut
ip default-gateway 10.1.1.1
!
vlan 10
 name Admin
vlan 20
 name Sales
vlan 30
 name Production
end
copy run start

!----------
!S2
!----------
enable
configure terminal
host B1-S2
!
vtp mode client
```

```
vtp domain XYZCORP
vtp password xyzvtp
!
interface range Fa0/1 - Fa0/4
 switchport mode trunk
!
!
interface vlan 1
 ip address 10.1.1.22 255.255.255.0
 no shut
ip default-gateway 10.1.1.1
!
end
copy run start


!-----------
!S3
!-----------
enable
configure terminal
host B1-S3
!
vtp mode client
vtp domain XYZCORP
vtp password xyzvtp
!
interface range Fa0/1 - Fa0/5
 switchport mode trunk
!
interface vlan 1
 ip address 10.1.1.23 255.255.255.0
 no shut
ip default-gateway 10.1.1.1
!
end
copy run start
```

Step 5   Verify that VLANs have been sent to B1-S2 and B1-S3.

```
!Output for B1-S2 is shown. Should be similar on B1-S3.
B1-S2#show vtp status
VTP Version                     : 2
Configuration Revision          : 0
Maximum VLANs supported locally : 64
Number of existing VLANs        : 8
VTP Operating Mode              : Client
VTP Domain Name                 : XYZCORP
```

```
VTP Pruning Mode              : Disabled
VTP V2 Mode                   : Disabled
VTP Traps Generation          : Disabled
MD5 digest                    : 0xCD 0xBF 0xDE 0x4E 0x0F 0x79 0x7D 0x3E
Configuration last modified by 10.1.1.21 at 3-1-93 00:43:41


B1-S2#show vlan brief


VLAN Name                        Status    Ports
---- ------------------------    --------- ------------------------------
1    default                     active    Fa0/5, Fa0/6, Fa0/7, Fa0/8
                                           Fa0/9, Fa0/10, Fa0/11, Fa0/12
                                           Fa0/13, Fa0/14, Fa0/15, Fa0/16
                                           Fa0/17, Fa0/18, Fa0/19, Fa0/20
                                           Fa0/21, Fa0/22, Fa0/23, Fa0/24
                                           Gig1/1, Gig1/2
10   Admin                       active
20   Sales                       active
30   Production                  active
1002 fddi-default                active
1003 token-ring-default          active
1004 fddinet-default             active
1005 trnet-default               active
```

Task 8: Assign VLANs and Configure Port Security

Step 1   Assign VLANs to the access ports on B1-S2.

```
interface fa0/6 - fa0/10
 switchport access vlan 10
interface fa0/11 - fa0/15
 switchport access vlan 20
interface fa0/16 - fa0/20
 switchport access vlan 10
```

Step 2   Configure port security.

```
interface fa0/6 - fa0/20
 switchport port-security
 switchport port-security maximum 1
 switchport port-security mac-address sticky
 switchport port-security violation shutdown
```

Step 3   Verify VLAN assignments and port security.

```
B1-S2#show vlan brief
```

```
VLAN Name                             Status    Ports
---- --------------------------       --------- -------------------------------
1    default                          active    Fa0/5, Fa0/21, Fa0/22, Fa0/23
                                                Fa0/24, Giy1/1, Giy1/2
10   Admin                            active    Fa0/6, Fa0/7, Fa0/8, Fa0/9
                                                Fa0/10
20   Sales                            active    Fa0/11, Fa0/12, Fa0/13, Fa0/14
                                                Fa0/15
30   Production                       active    Fa0/16, Fa0/17, Fa0/18, Fa0/19
                                                Fa0/20
1002 fddi-default                      active
1003 token-ring-default                active
1004 fddinet-default                   active
1005 trnet-default                     active
!
B1-S2#show port-security interface fa0/6
Port Security                : Enabled
Port Status                  : Secure-up
Violation Mode               : Shutdown
Aging Time                   : 0 mins
Aging Type                   : Absolute
SecureStatic Address Aging   : Disabled
Maximum MAC Addresses        : 1
Total MAC Addresses          : 1
Configured MAC Addresses     : 0
Sticky MAC Addresses         : 1
Last Source Address:Vlan     : 00D0.BCCA.9C3A:10
Security Violation Count     : 0
```

Task 9: Configure STP

Step 1   Configure B1-S1 as the root bridge.

```
!
spanning-tree vlan 1 priority 4096
spanning-tree vlan 10 priority 4096
spanning-tree vlan 20 priority 4096
spanning-tree vlan 30 priority 4096
!
```

Step 2   Configure B1-S3 as the backup root bridge.

```
!
spanning-tree vlan 1 priority 8192
spanning-tree vlan 10 priority 8192
spanning-tree vlan 20 priority 8192
spanning-tree vlan 30 priority 8192
!
```

Step 3   Verify that B1-S1 is the root bridge.

```
!Output should be similar for all VLANs.
B1-S1#show spanning-tree vlan 10
VLAN0010
  Spanning tree enabled protocol ieee
  Root ID    Priority    4106
             Address     00D0.BA3D.2C94
             This bridge is the root
             Hello Time  2 sec  Max Age 20 sec  Forward Delay 15 sec

  Bridge ID  Priority    4106  (priority 4096 sys-id-ext 10)
             Address     00D0.BA3D.2C94
             Hello Time  2 sec  Max Age 20 sec  Forward Delay 15 sec
             Aging Time  20

Interface        Role Sts Cost      Prio.Nbr Type
---------------- ---- --- --------- -------- ------------------------------
Fa0/2            Desg FWD 19        128.2    P2p
Fa0/1            Desg FWD 19        128.1    P2p
Fa0/5            Desg FWD 19        128.5    P2p
Fa0/4            Desg FWD 19        128.4    P2p
Fa0/3            Desg FWD 19        128.3    P2p
```

Task 10: Configure DHCP

Step 1   Configure DHCP pools for each VLAN.

```
!
ip dhcp excluded-address 10.1.10.1 10.1.10.10
ip dhcp excluded-address 10.1.20.1 10.1.20.10
ip dhcp excluded-address 10.1.30.1 10.1.30.10
!
ip dhcp pool B1_VLAN10
 network 10.1.10.0 255.255.255.0
 default-router 10.1.10.1
 dns-server 10.0.1.4
ip dhcp pool B1_VLAN20
 network 10.1.20.0 255.255.255.0
 default-router 10.1.20.1
 dns-server 10.0.1.4
ip dhcp pool B1_VLAN30
 network 10.1.30.0 255.255.255.0
 default-router 10.1.30.1
 dns-server 10.0.1.4
!
```

Step 2   Verify that the PCs have an IP address.

Use **ipconfig** on each PC to verify DHCP is working correctly. You might have to set the PC to automatically obtain an IP address and then use **ipconfig/release** and **ipconfig/renew** to obtain the IP address.

Step 3   Verify connectivity.

```
!From B1-PC1

C:\>ping 209.165.202.134

Pinging 209.165.202.134 with 32 bytes of data:

Reply from 209.165.202.134: bytes=32 time=234ms TTL=125
Reply from 209.165.202.134: bytes=32 time=184ms TTL=125
Reply from 209.165.202.134: bytes=32 time=230ms TTL=125
Reply from 209.165.202.134: bytes=32 time=228ms TTL=125

Ping statistics for 209.165.202.134:
    Packets: Sent = 4, Received = 4, Lost = 0 (0% loss),
Approximate round trip times in milli-seconds:
    Minimum = 184ms, Maximum = 234ms, Average = 219ms
```

Task 11: Configure a Firewall ACL

Step 1   Verify connectivity from Outside Host.

```
!-----------
!Outside Host
!-----------
!
C:\>ping www.xyzcorp.com

Pinging 209.165.200.246 with 32 bytes of data:

Reply from 209.165.200.246: bytes=32 time=45ms TTL=126
Reply from 209.165.200.246: bytes=32 time=115ms TTL=126
Reply from 209.165.200.246: bytes=32 time=124ms TTL=126
Reply from 209.165.200.246: bytes=32 time=101ms TTL=126

Ping statistics for 209.165.200.246:
    Packets: Sent = 4, Received = 4, Lost = 0 (0% loss),
Approximate round trip times in milli-seconds:
    Minimum = 45ms, Maximum = 124ms, Average = 96ms
!
```

Step 2   Implement a basic firewall ACL.

```
!-----------
!HQ
!-----------

ip access-list extended FIREWALL
 permit tcp any host 209.165.200.246 eq www
 permit tcp any any established
 permit icmp any any echo-reply
 deny ip any any
!
interface Serial0/1/0
 ip access-group FIREWALL in
!
```

Step 3   Verify connectivity from Outside Host.

The Outside Host PC should not be able to ping the server at www.xyzcorp.com. However, the Outside Host PC should be able to request a web page.

```
!-----------
!Outside Host
!-----------
!
C:\>ping www.xyzcorp.com

Pinging 209.165.200.246 with 32 bytes of data:

Request timed out.
Request timed out.
Request timed out.
Request timed out.

Ping statistics for 209.165.200.246:
    Packets: Sent = 4, Received = 0, Lost = 4 (100% loss),
!
```

CCNA Skills Challenge

For an extra challenge, try the following modifications to the CCNA Skills Practice:

- Change the routing protocol to RIPv2 or OSPF.

- Make up some different host requirements and change the addressing scheme.

- Configure the network with all static routes. No routing protocol.

- Change the encapsulation type from Frame Relay to PPP and verify functionality.

- Add switches to B2 and B3 with similar VLAN configurations as used on B1 switches.

- Add a new branch router through a T1 link. Assume the new branch router is not a Cisco router. You must use PPP with PAP authentication.

- Implement some of your own security policies by configuring more access lists.

- Configure SSH.

- If you have a friend you are studying with, take turns introducing errors to the network. Then practice using **show** and **debug** commands to verify and troubleshoot network.

Part IX

Exam Day and Post-Exam Information

Exam Day

Post-Exam Information

Exam Day

Today is your opportunity to prove that you know how to install, configure, operate, and troubleshoot medium-size routed and switched networks. Just 90 minutes and 50 to 60 questions stand between you and your CCNA certification. Use the following information to focus on the process details for the day of your CCNA exam.

What You Need for the Exam

Write the exam location, date, exam time, exam center phone number, and the proctor's name in the lines that follow:

Location: _____

Date: _____

Exam Time (arrive early): _____

Exam Center Phone Number: _____

Proctor's Name: _____

Remember the following items on Exam Day:

- You must have **two forms of ID** that include a photo and signature, such as a driver's license, passport, or military identification.

- The test proctor will take you through the agreement and set up your testing station after you have signed the agreement.

- The test proctor will give you a sheet for scratch paper or a dry erase pad. Do not take these out of the room.

- The testing center will store any personal items while you take the exam. It is best to bring only what you will need.

- You will be monitored during the entire exam.

What You Should Receive After Completion

When you complete the exam, you will see an immediate electronic response as to whether you passed or failed**.** The proctor will give you a certified score report with the following important information:

- Your score report, including the minimum passing score and your score on the exam. The report will also include a breakout displaying your percentage for each general exam topic.

- Identification information that you will need to track your certification. *Do not lose your certified examination score report.*

Summary

Your state of mind is a key factor in your success on the CCNA exam. If you know the details of the curriculum and the details of the exam process, you can begin the exam with confidence and focus. Arrive early to the exam. Bring earplugs in the off chance that a testing neighbor has a bad cough or any loud nervous habits. Do not let an extremely difficult or specific question impede your progress. You cannot return to questions that you have already answered on the exam, so answer each question confidently and keep an eye on the timer.

Post-Exam Information

The accomplishment of signing up for and actually taking the CCNA exam is no small feat. Many network engineers have avoided certification exams for years. The following sections discuss your options after exam day.

Receiving Your Certificate

If you passed the exam, you will receive your official CCNA certificate and wallet card about six weeks (eight weeks internationally) after exam day. Your certificate will be mailed to the address you provided when you registered for the exam.

You will need your examination score report to access the certification tracking system and set up a login to check your certification status. If you do not receive your certificate, you can open a case in the certificate online support located at the following web address:

http://ciscocert.custhelp.com/

When you receive your certificate, you might want to frame it and put it on a wall. A certificate hanging on a wall is much harder to lose than a certificate in a filing cabinet or random folder. You never know when an employer or academic institution could request a copy.

Your CCNA is valid for three years. To keep your certificate valid, you must either pass the CCNA exam again, pass one of the CCNA related exams (Security, Voice, or Wireless), or advance to the next level of certification before the end of the three-year period.

Determining Career Options

After passing the CCNA exam, be sure to add your CCNA certification to your resume. Matthew Moran provides the following advice for adding certifications to a resume in his book *The IT Career Builder's Toolkit* (Cisco Press, 2005. ISBN: 1587131560):

> I don't believe you should place your certifications after your name. It is presumptuous to pretend that your latest certification is the equivalent to someone who has spent 4–7 years pursuing a Ph.D. or some other advanced degree. Instead, place your certifications or degrees in a section titled *Education and Certifications*. A master's degree might be the exception to this rule.

Moran also discusses good strategies to break into the IT industry after you have earned your CCNA:

> The most important factor is that you are moving toward a career goal. You might not get the title or job you want right out of school. If you can master those skills at your current position, while simultaneously building your network of contacts that lead to your dream position, you should be satisfied. You must build your career piece by piece. It won't happen all at once.

Moran also outlines in his book that certifications such as the CCNA are part of an overall professional skill set that you must continually enhance to further your IT career.

Your CCNA certificate proves that you are disciplined enough to commit to a rigorous course of study and follow through with your professional goals. It is unlikely that you will be hired simply because you have a CCNA, but it will place you ahead of other candidates. Even though you have listed the CCNA on your resume, it is important to highlight your networking skills that pertain to the CCNA in your job and skills descriptions on your resume.

Examining Certification Options

Although passing the CCNA exam is not an easy task, it is the starting point for more advanced Cisco certifications, such as the CCNA Security (640-553), CCNA Voice (640-460), CCNA Wireless (640-721) or even CCNP-level exams. When you log in to the online certification tracking tool (use the exam report to do this), be sure to view the certification progress link. This link provides specific information about certifications you can achieve with your CCNA as the base.

If You Failed the Exam

If you fail your first attempt at the CCNA, you must wait at least five calendar days after the day of the exam to retest. Stay motivated and sign up to take the exam again within a 30-day period of your first attempt. The score report outlines your weaknesses. Find a study group and use the Cisco Learning Network online community to help you with those difficult topics.

If you are familiar with the general concepts, focus on taking practice exams and memorizing the small details that make the exam so difficult. If you are a Cisco Networking Academy alumnus, you have access to the curriculum, and Packet Tracer provides an excellent network simulator. Consider your first attempt as a formal practice exam and excellent preparation to pass the second attempt.

Summary

Whether you display your certificate and update your resume or prepare to conquer the exam on your second attempt, remember to marvel at the innovation and creativity behind each concept you learn. The ability of our society to continually improve communication will keep you learning, discovering, and employed for a lifetime.

Index

Symbols

3DES (Triple DES), 323
10BASE-T, 37
100BASE-TX, 37
802.00i (WPA2), 258
802.11g, 255
802.3. See Ethernet
1000BASE-T, 37

A

access attacks, 272
access control lists. *See* ACLs
access layer switches, 4
acknowledgment (ACK) packets,
  EIGRP, 213
ACLs (access control lists), 279
  adding comments to named or numbered
    ACLs, 287-288
  complex ACLs, 288
  configuring extended numbered ACLs,
    284-285
    deny FTP from subnets, 285
    deny only Telnet from subnets, 285-286
  configuring named ACLs, 286-287
  configuring standard numbered ACLs, 282
    deny a specific host, 283
    deny a specific subnet, 283-284
    deny Telnet access to routers, 284
    permit specific network, 282-283
  defining, 279
  design guidelines, 281-282
  extended ACLs, 280
  identification, 281
  interface processing, 279-280
  standard ACLs, 280
  troubleshooting, 291
    denied protocols, 292-293
    host has no connectivity, 291-292
    Telnet is allowed #1, 293
    Telnet is allowed #2, 294
    Telnet is allowed #3, 294-295
  types of, 280-281
  verifying, 289-290

AD (administrative distance), 153-154
ad hoc mode, wireless operations, 254
adding comments to named or numbered
  ACLs, 287-288
Address Resolution Protocol (ARP),
  16, 148
addresses
  broadcast addresses, 38
  Ethernet, 38
  IPv4, 109
    classes of addresses, 110-111
    header formats, 109-110
    subnet masks, 111-112
  IPv6
    conventions for writing, 139
    loopback addresses, 141
    managing, 142
    private addresses, 141
    reserved addresses, 141
  link-local addresses, 141
  multicast addresses, 38
  private IP addressing, 119-120
  public IP addressing, 119-120
  site-local addresses, 141
  static addresses, 123
  subnet addresses, summarizing, 118-119
addressing devices, 123
addressing schemes, 354
  EIGRP, 215
  OSPF, 233-234
  RIPv1, 198
administrative distance (AD), 153-154
  EIGRP, 214
Advanced Encryption Standard
  (AES), 323
advertisement request message, VTP, 78
AES (Advanced Encryption
  Standard), 323
AH (Authentication Header), 325
algorithms, OSPF, 231-232
analog dialup, circuit-switched
  connections (WAN), 314-315
ANDing, 112
antivirus software, 273
application layer (TCP/IP), 21

applications, network-based applications, 17

impact of voice and video, 18
increased network usage, 17
QoS (quality of service), 17

ARP (Address Resolution Protocol), 16, 124-126, 148

Frame Relay, 339

AS (autonomous system), 150

assigning VLANs, 358, 369-370

to interfaces, 89

asymmetric switching, 46

ATM, packet-switched connections (WAN), 317

attacker terminology, 267-268

attackers, thinking like, 268-269

authentication

PPP, LCP, 333
VPNs, 325
wireless security, 257

Authentication Header (AH), 325

auto-cost reference-bandwidth, 236

automatic summarization

EIGRP, 216-217
RIPv1, 204-205

autonomous system (AS), 150

autosummarization, disabling in RIPv2, 208

availability, balancing with security, 269

B

backing up IOS images, 184

backup DR (BDR), 230

backward explicitly congestion notification (BECN), Frame Relay, 339

balancing security and availability, 269

bandwidth command, 220, 236

Basic Rate Interface (BRI), 315

basic router configuration, 167-174

BDR (backup designated router), 230

BECN (backward explicit congestion notification), Frame Relay, 339

BID (bridge ID), configuring, 82-84

binary values, subnet masks, 112

black hats, 268

black hole VLAN, 73

boot system command, 186

bootup process, routers, 162-163

BRI (Basic Rate Interface), 315

broadband wireless, Internet connections (WAN), 319

broadcast addresses, 38

subnetting, 114

broadcast domains, 45

broadcast storms, STP, 78

broadcasts, 43

C

cable modems, Internet connections (WAN), 318

cables

crossover cables, 6, 164-165
straight-through cables, 6, 165

calculating Dijkstra algorithm (link-state routing protocols), 157-158

carrier protocols, 323

CDP, troubleshooting tools, 68-69

central office (CO), WAN, 309

channel service unit (CSU), 310

CHAP, configuring PPP, 335, 356, 362

cHDLC (Cisco HDLC), 329

CIR (committed information rate), Frame Relay, 339

circuit-switched connections, WAN, 314

analog dialup, 314-315
ISDN, 315-316

Cisco devices, configuring, 47

Cisco Enterprise Architecture, 10

Cisco HDLC (cHDLC), 329

Cisco Interim Solution, 258

Cisco IOS (Internetwork Operating System), 46. See also IOS

CLI EXEC sessions, 47
CLI navigation and shortcuts, 48
command history, 49-50
connecting to Cisco devices, 46-47
examination commands, 50
file naming conventions, 182-183
help facility, 48
storing and erasing configuration files, 51
subconfiguration modes, 50

Cisco IOS Integrated File System.
See **IFS**

Cisco IOS OSPF cost values, 236

**classes of addresses, IPv4 addressing,
110-111**

classful routing protocols, 151-152

classifying dynamic routing protocols, 150

   classful routing protocols, 151-152

   classless routing protocols, 152

   distance vector routing protocols, 150-151

   EGP, 150

   IGP, 150

   link-state routing protocols, 151

classless routing protocols, 152

CLI (command-line interface), 162, 261

   navigation and shortcuts, 48-49

CLI EXEC sessions, Cisco IOS, 47

clock rate command, 350

CO (central office), WAN, 309

codes, interface status codes, 65, 171

   LAN switches, 65-66

collision domains, 45

command history, Cisco IOS, 49-50

command syntax help, 48

command-line interface (CLI), 162, 261

commands

   auto-cost reference-bandwidth, 236

   bandwidth, 236

     EIGRP, 220

   boot system, 186

   clock rate, 350

   command history buffer commands, 49-50

   configure terminal, 50

   copy, 51

     managing configuration files, 182

   copy run start, 182

   debug eigrp fsm, 224

   debug frame-relay lmi, 348

   debug ip nat, 305

   debug ip rip, 247

   debug ppp authentication, 351

   default-information originate, 206, 238

   dir, 180

   dynamic auto, 91

   dynamic desirable, 91

   enable password, 55

   enable password password, 169

   enable secret, 55

   encapsulation ppp, 334

   erase startup-config, 51

   examination commands, Cisco IOS, 50

   frame-relay interface-dlci, 348

   interface range command, 55

   ip helper-address, 131

   ip ospf cost, 236

   ip ospf priority interface, 237

   ip route, static routes, 191

   ipconfig/release, 131

   ipconfig/renew, 131

   for managing configuration files, IFS, 182

   network, 215-216, 234-235

   no auto-summary, 208, 216

   no debug ip rip, 248

   no keepalives, 351

   no service dhcp, 129

   no shutdown, 58, 104

   passive-interface, disabling updates, 203

   ping, 11, 62, 132-133

   ppp authentication chap, 335

   ppp authentication pap, 335

   range, 89

   redistribute static, 219

   router ospf, 234

   show access-lists, 289

   show cdp, 68

   show cdp interface, 69

   show cdp neighbors detail, 69

   show controllers, 350

   show file systems, 179-181

   show flash, 185

   show frame-relay map, 348

   show frame-relay pvc, 348

   show interface status, 67

   show interfaces, 66, 172-174, 351

   show interfaces serial, 349

   show interfaces status, 66

   show ip eigrp interfaces, 248

   show ip eigrp neighbors, 245, 249

   show ip interface, 290

   show ip interface brief, 11, 170, 239

   show ip nat statistics, 304

   show ip nat translations, 304

   show ip ospf, 241

   show ip ospf interface, 242-243

   show ip ospf interface brief, 248

   show ip ospf neighbor, 240, 249

   show ip ospf neighbor commands, 245

   show ip protocols, 153, 239-240, 245, 248

     RIPv1, 200

show ip route, 11, 152, 170, 199, 239, 245
   RIPv1, 200
show port-security, 57
show port-security interface, 57, 94
show run, 304
show running-config, 170, 290
show spanning-tree, 83
show version, 162-163
show vlan brief, 88-90
show vtp status, 98
spanning-tree mode rapid-pvst, 84
spanning-tree portfast default, 84
switch configuration commands, 53-54
switchport mode access, 103
switchport mode dynamic desirable, 75
switchport mode trunk, 75
switchport mode trunk dynamic auto, 75
switchport nonegotiate, 75, 103
switchport port-security violation, 56
telnet, 11
tftpdnld, 187
traceroute, 133-134, 175, 246
undebug all, 248
username, 335
vtp pruning, 98
vtp version 2, 98
write erase, 51
xmodem, 187
**comments, adding to named or numbered
   ACLs, 287-288**
**committed information rate (CIR),
   Frame Relay, 339**
complex ACLs, 288
components
   of Frame Relay, 338-339
   of routers, internal components, 161-162
   for teleworker connectivity, 7
   of VPNs, 322
   of WAN, 309
configuration files
   Cisco IOS, 51
   commands for managing, 182
configurations, ISP, 355-356
configure terminal command, 50
configuring
   ACLs
      extended numbered ACLs, 284-286
      named ACLs, 286-287
      standard numbered ACLs, 282-284

Cisco devices, 47
default routing, 357, 364
DHCP, 359, 371-372
dynamic NAT, 301-302
EIGRP, 214-215
   automatic summarization, 216-217
   default routes, 219
   manual summarization, 217-218
   modifying EIGRP metrics, 219-220
   *modifying hello intervals and hold
      times, 220-221*
   network command, 215-216
EIGRP routing, 357, 365-366
firewall ACLs, 359, 372-373
Frame Relay, 343-344
   full mesh with one subnet, 344-347
   hub-and-spoke topology, 356, 360-362
   *partial mesh with one subnet per PVC,
      347-348*
HDLC, 330
inter-VLAN routing, 103-105, 357,
   364-365
NAT, 356, 362-363
NAT overload, 303
OSPF, 233
   controlling DR/BDR election, 237-238
   *modifying Hello intervals and hold
      times, 238-239*
   modifying metrics, 236-237
   network command, 234-235
   redistributing default routes, 238
   router ID, 235-236
   router ospf command, 234
port security, 56-58, 358, 369-370
PPP, 334
   CHAP, 335, 356, 362
   PAP, 335-336
RIPv1, 198-199
RIPv2, 207-208
   disabling autosummarization, 208
routers, as DHCP servers, 128-132
RSTP, 84
SSH access, 55-56
static NAT, 301
static routes, 191-193
   default static routes, 194-197
   with "Next Hop" parameter, 193
   with exit interface parameter, 193-194
STP, 82, 358, 370-371
   BID (bridge ID), 82-84
   PortFast, 84

trunking, 91-93
VLANs, 88-91, 357, 367-369
VTP, 97-100
Windows PC to use DHCP, 123

Connecting Cisco IOS to Cisco devices, 46-47

connection establishment, TCP/IP, 25

connection-oriented systems, WAN, 313

connectionless protocols, 26

connectionless systems, WAN, 313

connections

routers, 164-165
verifying network connectivity, 62-65, 175-176
WAN
circuit-switched connections, 314-316
dedicated connections, 314
Internet connections, 317-319
packet-switched connections, 315-317
WAN link options, 319-320

conventions

for writing IPv6 addresses, 139
for writing IPv6 prefixes, 139-140

converging with link-state protocols, link-state routing protocols, 158

copy command, 51, 182

copy run start command, 182

core layer switches, 4

CPE (Customer Premises Equipment), 309

CPU, 161

crackers, 268

crossover cables, 6, 164-165

CSMA/CA (carrier sense multiple access with collision avoidance), 256-257

CSMA/CD (carrier sense multiple access with collision detection), 34-35

CSU (channel service unit), 310

Customer Premises Equipment (CPE), 309

cut-through switching, 46

D

Data Communications Equipment (DCE), 309, 337

data encapsulation

MAC sublayer, 34
TCP/IP, 28

Data Encryption Standard (DES), 323

data service unit (DSU), 310

Data Terminal Equipment (DTE), 309, 337

data VLAN, 72

data-link connection identifier (DLCI), Frame Relay, 338

data-link protocols, WAN, 312

DBD (database description) packets, OSPF, 228

DCE (Data Communications Equipment), 309, 337

DDoS (distributed denial-of-service) attacks, 272

debug eigrp fsm, 224

debug frame-relay lmi, 348

debug ip nat command, 305

debug ip rip commands, 247

debug ppp authentication, 351

dedicated connections, WAN, 314

default file systems, 180

default routes

EIGRP, 219
redistributing in OSPF, 238
RIPv1, 206-207

default routing, configuring, 357, 364

default static routes, configuring, 194-197

default VLAN, 72

default-information originate command, 206, 238

demarcation point, WAN, 309

denial-of-service (DoS) attacks, 272

deny any statements, 279

DES (Data Encryption Standard), 323

design guidelines, ACLs, 281-282

designated router (DR), 230-231

device hardening, 273

devices, 3

Cisco devices, configuring, 47
connecting Cisco IOS to Cisco devices, 46-47
hubs, 3
switches. *See* switches
of WAN, 310

DHCP (Dynamic Host Configuration Protocol), 15, 127

configuring, 359, 371-372
configuring Windows PC to use, 123
verifying operations, 130
DHCP servers, configuring routers as, 128-132
DHCPv6, 142
Dijkstra algorithm, calculating, 157-158
dir command, 180
Direct Sequence Spread Spectrum (DSSS), 255
disabling

autosummarization, RIPv2, 208
updates, passive-interface command, 203
discontiguous networks, 246-247
distance vector routing protocols, 150-151
distance vectors, EIGRP versus, 211
distributed DoS attacks, 272
distribution layer switches, 4
DLCI (data-link connection identifier), Frame Relay, 338
DNS (Domain Name System), 15, 126-127
documentation for networks, 11
domains

broadcast domains, 45
collision domains, 45
top-level domains, 126
DoS (denial-of-service) attacks, 272
DR (designated router), 230-231
DR/BDR election, OSPF controlling, 237-238
DSL, Internet connections (WAN), 317-318
DSSS (Direct Sequence Spread Spectrum), 255
DSU (data service unit), 310
DTE (Data Terminal Equipment), 309, 337
DTP (Dynamic Trunking Protocol), 75
DUAL, EIGRP, 214
dual stacking, IPv6, 143
duplexes, switches, 66-67
dynamic 6to4 tunnels, 143
dynamic auto, 91
dynamic desirable, 91

Dynamic Host Configuration Protocol (DHCP), 15
dynamic NAT, 299-302
dynamic routing, 191

static routing versus, 149
dynamic routing metrics, 152-153
dynamic routing protocols, classifying, 150

classful routing protocols, 151-152
classless routing protocols, 152
distance vector routing protocols, 150-151
EGP, 150
IGP, 150
link-state routing protocols, 151
Dynamic Trunking Protocol (DTP), 75

E

E1 (External Type 1), 240
E2 (External Type 2), 240
EAP (Extensible Authentication Protocol), 264
EGP (Exterior Gateway Protocols), 150
EIA (Electronics Industry Alliance), 36
EIA/TIA-232, 311
EIA/TIA-449/530, 311
EIA/TIA-612/613, 311
EIGRP (Enhanced Interior Gateway Routing Protocol), 211

addressing schemes, 215
administrative distance, 214
configuring, 214-215
automatic summarization, 216-217
default routes, 219
manual summarization, 217-218
modifying EIGRP metrics, 219-220
modifying hello intervals and hold times, 220-221
network command, 215-216
distance vectors versus, 211
DUAL, 214
dynamic routing metrics, 153
message formats, 212
neighbor requirements, 249
packet types, 212-213
troubleshooting, 248
verifying
with show ip eigrp neighbors, 222-224
with show ip protocols, 221

EIGRP routing, configuring, 357, 365-366

electrical threats, 271

Electronics Industry Alliance (EIA), 36

eliminating routing loops, 155-156

employees, wireless security risks, 257

enable password command, 55

enable password password command, 169

enable secret command, 55

encapsulating protocols, 323

Encapsulating Security Payload (ESP), 325

encapsulation, 322

  HDLC, 329-330

  OSI models, 16

encapsulation ppp command, 334

encapsulation process, 16

encoding channels, wireless encoding channels, 255

encryption, 257, 322

encryption algorithms, VPNs, 323

Enhanced Interior Gateway Routing Protocol. See EIGRP

Enterprirse Architecture, 10

Enterprise Branch Architecture, 10

Enterprise Campus Architecture, 10

Enterprise Data Center Architecture, 10

Enterprise Edge Architecture, 10

Enterprise Teleworker Architecture, 10

environmental threats, 271

erase startup-config command, 51

erasing configuration files, Cisco IIOS, 51

error detection, LCP, 332

error recovery, TCP/IP, 24

ESP (Encapsulating Security Payload), 325

establishing VPN connections, 322

  authentication, 325

  encryption algorithms, 323

  hashes, 324-325

  IPsec Security Protocols, 325

  tunneling, 323

Ethernet, 16

  addresses, 38

  current Ethernet technologies, 36

  framing, 39

  Gigabit Ethernet, 37

  legacy Ethernet technologies, 34-36

    CSMA/CD, 35

  overview, 33-34

  physical layer, role of, 40

  switches, 37-38

  UTP cabling, 36-37

EtherType field, 74

EUI-64 format, IPv6, 141-142

examinations

  exam day information, 377

  post-exam information

    career options, 379-380

    receiving your certificate, 379

    retesting, 380

examination commands, Cisco IOS, 50

exit interface parameter, configuring static routes, 193-194

extended ACLs, 280

extended numbered ACLs, configuring, 284

  deny FTP from subnets, 285

  deny only Telnet from subnets, 285-286

Extensible Authentication Protocol (EAP), 264

Exterior Gateway Protocols (EGP), 150

external threats, 271

External Type 1 (E1), 240

External Type 2 (E2), 240

F

FC (Feasibility Condition), 223

FCC (Federal Communications Commission), 253-254

FD (Feasible Distance), 223

Feasible Successor (FS), 223

FECN (forward explicit congestion notification), Frame Relay, 339

FHSS (Frequency Hopping Spread Spectrum), 255

file naming conventions, IOS, 182-183

file systems, default file systems, 180

File Transfer Protocol (FTP), 15

firewall ACLs, configuring, 359, 372-373

firewalls, 273

flash memory, 162

flow control, TCP/IP, 25

forward explicit congestion notification (FECN), Frame Relay, 339

forwarding, frame forwarding, 45

asymmetric switching, 46
Layer 2 switching, 46
Layer 3 switching, 46
memory buffering, 46
switch forwarding methods, 45
symmetric switching, 46

FRAD (Frame Relay Access Devices), 337

frame format, PPP, 331-332

frame forwarding, 45-46

Frame Relay, 16, 337

backward explicity congestion notification (BECN), 339
committed information rate (CIR), 339
components of, 338-339
configuring, 344
   full mesh with one subnet, 344-347
   hub-and-spoke topology, 356, 360-362
   partial mesh with one subnet per PVC, 347-348
configuring and verifying, 343
data-link connection identifier (DLCI), 338
DCE, 337
DTE, 337
forward explicit congestion notification (FECN), 339
Inverse Address Resolution Protocol (ARP), 339
Inverse ARP, 341-343
LMI, 341-343
local access rate, 338
Local Management Interface (LMI), 339
NBMA (nonbroadcast multi-access), 340
packet-switched connections, WAN, 317
permanent virtual circuit (PVC), 338
switched virtual circuit (SVC), 338
topologies, 339
verifying, 348
virtual circuit (VC), 338

Frame Relay Access Devices (FRAD), 337

frame-relay interface-dlci command, 348

framing, Ethernet, 39

Frequency Hopping Spread Spectrum (FHSS), 255

FS (Feasible Successor), 223

FTP (File Transfer Protocol), 15

full-mesh topology, Frame Relay, 339

G

Gigabit Ethernet, 37

global unicast addresses, IPv6, 140-141

GUI (graphical user interface), 162, 261

H

hackers, 257, 267

hardware threats, 271

hashes, VPNs, 324-325

HDLC

configuring, 330
encapsulation, 329-330
verifying, 331

HDLC (High-Level Data Link Control), 329

header formats, IPv4 addressing, 109-110

hello intervals and hold times

modifying (EIGRP), 220-221
modifying (OSPF), 238-239

Hello packets

EIGRP, 213
OSPF, 228
   neighbor adjacency, 228-229

help facilities, Cisco IOS, 48

hierarchical network models, 9

High-Level Data Link Control (HDLC), 329

HIPS (host-based intrusion prevention), 273

history of commands, Cisco IOS, 49-50

HMAC (hashed message authentication code), 324-325

hold-down timers, preventing routing loops, 155

host and server security, mitigation techniques, 273

host ranges, subnetting, 114

host-based intrusion prevention (HIPS), 273

HTTP (Hypertext Transfer Protocol), 15

HTTP request, 21

HTTP response, 21

hub-and-spoke configuration, Frame Relay, 340

hub-and-spoke topology, Frame Relay (configuring), 356, 360-362

hubs, 3

Hypertext Transfer Protocol (HTTP), 15

I

ICMP (Internet Control Message Protocol), 16, 147

identification, ACLs, 281

IDS (intrusion detection systems), 273

IEEE, 253

IETF (Internet Engineering Task Force), 137, 227

IFS (Integrated File System)

commands, 179-181

commands for managing configuration files, 182

URL prefixes for specifying file locations, 181

IGP (Interior Gateway Protocols), 150

comparison summary, 154

images, IOS images, 183

backing up, 184

recovering with TFTP servers, 186-187

recovering with Xmodem, 187-188

restoring, 185-186

IMAP (Internet Message Access Protocol), 15

implementing WLAN, 261

checklist for implementing, 262-264

infrastructure mode, wireless operations, 254

inside global address, NAT, 297

inside local address, NAT, 297

Integrated File System. See IFS

Inter-Switch Link (ISL), 103

inter-VLAN routing

configuring, 103-105, 357, 364-365

troubleshooting, 105

verifying, 105

interface ID, IPv6, 141-142

interface processing, ACLs, 279-280

interface range command, 55

interface status codes, 65-66, 171

interfaces

assigning VLANs to, 89

passive interfaces, RIPv1, 203-204

routers, 164

unused interfaces, shutting down and securing, 58

up interfaces, layer 1 problems, 67

Interior Gateway Protocols. See IGP

internal threats, 271

Internet connections, WAN

broadband wireless, 319

cable modems, 318

DSL, 317-318

Metro Ethernet, 319

Internet Control Message Protocol (ICMP), 16, 147

Internet Engineering Task Force (IETF), 137

internet information queries, 271

Internet layer, TCP/IP, 26

Internet Message Access Protocol (IMAP), 15

Internet Protocol (IP), 16

Internetwork Operating System. See Cisco IOS

Intrasite Automatic Tunnel Addressing Protocol (ISATAP), 143

intrusion detection and prevention, mitigation techniques, 273

intrusion detection systems (IDS), 273

intrustion tools, wireless security, 257

Inverse Address Resolution Protocol (ARP), Frame Relay, 339

Inverse ARP, Frame Relay, 341-343

IOS (Internetwork Operating System), 162

file naming conventions, 182-183

IOS images

managing, 183

backing up, 184

restoring, 185-186

recovering with TFTP servers, 186-187

recovering with Xmodem, 187-188

IP (Internet Protocol), 16

IP addressing, 119-120

ip helper-address command, 131

IP multicast, 72

ip ospf cost command, 236

ip ospf priority interface command, 237

ip route command, static routes, 191

IP telephony, 72

ipconfig/release commands, 131

ipconfig/renew command, 131

IPsec Security Protocols, VPNs, 325

IPv4

  addresses

    classes of addresses, 110-111

    header formats, 109-110

    subnet masks, 111-112

  versus IPv6, 137

IPv6

  addresses

    conventions for writing, 139

    global unicast addresses, 140-141

    loopback addresses, 141

    managing, 142

    private addresses, 141

    reserved addresses, 141

  interface ID and EUI-64 format, 141-142

  versus IPv4, 137

  overview of, 137-138

  prefixes, conventions for writing, 139-140

  transitioning to, 142-143

ISATAP (Intrasite Automatic Tunnel Addressing Protocol), 143

ISDN, circuit-switched connections (WAN), 315-316

ISL (Inter-Switch Link), 103

ISP (Internet service provider), configurations, 355-356

ITU-R, 253

J–K–L

jitter, 18

LAN cabling, standards for, 6

LAN switches, 45

  interface status codes, 65-66

LANs (local-area networks), 7

Layer 1 problems, troubleshooting, 350

Layer 1 problems, up interfaces, 67

Layer 2 problems, troubleshooting, 350-351

Layer 2 switching, 46

Layer 3 problems, troubleshooting, 351-352

Layer 3 switching, 46

layers

  OSI models, 14-15

  TCP/IP models, 15-16

  troubleshooting with, 29

LCP (PPP Link Control Protocol), 332-333

legacy Ethernet technologies, 34-36

  CSMA/CD, 35

link-local addresses, 141

link-state advertisements (LSA), 228

link-state database (LSDB), building, 156-157

link-state protocols, converging with link-state routing protocols, 158

link-state routing process, OSPF, 232-233

link-state routing protocols, 151, 156

  calculating Dijkstra algorithms, 157-158

  convergence with link-state protocols, 158

  LSDB, building, 156-157

LLC (Logical Link Control) sublayer, 34

LMI (Local Management Interface)

  Frame Relay, 339-343

local access rate, Frame Relay, 338

local loop, 309

Local Management Interface (LMI), Frame Relay, 339

Logical Link Control (LLC) sublayer, 34

logical switching, 44-45

logical topologies, 9

loopback addresses, IPv6, 141

loopback configurations, OSPF, 235

looped link detection, LCP, 332

loss, 18

low delay, 18

LSA (link-state advertisements), 156, 228-229

LSack (link-state acknowledgment) packets, OSPF, 228

LSDB (link-state database), building, 156-157

LSR (link-state request) packets, OSPF, 228

LSU (link-state update) packets, OSPF, 228-229

M

MAC (Media Access Control) sublayer, 34

MAC addresses, switch forwarding, 45

MAC database instability, STP, 79

MAC sublayer, 34

maintaining security, 275-276

maintenance threats, 271

malicious code attacks, 272

man-in-the-middle attacks, 272

management VLAN, 73

managing
  addresses, IPv6, 142
  IOS images, 183
    backing up, 184
    restoring, 185-186

manual summarization, EIGRP, 217-218

MCT (manually configured tunnels), 143

media, 5-6
  networking, 5
  standards for LAN cabling, 6

Media Access Control (MAC) sublayer, 34

memory, 162

memory buffering, 46

message-of-the-day (MOTD), 169

messages
  EIGRP, 212
  OSPF, 227-228
  RIPv1, 197

methodologies, troubleshooting, 61-62

metrics, dynamic routing metrics, 152-153

Metro Ethernet, Internet connections (WAN), 319

MIST (Multiple Instances of Spanning Tree), 82

mitigation techniques, 273
  host and server security, 273
  intrusion detection and prevention, 273
  security appliances and applications, 273-274

models
  network models, benefits of, 13
  OSI models, 13
    layers, 14-15
    PDUs and encapsulation, 16
  TCP/IP models, 13-16

modes of VTP, 77

modifying
  EIGRP metrics, 219-220
  Hello intervals and hold times
    EIGRP, 220-221
    OSPF, 238-239
  OSPF metrics, 236-237

MOTD (message-of-the-day), 169

multicast addresses, 38

multilink PPP, LCP, 333

multiple frame transmission, STP, 79

Multiple Instances of Spanning Tree (MIST), 82

municipal Wi-Fi, 319

mutual authentication, wireless security, 257

N

named ACLs, configuring, 286-287

naming conventions, IOS, 182-183

NAT (Network Address Translation), 297
  benefits of, 300
  configuring, 356, 362-363
  dynamic NAT, 299-302
  example of PC1 sending traffic to Internet, 298-299
  inside global address, 297
  inside local address, 297
  limitations of, 300
  outside global address, 297
  outside local address, 297
  overloading, 300
  static NAT, 299-301
  troubleshooting, 304-305
  verifying, 303-304

NAT overload, 299-300, 303

native VLAN, 73

navigation, CLI, 48-49

NBMA (nonbroadcast multi-access), Frame Relay, 340

NCPs (Network Control Protocols), 332

neighbor adjacency issues, troubleshooting, 248-250

neighbors, OSPF

Hello packets, 228-229
verifying, 240

network access layer, TCP/IP, 27-28

Network Address Translation. *See* NAT

network admission control, 274

network command, 215-216, 234-235

network connectivity, verifying, 62-65, 175-176

Network Control Protocols (NCPs), 332

network documentation, 11

network interface card (NIC), 261

network layer testing tools

ping, 132-133
traceroute, 133-134

network management, 72

network models, benefits of, 13

network statements, 209, 247

network usage, network-based applications, 17

network-based applications, 17-18

networking, media, 5

networking icons, 7

networks

discontiguous networks, 246-247
OSPF, 230
threats to, 271

networks attacks, types of, 271-272

"Next Hop" parameter, configuring static routes, 193

NIC (network interface card), 261

no auto-summary command, 208, 216

no debug ip rip, 248

no keepalives command, 351

no service dhcp command, 129

no shutdown command, 58, 104

nonbroadcast multi-access (NBMA), 340

normal data, 72

NVRAM (nonvolatile random-access memory), 162

O

OFDM (Orthogonal Frequency Division Multiplexing), 255

Open Shortest Path First. *See* OSPF

operating system patches, 273

organizationally unique identifier (OUI), 38

Orthogonal Frequency Division Multiplexing (OFDM), 255

OSI models, 13

OSI layers, 14-15
PDUs (protocol data units), 16

OSPF (Open Shortest Path First), 227

addressing schemes, 233-234
algorithms, 231-232
configuring, 233
controlling DR/BDR election, 237-238
modifying Hello intervals and hold times, 238-239
modifying metrics, 236-237
network command, 234-235
redistributing default routes, 238
router ID, 235-236
router ospf command, 234
DR/BDR election, 230-231
Hello packets, neighbor adjacency, 228-229
link-state routing process, 232-233
loopback configurations, 235
LSA packets, 229
LSU packets, 229
message format, 227-228
neighbor requirements, 249-250
network types, 230
packet types, 228
troubleshooting, 239-240, 248
verifying, 240-243

OUI (organizationally unique identifier), 38

outside global address, NAT, 297

outside local address, 297

overloading NAT, 299-300

P

packet capturing sniffers, 271
packet forwarding, 147
  path determination and switching function example, 148-149
packet-switched connections, WAN, 315
  ATM, 317
  Frame Relay, 317
  X.25, 315
packets
  EIGRP, 212-213
  OSPF, 228
  RTP, 212-213
PAP, configuring PPP, 335-336
parameters
  exit interface, configuring static routes, 193-194
  "Next Hop," configuring static routes, 193
partial-mesh topology, Frame Relay, 339
passenger protocols, 323
passive interfaces, RIPv1, 203-204
passive-interface command, disabling updates, 203
password attacks, 272
passwords, recovering, 188
PAT (Port Address Translation), 299
path determination, packet forwarding, 148-149
PDUs (protocol data units), OSI models, 16
Per-VLAN Rapid Spanning Tree (PVRST), 82
permanent virtual circuit (PVC), Frame Relay, 338
personal firewalls, 273
phishers, 268
phreakers, 268
physical (MAC) addresses, ARP, 125
physical infrastructures, threats to, 271
physical layer
  Ethernet, 40
  WAN, 311
physical topologies, 8
ping, 11, 62, 132-133
  verifying network connectivity, 175

ping sweeps, 271
ping-of-death attacks, 272
Point-to-Point Protocol. *See* PPP
policies, developing security policies, 269-270
POP3 (Post Office Protocol), 15
Port Address Translation (PAT), 299
port mappings, VLAN, 355
port numbers, 23
port redirection, 272
port roles, RSTP and STP, 81
port scans, 271
port security, configuring, 56-58, 358, 370
port states, RSTP and STP, 81
port examination, post-exam information (receiving your certificate), 379
port-based memory, 46
PortFast, 84
ports, routers, 164
Post Office Protocol (POP3), 15
PPP (Point-to-Point Protocol), 329-330
  configuring, 334
    CHAP, 335
    PAP, 335-336
    with CHAP, 356, 362
  frame format, 331-332
  LCP (Link Control Protocol), 332-333
ppp authentication chap command, 335
ppp authentication pap command, 335
PPP Link Control Protocol. *See* LCP
prefixes
  IPv6, conventions for writing, 139-140
  URL prefixes for specifying file locations, 181
preshared key (PSK), 325
preventing routing loops, 155-156
PRI (Primary Rate Interface), 315
private addresses, IPv6, 141
private IP addressing, 119-120
privileged EXEC mode, 47
pruning, VTP, 78
PSK (preshared key), 325
PSTN (public switched telephone network), 310
public IP addressing, 119-120

PVC (permanent virtual circuit)
Frame Relay, 338
WAN, 313
PVRST (Per-VLAN Rapid Spanning Tree), 82

Q

QoS (Quality of Service), network-based applications, 17
quad-zero routes, 194
quartets, 139
query packets, EIGRP, 213

R

RAM, 161
range command, 89
Rapid Per-VLAN Spanning Tree (RPVST), 82
Rapid STP. *See* **RSTP**
reconnaissance attacks, 271
recovering
IOS images
with TFTP servers, 186-187
with Xmodem, 187-188
passwords, 188
redistribute static command, 219
redistributing default routes, OSPF, 238
reference bandwidth, 236
Reliable Transport Protocol. *See* **RTP**
remote-access VPNs, 321
reply packets, EIGRP, 213
reserved addresses, IPv6, 141
restoring IOS images, 185-186
RIP, 197
routes, interpreting, 200
troubleshooting, 247-248
RIPv1, 198
addressing schemes, 198
automatic summarization, 204-205
configuring, 198-199
default routing, 206-207
message format, 197
passive interfaces, 203-204
verifying, 199-202

RIPv2
configuring, 207-208
verifying, 208-209
Rivest, Shamir, and Adleman (RSA), 323
rogue AP, wireless security risks, 257
ROM, 161
router ID, configuring OSPF, 235-236
router ospf command, 234
routers, 5
AD (administrative distance), 153-154
basic router configuration, 167-174
bootup process, 162-163
configuring as DHCP servers, 128-132
connections, 164-165
internal components of, 161-162
ports and interfaces, 164
routes, tracing from Windows PC, 65
routing
EIGRP. *See* EIGRP
inter-VLAN routing, configuring and verifying, 103-105
OSPF. *See* OSPF
troubleshooting, 245
routing loop prevention, 155-156
routing methods, 149
dynamic routing protocols, classifying, 150-152
dynamic versus static routing, 149
RPVST (Rapid Per-VLAN Spanning Tree), 82
RSA (Rivest, Shamir, and Adleman), 323
RSTP (Rapid STP), 80-81
configuring, 84
port roles, 81
port states, 81
RTP (Reliable Transport Protocol), 212
packets, 212-213

S

satellite Internet, 319
scavenger class, 72
securing unused interfaces, 58
security, 267
attacker terminology, 267-268
balancing security and availability, 269
common threats
to networks, 271
to physical infrastructures, 271
vulnerabilities, 270

configuring, 369
developing security policies, 269-270
importance of, 267
maintaining, 275-276
mitigation techniques, 273-274
network attacks, 271-272
port security, configuring, 56-58
thinking like attackers, 268-269
wireless security risks, 257
wireless security standards, 258
**security appliances and applications,
mitigation techniques, 273-274**
security communications, 274
security violations, 57
service set identifier (SSID), 261
shared memory, 46
shortcuts, CLI, 48-49
show access-lists command, 289
show cdp commands, 68
show cdp interface command, 69
show cdp neighbor detail, 11, 69
show controllers command, 350
show file systems command, 179-181
show flash command, 185
show frame-relay map command, 348
show frame-relay pvc command, 348
show interface status, 67
show interfaces, 66, 171-174
show interfaces command, 351
show interfaces serial command, 349
show interfaces status, 66
show ip eigrp interfaces, 248
**show ip eigrp neighbors, 222-224,
245, 249**
show ip interface brief, 11, 170, 239
show ip interface command, 290
show ip interface e0 command, 290
show ip nat statistics command, 304
show ip nat translations command, 304
show ip ospf command, 241
show ip ospf interface brief, 242-243, 248
show ip ospf neighbor, 240, 245, 249
show ip protocols, 153, 239-240, 245, 248
   EIGRP, 221
   RIPv1, 200

show ip route, 11, 152, 170, 199, 239, 245
   RIPv1, 200
show port-security command, 57
show port-security interface command, 57
show portsecurity interface, 94
show run command, 304
show running-config command, 170, 290
show spanning-tree command, 83
show version command, 162-163
show vlan brief, 88-90
show vtp status command, 98
shutting down unused interfaces, 58
site-local addresses, 141
site-to-site VPNs, 320
SMTP (Simple Mail Transfer Protocol), 15
**SNMP (Simple Network Management
Protocol), 15**
spammers, 268
Spanning Tree Protocol. *See* STP
spanning-tree mode rapid-pvst, 84
spanning-tree portfast default, 84
speed mismatches, switches, 66-67
**split horizons, preventing routing
loops, 155**
SSH, configuring access, 55-56
SSID (service set identifier), 261
standard ACLs, 280
**standard numbered ACLs,
configuring, 282**
   deny a specific host, 283
   deny a specific subnet, 283-284
   deny Telnet access to routers, 284
   permit specific network, 282-283
star topology, Frame Relay, 340
stateless autoconfiguration, IPv6, 142
statements
   deny any, 279
   network, 247
static addresses, 123
static NAT, 299-301
static routes
   configuring, 191-192
      default static routes, 194-197
      with exit interface parameter, 193-194
      with "Next Hop" parameter, 193

static routing, dynamic routing versus, 149

store-and-forward switching, 46

storing configuration files, Cisco IOS, 51

STP (Spanning Tree Protocol), 79-80

broadcast storms, 78

configuring, 82, 358, 370-371

BID (bridge ID), 82-84

PortFast, 84

MAC database instability, 79

multiple frame transmission, 79

port roles, 81

troubleshooting, 84

straight-through cables, 6, 165

structured threats, 271

Structured Wireless-Aware Network (SWAN), 257

subconfiguration modes, Cisco IOS, 50

subnet addresses, summarizing, 118-119

subnet masks, IPv4 addresses, 111-112

subnet multipliers, 114

subnets, subnetting, 114

subnetting, 112-113

determining how many bits to borrow, 113

determining net subnet masks, 114

determining subnet multipliers, 114

examples, 114-116

listing subnets, host ranges and broadcast addresses, 114

VLSM. *See* VLSM

subset advertisement, VTP, 78

successor, EIGRP, 223

summarization

automatic summarization

EIGRP, 217

RIPv1, 204-205

manual summarization, EIGRP, 217-218

summary advertisement, VTP, 78

SVC (switched virtual circuit)

Frame Relay, 338

WAN, 313

SWAN (Structured Wireless-Aware Network), 257

switch configuration commands, 53-54

switch forwarding methods

based on MAC addresses, 45

frame forwarding, 45

switched virtual circuit (SVC), Frame Relay, 338

switches, 3, 37-38

access layer switches, 4

broadcast domains, 45

collision domains, 45

core layer switches, 4

distribution layer switches, 4

duplex and speed mismatches, 66-67

frame forwarding, 45-46

LAN switches, 45, 65-66

layer 1 problems on up interfaces, 67

VTP, 102

WAN switches, 310

switching

evolution to, 43-44

logical switching, 44-45

WAN, 312-313

switching function, packet forwarding, 148-149

switchport mode access, 103

switchport mode dynamic desirable command, 75

switchport mode trunk, 75

switchport mode trunk dynamic auto command, 75

switchport nonegotiate, 75, 103

switchport port-security violation command, 56

symmetric switching, 46

SYN flood attacks, 272

T

TCP (Transmission Control Protocol), 15

TCP header, 22

TCP/IP

application layer, 21

data encapsulation, 28

Internet layer, 26

layers, troubleshooting with, 29

network access layer, 27-28

transport layer, 21

connection establishment and termination, 25

error recovery, 24

flow control, 25

port numbers, 23

TCP header, 22

UDP, 26

TCP/IP models, 13-16
TCP/IP protocols, 15-16
TCP/IP stacks, testing on Windows PC, 63
Telecommunications Industry Association (TIA), 36
Telnet, 15, 176
telnet command, 11
Temporal Key Integrity Protocol (TKIP), 264
Teredo tunneling, IPv6, 143
termination, TCP/IP, 25
testing
    connectivity
        to default gateways on Windows PC, 63
        to destinations on Windows PC, 64
    TCP/IP stacks on Windows PC, 63
TFTP servers, recovering IOS images, 186-187
tftpdnld command, 187
threat control, 274
threats
    to networks, 271-272
    to physical infrastructures, 271
    vulnerabilities, 270
TIA (Telecommunications Industry Association), 36
TKIP (Temporal Key Integrity Protocol), 264
tools for troubleshooting, CDP, 68-69
top-level domains, 126
topologies, 8, 339
traceroute, 133-134, 175, 246
tracert, 132-134
tracing routes from Windows PC, 65
traffic types, VLANs, 72
transitioning to IPv6, 142-143
Transmission Control Protocol (TCP), 15
transport layer (TCP/IP), 21-22
    connection establishment and termination, 25
    error recovery, 24
    flow control, 25
    port numbers, 23
    TCP header, 22
    UDP, 26
Triple DES (3DES), 323

Trojan horses, 272
troubleshooting
    ACLs, 291
        denied protocols, 292-293
        host has no connectivity, 291-292
        Telnet is allowed #1, 293
        Telnet is allowed #2, 294
        Telnet is allowed #3, 294-295
    EIGRP, 248
    inter-VLAN routing, 105
    with layers, 29
    methodology, 61-62
    NAT, 304-305
    neighbor adjacency issues, 248-250
    OSPF, 239-240, 248
    RIP, 247-248
    RIPv2, 208-209
    routing, 245
    STP, 84
    tools, CDP, 68-69
    trunking, 93-94
    VLAN, 93-94
    VLSM, 246
    VTP, 102-103
    WAN implementations, 349
        Layer 1 problems, 350
        Layer 2 problems, 350-351
        Layer 3 problems, 351-352
    WLAN, 264
trunking
    configuring, 91-93
    troubleshooting, 93-94
    verifying, 91-93
trunking VLANs, 74-75
trust exploitation, 272
tunneling, 322. See also encapsulation
    IPv6, 143
    Teredo tunneling, IPv6, 143
    VPNs, 323

U

UDP (User Datagram Protocol), 15
    TCP/IP, 26
undebug all, 248
unshielded twisted-pair (UTP), 164
unstructured threats, 271
up interfaces, layer 1 problems, 67
update packets, EIGRP, 213

URL prefixes for specifying file locations, IFS, 181

usage of networks, network-based applications, 17

User Datagram Protocol (UDP), 15

user EXEC mode, 47

username command, 335

UTP (unshielded twisted-pair), 164

UTP cabling, 36-37

V

V.35, 311

variable-length subnet masking. *See* VLSM

VC (virtual circuit), Frame Relay, 338

verifying
  ACLs, 289-290
  BID, 82-84
  DHCP operations, 130
  EIGRP
    show ip eigrp neighbors, 222-224
    show ip protocols, 221
  Frame Relay, 343, 348
  HDLC, 331
  inter-VLAN routing configurations, 105
  NAT, 303-304
  network connectivity, 62-65
  OSPF, 240-243
  RIPv1, 199-202
  RIPv2, 208-209
  speed and duplex settings, 66-67
  trunking, 91-93
  VLAN, 88-91
  VTP, 99-100
    synchronized databases, 101-102
    VLAN configurations on VTP servers, 100-101

verifying network connectivity, 175-176

video, impact on network-based applications, 18

virtual circuit (VC), Frame Relay, 338

virtual private networks. *See* VPNs

viruses, 272

VLAN configurations and port mappings, 355

VLAN tag fields, 74

VLAN Trunking Protocol. *See* VTP

VLANs (virtual local-area networks)
  assigning, 358, 369-370
    to interfaces, 89
  benefits of, 71-72
  black hole VLAN, 73
  configuring, 88-91, 357, 367-369
  creating, 88
  data VLAN, 72
  default VLAN, 72
  DTP (Dynamic Trunking Protocol), 75
  management VLAN, 73
  native VLAN, 73
  overview, 71
  traffic types, 72
  troubleshooting, 93-94
  trunking VLANs, 74-75
  verification commands, 88-91
  voice VLAN, 73-74

VLSM (variable-length subnet masking), 116-118, 246
  troubleshooting, 246

voice, impact on network-based applications, 18

voice VLAN, 73-74

VoIP (voice over IP), 18

VPNs (virtual private networks), 320
  benefits of, 320
  components of, 322
  establishing connections, 322
    authentication, 325
    encryption algorithms, 323
    hashes, 324-325
    IPsec Security Protocols, 325
    tunneling, 323
  types of access, 320
    remote-access VPNs, 321
    site-to-site VPNs, 320

VTP (VLAN Trunking Protocol), 76-77, 97
  advertisement request message, 78
  configuring, 97-100
  modes, 77
  pruning, 78
  subset advertisement, 78
  summary advertisement, 78
  switches, 102
  troubleshooting, 102-103
  verifying, 99
    synchronized databases, 101-102
    VLAN on VTP servers, 100-101

VTP operation, 77-78

vtp pruning, 98

vtp version 2, 98

vulnerabilities, 270

W

WAN

components of, 309

connections, 165

circuit-switched connections, 314-316

dedicated connections, 314

Internet connections, 317-319

packet-switched connections, 315-317

WAN link options, 319-320

data-link protocols, 312

devices, 310

physical layer standards, 311

PVC, 313

SVC, 313

switching, 312-313

WAN implementations, troubleshooting, 349

Layer 1 problems, 350

Layer 2 problems, 350-351

Layer 3 problems, 351-352

WAN link options, 319-320

WAN switches, 310

WANs (wide-area networks), 7

war drivers, wireless security risks, 257

WEP (Wired Equivalent Privacy), 258, 261

white hats, 267

Wi-Fi Alliance, 253

Wi-Fi Protected Access (WPA), 258, 261

WiMAX (Worldwide Interoperability for Microwave Access), 319

windowing, 25

Windows PC

configuring to use DHCP, 123

testing

connectivity to default gateways, 63

connectivity to destinations, 64

TCP/IP stacks, 63

tracing routes, 65

Wired Equivalent Privacy (WEP), 258, 261

wireless access points, 261

wireless coverage areas, 256

wireless encoding channels, 255

wireless frequencies, 254

wireless LAN. *See* WLAN

wireless modes of operation, 254

wireless security risks, 257

wireless security standards, 258

wireless standards, 253

WLAN

implementing, 261

checklist for, 262-264

modes of operation, 254

speed and frequency reference, 256

standards for, 254

troubleshooting, 264

word help, 48

Worldwide Interoperability for Microwave Access (WiMAX), 319

worms, 272

WPA (Wi-Fi Protected Access), 258, 261

write erase command, 51

X–Y–Z

X.21, 311

X.25, packet-switched connections (WAN), 315

Xmodem, recovering IOS images, 187-188

xmodem command, 187